ISLAM
in an Era
of Nation-States

D1202626

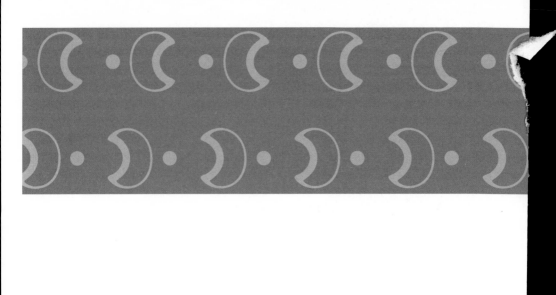

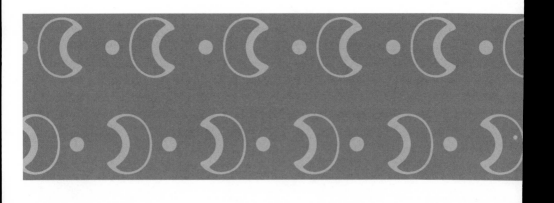

ISLAM
in an Era of Nation-States

Politics and Religious Renewal
in Muslim Southeast Asia

*Edited by Robert W. Hefner
and Patricia Horvatich*

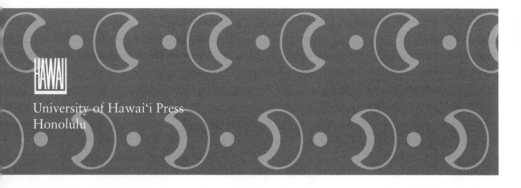

University of Hawai'i Press
Honolulu

© 1997 University of Hawai'i Press
All rights reserved
Printed in the United States of America
02 01 00   5 4 3 2

Library of Congress Cataloging-in-Publication Data
Islam in an era of nation-states : politics and religious renewal in
    Muslim Southeast Asia / edited by Robert W. Hefner and Patricia
    Horvatich.
      p.   cm.
    Includes bibliographical references and index.
    ISBN 0–8248–1901–2 (alk. paper). — ISBN 0–8248–1957–8 (pbk. :
alk. paper)
      1. Islam and politics—Asia, Southeastern.   2. Islam and state—
Asia, Southeastern.   3. Islamic fundamentalism—Asia, Southeastern.
4. Asia, Southeastern—Politics and government—1945–   5. Islam and
world politics.   6. Islam—20th century.   I. Hefner, Robert W.,
1952–   . II. Horvatich, Patricia, 1962–   .
BP173.7.I849   1997
322'.1'0959—dc21   97–8871
                                                        CIP

University of Hawai'i Press books are printed on acid-free paper and meet the guidelines for
permanence and durability of the Council on Library Resources

Designed by Angela Stanton

Contents

Acknowledgments

In recent years scholars in the fields of Southeast Asian and Islamic studies reflecting on the distinctive situation of Muslims in Southeast Asia have enlisted the help of colleagues working on Islam in other parts of the world. Many people have been part of that dialogue, which, for those of us involved in the creation of this book, intensified with a series of meetings over a twenty-month period from 1993 to 1995. For the genesis of the present volume, a key moment in these discussions was a conference held in August 1993 in Honolulu on "Islam and the Social Construction of Identities: Comparative Perspectives on Southeast Asian Muslims." For that meeting and the smaller discussions that followed over the next year and one-half, we especially want to acknowledge the assistance of the Center for Southeast Asian Studies and the School of Hawaiian, Asian and Pacific Studies at the University of Hawai'i at Mānoa. These departments, headed by P. Bion Griffin and Mark Juergensmeyer, respectively, provided some of the funding and resources needed to organize this international conference. The East-West Center also played an important role in the production of the conference by offering funding and making conference facilities available. We are particularly grateful to Geoffrey White, director of the Program on Cultural Studies; Charles Morrison, director of the Program on International Economics and Politics; Florence Lamoureux of the Center for Southeast Asian Studies; and Helen de Leon Palmore of the Program on Cultural Studies. The National Science Foundation, the Wenner-Gren Foundation for Anthropological Research, and the University of Hawai'i Foundation provided the majority of the funding for the Honolulu conference. We acknowledge their assistance with gratitude.

The discussions that preceded and followed the Honolulu meeting included many people, all of whom helped us to place Southeast Asian Islam in a broader perspective. We are especially grateful to the following individuals who participated in our meetings: Muthiah Alagappa, William Brinner, Dale Eickelman, Dru Gladney, Lenn Goodman, Anthony Johns, Mark Juergensmeyer, Clive Kessler, Bruce Lawrence, Barbara Metcalf, Mitsuo Nakamura, Amina Wadud-Muhsin, Lucy Whalley, and Mark Woodward. Special thanks are extended to Nurcholish Madjid and Michael Mastura, who brought a vital Southeast Asian perspective to our discussions.

Portions of Robert Hefner's Chapter 3 appeared in an article published in *Indonesia,* no. 56 (Fall 1993), titled "Islam, State, and Civil Society: ICMI and the Struggle for the Indonesian Middle Class."

Finally, we want to express our gratitude to Pamela Kelley at the University of Hawai'i Press for the energy and consideration she showed in spiriting this book to publication.

Introduction

Chapter 1

Islam in an Era of Nation-States
POLITICS AND RELIGIOUS RENEWAL IN MUSLIM SOUTHEAST ASIA

Robert W. Hefner

Ours is a time in which visions that animated an earlier era have faded, while those that will shape the coming age remain unclear. The most obvious causes of this world-changing transformation were the collapse of communism in Eastern Europe and the end of the cold war. In the aftermath of these events, the Western media were full of commentaries attempting to explain the causes and consequences of what had taken place. Some observers saw the events as evidence of an unprecedented shift in world politics, a veritable "end to history" as we know it. The defining feature of this development, at least as described by Francis Fukuyama (1989), was an end to the ideological struggles that had marked the late modern era and a new international consensus on the virtues of democratic governance and market-oriented development.

Unfortunately for this prognosis, world events quickly proved that, however much it might have marked the close of one era, this end of history was really just the beginning of another, animated by its own passions and polarities. The communist collapse was accompanied by growing ethnic, religious, and national conflict in the countries of the former Eastern Bloc as well as in much of the developing world. The genocide in Ruanda, the brutalization of Bosnia, religious and ethnic struggles in the Caucuses, interreligious strife in India—these and other conflicts served as painful reminders that, contrary to some optimistic ruminations, politics in much of the world had not yet reached a consensus on the means and ends of the modern age.

The intensity of international conflict eventually led other Western commentators to pull back from the optimistic forecasts of the immediate post–cold war era. Where before there was talk of a triumphant end to history, one now heard ominous predictions of a coming "clash of civilizations." In a widely read article published in Foreign Affairs in the summer of 1993, for example, the senior political scientist and State Department advisor Samuel Huntington suggested that international politics in the post–cold war era would be shaped not by modern ideology or economic interests, but by deeply irreconcilable "civilizational identities." "The fault lines between civilizations," Huntington observed, "are replacing the political and ideological boundaries of the Cold War as the flash points for crisis and bloodshed" (Huntington 1993, 29). Among the most likely trouble spots on the horizon, Huntington advised, was the Muslim world. "Conflict along the fault line between Western and Islamic civilizations has been going on for 1,300 years," he warned, citing the briefest of evidence to buttress this astounding claim, and in the future this *"military interaction between the West and Islam is unlikely to decline"* (emphasis added).[1]

Against this backdrop of international ferment, in general, and Western anxiety as to the political future of the Muslim world, in particular, the authors of these essays came together to discuss Islam and nation building in the Southeast Asian nations of Indonesia, Malaysia, and the Philippines.[2] In simple geographic terms insular Southeast Asia lies far from the Middle Eastern terrains conventionally associated in Westerners' minds with Islam. Indeed, many Middle Eastern Muslims are unfamiliar with Southeast Asia or uncertain as to the precise character of their fellow believers' faith. Notwithstanding this unfamiliarity, Southeast Asia is home to the most populous majority-Muslim country in the world (Indonesia) and contains an aggregate Muslim population greater than the Arab Middle East. The study of Islam in Southeast Asia thus presents an opportunity to deepen our understanding of the Muslim world's diversity and to challenge unitary characterizations of Islam's civilizational identity. Equally important, given the tenor of our times, this exercise allows us to disengage Muslim politics from histories and circumstances that owe more to the peculiarities of the Middle East than to Islam itself. All this is to say that Muslim Southeast Asia provides us with a much-needed opportunity to reevaluate the varied political potentialities of Islam in the modern era.

For the contributors to this volume, the more immediate benefit of such an intellectual inquiry is that it allows us to deepen our understanding of Islam in Southeast Asia in its own right. The nations in which Muslim Southeast Asians reside are characterized by extraordinary cultural and linguistic variety. Stretching across Indonesia, Malaysia, Singapore, southern Thailand, Brunei, and the southern Philippines, this region contains hundreds of ethnic groups, a similar variety of languages, representatives from most of the world's historic religions, and numerous tribal and localized traditions. Perhaps because of this dizzying diversity, Western scholars have until recently paid relatively little attention to Islam in Southeast Asia. Several years ago William Roff may have been guilty of hyperbole when he wrote that "there seems to have been an extraordinary desire on the part of Western social science observers to diminish, conceptually, the place and role of the religion and culture of Islam . . . in Southeast Asian societies" (1985, 7). But Roff's remark accurately conveys the conviction among many observers, Western and Southeast Asian, that Islam's influence on Southeast Asian society has been severely underestimated.

Recent developments in this region have made clear that such a neglect can no longer be justified. The economies of the two largest majority-Muslim countries in Southeast Asia, Malaysia and Indonesia, are today among the most rapidly growing in the world. Their economic dynamism has given both nations a heightened prominence in international affairs. Equally important, it has earned them the respect of Muslim leaders elsewhere in the world, many of whom have begun to wonder whether Southeast Asia might provide clues on how to manage market economies and cultural pluralism.

More significantly for the authors in this book, Islam in Southeast Asia can no longer be overlooked because since the late 1970s this region has experienced an unprecedented religious resurgence. Mosques have proliferated in towns and villages; religious schools and devotional programs have expanded; a vast market in Islamic books, magazines, and newspapers has developed; and, very important, a well-educated Muslim middle class has begun to raise questions about characteristically modern concerns, including the role and rights of women, the challenge of pluralism, the merits of market economies, and, most generally, the proper relationship of religion to state.

There have been many influences on this religious resurgence. Internationally, such developments as the Iranian revolution, the growth of Middle Eastern economic power since the 1970s, and the recent disenchantment in much of the Muslim world with secular nationalism have all played a role (see Esposito 1992, 11–24; Piscatori 1986, 26–34). However, at the center of all developments affecting Southeast Asian Islam looms one key institution: the modern nation-state. However rich its precedents, varied its influences, and diverse its motivations, the Islamic resurgence in Southeast Asia bears the imprint of this distinctly modern institution, with its projects for economic development and a state-shaped citizenry.

Though its policies and programs vary widely across national boundaries, the state in Southeast Asia, as in much of the modern world, has an "infrastructural reach" (Mann 1986, 114) far greater than the traditional states that once predominated throughout this region. Its capacity to shape public affairs and intervene in the most intimate domains of private life has presented Southeast Asian Muslims with a historically unprecedented challenge. It has reduced the territorial fragmentation long characteristic of this region, undercut the autonomy of Muslim social organizations, and, at times, deployed its forces to hunt down and eliminate Muslim rebels. For many political Muslims, however, there is also a romantic allure to this modern institution. Whatever its current uses, the state appears to offer the means for realizing long cherished dreams of religious and social transformation on a societywide scale. The idea of the nation has thus captured the Islamic imagination and intensified debate on what Muslim society should become (cf. Piscatori 1986; Moussalli 1995).

The resurgence also bears the imprint of something more uniquely Islamic: the emergence of a new style of religious activism that supplants or marginalizes the classically educated scholars of traditional Islam in favor of, as Dale F. Eickelman has described it, "religious and political activists who seek open religious discussion and whose authority is based upon persuasion and the interpretation of accessible texts" (Eickelman 1992, 652; cf. Meeker 1993; Yavuz n.d.). Though its precise influences vary from nation to nation, the ascent of these "new Muslim intellectuals" with their untraditional training and unconventional concerns is everywhere related to urbanization, mass education, new print and electronic media, and the growth of a Muslim middle class. These new movements build, of course, on the struggles of an earlier generation of Muslim reformers, who sought to open the door of religious interpretation *(ijtihad)* and make Islam responsive to the demands of the modern world, including the threat posed by the West (Keddie 1968; Piscatori 1986, 10). A century after the appearance of reformist Islam, however, developments in majority-Muslim nation-states have worked to create a new kind of Muslim discourse and a new kind of renewalist dynamic. The new discourse of renewal is oriented to the needs of a broad, mass-educated public rather than a narrow circle of religious adepts. In place of esoteric doctrine, the spokespersons for this reformation conceive of Islam in modern, quasi-ideological terms, as a source of practical and systematic knowledge "that can be differentiated from others and consciously reworked" (Eickelman 1992, 653; cf. Roy 1994, 3). This shift in religious rhetoric and its relevances is one more symptom of an Islam reinterpreted in the altered circumstances of the nation-state, national "publics," and the media that sustain both.

Though some Western and even Muslim observers speak as if they were a unitary phenomenon, these new Muslim groups do not speak with a single voice. On the contrary, one of the most striking features of the contemporary revival here in Southeast Asia is the diversity of its adherents and the vitality of its debate. Admittedly, the region has its radical militants and others who seem to conform to Western stereotypes of Islamic "fundamentalism." And, more generally, as in many other parts of the Muslim world, the resurgence has been characterized by intense "competition and contest over both the interpretation of symbols and control of the institutions . . . that produce and sustain them" (Eickelman and Piscatori 1996, 5). However, here in Southeast Asia, the dominant discourse to emerge from this contest has been marked not by theological totalism or strident authoritarianism, but by a remarkable combination of pluralism, intellectual dynamism, and openness to dialogue with non-Muslim actors and institutions.

However varied their emphases, most of these new Muslim intellectuals agree in their commitment to a developmental or activist understanding of their faith. Most show little enthusiasm for an Islam that is just a matter of pietistic study, personal morality, and ritual celebrations. Such conventional indices of religiosity remain important. But for new Muslim intellectuals and their followers, Islam must entail more than personal piety and public devotion. It must offer an alternative model of politics. It should provide moral discipline in the face of the anarchy and hedonism of the market. It can run schools, operate banks, and organize farmers' cooperatives. It may even provide an alternative, some say, to secular nationalism as the moral basis of the national community.

Unsympathetic observers might dismiss all this as the mere ideologization of religion. What is occurring, these critics might suggest, is the subordination of religion to the political needs of the moment or, worse yet, the ambitions of an unscrupulous leadership. Certainly there is such contestation and intrigue, as is the case whenever ethical ideas are drawn into the public sphere. But in Southeast Asia events have forced Muslims to confront a host of new questions and, in at least some instances, formulate new answers. Can Islam contribute to economic development? What posture should it adopt toward business and the market? And what of the status of women? The rights of non-Muslims? Is Islam compatible with pluralism and representative democracy? These questions emerge not from timeless theological doctrines, but from the efforts of Muslims to respond to the challenge of the nation-state and its associated projects for political and moral reconstruction.

Though Southeast Asian Muslims engage these issues with many of the scriptural, exegetical, and legal resources found elsewhere in the Muslim world, they do so within a social and historical horizon quite different from that of the Middle East. Their responses thereby reflect the creative tension everywhere characteristic of Islam (and, it should be said, all world religions) between the transcendent imperatives of the religion, as locally understood, and local histories, cultures, and identities. The latter heritage predisposes Muslims to selectively highlight certain elements of that heritage while neglecting others (cf. Bowen 1993; Eickelman 1987; Roff 1985). Such a creative tension is reflected in the essays in this volume. To understand its politics and meanings, we have to look into the history of Islam in this region and examine our own understandings or, as the case may be, misunderstandings of that history.

A Dual Marginalization

One of the most serious impediments to the development of a systematic understanding of Islam in Southeast Asia is the fact that the topic has long been marginalized in the fields of Islamic and Southeast Asian studies. In Islamic studies Western and Middle Eastern scholars alike have tended to place Southeast Asia at the intellectual periphery of the Islamic world. Still today in some overviews of Islamic history and civilization, Southeast Asian Muslims are mentioned briefly if at all. Though Southeast Asian Islam has almost two hundred million believers, it is not uncommon for observers, even learned specialists, to identify Islam with the Middle East and to regard Southeast Asia as, at best, intellectually and institutionally derivative of Middle Eastern Islam.[3]

There is a larger and, in one sense, understandable logic to this neglect. By comparison to Persia and the Arabian heartland, in insular Southeast Asia Islam became a civilizational force relatively late in Islamic history. Though Arab-Muslim traders traveled through island Southeast Asia as early as the seventh and eighth centuries, there was little settlement until the late thirteenth, when a Muslim town, inhabited in part by Arab-speaking foreigners, was established in the Pasai region of north Sumatra, an entrepôt for the trade with Muslim India and Arabia (Reid 1993, 133). Shortly thereafter, a Muslim presence appears to have been established in port towns along Java's north coast, territories still then under the control of the Hindu-Buddhist kingdom of Majapahit (Drewes 1968; Robson 1981). Ruling elites in the Malay peninsula were converted in the fifteenth and sixteenth centuries, and those in coastal Sulawesi and much of the southern Philippines were won to the faith in the seventeenth and eighteenth centuries.

The primary impetus for this wave of conversion was not conquest or religious warfare, as had been the case in Islam's early expansion in Arabia and North Africa, but trade and interethnic intercourse. Certainly, as Anthony Reid has noted, Muslim potentates (like their Theravada Buddhist counterparts in mainland Southeast Asia) regarded forcible conversion of neighbors as "an honourable motive for conquest" (1993, 170), and Muslim rulers periodically engaged in warfare with their Hindu-Buddhist, animist, or, in later times, Christian neighbors. However, as Thomas McKenna's essay in this volume illustrates, the causes of these conflicts were as much commercial and dynastic as they were religious.

More decisively, the rapid and relatively uniform spread of Islam to the insular world's maritime centers was related to broader historical developments, especially the growth of international commerce from the fifteenth to seventeenth centuries and the movement of large numbers of people out of localized societies into a multiethnic and interregional macrocosm (Reid 1993, 144; Robson 1981; cf. Hefner 1993a). Most of the map of modern Muslim Southeast Asia was laid out during this "age of commerce," as Anthony Reid (1988; 1993) has so aptly described it. A few remote corners of Southeast Asia have been converted to Islam in this century, some even in the last decades (see Rössler in this volume; Hefner 1987). In general, however, the dynamism of Islam in contemporary times has had less to do with a new wave of conversion than with the reform and rationalization of religion among established Muslim populations.

By itself, the comparatively late arrival of Islam in Southeast Asia neither explains nor justifies this region's marginalization within the field of Islamic studies. Given the genesis of what has come to be regarded as "classical" Islamic civilization within the Arabic- and Persian-speaking world, however, there was a tendency on the part of early Western Islamicists to devote their attention to regions where the classical tradition was first composed. This emphasis was reinforced by the focus of this early scholarship on Islamic "culture," not in the modern, social-historical or anthropological sense of this term, but in its great-traditional sense, as in written literature, philosophy, art and architecture, and law.[4] With several notable exceptions, the Orientalist commentaries that introduced Islamic civilization to a Western readership in the late nineteenth and early twentieth centuries were concerned with high culture, not the everyday meaning of Islam for ordinary Muslims. The focus of this writing was leading thinkers and civilizationwide achievements, especially those preserved for time in the printed word.

As a result of this textual emphasis, Southeast Asia—and other areas marginalized in the Orientalist understanding of the Muslim world, such as Central Asia, Bengal, and West Africa—was accorded only a minor role in early accounts of Islamic civilization. In some subfields of Islamic studies, such as jurisprudence *(fiqh)*, this perception of Southeast Asia as a late-comer and bit player in Islamic civilization seemed justified. As Hooker has noted (1983, 9), from the sixteenth century onward Muslim scholars in Southeast Asia were familiar with the standard works of Shafi'i law (one of the four schools of Sunni Muslim jurisprudence and the one most commonly applied in Southeast Asia). But local jurists confined their activities to the translation and interpretation of legal traditions codified in the Middle East; they never made an independent, distinctly Southeast Asian contribution to Islamic law. Equally important, the Shafi'i works familiar to Southeast Asian jurists were never used as the sole basis for legal deliberations in Southeast Asia's sultanates. Local potentates used a variety of legal systems, as was consistent with the cultural pluralism of their subjects (Milner 1983, 27; Reid 1993, 182–184).

This lack of originality in legal scholarship (if not legal practice), however, still tells us little about the ways in which Islam became part of the culture and lifeways of Southeast Asian Muslims. To understand this process requires that we distance ourselves from the legalistic, *"shari'ah-*centered" understanding of Islam that predominates in classical scholarship, Western and Muslim, and examine Islam in its local and regional context (cf. Munawar-Rachman 1994). From this perspective the diffusion of Islam into Southeast Asia looks more richly distinctive.

The first centuries of the Islamic expansion into Southeast Asia coincided with an era of great Sufi influence in Mecca, Medina, and northern India (Schimmel 1975, 344–363; Roff 1985, 20; Woodward 1989, 54–55). Not coincidentally, then, mystic literature and practices were conspicuous among the items first appropriated into popular Islamic culture in Southeast Asia. As Anthony Johns has noted (1961; 1993), the Sufi role in early Southeast Asian Islam was facilitated by the religious traditions already established in the region, which had an elective affinity with certain aspects of Sufism.[5] Most notable among these affinities was the monist disposition of many of this region's existing religious traditions, with their idea that rather than standing apart from this world, divinity infuses it.

The Southeast Asian response to Islamic mysticism was not passive or derivative, but complex and creative. In the works of such learned mystics as Hamzah Fansuri (al-Attas 1970) and Abd. al-Rauf (Johns 1955), Southeast Asian Muslims developed a literary and intellectualized variant of Islamic mysticism among the richest in the world. The impact of this thought reached far beyond esoteric circles, providing popular devotion with a nonlegalistic disposition (see Bowen 1993; van Bruinessen 1994) and influencing the practice and meanings of kingship (Hooker 1983, 11; Milner 1983, 35; Woodward 1989, 59). In court-based variants of this Southeast Asian Muslim tradition, the ruler, rather than independent religious scholars (ulama), came to be seen as the mystical anchor of the religious community. He was the defender of the faith, the shadow of Allah on earth, and a mystically powerful "perfect man." By virtue of his spiritual preeminence, he, not the *ulama,* was responsible for the transmission and implementation of

Islamic law. This prerogative provided rulers with discretionary leeway in deciding how strictly they wished to apply Islamic law. Though at times in early modern history (from the fifteenth to eighteenth centuries) *ulama* attempted to assert their authority against that of the court, sometimes in alliance with merchants hoping to limit the absolutist claims of rulers (Reid 1993, 263), the more general pattern resembled that Milner has described for Malay sultanates: "The Raja, not the Malay race or the Islamic *ummat* (community), was the primary object of loyalty" (1983, 31). And the raja himself was usually concerned with worldly interests more varied than the unitary conduct of worship and law (cf. Woodward 1989, 154).

Here, then, is at least one clue to the way in which the univeralist injunctions of Islam were accommodated to Southeast Asian culture. In modern times, however, our appreciation of this tradition's distinctiveness in Islamic civilization has been hampered by the obscurity of its literary sources and the embarrassment of some modern Muslims in the face of religious traditions regarded (much too simplistically) as undemocratic or heretical. For these and other reasons, it was all too easy for students of Islamic great traditions to perceive Muslim civilization in Southeast Asia as derivative or, worse yet, as the curious product of peoples who, somehow, weren't quite "real Muslims."

Islam in Southeast Asian Studies

The other marginalization to which the study of Islam in Southeast Asia has long been subjected unwittingly reinforced this neglect. This marginalization occurred within the field of Southeast Asian studies, particularly the form that took shape in the United States in the aftermath of World War II. In this emerging academic field, it was not uncommon for Islam to be portrayed as an intrusive cultural force or, as another widely used metaphor would have it, a late-deposited cultural "layer." The real Southeast Asia lay deeper and was somehow less Islamic.

This perspective on Islam in Southeast Asia had deep historical and, more specifically, colonial precedents. In colonial times, particularly in the Dutch East Indies, this notion of Islam as a "thin veneer" appealed to those who wished to justify the suppression of Islam on the grounds that it was a threat to colonial power (Ellen 1983, 65; Roff 1985, 13). In Java, for example, nineteenth-century colonial administrators developed a "structure of not seeing" (Florida 1995), overlooking Islamic influences in Javanese tradition, while exaggerating and essentializing the influence of non-Islamic ideals. In the aftermath of the brutal Java War (1825–1830), colonial scholars worked to create a canon of Javanese literature that romanticized pre-Islamic literature as a golden age and portrayed the coming of Islam as a civilizational disaster. These Dutch Orientalists conveniently overlooked the fact that the proportion of Islamic-oriented literature in modern court collections was vastly greater than the so-called renaissance literature (pre-Islamic classics rendered in modern Javanese verse) that colonial scholars portrayed as the essence of things Javanese (Florida 1995; cf. Day 1983; Ricklefs 1974, 176–226).

Colonial law effected a similar essentialization. Under the direction of Cornelis van Vollenhoven, the "*adat* (customary) law school" worked under state directive to develop what amounted to a system of legal apartheid. A classic example of the colonial "invention of tradition" (Hobsbawm and Ranger 1983), European experts divided the native peoples of the Indies into nineteen distinct legal communities. Islamic law was acknowledged in each community's legal traditions only to the extent that colonial scholars determined that local custom *(adat)* explicitly acknowledged Islamic law (Hooker 1983, 176). In this manner, colonial authorities reified the distinction between customary *adat* and Islam. As James Siegel's (1969) study of Aceh and Taufik Abdullah's (1966) of Minangkabau both demonstrate, however, this distinction between endogenous "custom" and exogenous "Islam" imposed an artificial polarity on a relationship that had always been dynamic (see Rössler and Peletz, this volume). In fact, in the decades preceding the European conquest, legal traditions in places like Malaya and Minangkabau (west Sumatra) had already begun to accord a greater role to textually based Islamic norms (Abdullah 1966, 10; Lev 1972, 250). It was precisely this growing Islamic influence that prompted anxious Dutch authorities to implement their *adatrecht* policy.[6]

British legal policies in Malaya differed from those of the Dutch. Drawing on their experience with Muslims in India, the British at first regarded Malay Muslims as "unheretical members of some idealized and uniform civilization" (Ellen 1983, 51). By treating *adat* as "custom that has no legal consequences" (Roff 1985, 16) and allowing the Malay sultans a measure of jural authority, the British allowed the formation of institutional structures in which Islamic law had a substantial albeit circumscribed role. Nonetheless, lacking a framework for integrating the study of local traditions and Islam, British scholars of the colonial era fell into an "anecdotal empiricism" (Ellen 1983, 53) that failed to grasp the dynamics of religious change in Malay society as a whole.

Though there was a tradition of Islamic studies in colonial Southeast Asia, then, it suffered from the subordination of scholarship to the needs of the colonial political order. In the early postwar era, a new and more contextual framework for the study of Islam in Southeast Asia came on the scene. Harry J. Benda's 1958 studies of the Muslim role in the struggle for

Indonesian independence provided rich insights into the relationship of Islam to Indonesian nationalism and the social bases for the fierce rivalries that pitted secular nationalists and communists against Muslims in the early independence era. Benda relied too uncritically on colonial historical scholarship in characterizing popular Javanese religion as "rooted in age-old pre-Hindu mysticism with accretions from later, including Muslim, religious elements" (1983, 14). Nonetheless, his research into Islam and nationalism provided a critical foundation for the reassessment of political Islam in the postcolonial era. A few years later, William R. Roff's (1967) analyses of Islam and Malay nationalism guaranteed that, in Malay historical studies at the very least, Islam would never again be assigned a peripheral role. In Islamic literary studies, finally, the pioneering scholarship of G. W. J Drewes (1968; 1969; 1978) and Anthony Johns (1957; 1965) revealed the depth of mystical writing in Southeast Asian Islam and its intimate relationship to South Asian and Middle Eastern sources.

However divergent their concerns, the works of Benda, Roff, Drewes, and Johns together laid the foundation for the revitalization of the study of Islam in Southeast Asia. In the end, however, their influence in the broader field of Southeast Asian studies was limited, in part because other scholars working in the region saw little need to devote further attention to Islamic matters and in part because all four men were soon overshadowed by the most famous American anthropologist and Indonesianist of the early postwar era, Clifford Geertz. At least in the United States, it was Clifford Geertz who set the agenda for the study of Islam in Southeast Asia from the 1960s until the mid-1980s. Later generations of Southeast Asianists would have to position themselves within and against Geertz' awesome legacy.

Geertz and Islam

Clifford Geertz' perspective on Islam is a complex and fascinating one, and, contrary to the claims of some of his critics, does not allow for easy dismissal. Geertz' early writings on Islam and Indonesian society (Geertz 1960; 1965; 1968) combine brilliant ethnographic insight with somewhat less careful historical generalization. Many of these works—particularly those written before the late 1960s, after which he distanced himself from the structural-functionalist methodologies in which he had earlier been trained —were strongly influenced by a sociological version of modernization theory adapted from the work of his mentors, Talcott Parsons and Edward Shils (Hefner and Hoben 1991). Whatever their shortcomings in light of today's preoccupations, Geertz' works were unparalleled in their ability to combine subtle ethnnography with provocative theoretical reflection.

Although one of his most widely read books compares Islam in Indonesia with that in Morocco (Geertz 1968; cf. Munson 1993), Geertz was generally impatient with the historical and literary scholarship long at the heart of Islamic studies. In retrospect, there can be little question that some of Geertz' skepticism was justified; whatever its logic, it allowed him to set off in new directions and make strikingly original contributions to the comparative study of Islam. In particular, by using an ethnographic approach and sensitizing Islam scholars to the issues it could illuminate, Geertz was better able than textually oriented Islamicists to explore the practice and meanings of Islam among ordinary Muslims. This concern with "everyday" or "practical Islam"—the activities and meanings through which ordinary Muslims experience their religion—has been a central and eminently welcome feature of Islamic studies since Geertz' work in the 1970s (Ellen 1983, 54; Eickelman 1976, 11–13; Munson 1993, 1–3).

In another respect, however, Geertz' estrangement from Islamicist scholarship had less fortunate, if largely unintended, consequences. Whatever its high-cultural biases, Orientalist scholarship had amply detailed the variety of religious styles and world views within Islamic civilization. By failing to take note of this "burden of complexity," as William Roff has described it (1985, 26), Geertz tended at times to draw on what was, in fact, a narrow standard for distinguishing what is and what is not Islam. This shortcoming is especially ironic in light of Geertz' stated concern with looking at Islam from an ethnographic point of view; however, it illustrates the dangers of any approach to Islam that erects too great a divide between ethnographic and textual study (Bowen 1993; Woodward 1989). The fact is that proper ethnographic characterizations of local Islam require familiarity with Islam's textual and normative sources.

Ironically, Geertz may have been influenced on this point not merely by his own disciplinary predilections, but by the biases of his modernist informants in Java, where he worked in the early 1950s. Many of these religious reformers were only too willing to describe the religious practices of their less orthodox Javanist rivals, the so-called *abangan*, as un-Islamic or "Hindu," since this allowed them to discredit those activities more thoroughly. Whatever the precise influences on his ethnographic vision, Geertz identified an array of devotional practices in Indonesia as non-Islamic because they were inconsistent with the modernist practice of Islam. Rather than talking of pluralism and subalterity within Islamic tradition, then, he tended to see the Javanese Muslim community as split between those whom he effectively regarded as true Muslims, the so-called *santri*, and those whom he thought only nominally Islamized, the *abangan* (lit. "red"). *Abangan* religious culture, Geertz felt, owed more to animism and Hindu-Buddhism than to Islam.

Inasmuch as it worked at all in Muslim Southeast Asia, Geertz' model really applied only to Javanese society. In a few areas of the Indo-Malaysian archipelago such as Lombok (Cederoth 1975; Krulfeld 1966), there existed religious divisions of equivalent severity to those found in Java. Until recently, however, throughout most of the region the more common religious opposition has been that John Bowen describes in his chapter in this book, between "old group" *(kaum tua)* traditionalists and "new group" *(kaum muda)* modernists (cf. Abdullah 1966; Bowen 1993, 21–30; Roff 1967). The modernists were strongly influenced by ideas of Islamic reform emanating from the Middle East, emphasizing the self-sufficiency of scripture and decrying what were regarded as unacceptable innovations *(bid'a)* in matters of worship. They were also critical of traditionalist religious jurists *(ulama).* The modernists felt that these caretakers of tradition had compromised their scholarship by relying too heavily on the scriptural and legal commentaries of previous scholars, especially as codified in the *madhab,* the recognized legal traditions of Sunni Islam. The modernists also felt that traditional *ulama* had been too tolerant of popular ritual practices that the modernists regarded as unacceptable innovations or, worse yet, polytheistic deviations *(shirk)* from true Islam (Noer 1973).

In light of more recent research, however, it is clear that Geertz' categorizations exaggerated Hindu-Buddhist influences and oversimplified Islamic ones. For example, he described premodern Javanese Islam in terms of what he called a "classical religious style," which he felt had predominated in Java from the sixteenth to mid-nineteenth centuries. Its characteristics, he said, were a quietistic mysticism, rather than legalism, and a decided nonchalance as regards Islamic ritual obligations. In a loose sense this characterization is consistent with the raja-centered Islam that, indeed, had once held true across Southeast Asia. However, the distinction overlooks the fact that even in Java there was from early on a vigorous legalistic tradition, associated most especially with the *pasisir* culture of Java's north and northeastern coasts (Pigeaud 1967–1980). While Geertz' account of one of the early apostles of Islam in Java, Sunan Kalijaga, emphasizes the aestheticized quietism of his conversion experience, other accounts of this saint *(wali)* emphasize his military and commercial prowess and his concern with the law (Graaf and Pigeaud 1974; Woodward 1989, 97). As Roff has observed (1985, 24), building in part on Pigeaud (1967–1980), the "classical style" of Javanese Islam had always been more richly differentiated and included a more significant legal-normative component than Geertz' rendering of the Kalijaga myth implies.[7]

These shortcomings in Geertz' analysis were summarized by the renowned Islamicist Marshall Hodgson: "Influenced by the polemics of a certain school of modern Shari'ah-minded Muslims, Geertz identifies 'Islam' only with what that school of modernists happens to approve, and ascribes everything else to an aboriginal or Hindu-Buddhist background, gratuitously labelling much of the Muslim religious life in Java 'Hindu.' He identifies a long series of phenomena, virtually universal to Islam and sometimes found even in the Qur'an itself, as un-Islamic; and hence his interpretations of the Islamic past as well as of some recent anti-Islamic reactions is highly misleading" (Hodgson 1974, 2.551.). Among other things, Hodgson is referring here to Geertz' tendency to see numerous aspects of Malayo-Indonesian mysticism, with its Sufi-derived topography of self and divinity, as "Hindu-Buddhist"; his identification of trafficking with local spirits as animist, even though such beliefs have been accommodated within Islam since the time of Muhammad (as the Qur'an itself makes clear); and his repeated identification of ritual festival meals *(slametan)* as animist or Hindu-Buddhist, even though similar rites (complete with incense) are common in other parts of the Muslim world. More recently, Mark R. Woodward (1989) has extended this line of criticism, revealing strongly Islamic elements within, most notably, the Javanese tradition of kingship, ritual, architecture, and the arts. In identifying mysticism, *slametan* feasts, the veneration of ancestors, and trafficking with tutelary spirits as invariably "animist" or "Hindu-Buddhist," Geertz may have conveyed a view of Islam consistent with that of his reform-minded informants. In doing so, however, he unwittingly diminished the civilizational pluralism of historic Islam.[8]

If, in the end, Geertz' categorization of things Islamic was too tightly drawn, this criticism is true in spades of Southeast Asianist scholars who followed in his wake, particularly in America-based Indonesian studies. By unwittingly sanctioning a restrictive view of Islam, Geertz seemed to confirm the suspicions of less careful scholars that Islam was of marginal or segmental importance to the study of Southeast Asian culture. In the Indonesian case, this impression seemed justified by the fact that the severe politicization of religion and politics in Java during the 1950s and the 1960s eventually led some nominal Muslims to repudiate Islam outright (see Pranowo 1991; Lyon 1977).

Not surprisingly, then, during the 1960s and 1970s some of the most influential essays on politics, personhood, and culture in Muslim Southeast Asia, especially in Indonesia, were written without serious exploration of Islamic influences. For example, Benedict Anderson's widely cited and otherwise remarkable essay, "The Idea of Power in Javanese Culture" (1972), drew extensively on Javanese literary and ritual traditions to develop a model of indigenous ideas of power in Java. In "A Note on Islam," which appears toward the end of the essay, Anderson cites Clifford Geertz to back up his claim that "the penetration of Islam *scarcely changed* the composition and recruitment of the Javanese political elite or affected the basic intellectual framework of traditional political thought" (Anderson 1972, 59; emphasis added). This observation raises complex and important issues. Its full assessment, however, would require at least some reference to Sufi notions of kingship, popular Islamic concepts of sainthood, and folk Islamic views of sacrifice and spiritual power, all of which exercise palpable influences on Javanese traditions (cf. Reid 1993; Lombard 1990, 176–208).

In a later and equally influential book on the origin and spread of nationalism, Anderson displays a similar blind spot. His comments on early Indonesian nationalism abound with insightful references to the "creole functionaries" who were recruited by the colonial state into institutions of modern learning and resocialized in the ways of European administration (1983, 105–106). These "functionary journeys," Anderson argues (p. 111), nurtured a sense of solidarity across linguistic and ethnic barriers that had previously segmented indigenous society, and thus created the links required for this group's leadership of the Indonesian nationalist movement. In this otherwise subtle account, however, we once again hear nothing about Muslim pilgrimages across ethnic and linguistic boundaries. In places like North Sumatra, Java, and South Sulawesi, these movements also shaped an anti-colonial imagination.[9] Though, like their non-Islamic counterparts, many of these Muslim pilgrims at first enunciated political visions premised on only pre- or protonationalist ideals, their religious pilgrimage and political struggles still worked to create a commitment to transethnic solidarities. Eventually, like their counterparts in most of the Muslim world (Piscatori 1986), Muslim leaders elaborated their own versions of the nationalist ideal. These were not secondhand derivatives of secular nationalism, but full-blown alternatives to the version created by Anderson's European-schooled, "creole nationalists." In religious centers in Aceh (Bowen 1993) and eastern Java (Hefner 1994), among others, Muslim thinkers elaborated a vision of the nation premised on shared religion, not merely common ethnic culture. They linked its meanings to Islam's ancient glories and the distant rumblings of Turkish, Persian, and Arab nationalism.[10]

In this and other examples, a generation of scholars went much further than Geertz had ever intended in marginalizing Islam in Southeast Asian studies. Slowly, however, the cumulative effect of scholarship by such pioneers as Benda, Roff, Drewes, and Johns led to a deeper appreciation of Islam in contemporary life. Renewed interest in Islam was not merely the result of accumulating scholarly wisdom, however. More significant was the impact of Islamic resurgence itself, which swept across Muslim Southeast Asia in the 1970s and 1980s. The evidence of those decades made all too clear that Islam was not a declining cultural force but an ascendant one.

Nationalism and the Secularist Juggernaut

Another reason Islam poses such problems for students of modern politics has to do with the conviction once widespread among Western political theorists that religion is, at best, a declining historical force, destined to give way to the twin forces of economic modernization and nation-state formation. One of the more remarkable facts of late-nineteenth- and twentieth-century Western political theory was the near universality of this belief. On the left and on the right, among Marxists and Weberians, and among modernization theorists and their postmodern critics, the view that modernity is inherently secularizing—or, at the very least, so thoroughly destabilizing of religious certitudes as to demand the privatization of religion within a realm of personal belief—has dominated all the important schools of modern Western social thought (Berger 1982; Casanova 1994).

Outside of Marxism, which had its own version, the most sustained expression of the secularization thesis was associated with the modernization theory of the 1950s and 1960s. Drawing on the works of Émile Durkheim and Max Weber, modernization theory asserted that modern political-economic development involves, above all else, the increasing differentiation and specialization of social and economic structures. Commerce and, later, industrialization bring about a growing division of labor, and this in turn promotes the differentiation of society into the pluralistic entities characteristic of much of the world today. It is the cultural consequence of this change that is the primary concern of secularization theorists. Where previously there was a "sacred canopy" (Berger 1967) stabilizing life experience and providing shared meanings, in modern times the canopy is rent and the collective bases of morality and identity are diminished or destroyed (cf. Beckford 1989, 74–107).

Given the severity of its forecasts, it is not surprising that from early on observers began to express doubts regarding the relevance of secularization theory for the Muslim world. Some theorists, such as the Turkish-born sociologist Bassam Tibi, continued to insist that secularization is intrinsic to modernization, and the Islamic world is no exception. How then to explain the Islamic revival occurring in the Muslim world today? Citing the experience of Christianity in Western Europe, Tibi notes that Protestantism, too, once had grandiose political aspirations, but it was eventually "domiciled within the sphere of interiority" (Tibi 1990, 139). Islam, he predicts, will develop in a "parallel direction" because this is what modern development requires. It would seem that only inasmuch as the Islamic world is commandeered by antimodernizing reactionaries can it evade this privatization.

Other observers of the Muslim world, however, appeared less certain of this prognosis. In his *Islam Observed* (a work that still shows the influence of his earlier training in modernization theory, which he subsequently rejected), Clifford Geertz argued that the "secularization of thought" is characteristic of the modern world (1968, 88). He attributed this trend to the "growth of science" and its destabilizing influence on revealed truths. Geertz qualified this generalization, however, by noting that "the loss of power of classical religious symbols to sustain a properly religious faith" can provoke the "ideologization of religion," as the bearers of revealed truths mobilize against secularist assault. While thus embracing a variant of the secularization thesis, Geertz recognized the possibility of antisecularizing movements. Contrary to what he might argue today, however, he also implied that these were by their very nature countermodernizations, rather than alternative modernities.

Some observers, such as the philosopher and anthropologist Ernest Gellner, have been even more adamant in rejecting the relevance of the secularization thesis for the Muslim world. Unlike Tibi or Geertz, Gellner attributes this exceptionalism not to Islam's antimodernizing dispositions, but to its uniqueness in adapting to the modern nation-state. The key, Gellner argues, is that Islam has been able to play a role in the nation-state functionally (but not substantively) equivalent to that of nationalism in the West. In the West, nineteenth- and early-twentieth-century nationalists revived and idealized popular ethnic culture, using it as an instrument of nation building. This change in political culture was facilitated by the social dislocation reshaping Europe, as the vertical allegiances of the feudal era were undermined and replaced by new lateral ones. Nationalism seized on the realities of vernacular language, folk customs, and myths of national origin to respond to this crisis and forge a new basis for the political order, one founded on the sovereignty of a "people" defined by common culture. In this manner, nationalism displaced Christianity as the key idiom of European political identity and, along the way, accelerated the secularization of modern European politics.

Gellner points out that a similar detraditionalization has altered social ties in the Muslim world. However, he argues that for several reasons Islam has been able to respond to the change while avoiding the secularist juggernaut. Islam, Gellner notes, had long been divided between an elite and a popular variant. The high tradition was associated with the transethnic and transregional clerisy, the *ulama,* who were responsible first and foremost for preserving and implementing the law, the master institution in Islamic tradition. By contrast, the low or folk tradition in Islam was grounded on tribal organizations, kinship politics, and the veneration of living Muslim saints (Gellner 1981, 75–76). While paying homage to the high tradition of scholarship and law, popular Islam had an only intermittent interest, at best, in its casuistic detail. Throughout history the two traditions flowed into and influenced each other. Periodically, however, they also erupted into conflict, when reformers "revived the alleged pristine zeal of the high culture, and united tribesmen in the interests of purification and of their own enrichment and political advancement" (ibid.). For a while thereafter, a purified Islam would dominate the political scene, but eventually it too would succumb to the twin corruptions of urban decadence and tribal parochialism.

With its industries, education, and, above all, powerful state, the modern era has irreversibly altered this "flux and reflux" (Gellner 1981; 1992, 14) in the life of Islam, shifting the historical advantage to the supporters of the clerisy-sustained high tradition. Modernizing reformists have blamed folk Islam for the Muslim world's backwardness. In reformers' eyes, the twin challenges of modernization and Western dominance demand that this backward tradition be replaced once and for all with a purified, high Islam. Only through such a total-cultural revolution can the Muslim world restore its lost glory and propel itself into the modern era. With the machinery of the modern state at their disposal, Gellner suggests, Muslim reformists can for the first time implement their programs of total-cultural revolution on a societywide scale. For Gellner, Islam is unique among the world's historic religions in being able to pull off this feat, using "a pre-industrial great tradition of a clerisy as the national, socially pervasive idiom and belief of a new style community" (Gellner 1983, 81).

There are several problems with Gellner's analysis. While emphasizing the vitality of religion in the modern Muslim world, Gellner preserves a too-Weberian understanding of religion's decline elsewhere. He thereby exaggerates the degree to which the non-Muslim world has been secularized, at least in the dual meaning of secularization as privatization and decline. Recently a number of scholars have commented on the inadequacy of this portion of the secularization argument for characterizing religious developments in the West, not least of all in the United States, where religious institutions have shown great resilience (Berger 1983; Wuthnow 1988; 1989). This resilience is not just another example of American exceptionalism. Throughout large portions of Latin America, Africa, and eastern Europe, Christianity has demonstrated an ability to project itself into the public arena with a vigor and expansiveness quite contrary to post-Enlightenment understandings of religion as essentially a matter of "private" belief or as a declining historical force (Casanova 1994; Martin 1990).

It is not just at the margins of the Christian world that one sees problems with secularist models of nation building and modernity. Recently India has witnessed the rise of a virulently anti-Muslim but broadly popular Hindu nationalism (van der Veer 1984; Juergensmeyer 1993). In Sri Lanka Theravada Buddhists have been at the vanguard of Sinhala nationalist efforts against the Tamil minority (Tambiah 1992). Even in Thailand, Burma, and Laos, Buddhism has been forcefully drawn into nation building (Keyes 1987; Reynolds 1978). All this leads to an obvious but important conclusion. Whereas in the 1950s and 1960s the marginalization of religion from northern European nation building was seen as the prototype for modern development, nation building now appears consistent with a wider array of moral-ideological regimes, including some in which religion plays an important public role (Casanova 1994).[11]

In half-century retrospect, then, it is clear that the secular nationalism of the postwar era was not the harbinger of a worldwide evolution, but the peculiar product of a particular historical epoch. Today, secularist modernism is being challenged in many parts of the world (Casanova 1994; Cohen and Arato 1992, 345–420; Juergensmeyer 1993). A general theory of religion and modernity must begin with this fact and with the more context-sensitive approach to religion it requires.[12] It is just such a contextualized understanding of the politics and meanings of nation building—and the plural nature of the project of modernity itself—that underlies the essays in this volume.

Islam and Nation

Each of the nations discussed in this volume is markedly different with regard to the role of Islam in the nation and in the public sphere more generally. As is the case throughout the Muslim world (Eickelman and Piscatori 1996; Esposito and Voll 1996), the ideals and activities of the new Islamic resurgence reflect not the irremediable influence of inalterable ideological forms, but country-specific patterns of civil and state organization. More specifically, most show the strong impact of state-society interactions that have evolved over the course of several decades of national independence.

In Indonesia, Muslim organizations played a pivotal role in anticolonial resistance from the very beginning of the nationalist movement; eventually, however, they had to resign themselves to a less central role in the institutions of government. At the beginning of the independence war in

1945, the Muslim leadership was itself divided on the question of an Islamic state. Some leaders advocated it; others merely wanted the government to enforce religious obligations among that portion of the population who professed Islam; and still others advocated a plural and liberal-constitutional democracy. In the face of bitter opposition from Christians and secular nationalists, the leadership opted for a compromise formulation, whereby there would be no unitary establishment of religion within the Indonesian state. Unlike a secular European state, however, the Indonesian constitution would require all its citizens to profess a state-recognized world religion, and it would otherwise promote religion through schools and other public institutions (Boland 1982; Hefner, Chapter 3, this volume). Though the precise nature of the state's support for religion was left vague at the time of independence, this principle of state support for religion provided Muslims with grounds for argument against secular nationalists in years to come.

During the 1950s, the nonsectarian compromise struck in 1945 was again the subject of intense debate. Some in the Muslim leadership felt that the spirit of the 1945 compromise violated Islamic doctrine and should therefore be repudiated in favor of a new drive for an explicitly Islamic state. Other Muslim leaders, however, strongly disagreed with this view. In the nation as a whole, as discussed in the essays by Feillard and Hefner below, the nationalist and communist parties eventually came to exercise greater influence than their Muslim rivals, at least until the cataclysmic violence of 1965–1966. The destruction of the powerful Indonesian Communist Party at that time set a new political dynamic in motion and once again raised questions regarding the proper role of religion in national life.

The military-dominated government that emerged after 1965–1966 came to power with the support of Muslim organizations, many of which actively participated in the physical liquidation of the Communist Party (Cribb 1990; Hefner 1990, 202–215). But the new regime soon marginalized its erstwhile allies by adopting policies designed to undercut the political capacities of the Muslim community as well as anyone else who might aspire to independent political organization. While suppressing political Islam, however, the regime was more tolerant of what it regarded as a depoliticized "cultural Islam"—especially those Muslim organizations that accepted the government's ideological principles of Pancasila pluralism, thereby renouncing the goal of establishing an Islamic state.

The latitude for civil (as opposed to explicitly political) organization provided by the government inadvertently worked to favor the efforts of those Muslims unhappy with the party-based rivalries of the 1950s. These advocates of nonpolitical activism wanted the Muslim community to concentrate its energies on education, social welfare, and the deepening of religious piety. Twenty years later, it is clear that this strategy of working in the system and promoting a moderate Islam has, for the moment, proved a success from the government's point of view, as well as for most of the Muslim community. Contrary to the hopes of some in the ruling elite, however, this government support for nonpolitical Islam helped to fuel an Islamic revival of unprecedented proportions (see Pranowo 1991, and Feillard and Hefner essays below). Moreover, as in other Muslim countries where the government has sponsored Islamic proselytization (Piscatori 1986, 138; Roy 1994, 125–131), it is by no means clear that the long-term consequences of this development will coincide with government strategists' intentions.

In Indonesia the consequences of these changes for state and society are as yet unclear. The New Order regime has consistently adopted a policy toward nonstate organizations that is centralizing, hierarchical, and corporatistic. In a pattern of heavy-handed cooptation that goes back to the Sukarno era (Reeve 1985), political, professional, labor, religious, and other civil associations are subjected to extensive state controls, including tests for ideological correctness and strong pressures to choose leaders amenable to government directives. In such circumstances, it is difficult for any civic organization to operate independently of strict state supervision. Indeed, as Indonesia's private business sector has grown in recent years, the government has sought to force even business associations to play by these corporatist rules (MacIntyre 1990).

Such a hierarchical authoritarianism creates a political atmosphere in which it is all too easy for rival claimants to power to conclude that the only rational way to engage in politics is to work behind the scenes, forging alliances with ascendant factions in the ruling elite and taking care not to push for broader political participation. It is important to emphasize that this corporatist policy is in fact quite contrary to the Muslim community's own organizational history. Prior to the patrimonial politics of the independence era, Muslim organizations had a long history of pluralism and extra-governmental independence. In precolonial and colonial times, most of the Islamic community stood apart from the state, in village schools and networks of trade, learning, and pilgrimage. Though the state had its hired clerics, often recruited from the ranks of the lesser aristocracy, most Islamic scholars kept a careful distance from state bureaucrats. In the face of Old Order patrimony and New Order controls, some Muslim organizations have had difficulty maintaining their independence. Nonetheless, in recent years such organizations as Nahdlatul Ulama and the Muhammadiyah have preserved a vital nonstate organization and have been among the most consistent advocates of social and political reform (see Feillard and Hefner, below).

Under the government's corporatist controls, however, it is understandable that some in the political arena, Muslim and non-Muslim alike, may be tempted to opt for a state-centered strategy aimed at capturing control of government, keeping the system closed, and using the state to suppress rival claimants to power. Were a vigorously Islamic leadership to move into a governing coalition and opt for such a strategy, it would destroy the Muslim community's historic role as a promoter of civil association and extra-governmental freedom. The Muslim world would have lost one of its brightest prospects for a democratic and pluralist Islam.

There is considerably less of a historic precedent for Muslim civil autonomy in Malaysia, though even here the situation is complex. Influenced by their longer experience with Muslims in India, from early on in the colonial era the British formally acknowledged the role of Islam among the Malay population. Primary responsibility for the management of Islamic affairs was left in the hands of the native elite, especially the sultans, under the watchful eye of British supervisors (Roff 1967; Mutalib 1990, 16). From an organizational perspective, then, Malay Islam in colonial times remained a more state-centered entity than was the case in Indonesia. In part as a result of this precedent, Malaysian Islam has tended until recently to display a more socially conservative, establishmentarian face than Islam in Indonesia.

This tendency to work through government rather than through civil institutions was reinforced in the late colonial era. At the end of the Second World War, Malayan society was shaken by events known as the "Emergency," a combination of ethnic and political disturbances provoked in the first instance by a Chinese-led communist insurgency against British occupation. In its first months, this struggle was marked by gruesome episodes of violence between Chinese and Malays. The Chinese had suffered under the Japanese occupation, and many among them resented what they regarded as Malay collaboration with Japanese authorities against the Chinese (Omar 1993, 34). The communist rebellion was suppressed by the British authorities after a long antiguerrilla campaign. In its aftermath, as Malaysia prepared for independence, the British instituted political and constitutional measures that effectively guaranteed Malay dominance in the government. (Malays make up just over 60 percent of the country's population, Chinese 30 percent). Equally important, they perpetuated the tradition of direct government involvement in the management of Islamic affairs. The three-sided dialogue seen in Indonesia between nationalism, state organization, and independent religious association was here replaced by a more unitary pattern of (limited) religious establishment and Malay political dominance.

It is important to note, however, that the British introduced legal institutions and constitutional balances into the Malaysian political system of a far more extensive sort than those developed by the Dutch in the East Indies. Indeed, the Dutch bequeathed a legal tradition that preserved large portions of the colonial system's police-state controls. However shaken they have been by recent developments, Malaysia's legal and political structures provide a significant counterweight to the establishmentarianism of the political order and have insured a greater measure of political and associational freedom than seen in Indonesia during the New Order. Nonetheless, the identification of Islam with Malayness and Malayness with political dominance has guaranteed that, unlike in Indonesia, there has been a strong tendency to coordinate Islam through state bureaus rather than through independent social organizations. As Peletz' essay in this volume indicates (cf. Jomo and Cheek 1992), many of Malaysia's new Muslim movements have focused not on building extrastate associations, but on challenging the government's Islamic credentials and calling for greater state involvement in religious affairs.

Some Malay religious organizations have responded to this situation by withdrawing from the political arena in favor of the purity and privacy of cult organization. However, as Malay politics in the Mahathir era has moved out of the hands of aristocrats and into those of new administrative elites, government Islam itself has been opened to people from a wider range of social backgrounds, even if its basic structures have remained unchanged (Crouch 1996, 246; Jomo and Cheek 1992; cf. Nagata 1984). The situation of Malaysian Muslims thus reflects two contrary influences. On one hand, Muslim interests have been premised on Malay political dominance and pursued in the corridors of state power rather than through civil association. On the other, Malaysia's remarkable economic boom and the growth of a more confident Malay middle class have served to mute demands for a more radical establishment of religion in the state. How much these latter qualities—and Malaysian democracy in general (see Crouch 1996, 236–247)—are dependent upon the country's continuing economic growth remains unclear.

In the third Muslim community represented in this volume, the Philippines, the relationship of Muslims to the nation-state has been different yet. If, in Malaysia, the state has been an official promoter of Islam and, in Indonesia, Muslims have struggled to guard their independence and project their influence into an otherwise nonsectarian state, in the Philippines the Muslim community has had to balance dominance within their own territories against marginalization within the institutions of the nation-state as a whole. In recent years, as a result of an influx of Christian Filipino migrants from the north, Muslim dominance even in regions of historic Muslim settlement has been severely threatened. As McKenna shows in his essay in this volume, this combination of regionalist vigor and national marginalization has given rise to armed movements for political secession. Yet, even here, the Muslim leadership has not been willing or able to agree on a unitary formula for Islam and state. As the essays by Horvatich and McKenna indicate, the Muslim community does not comprise a nation united around common religion and regionalism. On the contrary, it is cross-cut by competing affiliations, most notably those of ethnicity. These ties work to push segments of the Muslim community into alliance with non-Muslims. Even among those who joined the secessionist Moro National Liberation Front at the height of its armed struggle in the 1980s, there was strong disagreement as to whether the goal of their movement was the establishment of an Islamic state or a regionally encapsulated, nonsectarian state. Given the vulnerable position of Muslims in Philippine society as a whole, this contest of views among Philippine Muslims will be as much influenced by state actions as it will by ideological dispositions in the Muslim community itself.

Conclusion: Islam and the Public Sphere

These three examples should make us wary of talking about a single "Islamic politics" or, worse yet, "civilizational identity" in Southeast Asia (cf. Eickelman and Piscatori 1996). Islamic politics there is, but it spans a range of ideologies and organizations. Not insignificantly, it includes in its ranks a good number of ardent democrats and liberal-constitutionalists. "Civilizational identity" there is too in Muslim Southeast Asia. While providing for certain commonalities of worship, law, and custom, however, this identity is not the sort of thing that engenders commitment to a shared or totalizing political ideology.

These Southeast Asian examples also provide several more generalizable lessons on Islam in an era of nation-states. First and most basically, this region's diverse history demonstrates that the nation-state and nationalism have been as decisive an influence on Muslim politics as have any timeless principles of Muslim governance. It is important to stress this point, not to diminish the moral and transcendental truth of Islam, but to check the essentializing claims of those analysts, Western and Muslim, who would see Islam as an unchanging and all-encompassing blueprint for political order. Such a simplification does violence to the historical diversity of Islamic politics; more basically, it ignores that most Muslims in modern times have embraced the idea of the nation-state and incorporated its central ideological assumptions into their political world view (Piscatori 1986). Equally important, such a simplification overlooks the way in which the great majority of Muslim intellectuals in this region have embraced the ideals of popular sovereignty and citizenry participation.[13]

Just how Muslims should work to implement these ideals in the real world, however, is another, more complicated, matter. On this point there are great differences of opinion. Even as Muslim leaders have embraced principles of popular sovereignty, they disagree on what institutional structures might best realize that ideal. Even as they agree on the importance of respecting other religions, they disagree on how those religions should be accommodated within the nation.

In general terms, and leaving aside a few marginal groupings, one can distinguish two general views on these matters. The one—and in Southeast Asia it is held by a minority—would insist that anything short of a total Muslim state regulated by divine law *(shari'ah)* is a betrayal of Islam's promise. Islam, it is often said, is a "total way of life." The way in which this principle should be implemented, these advocates insist, is to subordinate all institutions to Islamic law *(shari'ah)* and to bring the full weight of the state to bear on its implementation. Hence, the argument goes, Muslims must seek to win control of the state and, once captured, reorganize its institutions in line with this total social plan. In absolute terms, government is not subject to the sovereignty of the people, but only to that of God (cf. Moussalli 1992; Norton 1995, 22).

Though advocates of this position insist that it is premised on the oldest of Muslim values, its manner of articulation here is distinctly modern. Often it is linked to the principle of God's oneness *(tauhid)*, an ideal that is, indeed, at the very core of Islamic belief. In the context of Muslim political theory, however, the concept of *tauhid* is applied by these conservative Islamists to an issue with which historically it has not been associated: the idea that society itself must reflect the unity and lordship of God through its subordination to a single body of divine principles supervised by the state. Interpreted in this way, *tauhid* becomes an argument against modern social differentiation and against, in particular, the open expression of divergent interests sanctioned under constitutional democracy. No social divisions should be allowed to destroy the unity of the Muslim community and nation. Both are subject to divine law, the supervision of which is the responsibility of modern government with all its intrusive power (cf. Moussalli 1995, 88–89).

Many people in the second group of new Muslim intellectuals also respect the idea that Islam is a total way of life; and they embrace the principle of God's oneness. But they interpret these principles quite differently from the first group of conservative Islamists. For these civic modernists, the ideal of *tauhid* requires precisely the opposite of the pluralism-denying unitarianism advocated by conservatives. God's oneness is such, it is said, that under no circumstance can it be profaned through its confusion with things nonsacral. On this point, these intellectuals are in general agreement with the great Egyptian reformer Muhammad Abduh, who insisted that Islam does distinguish between the religious and the secular, and who allowed great latitude for human reasoning in the organization of the latter —including, in this instance, the organization of modern government. According to this liberal interpretation of *tauhid*ic truth, then, it is imperative not to confuse the urgent reality of God's oneness with any particular state structure, political establishment, or, least of all, powerholder. Though God has provided guidelines, their interpretation is often difficult; pluralism and tolerance are thus imperative. Though Islamic tradition provides precedents regarding how specific principles should be interpreted, the precedents themselves demonstrate that Muslim thinkers must be responsive to historical context and their conceptual reformulation. The law demands freedom and pluralism, not an inalterable list of rules.

Most who advocate this latter position would reject the Western secularist argument that the way to resolve problems of religion and state is by erecting a high wall between the two and declaring religion a "private" matter, barring it from the public stage. But Western observers must remember that this rejection is by no means peculiar to Muslim modernists. In fact, on this point, these modernists sound a good deal like the Christian advocates of a post-Enlightenment "civil politics" described by Jose Casanova in his recent book on Christianity and civil society in the West (1994). Like these Christian critical theorists, these civic Muslims insist that to restrict religion to the private domain is to deprive it of its vital ethical role in public discourse and activity. Such a privatization of religion only cedes the moral high ground to the opportunistic instrumentalities of market forces and political entrepreneurs. Neomodernist Christians and Muslims thus agree in seeing virtue as vital to political life. Hence, as a source of moral guidance, religion is never just a matter of personal belief, but the most vital of public concerns.[14]

These Southeast Asian Muslims and their Western counterparts also agree in insisting that religion's public role is best served by maintaining a careful distance from any particular government or political faction. Religion's goals must not be profaned through their identification with efforts to seize state power. Religion must be anchored in the religious community and civil society, not in state bureaucracies, and from there it should work to inform public policy and discourse. For this Muslim variant of civic republicanism, then, the very principle of God's oneness *(tauhid)* mandates what is, in effect, a kind of secularization. But this secularization is not the same as that espoused by laicist secularists, with their privatization of religion and abandonment of the public domain. On the contrary, religion remains a vital element in public life, through its elevation above party politics and state structures into a more abstract moral ethos that pervades the whole of society.

It would be an exaggeration to claim that this latter view is now or will necessarily become dominant in Southeast Asian Islam. At the moment, the sense of political (not to mention military) crisis in the Muslim Philippines leaves little room for the luxury of such careful reflection. Similarly, for historical reasons noted above, such civic views tend to be more popular in Indonesia than in Malaysia. Nonetheless, it is remarkable that this view is as widespread as it is throughout the region. Could this pluralist Islam predominate in the long run? It is much too early to answer this question. At least in Malaysia and Indonesia, the Muslim community is just now emerging from a period of extraordinary and, in many ways, unexpected revival. Confident that it has secured a solid social base, it is only now beginning to grapple with the difficult questions posed by its increased influence.

At the very least, however, those of us with a sympathetic interest in the region would do well to acknowledge the significance of what has already been achieved in Muslim Southeast Asia. Though Western scholars once thought that the most distinctive feature of Southeast Asian Islam was the strength of so-called pre-Islamic survivals (some of which, we now realize, were actually subaltern variants of Islam), from a political perspective the more unusual feature of Islam in this region is its long-established tradition of intellectual and organizational pluralism. Even in an earlier era when virtually all Javanese, Malays, or Minangkabau called themselves Muslims, neither the courts nor the *ulama* exercised an effective monopoly of power over the Muslim community's moral and intellectual life. There were varied religious views even in premodern times and diverse ways of being a good Muslim. This pluralism was perhaps more pronounced in Indonesia than it was in Malaysia, and, as several chapters in this volume illustrate, certain forms of authoritarian cooptation threaten its vitality today. Nonetheless, it is remarkable to see how throughout this region the Muslim community has maintained its diversity and eschewed totalizing political formulae.

Though a few Muslim leaders occasionally lament this pluralism, seeing it as a fatal political weakness, from a democratic perspective, this pluralism is really a blessing in disguise. Much as with post-Reformation Christianity in Western Europe, this situation has led some Muslim leaders to the realization that the aspiration for monopolistic unity must be renounced in favor of pluralism, tolerance, and the abstraction of Islam into a deeply pervasive civic influence. There are other influences on this tradition of Islamic tolerance as well. In Indonesia, for example, the experience of Muslims since independence has impressed upon many the dangers of politicizing religion too directly. It was, after all, during the Old Order (pre-1966) period, when religious issues were politicized to an extreme, that one heard the loudest cries among some in the Javanist community for a turning away from Islam. Similarly, it was in the aftermath of the bloodshed of 1965–1966 that one saw some Muslims flee Islam for Hinduism and Christianity (Hefner 1993b; Lyon 1977). Conversely, there has been an unprecedented deepening of Islamic piety since the 1980s, a period during which political Islam has been far less influential than a civic-minded, cultural Islam. It is clear that for some Indonesians this dampening of political-religious passions, which is to say, the "desacralization" of certain kinds of party politics, has allowed for the realization of deeper Islamic ideals.

Though historical lessons of this sort may seem a fragile basis on which to build a consensus for democratic pluralism and tolerance, it is this same kind of heritage that promoted, and promotes, pluralist ideologies in the West. Conversely, where such a pluralist precedent is lacking, a modern society can easily slip into bitter civic discord. As Nazi Germany, contemporary Bosnia, and today's debates over the Muslim minority in France and Britain all illustrate,[15] the struggle for pluralism is not something the West resolved once and for all in the nineteenth century; as in the Muslim world, it remains a living challenge. Where precedents for civic tolerance exist—and especially where their principles have been abstracted from public culture and reinforced in legal-political charters—they are among the most vital of resources for civil accommodation. As in the early modern West, religious pluralism can also serve as a school in which young nations learn the habit of political tolerance (Martin 1978).

At the same time, Southeast Asia has other political precedents—most of them owing little to Islam—that look unfavorably at social autonomy and are little inclined to respect pluralism. We know, however, that, in the economic sphere, this heritage of a hierarchical and corporatist "bureaucratic polity" has proved itself less of an impediment to market dynamism than observers a generation ago would ever have thought possible (McVey 1992). Unfortunately, on the evidence of recent world history, it seems that the formulae required to manage religious and ethnic pluralism are considerably less certain than those required to manage capital and labor markets. Even today religious and ethnic absolutism has reappeared to ravage otherwise prosperous societies, including European ones.

The challenge for Southeast Asian Muslims is thus to build on and extend their tradition of pluralism and autonomy. The tradition can serve as a vital ingredient in any effort to devise a modern and democratic politics. Muslim success in this effort is no more guaranteed in Southeast Asia than that of Christians and Jews in the West. As in the West, however, the prospects for long-term success depend less on the timeless momentum of "civilizational identities" than on the fault lines of modern contests and, it is to be hoped, the creative efforts of willing men and women to make good on their religion's promise of universality and justice.

Notes

1. This and other statements gave rise to a small library of books and articles on the nature of political Islam in a post–cold war era. Among the most interesting overviews of this debate are Eickelman and Piscatori 1996, Esposito 1992, Fuller and Lesser 1995, and Halliday 1996. The Huntington debate, it should be noted, was widely covered in Southeast Asian Muslim newspapers and journals. To cite but one source, the liberal Islamic Indonesian journal *Ulumul Qur'an* published the full text of the Huntington article in translation and used the occasion to present a superbly balanced series of essays on Islam, Occidentalism, and modern politics. See *Ulumul Qur'an* 4:5 (1993) and 5:2 (1994).

2. The Muslim population of Southeast Asia is dispersed across Indonesia (whose population is 88 percent Islamic), Malaysia (55 to 60 percent), Singapore (about 16 percent), the southern Philippines (4 to 7 percent), Brunei (86 percent), and the four southern (and historically Malay) provinces of Thailand, near the border with Malaysia. There are also smaller Muslim populations in Burma, Cambodia, and Vietnam.

3. In his *History of Islamic Societies* Ira M. Lapidus presents one of the most sweeping characterizations of this sort, arguing that "for nearly 5,000 years Middle Eastern and Islamic societies have been based upon the constellation of lineage, tribal, religious, and political institutions first evident in the ancient cities of Mesopotamia in the third millennium B.C." (1988, 879). This is a view of culture that assigns unqualified primacy to historical precedent, rather than to the recreation of tradition in emergent and contextually renewed ways. As John Bowen remarked, Lapidus' image "becomes exceedingly shopworn by the time the author reaches the societies of modern Southeast Asia" (1993, 6). Even as sophisticated an observer as Olivier Roy is not immune to this peculiar geographic essentialism. In his recent *The Failure of Political Islam*, he observes that the Muslim world is divided into "three geographic and cultural tendencies: the Sunni Arab Middle East, the Sunni Indian subcontinent, and Irano-Arab Shiism" (1994, 2). Piscatori (1986) and Piscatori and Eickelman (1996) provide a welcome exception to this tendency.

4. As Roy F. Ellen has noted (1983, 50), an important exception to this emphasis in Islamic studies was the renowned Orientalist C. Snouck Hurgronje. In addition to his remarkable ethnography of the Meccan pilgrimage (Snouck

Hurgronje [1888] 1931), Snouck is famous for his careful ethnological study of society and religion among the Acehnese of northern Sumatra (Snouck Hurgone 1906). Unfortunately, until well into the postwar era, the work of this unusual ethnographic pioneer remained the exception rather than the rule within Islamic studies (cf. Benda 1983, 20–31).

5. For a more recent overview of Sufism's role in early Southeast Asian Islam, see Martin van Bruinessen 1994.

6. On all these points, Dutch cultural policies bore a striking resemblance to those of the French colonial administration in the Berber regions of Morocco (Munson 1993, 103). There too, in contradistinction to their policies among Arabs (with whom, it was assumed, an explicit policy of de-Islamization was too dangerous), colonial authorities overplayed ethnic "tradition" so as to downplay the influence of Islam.

7. All of this is not to deny, however, that Islamic cultural influence in Java has varied over time. M. C. Ricklefs' remarkable studies of Central Javanese history show there were periods of such variation in the early modern period; he also provides insight into the political reasons for this variation (Ricklefs 1974, 176–226; 1978, 154). In particular, Dutch colonialism caused a crisis of confidence among the Javanese aristocracy and a nostalgia for (a somewhat fantasized) pre-Islamic tradition (cf. Florida 1995). As Stuart Robson (1981) and Anthony Reid (1993, 181) have demonstrated, the decline was reinforced by the Mataram court's loss of the north coast mercantile trade, which isolated Javanese Muslims from the international ties through which legalistic and reform Islam were disseminated. Another period of decline for Islam in Java was the 1950s and early 1960s, when party rivalries in the countryside pushed some nominal Muslims toward the creation of explicit alternatives to Islam (Geertz 1973, 151; Hefner 1987). This politicization of religious ideologies culminated in the massacres of 1965–1966, prompting a significant flight of Javanists to Hinduism and Christianity (Lyon 1977; Hefner 1993b). From this historical perspective, one can appreciate that Geertz' characterization of Islam and Javanism was also influenced by the highly charged nature of religious politics during his fieldwork in the early 1950s.

8. Let me emphasize here that, even while agreeing with the spirit of Hodgson's critique, I want to avoid the converse error of identifying everything in Javanese culture or *abangan* religion as Islamic. To do so is to introduce a unitary holism to a cultural tradition that has long been marked by polyvalence, contest, and even violence. As I have discussed elsewhere (Hefner 1985), there are important elements of *abangan* tradition that clearly owed much to earlier non-Islamic traditions. Many of these, such as certain categories of spirits and offerings, were reconceptualized by many Javanese within a Javo-Islamic framework. But not all Javanese traditions were so assimilated, and not all ethnic Javanese were equally agreed on identification as Muslim. The incidence of apostasy and extreme heterodoxy apparent in nineteenth- and twen-

tieth-century Java shows that the Islamization of Java was ongoing and contested rather than a finished cultural event.

9. Anderson does make reference to Islamic educational pilgrimages, but only to deny that they might inspire nationalist sentiments as colonial schools did: "One has to remember that *in complete contrast* to traditional indigenous schools, which were *always local and personal* enterprises (even if, in good Muslim fashion, there was plenty of horizontal movement of students from one particularly well-reputed ulama-teacher to another), the government schools formed a colossal, highly rationalized, rightly-centralized hierarchy" (Anderson 1983, 110–111; my emphasis). Yet, as John Bowen has shown in Sumatra (1993, 55–73) and Dale F. Eickelman in Morocco (1985), Muslim religious schools were not "always local and personal"; and in the colonial era they became important centers for the nurturing of religious-nationalist sentiments (cf. Hefner 1994; Noer 1973).

10. Deliar Noer's *The Modernist Muslim Movement in Indonesia* (1973) provides an important overview of the role of Muslim schools in the development of Islam and nationalism in Indonesia; Omar's recent book (1993) provides a useful analysis of the somewhat more ambivalent relationship between Islam and nationalism among Malays.

11. Habermas' widely influential model of the development of Western civil society and "public" culture (1991) is notably flawed by a similar tendency to portray religion as a historically declining and essentially private concern.

12. Rather than seeking the causes of religious "disenchantment" in unilinear and irreversible processes of cultural evolution, then, it seems more prudent to recognize that secularization or, more precisely, desacralization, is reversible and contingent, depending as it does on the political and moral forces at work in a given time and place. While criticizing mainstream secularization theory, it is important to point out that the best among the secularization theorists in historical sociology always recognized this fact. David Martin's *A General Theory of Secularization* (1978) is exemplary in this regard, exploring European secularization not as a unilinear process, but as a consequence of the struggles for and against the establishment of church and state. More recently, Winston Davis has used a related approach in a fascinating study of modern Japanese religion (Davis 1992, 8–9). For Davis, secularization models formulated in terms of the general decline of religion are so grossly cast as to be meaningless. For him, a rehabilitated interest in modern secularization begins with the understanding that secularization operates to differing degrees in different social domains, creating a highly mottled pattern of religiosity and secularity in different societies.

13. This situation contrasts with Olivier Roy's observations on Islamism in the Middle East. There, he observes, the majority of Islamists reject the ideal of popular sovereignty as a Western idea, insisting instead that there can be no separation of religious and political authority because it is God and not the

people who is absolutely sovereign (Roy 1994, 40–41). Sayyid Qutb, a leading theorist for the Egyptian Muslim Brotherhood (until his execution by President Nasser in 1966), and, more recently, Hasan al-Turabi of the Sudan have made similar arguments (see Moussalli 1992; Muslih 1995). As Ahmad Moussalli has recently argued, however, it is equally clear that there is broader support for representative democracy among Middle Eastern Muslim intellectuals than such generalizations imply (Moussalli 1995; Norton 1995, 1). There are Muslim intellectuals in Southeast Asia who adopt a position opposed to the principle of popular sovereignty, but most prominent thinkers in Indonesia and Malaysia embrace variants of a prodemocracy "modernist" or "liberal" democratic view, close to that formulated by the influential Egyptian modernist Muhammad Abduh (Muslih 1995). These thinkers look to the concepts of consultation *(shura)* and the public interest *(al-maslahah)* as grounds for democracy within the Islamic tradition (cf. Esposito and Voll 1996, 18–32). Many also place great emphasis on the notion of God's oneness *(tauhid)* and sovereignty, a concept that Roy links to Islamist rejection of popular sovereignty. For an overview of debates on these issues among Muslim Indonesians, see Abdillah 1996.

14. In an intriguing essay on traditions of social criticism *(nasiha)* in Saudi Arabia, Talal Asad captures the spirit of this principle quite insightfully: "[A] well regulated polity depends on its members being virtuous individuals who are partly responsible for one another's moral condition—and therefore in part on continuous moral criticism" (1993a, 233). Though Asad goes on to argue that "modern [Western] liberalism rejects this principle," his characterization of Western liberalism overlooks the fact that the civic republican stream within Western liberalism invokes precisely the same principle of politics and virtue as expressed in his quote. In fairness to Asad, one can note that there is no shortage of Western proponents of just the atomized liberalism Asad generalizes to the whole of the West. But Western liberalism has its own contests and "subalterities," one of which is concerned with the question of just how to maintain the public virtues required for a vibrant civic life. See Taylor 1992, Rosenblum 1989, Douglass et al. 1990, and Putnam 1993 for recent perspectives on this issue.

15. On the challenges of Muslims to French society, see the collection of essays in Bruno Étienne 1990; for a highly critical discussion of the Muslim situation in Britain, see Asad 1993b.

References Cited

Abdillah, Masykuri. 1996. "Theological Responses to the Concepts of Democracy and Human Rights: The Case of Contemporary Indonesian Muslim Intellectuals." *Studia Islamika: Indonesian Journal for Islamic Studies* 3 (1): 1–41.

Abdullah, Taufik. 1966. "Adat and Islam: An Examination of Conflict in Minangkabau." *Indonesia* 2:1–26.

Anderson, Benedict R. 1972. "The Idea of Power in Javanese Culture." In Claire Holt, ed., *Culture and Politics in Indonesia,* pp. 1–69. Ithaca: Cornell University Press.

———. 1983. *Imagined Communities: Reflections on the Origin and Spread of Nationalism.* London: Verso.

Asad, Talal. 1993a. "The Limits of Religious Criticism in the Middle East." In Asad, *Genealogies of Religion: Discipline and Reasons of Power in Christianity and Islam,* pp. 200–236. Baltimore: Johns Hopkins.

———. 1993b. "Multiculturalism and British Identity in the Wake of the Rushdie Affair." In Asad, *Genealogies of Religion,* pp. 239–268. Baltimore: Johns Hopkins.

al-Attas, Syed Naguib. 1970. *The Mysticism of Hamzah Fansuri.* Kuala Lumpur: University of Malaya Press.

Beckford, James A. 1989. *Religion and Advanced Industrial Society.* London: Unwin Hyman.

Benda, Harry J. 1983. *The Crescent and the Rising Sun: Indonesian Islam under Japanese Occupation, 1942–1945.* 1958. Reprint, Leiden: Foris.

Berger, Peter L. 1967. *The Sacred Canopy: Elements of a Sociological Theory of Religion.* Garden City: Doubleday.

———. 1982. "From the Crisis of Religion to the Crisis of Secularity." In Mary Douglas and Steven Tipton, eds., *Religion and America: Spiritual Life in a Secular Age,* pp. 14–24. Boston: Beacon Press.

———. 1992. *A Far Glory: The Quest for Faith in an Age of Credulity.* New York: Free Press.

Boland, B. J. 1982. *The Struggle of Islam in Modern Indonesia.* The Hague: Martinus Nijhoff.

Bowen, John R. 1993. *Muslims through Discourse: Religion and Ritual in Gayo Society.* Princeton: Princeton University Press.

Bruinessen, Martin van. 1994. "The Origins and Development of Sufi Orders *(Tarekat)* in Southeast Asia. *Studia Islamika: Indonesian Journal for Islamic Studies* 1 (1): 1–23.

Casanova, Jose. 1994. *Public Religions in the Modern World.* Chicago: University of Chicago Press.

Cederoth, Sven. 1975. "Symbols of a Sasak Community in Northern Lombok." *Ethnos* 1 (4): 169–184.

Cohen, Jean L., and Andrew Arato. 1992. *Civil Society and Political Theory.* Cambridge, Mass.: MIT Press.

Cribb, Robert, ed. 1990. *The Indonesian Killings: Studies from Java and Bali.* Clayton, Victoria: Center for Southeast Asian Studies, Monash University.

Crouch, Harold. 1996. *Government and Society in Malaysia.* Ithaca: Cornell University Press.

Davis, Winston. 1992. *Japanese Religion and Society: Paradigms of Structure and Change.* Albany: SUNY Press.

Day, Anthony. 1983. "Islam and Literature in South-East Asia: Some Pre-modern,

Mainly Javanese Perspectives." In M. B. Hooker, ed., *Islam in South-East Asia,* pp. 130–159. Leiden: Brill.

Douglass, R. Bruce, Gerald M. Mara, and Henry S. Richardson, eds. 1990. *Liberalism and the Good.* New York and London: Routledge.

Drewes, G. W. J. 1968. "New Light on the Coming of Islam to Indonesia?" *Bijdragen tot de Taal-, Land-, en Volkenkunde* 124:433–459.

———. 1969. *The Admonitions of Seh Bari.* The Hague: Martinus Nijhoff.

———. 1978. *An Early Javanese Code of Muslim Ethics.* The Hague: Martinus Nijhoff.

Eickelman, Dale F. 1976. *Moroccan Islam: Tradition and Society in a Pilgrimage Center.* Austin: University of Texas Press.

———. 1985. *Knowledge and Power in Morocco: The Education of a Twentieth-Century Notable.* Princeton: Princeton University Press.

———. 1987. "Changing Interpretations of Islamic Movements." In William R. Roff, ed., *Islam and the Political Economy of Meaning,* pp. 13–30. London: Croom Helm.

———. 1992. "Mass Higher Education and the Religious Imagination in Contemporary Arab Societies." *American Ethnologist* 19 (4): 643–655.

Eickelman, Dale, and James Piscatori. 1996. *Muslim Politics.* Princeton: Princeton University Press.

Ellen, Roy F. 1983. "Social Theory, Ethnography, and the Understanding of Practical Islam in South-East Asia." In M. B. Hooker, ed., *Islam in South-East Asia,* pp. 50–91. Leiden: Brill.

Esposito, John L. 1992. *The Islamic Threat: Myth or Reality?* New York: Oxford University Press.

Esposito, John L., and John O. Voll. 1996. *Islam and Democracy.* New York: Oxford University Press.

Étienne, Bruno. 1990. *L'Islam en France: Islam, état, et société.* Paris: Éditions du Centre National de la Recherche Scientifique.

Florida, Nancy K. 1995. *Writing the Past, Inscribing the Future: Reading an Historical Prophecy of Nineteenth-Century Java.* Durham: Duke University Press.

Fukuyama, Francis. 1989. "The End of History." *National Interest,* summer, 13–24.

Fuller, Graham E., and Ian O. Lesser. 1995. *A Sense of Siege: The Geopolitics of Islam and the West.* A Rand Study. Boulder: Westview Press.

Geertz, Clifford. 1960. *The Religion of Java.* New York: The Free Press.

———. 1965. *The Social History of an Indonesian Town.* Cambridge: MIT Press.

———. 1968. *Islam Observed: Religious Development in Morocco and Indonesia.* Chicago: University of Chicago Press.

———. 1973. *The Interpretation of Cultures.* New York: Basic Books.

Gellner, Ernest. 1981. "Flux and Reflux in the Faith of Men." In Gellner, *Muslim Society,* pp. 1–85. Cambridge: Cambridge University Press.

———. 1983. *Nations and Nationalism.* Ithaca: Cornell University Press.

———. 1992. *Postmodernism, Reason and Religion.* London: Routledge.

Graaf, H. J. de, and Th. G. Th. Pigeaud. 1974. *De eerste Moslimse vorstendommen op Java*. The Hague: Martinus Nijhoff.

Habermas, Jurgen. 1991. *The Structural Transformation of the Public Sphere: An Inquiry into a Category of Bourgeois Society*. Translated by Thomas Burger. Cambridge, Mass.: MIT Press.

Halliday, Fred. 1996. *Islam and the Myth of Confrontation: Religion and Politics in the Middle East*. London: I. B. Tauris.

Hefner, Robert W. 1985. *Hindu Javanese: Tengger Tradition and Islam*. Princeton: Princeton University Press.

———. 1987. "Islamizing Java? Religion and Politics in Rural East Java." *Journal of Asian Studies* 46 (3): 533–554.

———. 1990. *The Political Economy of Mountain Java: An Interpretive History*. Berkeley and Los Angeles: University of California Press.

———. 1993a. "World Building and the Rationality of Conversion." In R. Hefner, ed., *Conversion to Christianity: Historical and Anthropological Perspectives on a Great Transformation*, pp. 3–44. Berkeley and Los Angeles: University of California Press.

———. 1993b. "Of Faith and Commitment: Christian Conversion in Muslim Java." In R. Hefner, ed., *Conversion to Christianity*, pp. 99–125.

———. 1994. "Reimagined Community: A Social History of Muslim Education in Pasuruan, East Java." In Charles F. Keyes, Laurel Kendall, and Helen Hardacre, eds., *Asian Visions of Authority: Religion and the Modern States of East and Southeast Asia*, pp. 75–95. Honolulu: University of Hawai'i Press.

Hefner, Robert W., and Allan Hoben. 1991. "The Integrative Revolution Revisited." *World Development* 19 (1): 17–30.

Hobsbawm, Eric, and Terence Ranger, eds. 1983. *The Invention of Tradition*. Cambridge: Cambridge University Press.

Hodgson, Marshall G. S. 1974. *The Venture of Islam*. 3 vols. Chicago: University of Chicago Press.

Hooker, M. B. 1983. "Muhammadan Law and Islamic Law." In Hooker, ed., *Islam in South-East Asia*, pp. 160–182. Leiden: Brill.

Huntington, Samuel P. 1993. "The Clash of Civilizations?" *Foreign Affairs* 72 (summer): 22–49.

Johns, Anthony H. 1957. "Malay Sufism." *Journal of the Royal Asiatic Society, Malayan Branch*, 30:2, no. 178.

———. 1961. "Sufism as a Category in Indonesian Literature and History." *Journal of Southeast Asian History* 2:10–23.

———. 1965. *The Gift Addressed to the Spirit of the Prophet*. Canberra: Australian National University Press.

———. 1993. "Islamization in Southeast Asia: Reflections and Reconsiderations with Special Reference to the Role of Sufism." *Southeast Asian Studies* (Tokyo), 31 (1): 43–61.

Jomo, K. S., and Ahmad Shabery Cheek. 1992. "Malaysia's Islamic Movements." In Joel S. Kahn and Francis Loh Kok Wah, eds., *Fragmented Vision: Culture and Politics in Contemporary Malaysia,* pp. 79–105. Honolulu: University of Hawai'i Press.

Juergensmeyer, Mark. 1993. *The New Cold War? Religious Nationalism Confronts the Secular State.* Berkeley and Los Angeles: University of California Press.

Keddie, Nikki R. 1968. *An Islamic Response to Imperialism: Political and Religious Writings of Sayyid Jamal ad-Din "al-Afghani."* Berkeley and Los Angeles: University of California Press.

Keyes, Charles F. 1987. *Thailand: Buddhist Kingdom as Modern Nation-State.* Boulder: Westview.

Krulfeld, R. 1966. "Fatalism in Indonesia: A Comparison of Socio-Religious Types on Lombok." *Anthropological Quarterly* 39:180–190.

Lapidus, Ira M. 1988. *A History of Islamic Societies.* Cambridge: Cambridge University Press.

Lev, Daniel S. 1972. *Islamic Courts in Indonesia.* Berkeley and Los Angeles: University of California Press.

Lombard, Denys. 1990. *Le carrefour javanais: Essai d'histoire globale.* 3 vols. Paris: Éditions de l'École des Hautes Études en Sciences Sociales.

Lyon, Margaret L. 1977. "Politics and Religious Identity: Genesis of a Javanese-Hindu Movement in Rural Central Java." Ph.D. dissertation, Department of Anthropology, University of California, Berkeley.

MacIntyre, A. 1990. *Business and Politics in Indonesia.* Asian Studies Association of Australia Publications Series, No. 21. Sydney: Allen & Unwin.

McVey, Ruth. 1992. "The Materialization of the Southeast Asian Entrepreneur." In McVey, ed., *Southeast Asian Capitalists,* pp. 7–33. Ithaca: Southeast Asian Program, Cornell University.

Mann, Michael. 1986. "The Autonomous Power of the State: Its Origins, Mechanisms and Results." In John A. Hall, ed., *States in History,* pp. 109–136. Oxford: Blackwell.

Martin, David. 1978. *A General Theory of Secularization.* Oxford: Blackwell.

———. 1990. *Tongues of Fire: The Explosion of Protestantism in Latin America.* Oxford: Blackwell.

Meeker, Michael. 1993. "The New Muslim Intellectuals in the Republic of Turkey." In Richard Tapper, ed., *Islam in Modern Turkey: Religion, Politics, and Literature in a Secular State,* pp. 189–219. London: I. B. Tauris.

Milner, A. C. 1983. "Islam and the Muslim State." In M. B. Hooker, ed., *Islam in South-East Asia,* pp. 23–49. Leiden: Brill.

Moussalli, Ahmad S. 1992. *Radical Islamic Fundamentalism: The Ideological and Political Discourse of Sayyid Qutb.* Beirut: American University of Beirut.

———. 1995. "Modern Islamic Fundamentalist Discourses on Civil Society, Pluralism, and Democracy." In Augustus Richard Norton, ed., *Civil Society in the Middle East,* vol. 1, pp. 79–119. Leiden: Brill.

Munawar-Rachman, Budhy, ed. 1994. *Kontekstualisasi Doktrin Islam dalam Sejarah* (The Contextualization of Islamic Doctrine in History). Jakarta: Yayasan Paramadina.

Munson, Henry, Jr. 1993. *Religion and Power in Morocco.* New Haven: Yale University Press.

Muslih, Muhammad. 1995. "Democracy." In John Esposito, ed., *The Oxford Encyclopedia of the Modern Islamic World*, vol. 1, pp. 356–360. New York: Oxford University Press.

Mutalib, Hussin. 1990. *Islam and Ethnicity in Malay Politics.* Singapore: Oxford University Press.

Nagata, Judith. 1984. *The Reflowering of Malaysian Islam: Modern Religious Radicals and Their Roots.* Vancouver: University of British Columbia Press.

Noer, Deliar. 1973. *The Modernist Muslim Movement in Indonesia, 1900–42.* Kuala Lumpur: Oxford University Press.

Norton, Augustus Richard. 1995. "Introduction." In Norton, ed., *Civil Society in the Middle East*, pp. 1–25. Leiden: Brill.

Omar, Ariffin. 1993. Bangsa Melayu: *Malay Concepts of Democracy and Community, 1945–1950.* Kuala Lumpur: Oxford University Press.

Pigeaud, Th. G. Th. 1967–1980. *Literature of Java.* 3 vols. The Hague: Martinus Nijhoff.

Piscatori, James P. 1986. *Islam in a World of Nation-States.* Cambridge: Cambridge University Press.

Pranowo, Bambang. 1991. "Creating Islamic Tradition in Rural Java." Ph.D. thesis, Department of Anthropology, Monash University.

Putnam, Robert D. 1993. *Making Democracy Work: Civic Traditions in Modern Italy.* Princeton: Princeton University Press.

Reeve, David. 1985. *Golkar of Indonesia: An Alternative to the Party System.* Singapore: Oxford University Press.

Reid, Anthony. 1988. *Southeast Asia in the Age of Commerce, 1450–1680*, vol. 1: *The Lands below the Winds.* New Haven: Yale University Press.

———. 1993. *Southeast Asia in the Age of Commerce, 1450–1680*, vol. 2: *Expansion and Crisis.* New Haven: Yale University Press.

Reynolds, Frank J. 1978. "Sacral Kingship and National Development: The Case of Thailand." In Bardwell L. Smith, ed., *Religion and Legitimation of Power in Thailand, Laos, and Burma*, pp. 100–110. Chambersburg, Penn.: ANIMA Books.

Ricklefs, M. C. 1974. *Jogjakarta under Sultan Mangkubumi, 1749–1792: A History of the Division of Java.* London: Oxford University Press.

———. 1978. *Modern Javanese Historical Tradition: A Study of an Original Kartasura Chronicle and Related Materials.* London: School of Oriental and African Studies.

Robson, Stuart. 1981. "Java at the Crossroads." *Bijdragen tot de Taal-, Land-, en Volkenkunde* 137:259–292.

Roff, William R. 1967. *The Origins of Malay Nationalism*. Kuala Lumpur: University of Malaya Press.

———. 1985. "Islam Obscured? Some Reflections on Studies on Islam and Society in Southeast Asia." *Archipel* (special issue on *L'Islam en Indonésie*), 29:7–34.

Rosenblum, Nancy L., ed. 1989. *Liberalism and the Moral Life*. Cambridge, Mass.: Harvard University Press.

Roy, Olivier. 1994. *The Failure of Political Islam*. Translated by Carol Volk. Cambridge, Mass.: Harvard University Press.

Schimmel, Annemarie. 1975. *The Mystical Dimensions of Islam*. Chapel Hill: University of North Carolina Press.

Siegel, James T. 1969. *The Rope of God*. Berkeley and Los Angeles: University of California Press.

Snouck Hurgronje, C. 1906. *The Achehnese*. Translated by A. W. S. O'Sullivan. 2 vols. Leiden: Brill.

———. 1931. *Mekka in the Latter Part of the 19th Century*. Translated by I. H. Monahan. 1888–1889. Reprint, Leiden: Brill.

Tambiah, S. J. 1992. *Buddhism Betrayed? Religion, Politics, and Violence in Sri Lanka*. Chicago: University of Chicago Press.

Taylor, Charles. 1992. *Multiculturalism and the "Politics of Recognition."* Princeton: Princeton University Press.

Tibi, Bassam. 1990. *Islam and the Cultural Accommodation of Social Change*. Boulder: Westview.

van der Veer, Peter. 1994. *Religious Nationalism: Hindus and Muslims in India*. Berkeley and Los Angeles: University of California Press.

Woodward, Mark R. 1989. *Islam in Java: Normative Piety and Mysticism in the Sultanate of Yogyakarta*. Tucson: University of Arizona Press.

Wuthnow, Robert. 1988. *The Restructuring of American Religion*. Princeton: Princeton University Press.

———. 1989. *The Struggle for America's Soul: Evangelicals, Liberals, and Secularism*. Grand Rapids: Eerdmans.

Yavuz, Hakan M. n.d. "The Role of Print and Media in the Islamic Movement: The Case of Turkey." Paper presented at the conference on "Print Islam and Civic Pluralism," Bellagio, Italy, March 1995.

Part 1
The State
and Civic Identities

Chapter 2

Appreciating Islam in the Muslim Philippines
AUTHORITY, EXPERIENCE,
AND IDENTITY IN COTABATO

Thomas M. McKenna

More than twenty years of attempts to elucidate the Islamic identity of Philippine Muslims have produced scant illumination. Those efforts, undertaken by a wide range of analysts, have been concerned almost exclusively with determining the origins and essence of an ethnoreligious identity presumed to be shared by the various Muslim ethnolinguistic groups of the Philippines (see, for example, Bauzon 1991; George 1980; Glang 1969; Gowing 1979; Madale 1986; Majul 1973). While many of these writers have made significant contributions to our knowledge of the political history of Philippine Muslims, an empirically grounded understanding of Islamic identity in the Muslim Philippines has mainly eluded them.

Philippine Muslims form a small religious minority (4 to 7 percent) in the only Christian-dominated nation in Southeast Asia. Although concentrated in the southern portion of the Philippine archipelago, the three major and ten minor Muslim ethnolinguistic groups are separated by considerable geographic and linguistic barriers. Virtually all works published in the past twenty-five years concerned with Philippine Muslims as a collectivity center on the development of a shared Islamic identity that presumably binds the various Muslim populations of the southern archipelago. In most of those works a specific term—"Moro"—is used to designate that postulated shared identity as Muslim Filipinos. "Moro" (or "Moor") was the term first used by early European mercantilists to refer to all the Muslim populations of Southeast Asia (Ellen 1983). It persisted among the Spanish colonizers of the Philippines. With their Reconquista of Muslim Spain a recent collective memory, the Spaniards assigned to the Muslim peoples of the South the label previously bestowed on their familiar Muslim enemies from Mauritania. American colonizers continued the usage even though that appellation had become an epithet among Christian Filipinos. In the past twenty-five years, Philippine Muslim nationalists have appropriated the term "Moro" and attempted to transform it into a positive symbol of collective identity.

Works treating Philippine Muslim identity have tended overwhelmingly to account for the evolution of that identity by recourse to a central historical narrative. In synoptic form the narrative declares that Islamic consciousness in the Philippines was uniquely forged in the course of more than three hundred years of Spanish aggression against the Muslim principalities of Mindanao and Sulu (Gowing 1979; Majul 1973). This consciousness was then either repressed or undermined during the American colonial period (see especially George 1980; Gowing 1979), but resurged in the early postcolonial period and eventually motivated a Muslim separatist rebellion (begun in 1972) against the Philippine Republic (see Bauzon 1991; George 1980; Gowing 1979; Madale 1986; Majul 1985).[1] That core historical narrative is confected from meager historical evidence. Nevertheless, it has been reiterated and embellished to support various interpretive stances on contemporary Muslim politics in the Philippines (see, for example, Bauzon 1991; George 1980; Gowing 1979; Majul 1985; Molloy 1988).[2]

The standard historical account in its various versions obscures what it means to illustrate by begging a host of questions about the historical construction of Islamic identity in the Philippines: How singularly intense was the Western aggression experienced by the Muslim polities of the Philippine archipelago? How uniformly was that aggression experienced throughout the Muslim regions of the archipelago? What does it mean to say that the Islamic identity of Muslim Filipinos has been shaped by a history of external aggression? What form did that shaping take? How reliable are the measures used to gauge the breadth, depth, and strength of "Islamic nationalism" (Molloy 1988, 61) in the Muslim Philippines?

My goal in this chapter is to attempt to cast some new light on Islamic identity in a single region of the Muslim Philippines—Cotabato.[3] Specifically, I wish to address two issues underlying the questions just posed concerning the historical construction and contemporary constitution of Islamic identity in the Muslim Philippines. The first has to do with the nature of the Islamic identity of Muslim notables and the various factors that have influenced that identity. The second concerns the congruity of the Islamic identities of Muslim leaders and followers. In addressing the first problem, I focus predominately on the construction of a transcendent ethnoreligious identity among Philippine Muslim elites during the American colonial period. In regard to the second—the coherence of dominant representations and subordinate beliefs about ethnoreligious identity—I offer ethnographic evidence from Cotabato to suggest that the conceptualizations of Islamic identity by Muslim elites and subordinates often fail to correspond.[4]

While I concur with the predominant view that Islamic identity in the Philippines has been uniquely shaped through a dialogue with external forces mostly absent elsewhere in Southeast Asia, I disagree about the nature and derivation of those forces as they have been presented in conventional treatments. For example, I argue initially that Spanish aggression against the Muslim polities of the archipelago did not, to any significant degree, stimulate the development of an overarching ethnoreligious identity self-consciously shared by members of various Muslim ethnolinguistic groups.

Islamic Identity and Western Aggression in the Philippines

Envisaging the Moro Wars ⟶not rel.

Although the anti-Spanish struggle played a role in shaping the contemporary Islamic identity of Muslim Filipinos, its effect was, in my estimation, limited and indirect. That view is entirely at odds with the prevailing opinion that the so-called Moro Wars were "fundamentally religious in character" (George 1980, 44). The same view is advanced by the foremost historian of Muslims in the Philippines, Cesar Majul, who notes that "the motivating force behind [the Spanish-Muslim] wars was religious difference" (1985, 18). He finds also a direct correlation between the anti-Spanish struggle and a "growing Islamic consciousness of the Muslims in the Philippines," remarking that "the role that Islam played in stiffening the resistance of the Muslims against Spanish effort to dominate them cannot be over-emphasized" (1973, 343).

The discourse of Spanish offensives against the Muslim South was undeniably religious in tone. Spanish attempts to reduce the southern sultanates to submission were voiced through an ideology of aggressive Christianization. Official documents extending from the earliest Spanish expeditions against the sultanates in 1578 to those associated with the military campaigns of the last decades of the nineteenth century order or advocate the destruction of mosques, the suppression of Islamic teaching, and the coercive conversion of Muslims to Christianity (Blair and Robertson 1903–1919, 4:174–181; de la Torre, quoted in Saleeby 1908, 252–253). Nevertheless, this religious rhetoric is most often inlaid in texts that also enunciate more mercenary objectives related to monopolizing trade, controlling resources, and collecting tribute.[5]

Marxist ⟶

While Islamic appeals were certainly employed to mobilize opposition to Spanish aggression in the southern sultanates, there is little historical evidence to suggest that indigenous resistance to the Spanish threat led to a heightened Islamic identity among the Muslim populace or that such elevated consciousness "stiffen[ed] the resistance of the Muslims" (Majul 1973, 343).[6] The conventional account stresses the role played by Islam in overcoming internal dissension and constructing a relatively unified front to foreign penetration of the Muslim South. Despite those suppositions, a united Muslim opposition of any significant extent or duration is nowhere evidenced in the historical record.

The term "Moro Wars" has been employed to describe an assortment of armed collisions, occurring over more than three hundred years, between individual Muslim polities in the southern archipelago and Spanish colonial forces. It has also been used to refer to the great number of slave raids made by various Muslim seafaring marauders (usually with no formal political ties to any of the southern sultanates) against Spanish-held territories in the North. These raiders were, in European parlance, freebooters—those engaged in plundering without the authority of national warfare.[7] If we exempt the private Muslim raids against the North, which occurred almost yearly between 1768 and 1846 (Warren 1985), the three-hundred-year conflict was primarily a "cold war" consisting of extended periods of mostly peaceful coexistence with the Spanish colonial intruders in the North coinciding with intersultanate rivalry in the South. That relative calm was only occasionally punctuated by armed confrontations between the Spaniards and particular sultanates, clashes that tended to be isolated events of relatively brief duration.

Relations between the Cotabato sultanates and the Spaniards provide illustration. Traditionally and for most of the Spanish period, the Cotabato River Basin contained two rival sultanates, one upstream and one downstream. In 1596 the Spaniards sent an expedition to subdue Cotabato. The Spanish forces prevailed in a series of battles against local rulers but soon retired from the region owing to heavy casualties and inadequate supplies. For a short period after this initial invasion attempt, the Cotabato sultanates sponsored a series of joint military campaigns cum slave raids against the North. Very quickly, however, a pattern developed whereby the two Cotabato power centers alternately aligned with the Spaniards against one another as their fortunes waxed and waned. In 1605 and 1635 the Spaniards signed treaties with the reigning upriver sultan recognizing him as the paramount ruler of Mindanao. In 1645 and 1719 similar agreements were made acknowledging the paramountcy of the downriver sultan. The 1719 agreement occurred as the result of a plea by the downriver sultan to the Spaniards to aid him in his war with the Sultan of Sulu and, later, to suppress an internal rebellion. In 1734 the successor to the Magindanao throne was crowned sultan by the Spaniards, and by 1837 the downriver sultanate was virtually incorporated into the Spanish colonial domain, with the government in Manila controlling trade and choosing the successor to the sultan (Ileto 1971). No large-scale armed clashes occurred in Cotabato until the last part of the nineteenth century, when the Spaniards mounted expeditions to subdue the upriver sultanate.

If Philippine Muslims shared a self-regarding Islamic identity in opposition to Spanish hostility, it was hardly ever manifested in concerted action against them after the first decade or so of Spanish intrusions. Historical evidence for such a heightened Islamic awareness is also fragmentary and unconvincing. While several accounts of religious observance by the high nobility of various sultanates can be found, descriptions of the level of religiosity of Muslim subordinates are scarce.[8] Before the late nineteenth century (see Blumentritt 1893; Ileto 1971), there is also no clear indication of Islamic clerics preaching anti-Spanish resistance to the general populace, and even after that date the evidence is incomplete.

There is no substantial basis in the historical record for the claim that the Moro Wars either engendered or significantly heightened a shared Islamic identity among Philippine Muslims that crosscut linguistic and geographic boundaries. There was little or no coordination among separate Muslim polities in the anti-Spanish struggle, and some inland areas of the Muslim South were barely affected by the wars for the greatest portion of the Spanish period. If Cotabato is at all typical, there is also no convincing evidence for an intensification of Islamic orthopraxy among the populace within any particular Muslim polity. Any elevation in religiosity among the rulers of those states was probably matched by an increasing Western influence (see Forrest 1969).[9]

Colonial Control and the Creation of a Transcendent Ethnoreligious Identity

Spanish colonial rule in the Muslim Philippines, when finally consolidated in the last decades of the nineteenth century, was short-lived and lightly felt. It was supplanted in 1899 by American colonialism, which worked profound changes on individual Philippine Muslim societies and induced the development of a transcendent ethnoreligious identity among certain Muslim elites. As the American occupiers extended their dominion over the southern archipelago, they fought battles at least as bloody as any waged during the period of Spanish aggression. Muslim objectors to American rule were promptly overcome and often slaughtered by devastating American firepower (Gowing 1983). In Cotabato, American rule was accomplished with a good deal less bloodshed than in much of the rest of the Philippines, north or south, because of the active assistance of key Muslim leaders who were the effective successors of the Cotabato sultans. The ruling nobility of both sultanates had been devitalized in the late nineteenth century and was largely replaced by a new local elite group that, while representing its rule with the same myths of nobility, had more tenuous ties to the traditional aristocracy. These new *datu*s (chieftains or notables) were cultivated by the Americans and became a dependent, collaborating elite whose power was ultimately predicated on resources derived from cooperating with American colonial authorities.

The course of colonial policy in the region that the Americans termed "Moroland" (Gowing 1983) was altered abruptly more than once as American aims in the rest of the archipelago (and Philippine nationalist opposition to those aims) evolved. The earliest American strategy in the Muslim South was indirect rule, modeled on colonial systems in British Malaya and the Dutch East Indies, an approach designed to neutralize Muslim groups while attempting to overpower Philippine independence forces in the North. In 1899 a formal treaty, the Bates Agreement, was signed with the Sultan of Sulu in which the Americans promised not to interfere in Sulu religion, law, and commerce (and to pay the Sultan and his *datu*s monthly stipends) in exchange for the sultan's acknowledgment of United States sovereignty.[10]

The colonial policy of indirect rule was soon modified and not long thereafter abandoned. In 1903 a tribal ward system was established in the newly constituted Moro Province wherein local headmen were placed under the direct supervision of a district governor (Gowing 1983, 114). The rationale for the administrative shift toward direct rule was given by General Leonard Wood, the first governor of the Moro Province, in a 1904 letter to an English friend:

> You are quite content to maintain rajahs and sultans and other species of royalty, but we, with our plain ideas of doing things, find these gentlemen outside of our scheme of government, and so have to start at this kind of proposition a little differently. Our policy is to develop individualism among these people and, little by little, to teach them to stand on their own two feet independent of petty chieftains. In order to do this the chief or headman has to be given some position of more or less authority under the government, but he ceases to have any divine rights.[11] (Wood, quoted in Gowing 1983, 115)

The Bates Agreement was unilaterally abrogated by the United States in 1905, with the Sultan of Sulu retaining colonial recognition only as the "religious head" of Sulu Muslims (Wood, quoted in Gowing 1983, 119). The policy of indirect rule was entirely abandoned in 1914, when the explicit recognition of the customary *(adat)* law of Muslim Filipinos included in the act that organized the Moro Province was expressly repealed (Thomas 1971).

One influential voice in the American colonial administration of the Moro Province opposed the move to direct administration and, though overruled, was instrumental in conditioning official attitudes about the governance of Philippine Muslims. Najeeb M. Saleeby was a Syrian-born physician who came to the Philippines as a U.S. Army doctor in 1900 (Thomas 1971). Saleeby was assigned to Mindanao and became fascinated with its Muslim inhabitants. He made the acquaintance of numerous prominent Muslims and learned two local languages—Magindanaon and Tausug. He used his knowledge of those languages and of Arabic to translate entitling genealogies *(Tarsila, Salsilah)* and law codes *(Luwaran)* for the two main sultanates of the region. Saleeby was quickly recognized by colonial authorities as the resident American specialist on Philippine Muslims and in 1903 was appointed Agent for Moro Affairs. In 1905, the same year he published his *Studies in Moro History, Law, and Religion* (the first scholarly work on Philippine Muslims published in English), he became the first superintendent of schools of the Moro Province.

Saleeby argued vigorously for a particular variant of indirect rule for Philippine Muslims. His views on indirect rule and on the "development" of the Muslims of the Philippines were expressed most cogently in a 1913 article titled *The Moro Problem*. In that work Saleeby disputes the widespread perception among American colonial administrators of the Moros as savages and religious fanatics. Moros, he observes, "have so little religion at heart that it is impossible for them to get enthusiastic and fanatic on this ground" (1913, 24). Moros do, however, possess relatively sophisticated, if "feudal," political communities ruled by *datus*. According to Saleeby: "The *datu* is God's viceregent on earth. He is of noble birth and the Prophet's blood runs through his veins. The people owe him allegiance and tribute" (p. 17). He notes further that, for the most part, the *datus* had not been actively opposed to American aims and that "religion has never been a cause of conflict between Americans and Moros" (p. 24). Moreover, "the Moros are greatly disunited . . . each district is inhabited by a different tribe and these tribes have never been united" (p. 15). It is in the Americans' interest, in fact, to unite the Moros under their traditional leaders in order to initiate a "process of gradual development" (p. 17). In furtherance of such a goal, Saleeby, himself a Christian, declares that "religion" (meaning

Islam) "can be encouraged and promoted" for the benefit of both the colonial government and the Moro people (p. 24). As envisioned by Saleeby, with the reestablishment of "*datu*ships" and "Moro courts,"

> the individual Moro would find himself well protected and would become more thrifty and intelligent. Moved by a natural tendency to imitate superior civilization, he would unconsciously reform his customs and home life and gradually acquire American ideas and new ambitions. An enlightened Moro community, wisely guided by efficient American officials, would undoubtedly work out its own destiny, and following the natural law of growth and development would gradually rise in wealth and culture to the level of a democratic [meaning Philippine Christian] municipality." (p. 30).

Saleeby's principal argument was that Moros, while lacking many of the "civilized" attributes of Philippine Christians, should not be treated as savages or simply be lumped with other non-Christian "tribes." Neither were Muslims religious fanatics unamenable to "development." To the contrary, they were capable of following a path of development parallel to that of Christian Filipinos, and they should be led on that path by their *datu*s. Inasmuch as *datu*s have legitimized their rule through Islamic ideology, Islam should be encouraged. But Moro religion, law, and customs require rationalization by imitation of "superior" culture. In this manner, American principles working on a unique Philippine population with a distinctive cultural history would achieve an outcome analogous to that devised for Christian Filipinos.

Although Saleeby's proposals were never incorporated as official colonial policy toward Philippine Muslims, many of his ideas strongly influenced the attitudes and practices of later colonial administrators. Those officials included Frank Carpenter, governor of the Department of Mindanao and Sulu from 1914 to 1920, who expressed his views in a 1919 letter requesting that a certain Sulu princess be sent to the United States as a government student. After reporting the "generally accepted" conclusion that it is "practically futile to attempt the conversion of a Mohammedan people as such to Christianity," Carpenter restates Saleeby's suggestions about guided development through the agency of Muslim notables.

> [It] is essential to the efficiency, commercially as well as politically, of the Filipino people that all elements of population have uniform standards and ideals constituting what may well be termed "civilization"; and as the type of civilization of the Filipino people in greatest part is that characteristic of the Christian nations of the world, the bringing of the Sulu people

from their primitive type of civilization to the general Philippine type may be stated as the objective of the undertaking of the Government in its constructive work among them. No more effective and probably successful instrumentality appears for this undertaking than the young woman who is the subject of this communication.

In suggesting particular arrangements for the American education of the princess, Carpenter goes on to list two considerations of "fundamental importance":

> That she be not encouraged nor *permitted* to abandon her at least nominal profession of the Mohammedan religion, as she would become outcast among the Sulu people and consequently her special education purposeless were she to become Christian or otherwise renounce the religious faith of her fathers. [emphasis mine] . . .
>
> That she be qualified to discuss intelligently and to compel respect from the Mohammedan clergy she should be encouraged to read extensively and thoroughly inform herself, so far as possible from the favorable point of view, not only the Koran itself and other books held to be sacred by Mohammedans, but also the political history of Mohammedanism.[12]

James R. Fugate, the American governor of Sulu from 1928 to 1936, also acted on some of Saleeby's suggestions by implementing colonial policies through individual Sulu *datu*s (Thomas 1971, 189). No colonial administrator was more apparently influenced by the views of Saleeby than Edward M. Kuder, who, beginning in 1924, spent seventeen years as superintendent of schools in the three Muslim provinces of Cotabato, Lanao, and Sulu. Like Saleeby, Kuder endeavored to learn local languages and eventually gained proficiency in Magindanaon, Maranao, and Tausug, the languages of the three main Muslim ethnolinguistic groups of the Philippines.

Kuder put Saleeby's ideas about *datu*-led development into practice by undertaking personally the training of a generation of Philippine Muslim leaders. In his travels throughout the Muslim provinces, he sought out honors students (all of them boys) from various Muslim groups, most usually the sons of datu families, and fostered them, bringing some of them to live under his roof and be tutored by him. In this manner, Kuder personally educated a considerable number of the second generation of Philippine Muslim leaders of this century. In my interviews with one of those leaders in 1986, he recalled with fondness his time spent as Kuder's "foster son" fifty years earlier, recollecting that he was "strengthened by Mr. Kuder's discipline." In the course of one of our conversations this former student produced a treasured keepsake, a beautifully bound volume of Burton's translation of *The Thousand and One Nights,* now tattered by time and climate. Kuder had presented the complete set to him when he left college, telling him it was important that he appreciate his religion.

In a scholarly paper published in 1945 titled *The Moros in the Philippines,* Kuder observes initially that the term "Moro" is an exotic label affixed by Europeans to Philippine Muslims in general and one not used among them. He also notes, echoing Saleeby, that more than three centuries of Spanish hostility had failed to bring about an overall alliance among the separate Muslim societies of the Philippines. There follows a revelatory passage: "Within the decade and a half preceding the Japanese invasion of the Philippines, increasing numbers of young Moros educated in the public schools and collegiate institutions of the Philippines and employed in the professions and activities of modern democratic culture had taken to referring to themselves as Mohammedan Filipinos" (Kuder 1945, 119). Kuder is here referring indirectly, but with detectable pride, to his protégés, the Muslim students he brought together and personally trained in the fifteen years preceding World War II. These young men, he avers, are the very first generation of Muslims in the Philippines who possess a shared and self-conscious ethnoreligious identity that transcends ethnolinguistic and geographical boundaries. Kuder's statement is an oblique assertion that he had accomplished in less than two decades what Spanish aggression was unable to provoke in more than three centuries. He had developed a core group of "Mohammedan" Filipinos. The use of that most emblematic of Orientalist terms discloses that the content of this new shared identity had been at least partly formed by his instruction. I have been unable to ascertain whether any of Kuder's students actually referred to themselves as Mohammedans, but it is apparent that Kuder, following Saleeby's suggestions, not only educated his students in the arts of "modern democratic culture," but also encouraged them to approach Islam (in Carpenter's words) "from the favorable point of view"—that is to say, through the eyes of Western arts and sciences.

Kuder's aim was to create an educated Muslim elite group trained in Western law and government and able to represent their people in a single Philippine state, a cohort ready to direct Muslim affairs through enlightened forms of traditional rule. That goal was realized in great measure in the careers of Kuder's students. Most became lawyers, civil servants and politicians, married Christians, and remained monogamous. At the same time, they conserved their traditional roles as Islamic adjudicators in what were now nongovernmental tribunals and as sources of moral authority. By the time the Philippine Republic was founded in 1946, they were well established with ties to the apparatus of national rule in Manila and able to command local allegiance on the basis of traditional social relations. They had also apparently developed a self-conscious transcendent identity as Muslim Filipinos. That consciousness derived not from opposition to American rule, but rather from studied adherence to its objectives.

The peculiar form of direct colonial rule established by the Americans for Philippine Muslims—combining official repudiation of the authority of traditional rulers with a wardship system for certain Muslim elites specifically designed to enhance their abilities as "Mohammedan" leaders—produced inverse effects from those found in another Southeast Asian colonial system attempting to rule Muslims. The Dutch development of adatrecht for colonial Indonesia was intended to deemphasize Islam by "constituting local particularisms in customary law [and] favoring the traditional authority structures linked to them" (Roff 1985, 14). While Dutch policies fostered (indeed created) ethnic divisions among Indonesian Muslims, the attempts by various American colonial agents to rationalize and objectify the Islamic identities of a generation of Muslim leaders provided the basis for ethnicizing Islam in the Muslim Philippines. That recently cultivated Muslim ethnic identity acquired particular saliency when Muslim political leaders found themselves representing a small and suspect religious minority in an independent nation dominated by Christian Filipinos.

Islamic Consciousness in the Postcolonial Philippines

Islamic Resurgence or Ethnic Affirmation?

The standard account of the postcolonial history of Islamic identity in the Philippines states in simplified form that, beginning circa 1950, an Islamic resurgence began to manifest itself throughout the Muslim areas of the Philippines (see, for example, Majul 1985, 28; Hunt 1974, 204; Gowing 1979, 69–71) and that this Islamic consciousness intensified and eventually culminated in an Islamic insurgency against the Philippine state (George 1980; Gowing 1979; Madale 1986; Majul 1979). A critical review of the available evidence suggests that, rather than witnessing the widespread development of a heightened Islamic consciousness, the early postcolonial period saw an intensification of ethnoreligious identity on the part of prominent Muslims. That ethnic assertion represented not a reversal of the tendencies of the colonial period, but their logical extension.

More than one chronicler of the postwar Muslim Philippines has commented that American war damage payments and back pay awards at the end of the Japanese War stimulated, among other things, a surge in mosque building, *madrasah* founding, and pilgrimages to Mecca (see, for example, Gowing 1979, 183; Madale 1986; Ravenholt 1956, 7; Thomas 1971, 316).

That link between the final American expenditures of the colonial period and an increase in Islamic-related investments by certain Muslims suggests something about the nature of the postwar Islamic resurgence in the Philippines.

The major share of American reparation payments were monopolized by established Muslim elites, especially those most closely aligned with the Americans before and during the war. The financial boon allowed many more of these individuals than ever before to make the pilgrimage to Mecca and enjoy the prestige that attached to *haji* status. The most prominent among them invested in more elaborate status enhancements, building mosques and opening Islamic schools (*madrasahs*). Muslim congressmen especially endeavored to become patrons of Islamic schools (see Mastura 1984, 99; Ravenholt 1956, 6–8). The competitive character of such sponsorships is revealed in a passage from Ravenholt relating the short history of a *madrasah* established in 1951 by a Maranao congressman: "For a time some 600 Moro students were enrolled in Mindalano's 'college.' . . . The school, however, was located too far from the main centers of Moro population on the Lanao Plateau, and when several competing Muslim 'colleges' were started in and around Dansalan by his political enemies Mindalano's enterprise foundered" (1956, 8).

The congressman's stated reasons for undertaking this and other enterprises in religious education exhibit considerable continuity with the development goals established by Saleeby, Kuder, and other American colonial officials. Ravenholt reports that "it is the conviction of Mindalano and the group working with him that if they are to bring constructive order to their people and make them full-fledged participating citizens in the [Philippine] Republic, this can only be accomplished by making them better Muslims" (p. 11). Similar statements can be found in the writings of Muslim intellectuals of the postwar period. In a representative piece titled "Modernizing the Muslims," Alunan Glang first restates the sine qua non of Philippine Islamic identity previously pronounced by Saleeby—the moral authority of *datu*s: "The system of *datu*ship has long kept the Muslims united and spiritually bound together. So deeply ingrained into the fabric of Muslim life is this institution that the faith and loyalty of the Muslims have withstood the severe vicissitudes of time and change. Down to this day, many of them still hold the *datu*s in characteristic religious awe and adulation" (1969, 33). Glang then proposes a prescription for "modernization" remarkably resonant with that proposed by Saleeby more than fifty years earlier: "One of the biggest single factors that may bring about the orchestration of the Muslim Filipino into the fabric of Filipino national life appears to be the Muslim leaders themselves whose pervasive influence had for centuries dominated and dictated much of the Muslim Filipino thinking and psychology" (p. 33).

There were some immediate and material incentives for prominent Muslims in the Philippine Republic to continue to pursue the goals first advanced by colonial administrators of parallel development within a single state. In general, independence significantly altered the structure of local and provincial politics in the Philippines. The electorate was expanded, campaigns became more expensive (at least partly because vote buying became more common), and politicians became more dependent on the distribution of funds from national political parties that, if the party controlled the government, came either from the national treasury or directly from American aid and international funds (Wolters 1984). Like Philippine politicians in general, Muslim *datu* politicians relied on national party funds and regularly switched parties to obtain improved access to such funds. However, Muslim politicians were uniquely constrained in that, as representatives of the largest single minority population, their acquisition of state and party funds was linked to the perception on the part of the Christians who controlled the state of how completely they were able to deliver Muslim compliance to state policies and practices, particularly those concerning Christian migration to traditionally Muslim lands. Muslim *datu* politicians endeavored, on the one hand, to provide evidence of Muslim acquiescence to state decrees, while, on the other, they encouraged the spread of rationalized emblems of a single Muslim ethnic identity as a way to project the impression of Muslim political might and thus ensure the continued need for the gatekeeper roles that they filled.[13]

It is also difficult to uncover evidence for the direct linkage suggested in the conventional account between the Islamic resurgence surmised for the earlier postwar period and the Muslim separatist rebellion begun in 1972. The antecedents of that rebellion are exceedingly complex, involving unlikely alliances and varied ambitions. However, two general tendencies can be discerned. First, established Muslim politicians, civil servants, and intellectuals—the same Muslim elites who had made the pilgrimage, sponsored Islamic schools, and founded Islamic organizations—overwhelmingly opposed the separatist rebellion. While some of them had previously provided material and ideological support to the underground Muslim separatist movement, when they were forced to choose sides in 1972 by the declaration of martial law and the start of the armed insurgency, virtually all aligned eventually with the martial law regime of Ferdinand Marcos (McKenna 1992).

Second, the ideological thrust of the armed separatist rebellion was not specifically Islamic, but rather nationalist. The leading figure of the Muslim separatist movement was Nur Misuari, a Tausug from Sulu and the son of a very poor, commoner family. He attended the University of the Philippines on a scholarship and then taught there as an instructor in the political science department. Misuari was one of a number of students to take advantage of a Philippine government scholarship program for Muslims begun in 1957. While political maneuvering ensured that many of these students were the sons of *datus*, the scholarship program also represented the first opportunity for considerable numbers of ordinary Muslims to attend universities. Misuari was active in progressive nationalist politics as a student but later focused his efforts on issues more specific to Philippine Muslims. In 1968 he helped to found the Philippine Muslim Nationalist League, and in 1971 he launched the Moro National Liberation Front (MNLF), an underground Muslim separatist movement that had as its goal the establishment of a single independent homeland for all the Muslim peoples of the Philippines.[14] The central symbolic appeal used by the MNLF was a cultural-historical appeal to the concept of Philippine Muslim nationalism. The term "Bangsamoro" (or "Moro Nation") was a distillation of the central components of the nationalist appeal. Separatist ideologues transformed the epithetic "Moro" into a positive symbol of collective identity. Moro culture heroes were identified, and the unity and continuity of the Moro anticolonial struggle was proclaimed. A policy statement from the first issue of *Maharlika,* an MNLF newsletter, illustrates the predominantly national character of the MNLF appeal:

> From this very moment there shall be no stressing the fact that one is a Tausug, a Samal, a Yakan, a Subanon, a Kalagan, a Maguindanao, a Maranao, or a Badjao. He is only a Moro. Indeed, even those of other faith who have long established residence in the Bangsa Moro homeland and whose good-will and sympathy are with the Bangsa Moro Revolution shall, for purposes of national identification, be considered Moros. In other words, the term Moro is a national concept that must be understood as all embracing for all Bangsa Moro people within the length and breadth of our national boundaries. (quoted in Noble 1976, 418)

Although various commentators have suggested a direct link between Islamic renewal in the Muslim Philippines and the Bangsamoro Rebellion (see, for example, Bauzon 1991; George 1980; Madale 1986), neither the rebellion (at least in its early years—see below) nor the unarmed separatist movement that preceded it exhibited any of the common features—essentialist reform of Islamic practice, the rejection of Western culture, the assertion of a political role for religion and religious scholars—usually associated with a resurgent Islam (Denny 1987). The Bangsamoro Rebellion does constitute a particular instance of ethnonationalism—a sweeping political phenomenon for which Brackette Williams has recently offered an innovative reading. According to Williams, any adequate analysis of ethnicity must treat ethnic differentiation as "an aspect of a total system of stratification" (1989, 421). In such a system, the most powerful members of any particular nation-state "determine who, among persons of different 'tribal pasts,' is trustworthy and loyal to the political unit" (p. 419). As a consequence of this selective creation of national homogeneity, "severely impure people aim to separate themselves . . . from those against whom they are judged unfavorably and/or in relation to whom they are materially disadvantaged. They proclaim themselves a new people" (p. 429).

Muslim separatism in the Philippines was propelled by much the same dynamic suggested by Williams. The Christian Filipinos who controlled the Philippine state regarded all unhispanicized citizens as impure and marked Philippine Muslims as especially untrustworthy because of their long history of mutual enmity.[15] In the first decade of the postcolonial period, the Philippine government sponsored Christian migration on a massive scale to the relatively underpopulated Muslim South—particularly to Cotabato. The inrush of subsidized migrants to Muslim regions generated economic differentiation and social tensions, and eventually undermined the political bases of Muslim politicians. As the problems ignited by large-scale migration became increasingly evident, the government responded with a publicized effort to "integrate" Philippine Muslims (as well as other "National Cultural Minorities") into national life through the creation of the Commission on National Integration (see Horvatich, this volume). One of the few substantive accomplishments of the commission was to provide scholarships for a significant number of Muslim students to attend universities in Manila. An unintended consequence of those scholarships was the creation of a group of disaffected young Muslims who had experienced firsthand the magnitude of anti-Muslim bias in the national capital, were schooled in political activism, and were prepared to circumvent established Muslim politicians and launch a movement for political independence from what had become an increasingly antagonistic Christian-dominated state. While the separatist endeavor was an Islamic movement advocating a separate, Muslim-controlled state, the Islamic identity that motivated it tended to be hyphenated, inclusive, and ethnicized. The Manila-educated leaders of the separatist movement inherited that ethnicized Muslim-Filipino identity from their colonial era seniors and lived its contradictions in their frustrated attempts at integration in the national capital. They chose to represent that identity by appropriating a previously pejorative appellation to denominate the citizens of their new nation; they proclaimed themselves

Moros—a term now transfigured to denote the descendants of those whom the Spaniards and their colonized subjects feared and distrusted.

The Emergence of an Independent *Ulama* and Endeavors for Islamic Renewal in Cotabato

The stimulus for the first sustained effort at Islamic renewal documented for Cotabato may be traced to a very different source of postwar largess. Between 1955 and 1978 the Government of Egypt, as part of the pan-Islamic programs of Gamel Abdul Nasser, granted more than two hundred scholarships to young Filipino Muslims, the majority of whom studied at al-Azhar University (George 1980; Majul 1979; Mastura 1984). Egypt had previously sent a few (mostly Indonesian) graduates of al-Azhar to teach in the Muslim Philippines, but it was only with Nasser's ascent to power in 1954 that significant numbers of Philippine Muslim students were able to undertake advanced studies. A number of those students were scions of *datu* families but many others were not, and the scholarships thus became another avenue for nonelite Muslim students to gain access to higher education. While the establishment of *datu*-sponsored *madaris* and the presence of foreign missionaries had minimal effect on Islamic consciousness in the region, the growth of an indigenous *ulama* educated in Islamic centers abroad has had profound and unprecedented consequences.

As in Manila, the Philippine Muslim student community in Cairo became a center for the development of activism in pursuit of social and political change in the Muslim Philippines, but, unlike that in Manila, student activism in Cairo was explicitly and exclusively Islamic in character. Although the first substantial numbers of Cotabato students educated in the Middle East began returning to the Philippines in the late 1960s, it was nearly 1980 before conditions there allowed the graduates to teach and preach relatively unconstrained by *datu* influence or military harassment. As the first cohorts of clerics returned to Cotabato from al-Azhar, they were almost immediately engulfed in the conflicts of the 1970s. Most joined the separatist movement and, with the outbreak of the armed rebellion, went underground either as active insurgents or to protect themselves from government persecution.[16]

Despite the circumscribed role of reformist Islamic views in the official ideology of the rebellion, Islamic clerics played a prominent role in the Cotabato rebel leadership, and one of their number in exile, Hashim Salamat, held the post of vice-chairman of the Central Committee of the MNLF. After the armed rebellion had been suspended with the signing of a cease-fire agreement between the MNLF and the Philippine government in 1977,

Salamat became frustrated with Nur Misuari's leadership, finally breaking with him in 1979. Six years later, Salamat officially changed the title of the organization he led to the "Moro Islamic Liberation Front" in order to "underscore Islam as the rallying point of the Bangsamoro struggle" (Salamat, quoted in Mastura 1985, 17). In a letter to the secretary-general of the Organization of the Islamic Conference, Salamat elaborated on those intentions: "All Mujahideen under the Moro Islamic Liberation Front (MILF) adopt Islam as their way of life. Their ultimate objective in their Jihad is to make supreme the WORD of ALLAH and establish Islam in the Bangsamoro homeland" (Mastura 1985, 18; emphases in the original). Salamat's principal aim of establishing Islam in Muslim Mindanao varied markedly from that of Misuari, who sought as his primary goal the creation of a separate state in the Moro homeland.

When finally they were able to speak out safely in public beginning in 1978, the Cotabato clerics both promoted Islamic equality and justice and strenuously advocated the reform of particular cultural practices. While the former endeavors were generally welcomed by ordinary Cotabato Muslims, the clerics' efforts at Islamic reform have been the source of some contention throughout Cotabato. The new Cotabato clerics have been singularly successful at shifting moral authority away from the *datus*. The close ideological and material association between traditional elites and religious leadership has, slowly but steadily, been weakened with the emergence of a new, independent *ulama*. The gradual severance of that linkage has been accomplished in part through preaching. Clerics have used Friday sermons to advance an alternative, egalitarian ideology as part of their program for Islamic renewal. As illustration, the following passage from my field notes paraphrases the contents of a Friday sermon given by Ustadh Ibrahim, a teacher at the largest *madrasah* in Cotabato City, at a mosque located in a poor urban migrant community at the edge of the city:

> The sermon given by Ustadh Ibrahim today concerned the true meaning of being a Muslim. His talk was based on the *ayah* [Qur'anic verse] "Do not die until you become a Muslim." He stated that to become a Muslim one must *act* like a Muslim at all times. Behaving like a Muslim consists of much more than merely praying and fasting. It means practicing social justice.
>
> He related a story about Caliph Ali. Ali was involved in a legal dispute with a non-Muslim, and both parties went before a *qadi*, an Islamic jurist, to resolve the matter. When Ali entered the hearing room, the *qadi* received him with lavish servility. When the non-Muslim entered, the *qadi*

acknowledged him brusquely. Ali became quite angered at this behavior and reminded the *qadi* of his duty to dispense justice and treat all men equally before the law.

In one of my conversations with Ustadh Ibrahim, he commented on the claims of traditional elites to politicoreligious leadership on the basis of descent from the Prophet Muhammad: "The *ustadh*s do not like such claims. Muhammad did not appoint his successor. He did not believe in blood relatedness as the criterion for leadership. The blood relation of the Caliphs to Muhammad was a distant one. What the *ustadh*s would like to see are equitable leaders, trusted leaders, not leaders chosen solely on the basis of blood inheritance. The issue of noble inheritance is a problem we [in Cotabato] have long had. Good people, with good minds, have had little chance if they were not royal descendants."

In Friday sermons and other public forums the independent *ulama* dispute the claim for nobility as the single criterion for politicoreligious leadership. This challenge is usually presented in an indirect manner, by emphasizing Islamic justice and equality, and by supporting "good *datu*s" —those few who meet the *ustadh*s' criteria for Islamic leadership. Cotabato *datu*s have responded to this challenge to their traditional authority by branding the *ustadh*s' message as Wahhabi extremism or, more commonly, Shi'a heterodoxy, arguing that it is improper for the *ulama* to speak for or to Cotabato Muslims on other than narrowly defined religious matters. That view was expressed in a radio campaign message by a *datu* politician running in 1988 against a newly formed Islamic political party supported by most of the independent *ulama* in Cotabato. "It is a Shi'a principle that the *ulama* participate directly in government. . . . In Iran, the *ulama* want to be political leaders. I am not saying that in Islam the *ulama* cannot participate in politics, but if the *ulama* form the political leadership, there will be no one to preach. . . . We do not want to create ayatollahs or mullahs here in the Philippines."[17]

The reform project of the independent *ulama* of Cotabato has not been significantly affected by the strong opposition of the *datu*s for two reasons. The first is that the *ulama* continue to be associated with MILF insurgents still under arms in remote camps in Cotabato. The existence of that armed force severely limits the ability of *datu*s to coerce the *ulama* or otherwise restrict their preaching. The second factor has been the increasing availability of external funding sources for religious purposes. External funds arrived first in the form of the scholarships from the government of Egypt in the 1950s and expanded rapidly in the 1970s and 1980s. Libya, the Organization of the Islamic Conference of Foreign Ministers, and the Kingdom of

Saudi Arabia have provided financial support for various religious projects, and Egypt continues to send missionaries for one- or two-year assignments in Cotabato. More significantly for the development of an independent local *ulama,* the governments of Libya and Saudi Arabia support a small percentage of local *ustadh*s as long-term missionaries. In addition, since the end of the armed rebellion, significant further funding has reportedly been made available from private institutions and individuals in the Middle East as the result of contacts developed by the MILF and local *ulama.*

Brief mention should be made of two related developments after 1980 in Cotabato: opportunities for secular higher education for Muslims were significantly expanded at the local level, and works on Islam in English (the language of higher education in the Philippines) became readily available. By 1986 those trends had led to the formation of organizations of young "Islamic activists" who were beginning to question the privileged position of the newly independent *ulama.* We thus find in Cotabato as in Tawi-Tawi (Horvatich, this volume) that within a few years of wresting moral authority from traditional leaders, the new religious scholars were themselves being challenged as part of a pan-Islamic transformation (examined recently by Dale Eickelman) in which religious authority is shifting "from elite specialists recognized as masters of religious texts . . . to religious and political activists who seek open religious discussion and action and whose authority is based upon persuasion and the interpretation of accessible texts" (Eickelman 1992, 652).[18]

The Islamic Identities of Muslim Subordinates

The ordinary Muslims of Cotabato possess their own accounts of local responses to American colonialism. They continue to tell their grandfathers' tales of answering American technical supremacy with magical prowess. Those stories recount how certain Muslims impressed the Americans by performing extraordinary feats: causing bullets to change direction in midflight or magically moving objects that Americans were unable to budge. Whereas the colonial narratives are almost entirely compensatory in nature, stories told of the recent Muslim rebellion in Cotabato concern direct confrontation with armed invaders. I have recorded numerous popular accounts of supernatural assistance provided to separatist rebels, most often through the intercession of local spirits (see McKenna 1990; 1996). Both sets of narratives indicate that popular notions of enchantment—notions that are in great measure independent of the ruling ideology of Muslim elites—have been an intrinsic element of the Islamic identity of Muslim subordinates in Cotabato.

That identity has been bound up with locality, with territory and its defense. It has been thus, potentially, an oppositional identity, but one rather different from that imagined in the conventional account. In a manner similar to that noted by Thomas Kiefer for the Tausug of Jolo Island, most Cotabato Muslims conceive of the World of Islam *(dar-ul-Islam)* as a form of social territory but have only the vaguest awareness of the actual geography of Islam (1986, 14). Although the concept of *dar-ul-Islam* as expressed by Cotabato Muslims distinguishes between a Muslim and a non-Muslim world, it does not correspond, in any significant sense, with an identity of Islamic (or Moro) nationalism. The ordinary Muslims of Cotabato have, in fact, never denominated themselves as Moros and, despite more than twenty years of appeals to Moro nationhood by separatist ideologues, still do not. That reluctance to embrace Morohood extends even to former rank-and-file insurgents, most of whom received considerable political instruction in rebel camps. As I have proposed elsewhere (McKenna 1996), the lyrics of popular rebel songs suggest that most ordinary Muslim insurgents were fighting for a familiar community *(inged)* rather than for an imagined Philippine Muslim nation *(bangsa Moro).*[19]

Cotabato Muslim subordinates identify themselves as "Muslims" as distinguished from Christians and other non-Muslims. Cotabato Christians refer to them reciprocally as Muslims and lump their various languages and dialects together under the single rubric "Muslim" (certain Christians vaunt their ability to "speak Muslim"). Yet their Muslim identity has not been their only or even their primary ethnic identity. Cotabato Muslims, who are divided into two ethnolinguistic and five dialect groups, commonly segment themselves for political purposes along linguistic, territorial, and status group divides. They also carefully distinguish themselves from the Muslim groups found in other regions of the South.

The Islamic identity of Muslim subordinates in Cotabato is not and probably never has been predicated upon their holding their traditional nobility in "religious awe and adulation" (Glang 1969, 33). At the same time, most ordinary Muslims are not the sort of Muslims the independent *ulama* would have them be. They are Muslims who rely on magical charms and amulets, and appease local spirits. They are Muslims whose religious practice exhibits a good deal of ritual impropriety, who may drink and gamble, neglect their prayers, and perform religious rituals quite at variance with Islamic orthopraxy. They are Muslims who embrace many elements of the highly Westernized culture of their Christian neighbors.

While ordinary Muslims have to a significant degree accepted the new source of moral authority represented by the independent *ulama*, they have done so despite its associated call for Islamic orthopraxy and the disenchantment of their world, not because of it. They tend to respect and admire the *ustadh*s for the Islamic learning they have acquired and approve when that knowledge is expressed in Friday sermons having themes such as "Allah will help the weak person to claim justice." In Campo Muslim, the urban migrant community where I conducted research in 1985, I found that there were core Islamic practices—fasting during the month of Ramadan, strict abstention from pork, ritual circumcision of males, and a virtual total absence of apostasy—that had existed prior to the emergence of the *ustadh*s and were little affected by them. There were other areas of religious practice and personal behavior that had reportedly undergone appreciable change that community members agreed to be entirely positive. The attendance of male community members at Friday noon worship had reportedly increased, and a greater number of individuals were attentive to daily prayers. Incidences of public drinking and gambling by community residents were also apparently reduced.

There were other aspects of the cultural life of the community, however, that tended to be strongly contested. These were (usually) traditional practices to which the *ustadh*s were adamantly opposed but that were equally resistant to emendation. They included traditional mortuary rituals, most especially the series of ritual feasts *(kanduli)* held at prescribed intervals of 3, 7, 40, 100, and 365 days after death.[20] After initially objecting to all such propitiation ceremonies for the deceased, the *ustadh*s later modified their position and have condoned the three-day (Telu a Gay) death commemoration ceremony. However, they have strongly criticized further ceremonies as unorthodox and wasteful of resources and do not approve of the traditional Sufic content of the *kanduli*. The traditional celebrations associated with two holy days—Maulid en Nabi (the birthday of the Prophet, Arabic Maulidu'n-Nabi) and the Layatul Kadir (the Night of Power, Arabic *Lailatu'l-Qadr)*—have been deemphasized or simplified, owing to the influence of the *ustadh*s. They have also disapproved of elaborate celebrations for pilgrims returning from the *hajj*. Additionally, clerics have strongly objected to certain cultural activities that are particularly enjoyed by young people. These include the death vigil traditionally kept by family, friends, and neighbors for seven nights after the death of a community member. Such vigils had been an important social occasion for young men and women. Another offending activity is the song duel, or *dayunday,* an exceedingly popular form of public entertainment most often found in association with wedding celebrations. The *dayunday* is a modern adaptation of a traditional song form, using Western instruments (guitar) and some aspects of Western showmanship, yet is still unmistakably an indigenous non-Western entertainment. It involves a song contest between a man and a woman, or more commonly a three-way competition between two women and one man (or vice versa), with the singers trading extemporaneous verses of romantic repartee. The *ustadh*s were disturbed at men and women performing together and singing openly about love and romance, and campaigned, without success, to ban the *dayunday*s. As clerics have denounced *dayunday*s, *datu*s have embraced them. Traditional elites sponsored every one of the *dayunday*s I attended, and they have become the most popular way to ensure large crowds at political rallies.

The various reforms attempted by the independent *ulama* have caused a good deal of confusion and anxiety in the community, particularly as identity-affirming rituals and practices have been assailed as un-Islamic behavior. The mediator in many of these cultural skirmishes in the community has been the local imam, who maintains close relationships with the *ustadh*s, and has been much influenced by their teachings. At the same time, he tends to identify with community members who are confused by the changes promoted by the *ustadh*s. In counseling community members, the imam distinguishes between behavior that is un-Islamic and that which is anti-Islamic, and suggests that there is nothing anti-Islamic in traditional rituals. He also expresses the sentiments of many community members by drawing a distinction between Islamization and Arabization. He advises members of his congregation that they are obliged to follow the injunctions of the Qur'an but not the practices of the people of the Middle East and that the *ustadh*s sometimes confuse these two. He has even commented that Allah revealed himself to the Arabs precisely because their behavior was so wicked. In general, the imam sincerely respects the *ustadh*s and counsels others to listen to their teachings. However, he does not urge community members to change traditional practices because, as he puts it, the *ustadh*s are still young and lacking in practical knowledge. The imam himself, a man possessed of considerable spiritual potency, has made his own compromise with the new ritual order by choosing not to exercise his supernatural powers, lest doing so be construed as a form of the sin of *shirk,* or attempted partnership with the divinity.

Among the independent *ulama* and other Muslim intellectuals concerned with Islamic renewal, there has developed a widely held notion that the Muslims of Cotabato have progressed partway toward the goal of becoming "genuine Muslims" (in Magindanaon, *tidtu-tidtu a Muslim*). The fact that so many are still becoming Muslims is used to justify, among other things, the allowance of local accretions to Islamic ritual and the extreme rarity of austere applications of Islamic law by nontraditional (i.e., independent *ulama*) adjudicators. That theology of incipience is not shared by ordinary Muslims. They are Muslims, they declare, because their forebears were Muslims, because they live in a Muslim homeland, and because they profess Islam.[21] Their "Muslimness" (Ellen 1983, 56) is not simply an oppositional ethnic identity constructed for them by political leaders.[22] Neither is it a universalistic religious identity that transcends nationality, or even locality. It is, as has been pointed out by a number of analysts (see, for example, Ellen 1983; Roff 1985), and recently and eloquently by Bowen, the product of a "dialogue between potentially conflicting cultural orders: the universalistic imperatives of Islam (as locally understood) and the values embedded in a particular society" (Bowen 1992, 667). The contemporary Islamic identity of the majority of Cotabato Muslims can actually be said to represent "only the current state of play" (p. 668) in three continuing and complexly intertwined dialogues: that between ordinary Muslims and the independent *ulama* over styles of religiosity, between traditional leaders and followers over the sources of political legitimacy, and between Muslims and the Christian-controlled Philippine state over the parameters of regional self-determination.

Conclusions

The conventional account of the development of a shared Islamic identity in the Muslim Philippines reinforces, intentionally or unintentionally, the ideological stance of Moro nationalists that a self-conscious oppositional identity as Philippine Muslims is ancient, deep, and broadly shared. Rather than being the consequence of a coordinated Muslim struggle against Spanish aggression, a transcendent ethnoreligious identity as Muslim Filipinos was developed and nurtured during the colonial period by representatives of the colonial state.[23] That identity was amplified and asserted during the early postcolonial period by Muslim elite politicians attempting to gain purchase in a nation-state controlled by Christian Filipinos. Beginning in the late 1960s, a new set of Muslim leaders advanced an expressly ethnonationalist identity as the footing for an armed separatist movement against the Philippine state. An adjacent but distinct development has been the emergence of an independent, formally educated *ulama* advocating comprehensive Islamic renewal.

The standard historical account has confused and conflated these discrete and differentially motivated attempts at forging a potent and inclusive Philippine Muslim identity. It has also virtually ignored consideration of the practical[24] and continuously reformulated Islamic identities of Muslim subordinates—cultural identities that, while intensely local, also encompass considerable regional resonances in that Muslim subordinates throughout the South, at least for the past hundred years or so, have been similarly affected by extralocal forces. The perceptions and voices of ordinary Muslims are neglected in the conventional account because its core premise of a single Islamic identity widely shared by Philippine Muslims precludes notice of contested meanings and conflicting discourses. I have drawn on ethnographic and ethnohistoric data from Cotabato to show that ordinary Muslims have never uncritically embraced any of the dominant meanings of Islamic identity either ascribed or proposed to them. Their Muslimness is self-sufficient and has resisted symbolic definition or moral supervision by either *ulama* or *datu*s. The message conveyed by such data is that analyses of Islamic identity in the Muslim Philippines should be keyed to ordinary understandings of historical experience rather than to suppositions about cultural homogeneity and regional solidarity.

Notes

This essay draws on research conducted in the southern Philippines from June 1985 to September 1986, supported by a grant from the National Science Foundation (grant no. BNS-8405717), and in January and February of 1988, supported by the University of California at Davis. Additional archival research was conducted at the Newberry Library in July 1992 and at the National Archives in November 1993, supported by a Faculty Research Grant from the University of Alabama at Birmingham.

1. A representative capsule expression of this narrative is found in a recent piece concerned with the contemporary politics of Muslim separatism in the Philippines.

    > For over 400 years the Moros perceived their struggle as a fight to protect their religion, cultural identity and homeland against foreign invaders. They have fought many wars for political independence against the Spanish, Americans and lastly, the Christian Filipino governments in Manila. With their strong sense of Islamic nationalism, the majority of the Muslims regard themselves simply as Moros and not Filipinos at all. Over the centuries Islam has been important to the Muslim people in the Philippines not only in forging the basis of their self-identity, but also in acting as the cement between deep ethnic divisions that exist among the many cultural-linguistic groups that make up the Moro people. (Molloy 1988, 61)

2. The frail foundation provided by the standard historical accounts has not deterred attempts to perch elaborate explanatory structures upon it with predictably awkward outcomes. As illustration, a recent work by Bauzon (1991) expressly concerned with Islamic identity in the Philippines presents (on the basis of secondary sources) a depiction of Islamic culture and politics in the Philippines so inaccurate as to be unrecognizable to anyone familiar with ethnographic or ethnohistorical accounts of particular Muslim Filipino populations.

3. The region of Cotabato, formerly constituting a single province, comprises the entire southwestern portion of the island of Mindanao. Its traditional population center was the Cotabato River Basin. Cotabato is the traditional

homeland of the Magindanaon, the largest Philippine Muslim ethnolinguistic group. The region is now divided into four separate provinces, only one of them—Maguindanao Province—with a majority Muslim population.

4. This latter issue I have addressed in more detail and with considerably more theoretical elaboration in two other works. See McKenna 1990; 1996.

5. See, for example, the instructions given to Captain Esteban Rodriguez de Figueroa, who, in 1578, was commissioned to subdue the Moro sultanates of Sulu and Mindanao. These instructions direct Rodriguez to promote trade with the Moros, explore their natural resources, Christianize them, and compel them to acknowledge Spanish sovereignty (Blair and Robertson, 1903–1919, 4:174–181).

6. With respect to the frequency and importance of Islamic appeals, the two most famous anti-Spanish appeals on record—the 1603 address by Datu Buisan to the Leyte Chiefs and Sultan Kudarat's 1639 exhortation to the Iranun *datus*—contain no reference to Islam or any mention of religion whatsoever (Majul 1973, 118, 141). Those speeches were reported by the Spanish Jesuits who witnessed them. One presumes these diarists to have scrupulously recorded any religious references they might have heard.

7. In his superb book *The Sulu Zone, 1768–1898*, James Warren examines and rejects the argument that Muslim raiding and slaving in the sixteenth to eighteenth centuries should be viewed within the framework of the "Moro Wars" as "retaliation against Spanish colonialism and religious incursion" (1985, xvi).

8. Majul features the single historical account that can be interpreted to indicate a fairly high level of orthopraxy among the Muslim populace in fifteenth-century Cotabato (see de la Costa 1961, 85–86). He dismisses the remainder, among them a seventeenth-century account of Cotabato by William Dampier (generally considered to be a careful observer) that comments on the lack of mosque attendance by commoners: "Friday is their Sabbath; but I never did see any difference that they make between this Day and any other Day, only the Sultan himself goes to the Mosque twice. . . . The meaner sort of people have little Devotion: I did never see any of them at their Prayers, or go into a Mosque" (1906, 344–345).

9. Cesar Majul's 1973 book *Muslims in the Philippines* is a Muslim nationalist history and is best evaluated in the context of the political environment in which it was written. As with other nationalist discourses (it compares favorably with Philippine nationalist histories, which essentially ignore the existence of Philippine Muslims—see Agoncillo 1969; Constantino 1975), its rhetorical effect "is the subjugation of a threateningly unruly history" (Spencer 1990, 287). Majul's corpus of work in general (see especially his 1985 work *The Contemporary Muslim Movement in the Philippines*) is a rich and impressive collection of carefully researched historical writings on Philippine Muslims.

10. Informal agreements of a similar nature were made during that period with other sultans and *datus* in the rest of the Muslim South (Gowing 1983).

11. The short-lived tribal ward system seems to have been a compromise between the views of colonial administrators such as General Wood, who generally disdained Philippine Muslims and had little use for traditional leaders, and those of men like General George W. Davis, who in a 1901 report argued that "it seems to me that the worst misfortune that could befall a Moro community and the nation responsible for good order among the Moros would be to upset and destroy the patriarchal despotism of their chiefs, for it is all they have and all they are capable of understanding" (Report of Brigadier General George W. Davis to Luke E. Wright, Vice Civil Governor of the Philippine Islands, 4 December 1901, Bureau of Insular Affairs Records, file no. 5075-2, National Archives).

12. Carpenter to Secretary of the Interior Rafael Palma, 27 January 1919, Bureau of Insular Affairs Personal File—Tarhata Kiram, National Archives.

13. In respect to my contention that these emblems of Islamic resurgence were primarily signs rather than practices, it can be noted first that the *madrasah*s established in the immediate postwar period had minimal results in heightening the Islamic consciousness or religiosity of ordinary Muslims (see Hassoubah 1983). Second, the great majority of the Islamic organizations created in the postwar period, organizations often cited as tangible indicators of Islamic resurgence (see Gowing 1979; Mastura 1984; Majul 1979), seem to have been little more than paper organizations with no genuine existence apart from an organizational name and a set of by-laws.

14. In a 1968 editorial in the official organ of the Philippine Muslim Nationalist League, Misuari writes: "Separatism is a costly and painful process and few ordinary mortals are prepared to pay the price. But this world has been a witness time and again to the division of certain countries into smaller ones. For, political division is a matter which is not fully within the control of men, nor yet a sole product of their whims and caprices. It is in fact mainly the creation of the actual conditions in which men find themselves. It is the creation of the system" (quoted in George 1980, 200). The rhetoric employed here by Misuari appears more inspired by the language of revolutionary Marxism, an ideology motivating numerous other nationalist struggles, than by the discourse of Islamic renewal. Those two opposed ideologies are equivalently indisposed (at least in their more orthodox embodiments) toward nationalist strivings.

15. That history was frequently recalled and reenacted by Christian Filipinos through the public performance of the *"Moro-moro,"* a form of folk theater in which Christian heroes battled Muslim villains depicted as savage and treacherous pirates.

16. The Muslim separatist movement was, to a significant degree, ignited by the aspirations engendered by both secular and Islamic higher education. The coalescence (at least for a time—see below) of Middle East– and Manila-educated activists in the MNLF leadership represents a distinctive variant of a pan-Islamic development recently analyzed by Dale Eickelman: the relationship between mass higher education, political and religious activism, and

transformations of religious authority (1992; see also Horvatich in this volume).

17. Despite the implication in this speech of widespread *ulama* participation in political office seeking, only one Cairo-educated cleric ran as a candidate in the Islamic political party in 1988 in Cotabato, even though many *ustadh*s were active officers or members of the party.

18. The Cotabato case contains an additional ironic element. In the mid-1980s many Muslim university students in Cotabato were avidly reading, in English translation, the words of the Egyptian fundamentalist thinker Sayyid Qutb. More than a few of those students had been named Nasser by their parents, after the Egyptian leader who provided significant Islamic assistance to Philippine Muslims—the same man who ordered the execution of Sayyid Qutb in 1966 (Eickelman 1992, 646, and personal communication).

19. While the figurative language and recurrent themes found in rebel songs are not inconsistent with official representations of the Bangsamoro Rebellion, virtually none of the key symbols and images advanced by the core leadership of the MNLF are evident. Those songs as well as other popular narratives of the rebellion exhibit a strong sense of collective identity as Muslims and a willingness to struggle for the separatist cause, but also reveal both ambivalence toward the subsumption of local identities within a Moro national identity and apprehension about the subordination of local concerns to national interests (McKenna 1996).

20. Similar sorts of ritual feasts *(kanduli, kenduri, kenduren/slametan)* held for various occasions have been described for numerous other Southeast Asian societies. See, for example, Bowen 1992; Geertz 1960; Horvatich 1993; Reid 1984.

21. Michael Peletz, in this volume, provides a fascinating discussion of the ambivalence of ordinary Muslims toward Islamic resurgence in contemporary Malaysia. While ordinary Muslims in Cotabato expressed ambivalence toward Moro nationalism (both desiring and distrusting it), I did not find the same sort of responses in respect to the Islamic renewal efforts of the independent *ulama*. Instead, like Patricia Horvatich in this volume, I've noted some aspects of the renewal program were accepted and others resisted, in some cases openly. I would suggest at least two reasons why the Cotabato case differs from that described by Peletz for Kelantan. First, the independent *ulama* were openly opposed in Cotabato by established Muslim politicians who advanced an alternative ideology of moral authority. The existence of this powerful opposition allowed ordinary Muslims the opportunity for "fence sitting" and permitted potential mediators such as the community imam to explore the middle ground between the polar positions. Second, the struggle over Islamic renewal was separable from issues of Muslim identity in the Philippines. Muslim nationalist (Moro) identity remains the most significant publicly promoted Islamic identity in the Philippines, and, for ordinary Muslims at least, no alternative primary ethnic identity is feasible. While all ordi-

nary Muslims are expected to be Muslim nationalists, it is possible for an individual to be a "Moro" without being a "genuine" Muslim. In fact, one can be a Moro, at least according to the MNLF leadership, without being a Muslim at all.

22. It is important to clarify the nature of the difference between the self-conscious and objectified Muslim-Filipino identity enunciated by most Philippine Muslim political leaders in the postcolonial period and the unself-conscious cultural identity of ordinary Muslims. The latter sort of identity is illustrated by Patricia Horvatich's observation that the Sama (a Philippine Muslim population) "define almost everything they do [including gathering sea urchins] as Islamic because they are Muslim" (forthcoming). Jonathan Friedman has made a similar distinction between two forms of Greek identity in a recent discussion of the phenomenon of Hellenism in the ancient world. In reference to Greek colonists in Asia he notes: "Colonists tend to develop a strong cultural identity, primarily as a means of distinction: 'I am Greek because I live like this, have these symbols, practice such-and-such a religion, etc.' But this kind of identity expresses a separation of the person from that with which he identifies. The content of his social selfhood may become distanced from his immediate subjectivity: 'I am Greek because I do this, that and the other thing' does not imply the converse, i.e., 'I do this, that and the other thing because I am Greek' " (Friedman 1990, 26).

23. Similar developments of ethnic entities by colonial authorities occurred in various parts of the region during the late colonial period. See Benedict Anderson (1987) for a description of that process among the Karens and the Moluccans.

24. For a definition and discussion of "practical Islam" in Southeast Asia, see Ellen 1983.

References Cited

Agoncillo, Teodoro A. 1969. *A Short History of the Philippines*. New York: Mentor Books.

Anderson, Benedict R. O'G. 1987. "The State and Minorities in Indonesia." In Anderson, ed., *South East Asian Tribal Groups and Ethnic Minorities: Prospects for the Eighties and Beyond*, pp. 1–13. Cultural Survival Report 22. Cambridge, Mass.: Cultural Survival Inc.

Bauzon, Kenneth E. 1991. *Liberalism and the Quest for Islamic Identity in the Philippines*. Durham: Acorn Press.

Blair, E. H., and J. A. Robertson, eds. 1903–1919. *The Philippine Islands, 1493–1898*. 55 vols. Cleveland: A. H. Clark Co.

Blumentritt, Ferdinand. 1893. "Los Maguindanaos: Estudio etnográfico." *Boletín de la Sociedad Geográfica de Madrid* 35:267–285.

Bowen, John R. 1992. "On Scriptural Essentialism and Ritual Variation: Muslim Sacrifice in Sumatra and Morocco." *American Ethnologist* 19 (4): 656–671.

Constantino, Renato. 1975. *The Philippines: A Past Revisited*. Manila: By the author.

Costa, S. J., Horacio de la. 1961. *The Jesuits in the Philippines, 1581–1768*. Cambridge, Mass.: Harvard University Press.

Dampier, William. 1906. *Dampier's Voyages*. Edited by John Masefield. London: E. Grant Richards.

Denny, Frederick M. 1987. *Islam and the Muslim Community*. San Francisco: Harper and Row.

Eickelman, Dale F. 1992. "Mass Higher Education and the Religious Imagination in Contemporary Arab Societies." *American Ethnologist* 19 (4): 643–655.

Ellen, Roy F. 1983. "Social Theory, Ethnography, and the Understanding of Practical Islam in South-East Asia." In M. B. Hooker, ed., *Islam in South-East Asia*, pp. 50–91. Leiden: Brill.

Forrest, Thomas. 1969. *A Voyage to New Guinea and the Moluccas, 1774–1776*. Kuala Lumpur: Oxford University Press.

Friedman, Jonathan. 1990. "Notes on Culture and Identity in Imperial Worlds." In Per Bilde et al., eds., *Religion and Religious Practice in the Seleucid Kingdom*, pp. 14–39. Aarhus, Denmark: Aarhus University Press.

Geertz, Clifford. 1960. *The Religion of Java*. Chicago: University of Chicago Press.

George, T. J. S. 1980. *Revolt in Mindanao: The Rise of Islam in Philippine Politics*. Kuala Lumpur: Oxford University Press.

Glang, Alunan C. 1969. *Muslim Secession or Integration?* Quezon City: Alunan Glang.

Gowing, Peter Gordon. 1979. *Muslim Filipinos—Heritage and Horizon*. Quezon City: New Day Publishers.

———. 1983. *Mandate in Moroland: The American Government of Muslim Filipinos—1899–1920*. Quezon City: New Day Publishers.

Hassoubah, Ahmad Mohammad H. 1983. *Teaching Arabic as a Second Language in the Southern Philippines*. Marawi City: University Research Center, Mindanao State University.

Horvatich, Patricia. 1993. "Keeping up with the Hassans: Tradition, Change, and Rituals of Death in Tawi-Tawi, Philippines." *Pilipinas: A Journal of Philippine Studies* 21:51–71.

———. Forthcoming. "The Martyr and the Mayor: On the Politics of Identity in the Southern Philippines." In Renato Rosaldo, ed., *Cultural Citizenship in Southeast Asia*.

Hunt, Chester L. 1974. "Ethnic Stratification and Integration in Cotabato." In Peter G. Gowing and Robert D. McAmis, eds., *The Muslim Filipinos: Their History, Society, and Contemporary Problems*, pp. 194–218. Manila: Solidaridad Publishing House.

Ileto, Reynaldo C. 1971. *Magindanao: 1860–1888: The Career of Datu Uto of Buayan*. Data Paper No. 82. Ithaca: Cornell University Southeast Asia Program.

Kiefer, Thomas M. 1986. *The Tausug: Violence and Law in a Philippine Moslem Society*. Prospect Heights, Ill.: Waveland Press.

Kuder, Edward M. 1945. "The Moros in the Philippines." *Far Eastern Quarterly* 4 (2): 119–126.

Madale, Nagasura. 1986. "The Resurgence of Islam and Nationalism in the Philippines." In Taufik Abdullah and Sharon Siddique, eds., *Islam and Society in Southeast Asia.* Singapore: Institute of Southeast Asian Studies.

Majul, Cesar Adib. 1973. *Muslims in the Philippines.* Manila: St. Mary's Publishing.

———. 1979. "Minorities in the Philippines: The Muslims." In *Trends in Ethnic Group Relations in Asia and Oceania.* Paris: UNESCO.

———. 1985. *The Contemporary Muslim Movement in the Philippines.* Berkeley: Mizan Press.

Mastura, Michael O. 1984. *Muslim Filipino Experience: A Collection of Essays.* Manila: Ministry of Muslim Affairs.

———. 1985. "Perspectives and Approaches to Muslim Studies in the Philippines: The Ummatic Science Imperatives." Unpublished paper presented at the First National Conference in Philippine Studies, February 11–13, 1985, Quezon City, Philippines.

McKenna, Thomas M. 1990. "Islam, Elite Competition, and Ethnic Mobilization: Forms of Domination and Dissent in Cotabato, Southern Philippines." Ph.D. dissertation, University of California, Davis.

———. 1992. "Martial Law, Moro Nationalism, and Traditional Leadership in Cotabato." *Pilipinas* 18:1–17.

———. 1996. "'Fighting for the Homeland': National Ideas and Rank-and-File Experience in the Muslim Separatist Movement in the Philippines." *Critique of Anthropology* 16 (3): 229–255.

Molloy, Ivan 1988. "The Decline of the Moro National Liberation Front in the Southern Philippines." *Journal of Contemporary Asia* 18 (1): 59–76.

Noble, Lela Gardner. 1976. "The Moro National Liberation Front in the Philippines." *Pacific Affairs* 49 (3): 405–424.

Ravenholt, Albert. 1956. "The Amir Mindalano—Profile of a Filipino Mohammedan Leader." *American Universities Field Staff Reports, Southeast Asia Series* 4 (10): 162–171.

Reid, Anthony. 1984. "The Islamization of Southeast Asia." In Muhammad Abu Bakar et al., eds., *Historia: Essays in Commemoration of the Twenty-fifth Anniversary of the Department of History, University of Malaya.* Kuala Lumpur: Malaysian Historical Society.

——— 1988. *Southeast Asia in the Age of Commerce, 1450–1680,* vol. 1: *The Lands below the Winds.* New Haven: Yale University Press.

Roff, William R. 1985. "Islam Obscured? Some Reflections on Studies of Islam and Society in Southeast Asia." *Archipel* 29:7–34.

Saleeby, Najeeb M. 1905. *Studies in Moro History, Law, and Religion.* Ethnological Survey Publications 4 (1). Manila: Dept. of the Interior.

———. 1908. *The History of Sulu.* Division of Ethnology Publications, 4 (2). Manila: Dept. of the Interior.

———. 1913. *The Moro Problem*. Manila: Bureau of Printing.

Spencer, Jonathan. 1990. "Writing Within: Anthropology, Nationalism, and Culture in Sri Lanka." *Current Anthropology* 31 (3): 283–300.

Thomas, Ralph Benjamin. 1971. *Muslim but Filipino: The Integration of Philippine Muslims, 1917–1946*. Ann Arbor: University Microfilms.

Warren, James F. 1985. *The Sulu Zone, 1768–1898: The Dynamics of External Trade, Slavery, and Ethnicity in the Transformation of a Southeast Asian Maritime State*. Quezon City: New Day Publishers.

Williams, Brackette. 1989. "A Class Act: Anthropology and the Race to Nation across Ethnic Terrain." *Annual Review of Anthropology* 18:401–444.

Wolters, Willem. 1984. *Politics, Patronage, and Class Conflict in Central Luzon*. Quezon City: New Day Publishers.

Chapter 3

Islamization and Democratization in Indonesia

Robert W. Hefner

One of the most remarkable developments in Indonesian politics in recent years has been the rapprochement of the post-1966 "New
Order" government with important segments of the Muslim community.
Prior to the decade of the 1990s, many foreign specialists of Indonesia were
convinced that the Suharto government was a resolute defender of *abangan*-
Javanese values,[1] deeply opposed to anything that might expand Muslim
influence in Indonesian politics and society. Yet it was President Suharto
himself who on December 6, 1990, authorized the formation of Indonesia's
newest and most controversial Muslim social organization, the Association
of Indonesian Muslim Intellectuals (ICMI, Ikatan Cendekiawan Muslim Se-
Indonesia). Though the action caught many Western observers by surprise,
most Muslim Indonesians were aware that the president's act was merely
the latest in a series of overtures directed at the Muslim community. Nonetheless, for many non-Muslim and secular Indonesians, the president's
actions seemed a dangerous departure from the nonsectarian principles of
the New Order. After all, they noted, ICMI was not merely a politically neutral cultural organization. Many of its members declared quite openly that
the organization's primary purpose is to promote the Islamization of Indonesian state and society.

Many ICMI critics at first reassured themselves that the president's
actions were part of an only momentary effort to court Muslim support in
advance of the 1992 national elections; once the elections were over, they
forecast, the organization would disappear. When, in the months following
the elections, it became clear that ICMI was not only going to survive but
would play an expanded role in the president's new cabinet, these observers
realized that ICMI must be part of a longer-term presidential strategy. They
correctly noted that, since the late 1980s, President Suharto had faced

growing challenge from segments of a military who up to that time had provided his most important base of support. As military and civilian opposition to his rule grew, it was argued, the president chose to "play the Muslim card." In so doing, he fell back on his often-used strategy of alternately coopting and dividing his opposition. In this instance, it was said, the president's courtship of Muslims was intended to deflect challenges from his military opposition, while simultaneously splitting Muslim democrats from their Christian and secular allies.

The ICMI leaders with whom I spoke over summers from 1991 to 1995 had varied opinions on the president's motives.[2] Most insisted, however, that the president's intentions were of much less importance than the benefits ICMI might provide for individuals, the Muslim community, and the nation. Even on these issues, however, there was a sharp range of opinion among the ICMI membership. Many of the government officials who rushed to join the organization after 1993 confessed privately that they did so because membership had come to be seen as obligatory for upwardly mobile Muslim officials. Though some officials of nominal or *abangan* Muslim persuasion resisted the trend, all were aware that a sea change in bureaucratic attitudes toward ICMI had taken place after the installation of the sixth development cabinet in March 1993 (notable for its large number of ICMI sympathisizers). Concerned about the risks of aligning oneself with the wrong government faction, many prior to 1993 had still hesitated to join the Muslim organization. By the end of 1995, however, all such hesitation had ended: ICMI had come to be seen as the dominant civilian faction within the bureaucracy, and Muslim government officials not otherwise allied with the military or nonsectarian nationalists felt great pressures to join.

However significant its government faction, ICMI's membership does not comprise career bureaucrats alone. From the very beginning, many independent-minded Muslims also joined the organization, both from the ranks of government and from independent social organizations. Their motives for doing so were varied but, in general, fell into one of three groupings. The first group, which we might call "cultural Islam," consisted of pious individuals strongly opposed to any effort to drag Islam into politics. Citing the disastrous consequences of the politicization of religion during the 1950s and early 1960s, supporters of cultural Islam wanted ICMI (and Muslims in general) to remain outside and above politics, acting as a moral rather than political influence on society. For them, ICMI was but one more instrument in this effort to promote social decency, political moderation, and piety.

Drawn primarily from the ranks of the modernist Muslim community, a second group within the independent Muslim community agreed with this emphasis on Islam as a source of ethical guidance, but also spoke of the need to address long-term political concerns. They were troubled by the arbitrary and undemocratic nature of the presidential regime. However, marginalized from Indonesian politics since 1960 (see below), these modernist supporters of ICMI had concluded that, over the long run, the most important measure for the long-term transformation of Indonesian politics was a deeper Islamization of society. They felt that, if this ethical change could be achieved, a more just and democratic political system would inevitably follow. Muslims should therefore take advantage of the resources and political protection provided by the president's actions, whatever his motives, and work to promote a deeper Islamization of Indonesian society.

A third group among the independent ICMI membership, the smallest, consisted of prodemocracy activists convinced the organization could play a vital role in the demilitarization of the Indonesian state. These people agreed with the ethical concerns of the first two groups and also recognized that the president's administration was rampant with corruption. However, they emphasized, Suharto's rule is inevitably limited. Over the long run, then, the most serious obstacle to Indonesian democratization is less the person of the president than it is military dominance of the political system as a whole. Inasmuch as this is the case, they argued, it is important to take advantage of the resources provided by the president's actions, whatever his motives, so as to consolidate nonmilitary influence within the government. Only by taking advantage of the cracks in the system in this way could one hope to lay the grounds for a reduction of the military's role in state and society.

In what follows, I examine the issues raised by these varied perspectives on Islamization and democratization in contemporary Indonesia by considering the circumstances of ICMI's founding and its first years of operation. At its most basic level, the example provides insight into the changing nature of elite attitudes on Islam in the New Order era and counsels against the long-familiar view that the Suharto regime is in some way irrevocably committed to *abangan* values. ICMI's ascent suggests that the political elite is much less committed to Javanist values than it is to preservation of its own political and economic interests. More generally, and of far greater relevance for the comparative study of Islam, the ICMI example also sheds light on the dilemmas faced by Muslim reformers where the cause of Islamization is embraced by an authoritarian regime. In such circumstances, ruling elites can easily play the interests of Muslim reformers off against those of secular democrats. As in Indonesia, such manipulation inevitably unleashes a difficult debate among Muslims about the relative importance of democracy to Islamization and the proper means to achieve both.

Javanism and Islam in the Early New Order

For many years it was a truism of Indonesian studies in the West that the military-dominated, New Order government that has ruled Indonesia since 1966 was essentially hostile to Islam. "Suharto and the generals on whom he relies were brought up in a Hindu-Javanized milieu that made them more nominal *(abangan)* than practicing *(santri)* Muslims" (Emmerson 1978, 96; cf. Hassan 1980, x). The putative opposition of the ruling elite to "orthodox" Islam is thought to have shaped government initiatives in the late 1960s intended to undercut the influence of Muslim political parties. Confounding Muslim expectations, for example, the government in 1968 refused to recognize the Jakarta Charter as the preamble to the national constitution, thereby dashing Muslim hopes that (as the charter specifies) the state *(negara)* would be obliged to "carry out" *(menjalankan)* Islamic law *(shari'ah)* among the Muslim portion of the populace (Samson 1971–1972; cf. Feillard, this volume).

Not long after this incident, the government again frustrated Muslim hopes by refusing to rehabilitate Masyumi, the party of Muslim modernists suppressed by the late President Sukarno in 1960 for its alleged involvement in regional rebellions. Adopting an even harder line, the government then barred Masyumi leaders from participating in the newly formed Partai Muslimin Indonesia (PMI), an organization intended by its sponsors to be the electoral voice of modernist Muslims (Ward 1970). In the two years following the 1971 elections, finally, the government moved once more against Muslim power by consolidating the nine political parties still operating in the political arena into two, one of which was supposed to represent the interests of Muslims. Both of the newly reorganized parties were subject to extensive government controls. In the face of these restrictions, Muslim party activists—who at the beginning of the New Order had dreamed of greatly expanded influence, since they had played so central a role in the crushing of the Indonesian Communist Party during 1965–1966—could only conclude that the ruling elite was determined to prevent Muslims from ever again becoming an independent political force.

Faced with these and other measures, many in the Muslim community came to the additional conclusion that the New Order government had been hijacked by an anti-Muslim alliance of Chinese Catholics, former PSI socialists, and army officers. Most fingers pointed to Major General Ali Murtopo as the mastermind behind these policies. The head of the powerful OPSUS, a special operations intelligence bureau linked to the Army Strategic Reserve Command (Kostrad), Murtopo was one of President Suharto's two closest aides during the first years of the New Order (Robison 1986, 148–152). General Murtopo was known to have Chinese Catholics among his most trusted advisors, several of whom went on in 1971 to establish the influential Center for Strategic and International Studies (CSIS). Murtopo and his aides are also credited with having developed the strategies behind the 1971 elections, the formation of Golkar (the government party), and the application of draconian restrictions on Muslim and other political parties in 1973 (Ward 1974; Boland 1982, 150–153).

Subsequent events in these first years of the New Order only deepened this sense of disappointment among Muslims. In 1973 the People's Consultative Assembly (Majelis Permusyawaratan Rakyat or MPR) seemed poised to rebuke Muslims by proposing to elevate mystical belief *(kepercayaan)* to the same status as "religion" *(agama)*, that is, to a position of equality with the scripturally based monotheistic religions officially recognized by the Indonesian state. This legislation caused deep concern among Muslim leaders, since many regarded the mystical Javanism that was to benefit from this elevation as a heterodox threat to Islam. During the same legislative session, the Assembly moved to "unify" laws on marriage and divorce by greatly limiting the jurisdiction of Islamic courts. Though the force of the Muslim response to both of these measures eventually made the government back down, many Muslim observers were convinced that these initiatives were proof of an ominous new turn in New Order policy, designed not merely to limit Muslim political power, but to restrict Islam's influence in Indonesian civil life as well (Emmerson 1978, 97; Hassan 1980, 143–156).

Islamic Renewal and the Politics of "Cultural" Islam

There were always Muslim intellectuals who took a less pessimistic view of the New Order government. They insisted that restrictions on "political Islam"—that is, on the Islamic parties that aimed to capture the reins of government—should not be equated with government opposition to "cultural" or "civil" Islam, which is to say, an Islam whose primary role in the life of the nation is to serve as a source of ethical and cultural guidance.

One group of young Muslims among whom this view was popular consisted of development-oriented economists and technocrats who emerged from the student groups known as the "generation-of-'66." The generation-of-'66 were student activists who, in the months following the failed left-wing officers' coup of September 30, 1965, joined forces with reform factions of the military in a successful campaign to outlaw the Communist Party and topple President Sukarno. Though generation-of-'66 activists came from many different religious backgrounds (and even included a number of Chinese Catholics), the single largest grouping in their ranks consisted of students from Muslim organizations. The two most important among these were the university-based Islamic Students Association (HMI) and the high-school based Indonesian Islam Students (PII). Though modernist in theological orientation, some among the HMI and PII activists were known to be sympathetic to the liberal ideals of the Indonesian Socialist Party (PSI). Over the years the PSI had become more social democratic and developmentalist than socialist in orientation and had attracted many Western-oriented modernizers to its ranks (Liddle 1973). A fierce critic of President Sukarno's authoritarianism, the PSI had been banned by Sukarno in 1960. When, in 1966–1967, the Suharto regime turned to Western-trained economists to devise policies to extricate Indonesia's economy from its woes, many among the high-ranking economists it recruited were specialists with known ties to the Socialist Party. These men in turn provided the opportunity for a small number of Muslim technocrats from the HMI and the PII to secure employment in New Order planning agencies in the mid-1960s. In years to come, these government Muslims would act as quiet but persistent advocates of an accommodating, development-oriented Islam.[3]

From very early on, then, there were Muslim activists who chose to cooperate with the New Order regime and work for change from within the system. Besides the technocrats, however, there was a second group of young Muslims from the ranks of the generation-of-'66 who were also sanguine about the prospects for a long-term accommodation with the government. Though the most influential of these individuals also came from the ranks of the HMI and the PII, they were neither technocrats nor economists. Most worked with Muslim social associations and nongovernmental organizations (NGOs) rather than in government, serving as activist-intellectuals in the liberal wing of the Muslim community. Precisely because of their independence from government and their prominence as writers and activists, over the long run they would exercise a more decisive influence on Muslim political attitudes than the Muslim technocrats.

In the late 1960s this second grouping included such young Muslim intellectuals as Usep Fathudin and Utomo Danadjaja from the PII, Ahmad Wahib, Dawam Rahardjo, and Djohan Effendi from the "Limited Group" discussion circle in Yogya, and Nurcholish Madjid from the Jakarta headquarters of the Himpunan Mahasiswa Islam, or HMI. Though most came from modernist theological backgrounds and had had at least indirect ties to Masyumi leaders in the late 1950s and early 1960s, their polical situation was quite different from that of the senior Masyumi leadership. During the first years of the New Order, senior Masyumi chiefs had staked their political reputations on the unsuccessful campaign to rehabilitate the party. As the depth of their failure became more apparent, which is to say as the New Order regime made clearer its determination to prevent the reemergence of any independent Muslim party, their frustration with the new government deepened. At the same time, their leadership positions were threatened by hardline critics in their own ranks, who had always been skeptical of the leaders' commitment to Western-oriented principles of constitutional government and a separation of powers. The hardliners wanted a more uncompromising commitment to Islamist political ideals. With nothing to show for their long years of dedication to the ideals of constitutional democracy, the senior Masyumi leaders were obliged in the aftermath of their defeat to denounce the regime and adopt some of the rhetorical idioms of radical Islamism. They withdrew from politics to dedicate themselves to religious proselytization *(dakwah)*. They did so, however, with the explicit recognition that Islamization was itself a form of politics. Barring a change of national leadership, it was only the latter, they felt, that could bring about the cultural change required to restore political Islam to its proper place (see Samson 1973).

The young Muslim activists from the generation-of-'66 were familiar with the plight of their elders. During the first two years of the New Order, most had participated, if often halfheartedly, in the effort to rehabilitate Masyumi. However, when it became apparent that this strategy had failed, these young activists were unwilling to follow the senior leadership into opposition. They felt there was still sufficient room to work within the system for changes beneficial to Muslim Indonesians.

There was a larger reason that these young activists were less enthusiastic about the struggle to revive the party system or directly oppose the government. Many were convinced that the mass politics of the late 1950s had only wrecked the economy, politicized religion, and driven many nominal Muslims into the arms of the Communist Party. Like their colleagues in the youth groups of the Socialist Party, many of these young Muslim intellectuals had grown deeply disenchanted with populist politics. Not having invested all their energies in party organization, they found it easier than their elders to contemplate a national politics based on forms of participation other than electoral politics alone.

Equally important, many of these same young modernist Muslims had, like some PSI socialists, concluded that collaboration with the military was not necessarily an evil thing. During the lean years from 1960 to 1965, when the Masyumi and the PSI were banned and the Communist Party became the nation's most powerful party, military officers in many parts of the country had secretly provided resources and protection for Masyumi and PSI youth. This support was particularly vital for youth from the Islamic Students Association (HMI), since, in the aftermath of Sukarno's ban on the PSI and Masyumi, the Communist Party launched a ferocious campaign to have the HMI banned. The rewards of this behind-the-scene collaboration seemed confirmed after the failed left-wing officers' coup of September 30, 1965. Having blamed the communists for the coup attempt, the military turned to Muslim social organizations and student activist groups (Christian and Muslim) to help in its campaign against the Indonesian Communist Party (PKI). In the course of this struggle, the military provided the anticommunist students with extensive financial and material resources, and left them with the impression that they could play a significant role in national politics.

For all these reasons, many Muslims in the generation-of-'66 had concluded that the military could be a force for progress. Hence, in the face of continuing government restrictions on political parties in the late 1960s, they found it easy to distance themselves from mass politics in favor of a new strategy of Islamic revitalization. At its heart lay the conviction that only a long-term, "cultural" approach to revitalization could neutralize military suspicions while slowly deepening the roots of Islam in the nation as a whole.[4]

The young intellectuals responsible for developing this strategy at first did so in several separate discussion groups in Jakarta, Bandung, and Yogyakarta. However, the man whose name has come to be most widely associated with this strategy is Nurcholish Madjid, the former leader (1966–1971) of the Islamic Students Association (see Tanja 1982; Sitompul 1986). In a series of public presentations in the late 1960s and early 1970s, Madjid asserted that the Muslim community itself bore much of the responsibility for its failure to achieve political influence under the New Order. The party organizations that Muslim politicians were attempting to revive, Madjid argued, had in the 1950s already demonstrated their inability to capture the hearts and minds of the majority of Indonesians. Rather than perpetuating this failure, the Muslim community should develop new organizations capable of winning the allegiances of all Indonesian Muslims. Only through such a revolution in values, Madjid claimed, could Indonesia escape the debilitating cycle of polarization whereby party-based Islam inveighed against a government and military deeply suspicious of political Islam.[5]

As in his writings still today,[6] Madjid's style of argument in these presentations was a complex mix of theology, political analysis, and academically informed historical sociology. The novelty of this unconventional blend was especially evident in Madjid's remarks on what Western observers might have thought an academic issue, the phenomenon of secularization. Madjid accused his fellow Muslims of having "sacralized" profane institutions, such as, most notably, Islamic political parties and an Islamic state *(negara Islam)*. Noting, quite correctly, that there is no Qur'anic injunction mandating an Islamic state, Madjid criticized Indonesian Muslims for sanctifying an idea that was in fact a human fabrication. Muslims, Madjid concluded, should "secularize" this commitment while preserving Islam's lasting values.

According to Madjid, this effort at desacralization or "secularization" is necessitated by the most central of Muslim doctrines, *tauhid,* belief in the uncompromised oneness of God. "Islam itself, if examined truthfully," Madjid wrote, "was begun with a process of secularization. Indeed the principle of Tauhid represents the starting point for a much larger secularization" (Madjid 1984, 222). This commitment to *tauhid* requires a vigilant and never-ending effort to distinguish what is divine from what is merely human in Islamic tradition. By this requirement, Madjid argued, *tauhid* also implies a commitment to reason, knowledge, and science, all of which can be understood as acts of devotion to a Creator whose majesty is immanent in the natural laws of the world. "Thus modernity resides in a process, a process of discovery of which truths are relative, leading to the discovery of that Truth Which Is Absolute, that is Allah" (p. 174).

From a theological perspective, Madjid's comments on *tauhid* lay well within the tradition of Islamic modernism and neomodernism, with their emphasis on the unity of God and the compatibility of science and progress with Islamic revelation. Where Madjid disagreed with his Indonesian modernist elders, however, lay in his insistence that, while paying lip service to these ideals, Muslim leaders had done little to insure their practical implementation. Rather than taking steps to bring about intellectual and economic renewal, Madjid implied, Indonesia's Muslim leaders had wasted their time on ideological bickering and frivolous political adventures. By prioritizing political concerns in this manner, Madjid asserted, Muslims had failed to develop the "psychological strike force" needed to meet the challenge of the new era. The quest for state power, Madjid wrote, led to a fetishism of the Muslim community's "quantity" rather than a nurturing of its educational, social, and economic "quality" (Madjid 1984, 175–181, 204–214).

The cumulative result of this failed strategy, Madjid argued, was that Muslims were left unprepared to compete with more modernized groups in Indonesian society. Surveying the New Order scene, Madjid took note of the preponderance of Chinese, Christians, and Western-oriented technocrats in private and public enterprise. Rather than condemning this disparity as evidence of a government bias against Muslims, Madjid implied that it was in part the result of the Muslim community's own blunders. If Muslims continued to invest all their energies in bankrupt political initiatives, they would only further marginalize themselves from centers of influence in New Order society.

Enunciated as it was in the face of the government's continuing suppression of Muslim political activity, some observers, including many senior Muslim leaders, concluded that Madjid's stance was little more than an effort to court government favor (see Hassan 1980, 121–123; Ali and Effendy 1986, 134–143). But Madjid's long involvement in the religious community *(ummat)* and his reputation as a thoughtful, principled, and pious activist suggested that he was genuinely concerned about Muslims' long-term prospects in a fast-changing Indonesia. Often described in the Muslim media in the late 1960s as the youthful heir to the modernist leader Muhammad Natsir (the former chairman of the Islamic political party Masyumi), Madjid was well aware that confronting the Muslim establishment might imperil his political career. Yet he felt that the Muslim community was reacting in a self-defeating manner to the challenges of the New Order; what was needed, therefore, were bold words to shock the leadership into new ways.

In the months following his well-publicized broadsides, the risks implicit in his initiative seemed confirmed. Madjid was denounced by such formidable modernist leaders as H.M. Rasyidi, Hamka, and Muhammad Natsir.[7] Several supporters of Madjid in other youth organizations, such as Utomo Danadjaja and Usep Fathudin from the PII, were also expelled from their organizations. Many observers concluded that Madjid's career as an Islamic leader was finished, and he and his associates would play no future leadership role in Indonesian Islam.

As is often the case in Islamic debates, the theological, not just the political, elements in Madjid's argument excited some of the most furious criticism. Madjid and the "renewal" *(pembaruan)* group's support for secularization provoked especially bitter controversy. Critics argued that this idea amounted to a Westernized interpretation of Islam. By understanding *tauhid* as the desacralization of all but God's oneness, it was said, Madjid and his friends ignored Islamic Sunnah, the tradition of the community as sacralized by the example of the Prophet. The Sunnah, critics said, provides clear normative precedent for how society should be organized. As one Malaysian critic of the renewal movement asserted (Hassan 1980, 114, 123), to deny this precedent is to rid Islam of its sociological wholeness, transforming it into a mere "spiritual personalist ethical system" akin to what Christianity has become in the West. This may be conveniently accommodating to New Order interests, these critics said, but it is deeply contrary to Islam's claim to being an integrated way of life.

In fact, much of the detail of Madjid's argument was lost in the sound and the fury of the subsequent debate. Though he and his colleagues were accused of being secularists, they consistently distinguished secularization, described as the desacralization of domains wrongly valorized as sacred, from secularism, a Western ideology advocating a rigorous separation of religion from social life. They condemned the latter, while insisting that the former was required by the spirit of Islamic monotheism. In the aftermath of the controversy, however, Madjid himself expressed some misgivings at his choice of terms, commenting publicly that his reference to "secularization" had invited misinterpretation (see Madjid 1984, 221–233, 257–260).

Much as his critics suggested, Madjid's understanding of secularization did show Western influences, at least in the sense that it cited the work of such liberal theorists as the American sociologist Robert Bellah and the Protestant theologian Harvey Cox. But rather than expressing uncritical enthusiasm for the West, Madjid's appeal to these authors was illustrative of the way in which he and his colleagues felt that Muslims should not hesitate to draw on scientific and religious literature from outside Islam, both to broaden their own understanding and to demonstrate Islam's universality. This affirmation of an inclusive and universal Islam has remained a key theme in Madjid's writings to this day and underlies much of his popularity among liberal members of the educated middle class. In the early 1970s, however, the subtlety of such a message was lost amidst a debate that seemed to equate secularization with secularism and secularism with the relegation of Islam to a position of political impotence.

Though conceding, then, that his choice of terms had caused some confusion,[8] Madjid never drew back from his broader position on the attitude the Muslim community should take toward the New Order government and toward Islamic renewal generally. Though his influence temporarily waned in the mid-1970s, Madjid is important because he provided intellectual grounds for justifying something much larger than his own views. In effect, he reassured Muslim members of the generation-of-'66 that their disenchantment with party politics did not amount to a betrayal of Islam, and piety did not require that they work for the establishment of an Islamic state. In this sense, the initiatives of what had come to be known as "renewal" (pembaruan) Islam legitimated the efforts of a larger community of nonparty activists seeking to develop new Islamic initiatives, especially in the fields of education, the economy, and social welfare.

Equally important, the efforts of the renewal group also served to provide moral sanction for the growing numbers of educated Muslims who, beginning in the mid-1970s, saw fit to take up government service. The 1960s' trickle of Muslims moving into the bureaucracy had, by the 1980s, turned into a flood. Many of these officials labored behind the scenes to promote Muslim interests, while awaiting a softening of attitude on the part of a government determined to prevent any reinvigoration of mass-based party politics.

Fruits of Renewal

This effort at "new thinking" *(pemikiran baru)* was but one of several related developments in the Muslim community at this time, the importance of which lies less in their specific detail or associated personalities than in their sanctioning of a shift of Muslim energies out of formal politics and into social and educational activities. Commenting on Madjid's impact on younger activists, Fachry Ali and Bahtiar Effendy—Muslim scholars and activists themselves—make the point that Madjid's understanding of Islamic renewal encouraged a more "empirical" attitude toward Islam (Ali and Effendi 1986, 133).[9] Rather than quibbling over doctrine or ideological details, Muslims were enjoined to recognize the reality of the New Order and undertake initiatives that could enhance their influence within its institutions.

The political consequences of this change in Muslim attitudes were quite real. Although there were a handful of uncompromising Islamist movements in Indonesia during the 1980s (see Abdulaziz et al. 1991; Tamara 1985, 23–25), the really notable feature of the period was the patient effort of moderate Muslims to build institutions for Islamic education and socioeconomic advance. Indeed, on this point, Indonesia was unusual among Muslim societies during the tumultuous decade stretching from 1978 to 1988. The country witnessed a general decline in the influence of Muslim political parties but saw a great leap forward in the social and intellectual vitality of the community.[10]

It is important to emphasize, however, that Muslim civil associations were not the only agencies involved in these renewal initiatives. The New Order state also supported a number of cultural-Islamic programs, usually under the auspices of its enormous Ministry of Religion. At first sight, the state's role in the strengthening of Islamic institutions and piety may appear surprising in light of the government's reputation among Western scholars as a bastion of *abangan*ism and, more significantly, in light of its very real restrictions on political Islam. In the opinion of Muslim intellectuals, however, the expansion of state support was related to a gradual change in government attitudes that first became noticeable in the mid-1970s, in part as the result of a curious synergy between "renewal" leaders and moderate Muslim officials in the Ministry of Religion.[11]

The first hints of this change were seen in 1972–1973, when the government intervened to tone down MPR initiatives on Javanist "belief" *(kepercayaan)* and marriage laws, reversing legislation that devout Muslims had regarded as deeply hostile to their interests. By most accounts this reversal was little more than a strategic and limited concession in the face of overwhelming Muslim protest. Indeed, the government seems at first to have been divided on how forcefully to push for the new regulations. In the case of the marriage law, for example, the legislators in the ruling party (Golkar) who sponsored the legislation were initially confident they had the full support of the government in their efforts to limit polygamy and restrict the role of Islamic courts in marriage and divorce. As the scale of the Muslim unrest became apparent, however, high-ranking military officials—with the clear encouragement of Suharto advisors—intervened, pushing aside the legislators and negotiating a compromise solution with Muslim politicians on their own (see Feillard 1995, 145–150).

If these early government concessions looked like little more than strategic retreats, the Ministry of Religion's Decision No. 70 in 1978 seemed to reflect a more deliberate opening to Muslim interests. The decision banned missionizing by the members of any one religion (Christians being the main target) among citizens who already professed, however nominally, another government-recognized religion. Christians protested that many Javanese are Muslim in name only and thus should not be subject to the stricture. But the government brushed these objections aside. Indeed in 1979 the ministries of Religion and Home Affairs joined forces to strengthen the restrictions with their Joint Decision No. 1 of that year. As Bambang Pranowo has observed, "The Islamic groups enthusiastically welcomed these decisions, for they were directed especially toward the Christian missionaries actively carrying out religious propagation amongst the Muslim community" (1990, 493). Conversely, Indonesian Christian missionaries whom I interviewed in East Java in the late 1970s, 1985, and 1991 acknowledged these restrictions had a disastrous impact on their missions to Javanists (Hefner 1993, 99–125).

The significance of these new policies is readily apparent if one remembers that, just ten years earlier, the same ministries of Religion and Home Affairs had joined forces to implement a program of ideological "construction" *(pembinaan)* that openly encouraged access by Christian missionaries to villages identified as former strongholds of the Indonesian Communist Party (PKI). Missionaries were also given access to PKI prison camps.[12] Still today Muslim commentators, including some among the ICMI leadership, regard this unrestricted access of Christian missions to nominal Muslims as a clear indication that Christians and secular modernizers wielded disproportionate influence in the early New Order. Conversely, reversal of the policy in 1978–1979 is seen as an indication that, despite controls on political Islam, segments of the ruling elite were beginning to recognize the need for a more sympathetic accommodation with Muslims, especially those willing to work within the framework of Pancasila politics.

The other program to which Muslim leaders today point as evidence of a basic change in attitude on the part of the government was the Ministry of Religion's efforts to expand the institutional resources for Islamic education and *dakwah* (religious predication; see Feillard, this volume). One important feature of this effort was the enormous expansion in State Islamic Institute Colleges (IAIN), which began in the 1960s and which, during the 1970s and 1980s, produced large numbers of graduates trained in Islamic theology, law, arts, and pedagogy (Lombard 1990, 2:123, 126). As in the Middle East (Eickelman 1992), mass education of this sort contributed significantly to the Islamic renewal.

These efforts in higher education were accompanied by an equally impressive program of infrastructural development sponsored by the Ministry of Religion, focusing on the construction of mosques, prayer halls *(musholla),* and Islamic schools *(madrasah),* especially in areas regarded as weakly committed to Islam. The construction of mosques in East and Central Java shows the clear and unrelenting progress of this program. In East Java, the number of mosques increased from 15,574 in 1973 to 17,750 in 1979, 20,648 in 1984, and 25,655 in 1990. By comparison, over the same seventeen-year period, the number of Catholic churches increased from 206 to 324. Protestant churches (including many small, evangelical meeting halls) increased from 1,330 in 1973 to 2,308 in 1984, but then declined again to 1,376 in 1990. There was a similarly effective program of mosque construction in Central Java, where, between 1980 and 1992, the number of mosques almost doubled, from 15,685 to 28,748.[13] In addition to ministry programs, there was a smaller but more conspicuous program sponsored by President Suharto himself, under the auspices of a presidential foundation for the support of Islamic initiatives, the Amal Bakti Muslimin Pancasila. The Amal Bakti program sponsored the construction of four hundred mosques and provided support to one thousand Muslim proselytizers *(dai),* posted to areas of Indonesia that were deemed devotionally weak, including many on the island of Java.[14] In all this, proponents of cultural Islam felt that they saw visible confirmation of the wisdom of their strategy of working within the system.

The progress of cultural Islam was not matched in the official political arena. Indeed, in the early 1980s the government escalated its efforts to force all social and political organizations to acknowledge the national ideology (the "Five Principles" or Pancasila) as their "sole foundation" *(asas tunggal).* The government's effort caused deep resentment among Muslims and even some Christians. In the Muslim case, however, the policy had an especially devastating impact. It splintered an already fractured Muslim leadership, as fierce disputes erupted over the proper response to the government policy (Hari 1990; van Dijk 1985; *Tempo* 1986). In the electoral arena, these developments reinforced the domination of Golkar, the government-supported party. Despite the occasional defection of supporters during the 1980s, Golkar generally improved its share of the Muslim vote at the expense of the putatively Muslim party, the Partai Persatuan dan Pembangunan or Party of Unity and Development (PPP). Election observers decried what was widely regarded as governmental manipulation of the leadership of the opposition parties. But the result, in any case, was the continuing atrophy of Muslim electoral muscle (Crouch 1988, 245–272; Ward 1974).

Some observers have described these government actions as reminiscent of the earlier Dutch colonial policy of tolerating Islamic religion but ruthlessly repressing all forms of political Islam. There is a measure of truth to the analogy. It obscures, however, a fact that the renewal leaders and other moderate Muslims seem to have understood: though they tolerated Islamic devotion, the Dutch never provided the massive infrastructural support to Islamic piety that the New Order has. Despite political setbacks, then, Muslim leaders today look back on the 1980s as a decisive turning point for Islam and at least a partial vindication of the accommodative group's attitude toward the government.

Indeed, the great majority of Muslim intellectuals today believe that their acceptance of the *asas tunggal* policy had an important unintended consequence. Once Islam was no longer associated with any single party and once politicians recognized that the nation was experiencing an Islamic resurgence, all of the political parties began to advertise their commitment to Islam. This "greening" (*penghijauan,* green being a symbol of Islam) of the campaign process was most dramatically evident during the 1992 electoral campaigns and received widespread comment in the national media. Lukman Harun, a Muhammadiyah leader and director of the Center for Islamic Studies at Jakarta's National University, summarized what is perhaps the most general view among Muslim intellectuals on this change: "Yes, we compromised in accepting the Pancasila, and there were many people who disagreed. But at first we didn't really understand what the consequence of this would be. Before there was one party identified with Islam. But look at what has happened. After being depoliticized, suddenly Islam is no longer confined to any one party but promoted by all of them."[15]

There was another, perhaps deeper dimension to the cultural changes of the 1980s. In Java, where the nominally Islamic Javanist community had long posed a serious obstacle to Islamic reform, media and academic reports in the 1980s took note that many former strongholds of Javanist Islam were beginning to take on a *santri* (pious Muslim) face. The type of Islam being promoted in most such cases, it should be emphasized, owed more to the politically neutral, "neo-*santri*" Islam supported by the government than it did to the party-based Islam of the 1950s or the decentralized, fiercely independent Islam of colonial times. Nonetheless, the growth of Islamic devotionalism in areas previously renowned for their Javanist heterodoxy was welcomed by Muslim leaders. Indeed, for many, this change in religious culture is a far more meaningful achievement than anything that might be accomplished in the electoral arena.[16]

On all these points, the contrast with the first ten years of the New Order government is striking. While those early years had been marked by a small but controversial movement of Javanese from Islam to Hinduism and Christianity, by the 1980s there was clear evidence of Islamic revival and Javanist decline. Indeed, reports since the late 1980s have suggested that some of the earlier converts to Christianity and, especially, Hinduism were returning to Islam, as the Islamic revival reached into the very heartlands of Javanism.[17] The impact of "cultural" Islam was thus reaching into civil society; unbeknownst to many, it was also preparing the ground for an important shift in Indonesian politics.

The Quest for the Middle Class

It was in the booming metropolitan regions of Indonesia, however, that the most spectacular evidence of cultural Islam's advance was visible. In Indonesia's large cities, a new middle class was taking shape, even as the gap between rich and poor increased (Dick 1990, 96–122). Not surprisingly, universities were at the forefront of this trend. Earlier, in the 1950s and early 1960s, Indonesia's national universities had been centers of secular nationalism, in which the *santri* community, though represented, was typically among the weaker of the factions in the student body. The 1970s, however, saw the rapid growth of the so-called Salman movement *(gerakan Salman)* and related Muslim initiatives on state university campuses. Salman students rejected the scholastic arguments of traditionalist Islam and the exclusivism of modernism. In order to Islamize the secular university, they adopted relaxed, democratic forms of dress and amusement, while encouraging strict adherence to Muslim devotional acts *(ibadah),* including daily prayers, the fast, and payment of alms *(zakat)* to the poor.

The model for this campuswide devotional movement was developed at the Salman Mosque, located at the Bandung Technological Institute, under the guidance of M. Imaduddin Abdulrahim, a charismatic intellectual who, years later, would play a central role in the establishment of ICMI (see below). Conducting an extensive campaign of religious outreach, the Salman Mosque Committee invited pop bands to play at the mosque, sponsored seminars on religion and development, published a small journal of culture and economic affairs, and developed a variety of educational and economic programs for poor residents living near the university.[18]

By the early 1980s Salman-inspired religious activities had become a conspicuous feature of campus life at virtually every major university in Java and Sumatra. The movement also led to the formation of discussion groups that sought to formulate Muslim political and economic policies. A few of these smaller groupings provided the nucleus for the more radical Islamic movements that attracted attention, if not significant public support, in the 1980s and 1990s.[19]

The mainstream movement for Islamic revival, however, eventually reached far beyond the university and touched the lives of the urban poor and the middle class. A decade earlier, in the 1970s, few Indonesians could have predicted such a development. Those years had witnessed a rapid expansion in urban wealth and an infusion of Western and East Asian consumer styles into elite and middle-class circles. Night clubs proliferated, alcohol became widely available, and rebellious youths affected permissive lifestyles that their elders, even non-*santri,* found shocking. Urban society was widely regarded as becoming more "monied," and many people took offense at the callous disregard of elite youth for traditional mores and etiquette.

Benedict Anderson's analysis of cartoons and media images from this period captures the widespread ambivalence toward these changes in certain urban circles. Anderson's discussion focuses on the unease felt by elite Javanese officials in the face of their own privileged children abandoning the reassuring, if hierarchical, etiquette learned by their parents in small-town Java. Ripped from their earlier social background and unable to fall back on the assertive nationalism of the 1950s, the senior generation's neotraditionalism seemed quaintly obsolete to a generation of privileged offspring. Anderson describes the anxiety this caused among the Jakartan elite: "Such events suggest to Indonesia's rulers that the future threatens to elude them, and so the past is summoned to their aid. Most of them are deeply aware of the far journey they have made in their lives from the rural townships of late colonial Java to the metropolitan pomp of the 'cosmopolitan' Jakarta they now enjoy. . . . Their past has also not prepared them morally for the lives they now lead. Most of them grew up in the sphere of provincial Javanese society, and the norms and values of that society have left powerful residues at the core of their consciousness" (1978, 315).

It was against a less privileged but otherwise similar background that many middle-class Muslims came to feel uncomfortable with what they regarded as a narrowing or "privatization" *(pribadisasi)* of moral concerns during the 1970s. Unlike the Javanese officials whom Anderson describes, however, Muslim urbanites tend to carry a less amorphous experiential "residue" from their early years. Rather than diffuse existential anxiety and appeals to an invented Javanese "tradition," they typically respond to the anomie and hedonism of urban life with precise ethical prescriptions and calls for a deepening of faith. For them, Islam seems better suited to the challenges of urban existence than Javanist traditions, which they see as incapable of responding to the social and economic needs of ordinary Indonesians. Unlike the elite's ersatz Javanism, they point out, Islam—especially the neatly modularized and eminently educable variant associated with Islamic modernism and neomodernism—is both modern and transethnic. Even in the absence of the tranquil communities of yesteryear, it can work to instill ethical discipline and restraint. Yet Islam is also thoroughly Indonesian. Its roots reach back to precolonial society and into most, if not all, of the ethnic communities of the archipelago. Equally important, however much certain Western observers have identified Islam as an opponent to Indonesian nationalism, Muslim intellectuals know that they too can rightly claim the mantle of Indonesian nationalism, albeit a nonsecularist version (cf. Bowen 1993; Noer 1987).

One need only compare Anderson's portrait with that of Kuntowijoyo in the epilogue to his *Paradigma Islam: Interpretasi Untuk Aksi* (Islamic Paradigms: Interpretations for Action; 1991) to discern that, however much they shared a similar sense of moral anxiety, Muslim intellectuals were not plagued by the existential vagueness afflicting the Javanist elite. A Yale-educated historian from Gadjah Mada University, Kuntowijoyo describes the moral crisis among urban youth in terms strikingly similar to those of Anderson and attributes its origins to similar causes. "Apparently social changes since 1965 have given birth to a new social class, a middle class, one that is almost without roots in any prior historical period" (Kuntowijoyo 1991, 370–371). But Kuntowijoyo's analysis goes on to suggest that there is a complex dialectic to the crisis, one not apparent in Anderson's descriptions of the Javanist elite. Alongside the self-indulgent hedonism of privileged youth, Kuntowijoyo observes, there is an emergent counterculture of high moral idealism and principled criticism. This critical culture is not based on traditional Javanese notions of power; indeed, Kuntowijoyo claims (referring to Anderson's work on ideas of power in traditional Java), it self-consciously rejects these in favor of an unhierarchical tradition that, for Kuntowijoyo, originates in modern Islam.

When the New Order government brought this new middle class into existence, Kuntowijoyo writes, it expected it to be "faithful" *(mempunyai kesetiaan)* to its policies. But among those making the pilgrimage from village to city, there were some who brought an Islamic ideology contemptuous of the elitist values of government bureaucracy. Thus, in Kuntowijoyo's view, this neo-*santri* tradition acts as an antihegemonic subculture, quietly subverting elite culture from within: "The process of decolonizing and detraditionalizing consciousness has already gone so far that the bureaucracy cannot assume [popular acceptance of] a concept of power like that of a magical source radiating invulnerability. . . . The social and moral basis of the authoritarian bureaucracy is finished" (p. 373).

This theme of *santri* subversion of Javanist elitism was common in the critical Islamic literature of the 1980s.[20] The confidently assertive attitude of Kuntowijoyo's commentary is equally characteristic of this writing, distinguishing it from the more tentative tone of the 1970s renewal literature. Like many in this new generation of scholar-activists, Kuntowijoyo shows little of the self-doubt of the earlier period. Muslims have joined the ranks of government and business, he notes, and they are prepared to Islamize not only the peasantry, but large segments of the middle class and ruling elite.

Not surprisingly, a now-middle-aged Nurcholish Madjid has himself been at the forefront of this newly robust cultural Islam, with its eyes set on government officials and the middle class. In 1986, Madjid established an association for urban proselytization known as Paramadina (from the Spanish *para*, "for," and the Arabian city of Madinah). Zifirdaus Adnan has wryly observed that, though the Paramadina officials "explained that the target of the *dakwah* (missionary activity) was the middle class people who have not received sufficient understanding of Islam," the presence of the ministers for religion, education and culture, environment, and youth affairs at the organization's inaugural celebration indicates that "the target is not only the middle class but also the elite class" (1990, 459). The organization counted no fewer than eight cabinet members on its first advisorial board. In interviews during 1992 and 1993, Cak Nur, as he is affectionately known, openly acknowledged this desire to deepen the faith of the urban elite. He pointed to the expansion of mosques and prayer halls in businesses, hotels, government offices, and Jakarta's affluent southern suburbs as dramatic evidence of success.

An additional feature of the Islamic advance into the middle class has been the emergence of a new kind of revivalist proselytizer *(dai)*. Many of these pop revivalists come from backgrounds in film, music, literature, and other mass media rather than from Muslim schools. They use deeply emotional accounts of their conversion experience rather than complicated exegesis of doctrine to move people to a deeper faith. Their prominence testifies to a dispersion of religious authority beyond the ranks of traditionally trained Islamic scholars, a trademark of the Muslim revival in other Muslim countries as well (see Eickelman and Piscatori 1996).[21]

Despite setbacks in the formal political arena, then, by the late 1980s Muslim activists and intellectuals showed a new confidence about their long-term prospects under the New Order. It is this air of confidence that is so powerfully evident in Kuntowijoyo's article, with its open contempt for ersatz Javanism. By itself, the critical tone of this article is, again, not unusual, as it was a regular feature of Muslim criticism in the 1980s. More distinctive than the message of Kuntowijoyo's broadside, however, was its medium. The paper was first presented at ICMI's inaugural meeting in Malang, East Java, in December 1990. It was then reprinted in the published proceedings of the conference, alongside more cautious articles by government intellectuals (ICMI 1991, 203–210).

The example is telling. Inaugurated to the beat of the president's drum, some of the ICMI membership showed a marked inclination to march to a different drummer. From the start, however, there was a tension in the organization between those who wished to work closely with the government and those who hoped to see ICMI act more independently. This tension would become increasingly apparent in the months following ICMI's founding.

State and Society in ICMI's Founding

Media reports on ICMI's genesis often portray it as the spontaneous creation of five students from the Universitas Brawijaya in Malang, East Java (*Kompas* 1990; *Pelita* 1990). The five students, the story goes, were devout but otherwise unexceptional Muslim youth who yearned to bring Muslim intellectuals together to talk about the future of the nation and the *ummat*. To do so, they proposed a meeting to which leaders from all of Indonesia's major Islamic associations as well as from government and the media would be invited. Having come up with the idea in early 1990, the students then proposed the plan to the rectors of the state-run Brawijaya University and Malang's Muhammadiyah University. The rectors responded favorably but hesitated in face of the expense and political sensitivity of such a symposium. Undeterred, the five youths set out at their own expense to visit centers of Islamic education in Java, to promote their idea with leading intellectuals and to raise funds for the conference. In the course of their travels, they met with prominent Muslim intellectuals, including, most notably, Dr. M. Imaduddin Abdulrahim and Drs. M. Dawam Rahardjo, who jointly suggested that the students move beyond the idea of a mere symposium and promote the formation of a national association of Muslim intellectuals.[22]

Sensing the importance of government sponsors if the organization was to survive, Imaduddin proposed that the students invite the minister of the environment, Emil Salim, and the minister of research and technology, Dr. B. J. Habibie to act as chairmen of the national organization. Emil Salim was one of the architects of the New Order's early economic policies. A kindly, mild-mannered gentleman, he was among the technocrats who had sponsored the admission of development-minded Muslims into government planning bureaus in the late 1960s and 1970s; he had long been known as a gentile proponent of better government-Muslim relations. Imaduddin and the students were not personally acquainted with Dr. Habibie. Quite unlike Salim, Habibie was best known for his passionate commitment to technology; indeed, though a mutual friend, he was indirectly critical of the policies technocrats like Salim had helped to craft. He favored government-supported high-technology industries rather than labor-intensive export industries. Though less well known for his piety, Habibie had recently been featured in several television interviews and a story in the popular Muslim magazine *Kiblat,* where he spoke warmly of his devotion to Islam.

In subsequent meetings, Emil Salim agreed to attend the national symposium but declined to play a leadership role in any organization, insisting that he was "too old" and that Habibie would be more energetic and effective. The students thus turned to Habibie to lead the proposed organization, which, at Nurcholish Madjid's suggestion, had tentatively acquired the title of ISMI—Ikatan Sarjana Muslim Indonesia (Association of Muslim Indonesian Scholars). Contacted through letters and by telephone, Habibie at first declined to meet with the students. According to the reports of his aides, Habibie said privately that, though his devotion to Islam was real enough, he was not sufficiently well versed in Islamic doctrine to play such a leadership role. "How can I do it? I am an engineer and a builder of airplanes, not an Islamic scholar!" More important, no doubt, he is also reported to have expressed fears that by agreeing to lead the organization he might contradict the wishes of President Suharto.

It was only after Habibie was contacted by the former minister of religion and Suharto confidant (retired) General Alamsyah Ratu Perwiranegara that he agreed to meet with the students. It was Imaduddin who urged the students to overcome Habibie's reluctance by working through Alamsyah. Though the retired general was well known for his unswerving devotion to the president, he had over the course of his career maintained open lines of communications with Muslims. In any case, Imaduddin's suggestion proved effective; the students and their supporters were granted a meeting with Habibie.

On August 23, 1990, the students, accompanied by Imaduddin, Dawam Rahardjo, and M. Syafi'i Anwar (a close associate of Rahardjo and a former reporter for the Muslim newsweekly *Panji Masyarakat*), traveled to Dr. Habibie's office on Jalan Thamrin to present their formal request to the minister. The group had been granted one half hour from Habibie's busy schedule. The students and their supporters presented their ideas directly, in what one of the participants later described as a long and slightly anxious monologue. Afterwards, Habibie commented positively on the idea of the association, but again protested that he was not the most appropriate figure for the role, saying, as before, that he was not sufficiently learned in Islamic matters. But he did not turn down the students' request outright. Instead, he asked that a petition be drawn up and circulated among prominent Muslim intellectuals to express support for his leadership of such an organization, so as to impress upon the president (and, no doubt, the Indonesian public) that their appeal had broad support in the Muslim community. In addition, he asked for an outline of the association's organization and goals, which he would then present to the president. "I am a servant of the president," he said (according to the reports of some present at the meeting), "so I must go to him to request permission to work with you."

Over the next week, Imaduddin, Dawam Rahardjo, and Nurcholish Madjid drew up a document outlining the organization's goals and expressing support for Dr. Habibie's chairmanship. The document was circulated among prominent Muslim intellectuals in Jakarta, Bogor, Bandung, and Yogyakarta; eventually forty-nine individuals signed it. In the meantime, too, Habibie talked with several of his colleagues in the cabinet, soliciting their advice on the wisdom of his joining the organization. Most, I was told, urged him to decline the invitation. One, Dr. Saleh Afiff (state minister for national development planning), advised him not to turn down the request but to seek President Suharto's counsel directly. Habibie agreed and arranged an appointment with the president, sending him the petition and the outline of the association's goals.

Only Habibie and Suharto were present during their meeting, but a more or less uniform account of their exchange has become common knowledge among cabinet officials and ICMI officials whom I interviewed. According to this report, Habibie began the meeting by repeating his disclaimer that he is an engineer, a maker of airplanes, and unqualified to lead an association of Islamic intellectuals. Then, more quietly, he is reported to have turned to the president and said, "Also, if I lead this organization, maybe I will be separated *(terpisah)* from Bapak (father, sir). Perhaps my and Bapak's understanding of Islam differ?" Throughout his public life, Habibie has made a point of demonstrating his unswerving loyalty to the president. His close relationship has been an especially crucial political resource for Habibie because, until ICMI's founding, he has had no significant political base outside the bureaucracy. So Habibie's question struck to the heart of his own political future.

President Suharto is reported to have responded without hesitation to Habibie's query, saying, "This is good; you can do it." Then, in a demonstration of his own mastery of Islamic knowledge, the president told Habibie to take a pen, open his notebook, and record what follows. The now-mythic account of this meeting recounts that, over the next two hours, the president "dictated" *(mendikte)* a long discussion of the basic principles of Islam, including the meaning of the Sunnah, obligatory prayer *(sholat),* and passages from the Qur'an. At the end, the president said, "Now you understand what I know." From this demonstration Habibie was to appreciate that the president's knowledge of normative Islam was great and consistent with his own. The whole meeting lasted six hours, and, from it, Habibie emerged with a clear presidential mandate to lend his hand to the Islamic association.

After this, Habibie invited several ministers to his home, where he described ICMI and invited them to join in its establishment. Those present included the minister of internal affairs, Rudini; Fuad Hasan, the minister of education and culture; Azwar Anas, the minister of transportation; Emil Salim, minister of the environment; Nasruddin Sumintapura, vice-minister for finance; Saleh Afiff, state minister for national development planning and chairman of the National Development Planning Agency (Bappenas); and H. Munawir Sjadzali, minister of religion. Also present were two people without ministerial ties: Nurcholish Madjid and Professor Dr. Insinyur Ahmad Baiguni, an advisor to Habibie from the Agency for the Assessment and Application of Technology (BPPT). Of those present, Minister Rudini, who was a military man known for his Javanist sympathies, initially expressed reservations about the organization. However, on learning of the president's support for ICMI, he quickly agreed to join.

Now with presidential and cabinet support, on September 27 Habibie again met with the students and their supporters, informing them that the plan had the president's blessing. As a condition of his becoming chairman, however, Habibie requested that he be allowed to bring some of his administrative staff from BPPT to work in ICMI. Among those assistants was Dr. Wardiman Djojonegoro, an engineer and close assistant to Habibie at the

BPPT, later to become Habibie's right-hand man within ICMI. A Madurese of aristocratic *(priyayi)* background, Wardiman had a reputation for having decidedly "nationalist" views on Islam. Some Western observers thus saw in Wardiman's appointment an effort to "*abangan*ize" ICMI. Those familiar with Wardiman, however, note that he is better known for his loyalty to Habibie and his reputation as a cool-headed administrator than as an ideologue. Whatever his background, he quickly demonstrated his loyalty to the Islamic cause. Among other things, during the first year of ICMI's existence, Wardiman was a bold but even-handed critic of Christian dominance in education and the media.[23]

In this case, as in many of his subsequent appointments, Habibie revealed his preference for a loyal and controlled managerial team, like that which he had built at the national technology institute, the BPPT. His appointment of trusted BPPT staff to ICMI steering committees also reflected his determination in the face of continuing military suspicion to demonstrate that the organization was not political, but technoscientific and educational . At this same meeting, Habibie suggested that the term *sarjana* ("scholar") in the organization's title be changed to *cendekiawan* ("intellectual"), so as to avoid the impression that the organization was only open to people with academic degrees. He also suggested that the organization's first national symposium be held at the beginning of December. All those present agreed, and three teams were set up to coordinate preparations for the symposium, which was to take place on the campus of Brawijaya University in Malang, East Java.

With presidential blessing, preparations for the December meeting proceeded apace. What had begun as an extragovernmental initiative launched by a few Muslim intellectuals—some of whom had once had a less than cordial relationship with the regime (see below)—had now evolved into a top-heavy, if still unsteady, coalition of government and extragovernment Muslims. Officials from the state-sponsored Council of Islamic Clerics (Majelis Ulama Indonesia) were drawn into planning meetings during October and November, as were the minister of religion, H. Munawir Sjadzali (a political moderate and a theological liberal), and his staff. A close supporter of the president and a Habibie ally, Harmoko, minister of information, was also active in the planning meetings.

Far more interesting than the government officials recruited to the planning committees were the nongovernmental Muslims drawn in. They continued to play a central, if somewhat less visible, role in meeting preparations. The appointees to the main planning committee, for example, included Dawam Rahardjo, Sri Bintang Pamungkas, and Muslimin Nasution. Nasution was head of the Bureau of Research and Development in the government's Department of Cooperatives and thus (despite otherwise impressive credentials as a Muslim intellectual and an ideological liberal) could be regarded as a "government" Muslim. Dawam and Bintang , however, were known for their outspokenness and prodemocracy views. Dawam was a well-known social and theological progressive, linked in the 1980s to the NGO community and the struggle for equitable development (see below).

Bintang was, in theological terms, a more conventional modernist than Dawam; however the strength of his public commitment to democratization and clean government often placed him at the edge of allowable discourse in Indonesia. Educated at the Bandung Technological Institute and then at Iowa State University, Sri Bintang in 1990 was employed in the Department of Economics at the Universitas Indonesia.[24] In the late 1980s he acquired a reputation among Muslim and NGO activists as a courageous and principled critic of government policies. His denunciations of corruption in government were regularly featured in the national press. Moreover, having refused in 1988 to join Golkar, the government-sponsored party that most public employees are required to support, Sri Bintang went on to run for and win a seat in the the National Assembly (DPR) under the banner of the opposition Muslim party, the PPP. His campaign during 1992 was, by all measures, remarkable for its blunt criticisms of corruption, economic inequality, and the continuing involvement of the military in national politics (see *Editor* 1993, 74–75). The appointment of two such public figures to key planning posts for the new organization surprised many skeptics and was taken as a sign that, whatever the president's intentions, Habibie was intent on building a broad coalition reaching beyond the halls of government.

Imaduddin Abdulrahim was another, equally remarkable appointment to the various steering committees for the December meeting. Up to that year (1990) Imaduddin had had a troubled relationship with the government security agencies. A founder and leader of the Salman movement at the Bandung Technological Institute, Imaduddin had been detained by security forces on several occasions in the early 1970s, denounced as "fundamentalist and anti-Catholic," and arrested and held without charges during fourteen months of 1978–1979. Eventually he was barred from state employment. After his detention, he traveled to the United States to take a Ph.D. in management at Iowa State University, hoping that upon return to Indonesia the employment ban would be lifted. On completing his degree in 1984, however, he learned that the ban still applied. He thus taught for two years in the United States, returning to Indonesia only in 1986. Still unable to get state employment, he eventually formed his own management company, where he has enjoyed considerable financial success.

Not all Muslim critics were won to the ICMI cause. Deliar Noer, for example, a distinguished intellectual of the senior (pre-Madjid) generation, refused to join on two grounds: first, that Habibie himself had previously demonstrated no deep commitment to Islam and, second, that ICMI was not a truly representative organization, but was designed to promote President Suharto's reelection. Others with ties to the NGO community, such as M. Billah, preferred to remain outside the organization for fear that membership might compromise their ability to act independently. Still others, like the respected historian Taufik Abdullah, declined to join despite repeated invitations, on the ground that ICMI was too closely controlled by the bureaucracy. Like many other independent intellectuals, however, Abdullah has also refrained from publicly criticizing ICMI. In private, he acknowledges that the organization has done some real good, such as sponsoring public discussion of human rights.[25]

Others, however, have not hesitated to criticize ICMI on the grounds that it encourages exclusivistic and sectarian attitudes at a time when what is needed is interreligious tolerance and a nonreligious nationalism. For example, Djohan Effendi, a Muslim liberal associated with Madjid and Rahardjo during the earlier movement for Islamic renewal and now employed in the Ministry of Religion (and, as of April 1993, a special assistant for religious and social affairs to State Secretary Drs. Moerdiono, an outspoken ICMI critic), has quietly but repeatedly warned that ICMI is once again politicizing Islam. In doing so, he has said, ICMI risks undermining the hard-won accomplishments of cultural Islam and indeed may eventually provoke the military to move against those who use Islam for political ends.[26]

The outspoken chairman of Nahdlatul Ulama, Abdurrahman Wahid, also accused ICMI of sectarianism (see Feillard, this volume). Despite a personal appeal by Habibie, who visited Wahid when he was hospitalized in February of 1991, Wahid has refused to join ICMI, saying its focus is "exclusivistic" and elitist rather than pan-Indonesian. Ridwan Saidi, chairman of HMI from 1974 to 1977 and a former PPP activist who had joined Golkar (only in 1995 to try to form a new Islamic party), criticized ICMI on similar grounds, claiming that ICMI reflects a peculiarly bureaucratic vision of Islam.[27]

Wahid's comments have been widely featured in the media. He argues that at this juncture in history the struggle for democracy and justice must take precedence over less inclusive concerns, including those of the Muslim community. He phrases this argument in unusually blunt terms, shocking even some of his own supporters in the Muslim community. "I am for an Indonesian society, not just an Islamic one," he has said in several public assemblies. Islam, he argues, should not be idealized so that it is regarded as the only ground for democracy, law, or economic justice. Rather, Islam should serve as an "inspirational base for a national framework of a democratic society" (Wahid 1990, 29). In interviews Wahid expressed his additional concern that, with the support of some government officials, ICMI might be used to promote a rigidly exclusivistic Islam contrary to Indonesian Islam's long history of tolerance. It is significant that, despite his criticisms, Wahid did not forbid Nahdlatul Ulama members to join ICMI, and several prominent figures did join.

In April 1991, however, Wahid made his own position all the clearer, with his participation in the founding of a nongovernmental and nondenominational coalition known as the Forum Demokrasi. Some of Wahid's sternest critics launched a vicious rumor campaign, implying this effort was related to a putative "alliance" with Christians in general and the minister of defense and security, Benny Murdani, in particular. Wahid's defenders vigorously deny these charges of a political alliance with Murdani. Though the Democratic Forum was not banned, the government made clear its displeasure with Wahid's initiative. Among other things, it refused to reappoint him to the MPR on October 1, 1992. Conversely, the new MPR had a large number of Muslim leaders with ties to Minister Habibie and ICMI.[28]

It is striking that, during this first phase of ICMI's formation, even as aides to Minister Habibie came to exercise growing influence in its administration, ICMI managed to mobilize a diverse array of Muslim intellectuals. They included what Wardiman Djojonegoro, the general secretary of ICMI and one of Habibie's closest aides, referred to in interview with me as the "right and left wings" of the Muslim opposition.[29] This diversity reinforced the sense of spirited exchange so evident during the first ICMI congress, from December 6 to 8, 1990. Most of the speeches presented were scholarly, cautious, and even dryly academic in tone; the published versions of several came with long bibliographies. The substance of the papers, however, was more varied. Most respectfully echoed President Suharto's speech, endorsing the government's goals for twenty-first-century development. This emphasis was consistent with the title of the symposium, "To Build a Twenty-First-Century Indonesian Society," equally notable for its developmentalist emphasis and its lack of reference to Islam. The papers presented by Habibie's associates stressed this same theme, underscoring the importance of science and technology in the next phase of Indonesia's industrialization and urging Muslims to assure themselves a greater role in national development by mastering new information and technologies.

As Kuntowijoyo's above article indicates, however, much of the discussion was considerably less technodevelopmentalist in tone. Several discussants raised pointed questions about economic justice and echoed Kuntowijoyo in criticizing the bureaucratic values of the Javanist elite. Rather than simply endorsing the government's developmentalist goals, these independent scholars emphasized the need to use Muslims' political and intellectual influence to democratize Indonesian society.

The Politics of Cultural Breakthrough

The effort to unite Muslim intellectuals under a single, all-embracing organizational banner has historic precedent. Previously the most notable initiative was the formation of Persami, the Union of Muslim Scholars (Persatuan Sarjana Muslim Indonesia). Founded in 1964 to combat the growing influence of the Communist Party, Persami played an active role in supporting then-General Suharto in his rise to power during 1966–1967. It declined after 1968, however, as the result of leadership disputes and the regime's interest in limiting social organizations that might prove inclined to criticize its programs (*Tempo* 1990, 36).

ICMI's umbrellalike organization also replicates a pattern of corporatist control that, as Benedict Anderson (1983) and David Reeve (1985, 322–364) have emphasized, is a long-standing characteristic of Indonesian politics, elaborated to its most effective degree under the New Order. However, if bureaucratic control was an intent, its imposition nonetheless had unintended effects. One was that Muslim activists previously regarded as enemies of the state and thus subject to political controls suddenly had unprecedented freedom of movement and access to the press. In the months following the first ICMI congress, the media gave prominent attention to Islamic discussions of politics and development, discussions that, just a few years earlier, would have been regarded as dangerously sectarian.

Here again, Imaduddin Abdulrahim's experience provides a telling illustration of the depths of this change. In interviews in August 1992 and June 1993, Dr. Imaduddin commented that before ICMI's founding he had great difficulty giving public lectures. Wherever he went, his sponsors were required to obtain permits from the national police, and these were often denied. Since his association with ICMI, he noted, all this has changed. Now he travels freely around the country, "from Aceh to Java," as he put it, and not once has he had to secure police permits.

Dr. Imaduddin's testimony is all the more striking inasmuch as, by his own and others' accounts, before 1990 he had made several unsuccessful attempts to establish an association of Muslim intellectuals. The most recent of these occurred in January 1989, when Imaduddin and Dawam Rahardjo invited fifty intellectuals to the town of Kaliurang, near Yogyakarta, to discuss establishing such an organization. Forty of the fifty invitees showed up. On the second day, however, police arrived too and closed down the meeting, insisting that it had not received prior clearance and was thus illegal. Participants in the conference blamed the action on Benny Murdani, the Catholic-Javanese minister of defense and security.

Another effort to create an association of Muslim intellectuals had been made considerably earlier, in 1984, at a meeting in Ciawi, Bogor. The meeting had been organized through the joint efforts of the government-sponsored Majelis Ulama Indonesia (Council of Indonesian Ulama) and Dawam Rahardjo's respected (and theologically liberal) Institute for Religious and Philosophical Studies. At the meeting, Rahardjo expressed the view that the time seemed right for such an organization. Representatives from the MUI and the Ministry of Religion balked, however, fearing government disapproval, and the plan was eventually shelved. A similar effort was made in 1987. This time the activists behind the effort reached even higher into the upper echelons of the New Order elite, hoping that with General Alamsyah Ratu Perwiranegara (the Suharto confidant) as one of its official sponsors, the organization would secure government approval. Once again, however, the initiative was stopped when security officials expressed their concerns that the organization might give rise to "sectarian" influences.[30]

From this brief historical account, it can be seen that press reports on the role of the five Brawijaya students in ICMI's founding hid what was, in fact, a more complex history. From the start, prominent Muslim intellectuals were deeply involved in the effort to establish an ICMI-like organization. For political reasons, however, they chose to distance themselves from the publicity surrounding ICMI's founding. Indeed, the initial Malang meeting in early 1990 at which the five Brawijaya students were supposed to have come up with the proposal for an ICMI-like organization was not simply a private campus event. It occurred in the context of a visit to the campus by none other than Dr. Imaduddin. Not coincidentally, the rector who had approved Dr. Imaduddin's visit to the campus of Brawijaya University—at a time when Imaduddin was still barred from most campuses—was an alumni of the Association of Muslim Students (HMI), of which Nurcholish Madjid had been chairman and Imaduddin himself a member in the late 1960s. After the talk, Dr. Imaduddin urged the students to approach the dean with the idea for a national symposium, saying that they would be remembered in history for such a pathbreaking initiative.

The media story of the students' role correctly underscores that the effort to establish an association of Muslim intellectuals, at least in the first instance, originated within the independent Muslim community. However much it was to be drawn into bureaucratic intrigues, the original idea for

ICMI was not simply a matter of government political engineering, but the product of a state-society interaction with a longer and more contested history. Rather than being the brainchild of five anonymous students from a provincial university, however, the original plan for the association originated with well-placed but independent Muslim intellectuals. Some of those intellectuals had a reputation with the security forces that might have compromised efforts to establish the organization, had their names been given too much prominence. An activist like Imaduddin openly acknowledges this fact, noting that it was his idea to look to Minister Habibie for support, since he feared that his own reputation in security circles might jeopardize the organization's prospects.

The question that remains is, what had changed between 1988 and late 1990 so that the government, and the president in particular, felt compelled to support an organization that just eighteen months earlier security forces had sought to suppress? Surprisingly, on this point both supporters and critics of ICMI share similar views. Both groups acknowledge that the president's rivalry with segments of the military, in particular Benny Murdani and his allies, intensified in 1989 and 1990, in anticipation of the 1992 elections. As several interviewees commented, one had to look all the way back to the early 1960s, to the conflict between President Sukarno and the military, to find a breech between government and the military of similar proportions (cf. Anderson 1989; *Indonesia* 1992).

It is noteworthy in this regard that numerous high-ranking military officers are reported to have advised against government legalization of the organization. In the days before the president's approval of ICMI's formation, Vice-President Try Sutrisno is said to have urged the president to reject the proposal. Eventually, as it became clearer that ICMI had the support of the president, the military stopped its public sniping, and Try Sutrisno himself attended the Malang meeting.[31] Despite this apparent accommodation, military criticism of ICMI continued. Rather than attacking the organization as a whole, however, military critics over the next months warned of factions within ICMI who want to use it and Islam itself for their own political ends. In a widely publicized speech presented on June 18, 1993, Vice-President Try Sutrisno warned, without mentioning names, that there were signs that some people were using Islam as an "instrument of legitimation."[32] In April 1993—one month after the installation of a new cabinet heavy with ICMI sympathizers—the vice-president participated in an even bolder challenge to ICMI, giving his blessing to the formation of an "Association of Nusantara Intellectuals" (ICNU). This was a nondenominational organization of intellectuals intended to fight "sectarianism" and other challenges to Indonesia's "five principles" (Pancasila) of government. Despite the vice-president's blessing, however, ICNU failed to take off. However, there were two additional efforts to launch nonsectarian, militaronationalist alternatives to ICMI in 1994 and 1995.

Many independent Muslims have also continued to criticize ICMI. Critics such as Deliar Noer and Ridwan Saidi have cited the president's role in ICMI's founding to buttress their claim that ICMI was little more than a vehicle for the mobilization of presidential support. Other critics have complained that Habibie has used ICMI for his own political ends, including what some people regard as his failed effort to win nomination to the vice-presidency in March of 1993. In retrospect, it seems unlikely that Habibie ever seriously thought he could win the vice-presidency in 1993. But there clearly were political advantages to his involvement with ICMI. In particular, before his appointment to the ICMI chairmanship, Habibie enjoyed the confidence of President Suharto but lacked ties to any national organization that might provide a mass base. ICMI has provided him with that.

Over the years since the organization's founding, ICMI's activities have continued to expand. As Imaduddin commented above, ICMI's prominence has allowed previously marginalized Muslim intellectuals to air their views in public settings.[33] It has also provided Muslims with the resources and political latitude to undertake initiatives that were heretofore unthinkable. These have included the establishment of an Islamic Bank, the Bank Muamalat, and of a respected national newspaper, *Republika;* a national Islamic Center is also being planned.[34] Whatever ICMI's long-term fate, these initiatives have allowed an important institutional consolidation of the new Muslim middle class.

It should be noted, finally, that there is a broader, economic dimension to Habibie's appeal. Many Indonesians see Habibie as one of the few government leaders speaking to the problem of the continuing marginalization of Muslims in Indonesian enterprise. The economic liberalization of the late 1980s has unleashed a new entrepreneurial dynamic, but Muslims and *pribumi* (indigenous, non-Chinese) Indonesians remain, with a few exceptions, but secondary players in it. Though his economic ideas have been criticized as elitist, wasteful, and, ultimately, self-defeating, Habibie's impassioned discourses on technology and "value-added" industry appeal to many middle-class Indonesians who fear that the low-wage, export-oriented industrialization favored by economic technocrats may provide low-paying employment for the poor but very little for the indigenous middle class. From this perspective, Habibie has sought to present himself as but one in a long line of Indonesian bureaucratic nationalists who would bend the rules of the market to allow state intervention to improve the position of Indonesia's indigenous majority. Ironically, the great majority of his enterprises, such as airplanes and shipbuilding, are capital-intensive and labor-poor. They offer few employment opportunities and do little to provide the native community with the business skills with which they might compete with Sino-Indonesians (Sjahrir 1993; *Economist,* April 17, 1993).

Despite all these controversies, Habibie's national influence has continued to grow. So too have the questions surrounding his commitment to openness and liberalization. In his role as director of the state airplane manufacture industry (IPTN), Habibie has consistently supported large and unaccounted state subsidies to his own enterprises. Critics of his enterprises suggest that the strategic industries under Habibie's direction receive subsidies totaling more than a billion dollars each year. In April 1994 Minister Habibie was also strongly criticized in the press for secretly "borrowing" 300 million dollars from funds designated for reforestation to plough into his capital-hungry state firms. These and other incidents, discussed below, have shaken public confidence in Habibie's commitment to governmental reform and led even some of his supporters to wonder whether he can avoid being compromised by the culture of corporatist cronyism.[35]

Developmental Tensions

However extraordinary ICMI's ascent, several incidents in the months following its founding illustrated its vulnerabilities to elite control. The examples also suggest that, though ICMI may succeed in winning concessions from the government, the long-term impact of the organization will depend entirely on broader political developments, including the president's willingness to make concessions to those demanding greater political participation and Muslim leaders' interest in promoting those demands.

From the beginning certain incidents revealed serious tensions within ICMI over the organization's proper structure and political posture. For example, as Habibie and his aides laid out ICMI's organizational structure in early 1991, it became clear that they were under pressure from above to limit the organization's autonomy by bringing ICMI under tight executive control. Up to that time, the print media had almost uniformly speculated that Dawam Rahardjo was the top candidate for the important post of general secretary (see *Tempo* 1990, 27; *Fajar,* December 8 1990, p. 1). Unlike other independent Muslims, Dawam had never been regarded by security forces as an extremist or an antigovernment activist. He has strong ties to the NGO community and for years has managed to walk a fine line between criticism of specific government policies and support for the general goals of national development. Like Imaduddin, however, Dawam also had a long history of involvement in efforts to establish a national association of

Muslim intellectuals. He also had impeccable credentials as a devout Muslim, an accomplished scholar, and someone who, though occasionally cooperating with the government on development projects, maintained a careful distance from the bureaucracy. Over the years, finally, Dawam had also distinguished himself as development theorist (his academic training was in economics), a credential well suited to the kind of pragmatic role Habibie hoped ICMI would play. For all these reasons, Dawam's election to general secretary appealed to independent Muslims and seemed acceptable, it was thought, to the government.

In the first weeks of January 1991, Habibie supporters leaked hints to the press of the eventual organization of ICMI. Claiming that it would have a state-of-the-art "matrix" structure like that common in Western high-tech enterprises, Habibie's assistants indicated that ICMI would not have a general secretary, because none was needed under a matrix system. While independent intellectuals would figure prominently within each matrix sector, the crucial managerial positions at the top of the organization were to be recruited from Habibie's Agency for the Development and Application of Technology (BPPT).

Independent prodemocracy intellectuals, including Sri Bintang Pamungkas and Dawam Rahardjo, were quick to criticize Habibie's plan. In public statements they complained that the proposed structure was undemocratic and denied independent Muslims their right to positions of influence in the organization. Speaking in unusually blunt terms, Dawam accused Habibie of allowing ICMI to be taken over by bureaucrats.[36] Over the next three weeks there was great tension; many observers thought the fledgling organization was about to collapse. The criticism seemed to seal Dawam's fate, guaranteeing that he would not be accorded a truly influential leadership position in the organization. The most important leadership position in the organization thus went not to Dawam, but to Habibie's trusted advisor (and the future minister of education) Wardiman Djojonegoro.

To the surprise of many observers, however, ICMI survived, indeed with relations among Habibie, Dawam, and others still intact. Rahardjo was given a prestigious if somewhat symbolic position in the ICMI leadership. More significant, his journal, *Ulumul Qur'an*—a well-respected mouthpiece of liberal Islam, which to this day continues to serve as a forum for democratic and theologically liberal ideals—was provided with some ICMI subsidies. At the same time, Habibie took great pains to insist that, in obvious contrast with others in the president's inner circle, he welcomed criticism and debate (see *Media Indonesia*, February 7, 1991, p. 1; *Berita Buana*, February 6, 1991, p. 2). Despite criticisms over his choice of officials in

ICMI, leading figures associated with the prodemocracy wing of ICMI thus relented and continued to give Habibie their public, if somewhat shaken, support.

Two subsequent incidents highlighted once again tensions between reform-minded independents and Habibie aides. In May of 1991 Emha Ainun Najib, a popular Javanese playwright, social critic, and director of the "Cultural Discussion" bureau within ICMI, sought to have ICMI sponsor a small conference on the Kedung Ombo dam project in West Java, a highly controversial development project that has displaced thousands of rural dwellers from their lands. Before the conference could take place, Najib received a notice from an ICMI higher-up, warning that ICMI could not properly sponsor such an event. Behind the scenes, other independents were reminded that this kind of activity was foolish, embarrassing Habibie and needlessly squandering ICMI's political capital on an initiative doomed from the start. Eventually, Emha Najib resigned from ICMI.

On May 2, 1992, another incident revealed much the same tension between independent reformers and government officials. In the seminar room of the ICMI Secretariat on Jalan Thamrin in Jakarta, several dozen people gathered to discuss human rights in Indonesia. Among them were independent ICMI members; prominent and, from the government's perspective, controversial human rights advocates such as Mulya Lubis, Aswab Mahasin, and H. J. C. Princen; and longtime critics of the Suharto government, such as Chris Siner. As the event's opening address was coming to an end, ten uniformed officers appeared and requested to see the conference permit. The ICMI members explained that no such permit was needed because the seminar was an internal ICMI affair, like others that had taken place at the headquarters. The police insisted that all meetings of more than five people required a permit, and they politely but firmly insisted that the meeting stop. The organizers relented and the meeting ended without further incident.[37]

Events such as these have prompted a handful of individuals to quit ICMI so as to maintain their independence from the bureaucracy. However, through early 1994, most reform-minded independents remained optimistic about the organization, believing that it could work to enhance democracy and economic equity simultaneously. To justify their hopes, they pointed to examples like an ICMI-related research center's sponsorship of a controversial seminar on human rights. The research center, known as CIDES, the Center for Information and Development Studies, had on its steering committees such outspoken Muslim liberals as Adi Sasono and Dewi Fortuna Anwar. Shortly after its founding in September 1992, Adi Sasono took what was, in light of the previous failure in May of 1992, the rather bold step of announcing that CIDES would sponsor a one-day seminar on human rights after ICMI's annual national meeting in December. The fact that this was the first national event to be sponsored by CIDES prompted some observers to wonder whether the meeting would be allowed. Despite rumors that it was to be banned by security officials, the meeting took place. Moreover, as with the attempted May meeting on human rights, this conference included presentations by prominent human rights activists from outside ICMI, such as T. Mulya Lubis.

This bold commitment of the CIDES leadership to human rights issues did not end there. CIDES publishes two newsletters and a journal, *Afkar*. When the first issue of *Afkar* appeared in February of 1993, it astounded even many ICMI members by reprinting the texts of six of the panelists at the December human rights meetings, several of which contained unusually blunt assessments of human rights in Indonesia. At first, Minister Habibie privately expressed concern that the pilot issue of a journal promoted as ICMI's flagship publication should concentrate on such a controversial issue. Forced to decide whether he would go along with the journal's publication, however, Habibie affirmed his stance that CIDES should be independent and willing to take on timely issues. Although some observers had speculated that Adi Sasono's daring action might cost him his job, Habibie made a point of expressing his confidence in Sasono and his discussion of human rights.

These and other developments reassured many in the Muslim community that ICMI could continue to play an important role in the cause of democratization and justice. However, events over the course of 1994 shook the confidence of these democratic Muslims once again. In early 1994 there were a series of press stories questioning Habibie's role in the purchase of naval ships from Germany, the "borrowing" of reforestation funds from the Department of Forestry to finance Habibie's technology programs, and several other schemes. What these events had in common was their outspoken criticism of Habibie's behind-the-scenes maneuvering and his reluctance to provide a public accounting of expenditures. To many observers, including many independent Muslims, these incidents suggested that, rather than working to open up the system, Habibie was perpetuating a longstanding pattern of government mismanagement, corporatist cooptation, and bureaucratic cronyism.

A move that shocked even Habibie's closest supporters seemed to confirm the worst of these fears when, on June 27, 1994, the government, with clear presidential support, banned three of Indonesia's most respected news magazines, *Tempo, Editor,* and *DeTik.* All three had been in the forefront of efforts to raise questions about Habibie's offstage deals. Sources close to

Habibie insist that he opposed the bans, preferring to challenge the press account through the courts. President Suharto, however, insisted that such a tedious legal procedure made no sense; he thus insisted on the immediate closing of all three news establishments.

In the aftermath of these shocking events, most ICMI leaders made no public comment on the bans. In private, most liberals were deeply embarrassed or even outraged. However, with an air of sad resignation, one liberal ICMI cadre explained in June of 1995 that the president's supporters in ICMI had viewed the press bannings as a litmus test of loyalty. Politics is politics, ICMI leaders were told, and they were obliged to give no hint of disloyalty to either Habibie or the president. One high-ranking official commented to me, "Look, you have to realize politics is not perfect; our option is either support Habibie or give up and let the military control the whole show." This calculated realpolitik had an understandable logic. However it provided little consolation to the many prodemocracy activists who had hoped that ICMI reformers would act as principled advocates of democracy and the rule of law.

There were important exceptions to the deafening silence from ICMI ranks. While avoiding direct criticisms of Habibie, Dawam Rahardjo and Nurcholish Madjid continued to speak intelligently and courageously of the need for tolerance, openness, and a renewed commitment to democratization. However, the majority of ICMI leaders remained silent, and a few even hinted at their support for the press closures. Most astounding among those in the latter group was Adi Sasono, the former student activist turned dependency theorist, NGO champion, and proponent of the demilitarization of government. In public comments that astonished people in the prodemocracy movement, Adi suggested that Muslims had to be cool-headed about the closings and clear about their priorities. None of the news magazines affected by the closure was Muslim, and thus Muslims were still free to promote their views in the media. These comments were seen by secular democrats as sad evidence that the regime's strategy of dividing the democratic opposition had borne bitter fruit indeed.

Epilogue: Islam and Democratization

We are so accustomed to thinking . . . only of politicians using religion for political ends, that it is extremely hard for us to understand what politics might look like if we could see it through religious eyes, or in a religious perspective, and thus imagine the possibility of religious people using politics for religious ends.

Anderson 1977, 21

Marginalized from real influence since the late Sukarno era, Indonesia's Muslims, especially the modernist community, are understandably relieved that they are finally being accorded a measure of influence in national policies and programs. Few have illusions about the degree to which real reform of the Indonesian political system is, at this point, possible. Many are troubled by their accommodation with the president and recognize that theirs is an alliance of unequals in the extreme. They can point nonetheless to genuine social, if not structuropolitical, achievements. The Ministry of Religion continues its programs for the construction of mosques and Islamic schools. Its support for *dakwah* proselytization stemmed the tide of Hindu and Christian conversion and reinforced a reverse process of Islamization that has had significant impact even in Javanist portions of the countryside. Governors and regency officials now regularly exchange Islamic greetings at public events and are prominently featured in television coverage celebrating Muslim holidays. In 1988 rules for religious education in the schools were reinforced. In 1989 the authority of the nation's Islamic courts was strengthened, over the strenuous objections of secular-nationalist members of parliament. In 1990, after months of stormy protest, the government allowed Muslim schoolgirls to wear *jilbab* (religious scarves) to classes. In 1991 an Islamic bank was established. Also in 1991, President Suharto became Haji Muhammad Suharto, after his celebrated pilgrimage to Mecca.[38] Finally, in several sensational cases between 1990 to 1993, the government secured harsh prison terms against journalists and performers accused of slandering Islam.[39]

Whatever the precise balance of forces in government, these developments provide clear evidence that Western scholars can no longer fall back on their familiar characterizations of government cultural policies as *abangan* or, worse yet, "secularist." It is doubtful that such monolithic characterizations were ever fair to the complexity of religious interests at work within the government. Such pioneering figures as Djohan Effendi, Dawam Rahardjo, and Nurcholish Madjid seem to have sensed this from the start and maneuvered accordingly. Their strategy of Islamic renewal has borne fruits that, ten years ago, most Western Indonesianists would have thought unimaginable.

For the Muslim community itself, the growing influence of Muslim social styles has, as the human rights advocate Aswab Mahasin once explained to me, "made many people who were previously embarrassed about their faith, because it looked backward and unmodern, proud to act like Muslims." For Western scholars who see religion as no more than an instrument for achieving political-economic ends, such accomplishments may seem trivial because they are peripheral to the real flesh and blood of politics. However, many devout Muslims view the matter differently. Many see the state and politics not as ends in themselves, but as means for the creation of a greater good, the realization of Islamic ideals in society. For such people, the symbolism of Islamic devotionalism is not just symbolic, but the very basis for an ethical order.

Inevitably, however, recent Muslim successes have also raised questions. In a Western historical idiom, these questions have to do with the nature of the "civil" society toward which Indonesia may be moving, however haltingly. The idea of civil society refers to a sphere of action and interests between the level of the household and the institutions of the state, one that in certain circumstances can work to counterbalance the state's monopoly of ideological and coercive power (Cohen and Arato 1992; Hall 1986; Seligman 1992). By itself such an intermediary domain guarantees neither democracy, justice, nor pluralist tolerance. It becomes a vital support for all three, however, if and when it serves to strengthen the presence of two other elusive social arrangements: extragovernmental associations that act as counterweights to the state's monopoly of power and a social pluralism that helps to legitimate the idea that people have a right to their own ideas and actions.

For a few Islamist purists the idea of a civil society is itself suspect because it is seen as a Western creation. It first emerged in European historical experience, after all, the product of a long social evolution whereby, in a few (and, at first, very few) corners of Western Europe, a complex social compromise emerged. Despite the best efforts of tyrants and the deepest hopes of clergy, no single estate, class, or religious community found itself strong enough to impose its will on the whole of society. Out of this happenstance stalemate, a "pluricentric" (Hall 1986, 111–188) balance of social powers emerged. With it—though subject to unending challenge by its ideological rivals—there emerged an idiom of rights and freedoms that placed serious limitations on the authority of the state (Dunn 1969; Seligman 1992; cf. Habermas 1989).

Given its Western genesis, it is not surprising that some Muslims regard the concept of civil society as an abnegation of one of their most cherished ideals: that religion can and should serve as the groundwork for the reformation of society as a whole. The concept of religion implicit in the idea of civil society is a deliberately uncomprehensive one. Rather than providing a master plan for the whole of society, religion under this model serves primarily as a moral compass for legal, economic, and political structures. "Civil" religion may be influential and informative, but it is not exhaustively determinative of state and societal institutions.[40]

Most devout Muslims profess allegiance to the idea that Islam is a total way of life. But the implications of this truism for Muslim visions of modern society are varied, as different Muslims interpret its truth in profoundly different ways. For those for whom it means that Islam can and should impose an all-encompassing political system on society, the Western notion of civil society seems decidedly anemic. It suffers from the same deficiency that, in some Muslims' eyes, modern Christianity does: it places religion too much at the margins, making it appear as if religion lacks the capacity to reform the whole of social life.

Whatever ICMI's fate, Muslim intellectuals in Indonesia will continue to confront this question of just how comprehensive a role Islam can and should play in societal reformation. With unusual insight into a process about which Western scholars had only vague ideas at the time, Abdurrahman Wahid, the renewal-oriented leader of Nahdlatul Ulama, anticipated this question in a modest paper presented at a conference at Monash University four and one-half years before ICMI's founding:

> Different Muslim groups have responded [to this rising consciousness of Islam] by formulating two main strategies to achieve those objectives. The first is by idealizing Islam as the only feasible social system able to maintain true democracy, strict adherence to law and economic justice. The so-called "Islamization process" taking place in the life of the whole nation should be used to promote the idea of an "Islamic society" in Indonesia. This strategy of struggling for an Islamic society in Indonesia naturally collides with the other strategy. According to the so-called "soft" groups, Islam plays an important role in the life of the nation, if only for the reason that Muslims constitute the overwhelming majority of the population. But the role Islam should play is not derived from the idealization of itself as the only alternative to the existing situation, but rather as the inspirational base for a national framework of a democratic society. As such, Islam is not an alternative to other social systems, but a complementary factor among a wide spectrum of other factors in the nation's life. A bitter debate is therefore unavoidable between those opposing views. . . . As of now, it is not clear where the support of the Muslim middle class will go to. (Wahid 1990, 24)

As this quote implies, Wahid is an outspoken proponent of the "national" rather than the "Islamic" society idea. In recent years, he has expressed concern over the way the government has courted conservatives in the Muslim community. He has cautioned that the government should make clear its opposition to fundamentalism and support Muslims, like himself, committed to the idea of Islam as a moral influence within a plural society. Having resisted pressures to affiliate with ICMI and having loudly proclaimed his support for the prodemocracy movement, Wahid has since 1994 been the subject of an intense government campaign to topple him from the Nahdlatul Ulama leadership and marginalize him in the Muslim community.

Other intellectuals, like Sugeng Sarjadi, a former Muslim student activist who, in 1992, shocked his Muslim friends by joining the nominally democratic-nationalist PDI (Indonesian Democratic Party) and running for the DPR, go even further than Wahid. Recently Sarjadi has publicly criticized his Islamic colleagues for, in his view, once again confusing incidental opportunities with Islam's deeper values. In an interview with me during July of 1992, he said that Muslims have been seduced by the government's embrace of Islamic symbolism. What is really needed, he claimed, are principles of justice and fair play that can be implemented for Indonesians of all faiths: "What's the meaning of this religion, Islam? If an *abangan* makes the pilgrimage and becomes a *santri,* what's the point? Is that Islam? Make the pilgrimage but add to it corruption, what do you get? Isn't Islam really about universal values of justice? Can you buy the symbolism of Islam without its ideals of justice?"

This is the crux of the matter. Observers of Islamic politics since the time of Ibn Khaldun have noted that Islamic values (like those of the other world religions) can be interpreted to support the most varied of political orders. The critical matter in determining which interpretation of Islamic values predominates in society depends on a process of "competition and contest over both the interpretation of [Islamic] symbols and control of the institutions, formal and informal, that produce and sustain them" (Eickelman and Piscatori 1996, 5; cf. Esposito and Voll 1996). It is just such a contest that is unfolding in Indonesia right now. The question is not just the simplistic matter of whether Muslim leaders will be accorded greater influence in the government's inner circle. The question is, how those leaders, once accorded influence, will interpret their responsibility to Islam and nation.

The two years that followed the 1994 press bannings saw discouraging developments in this regard. While Muslim leaders continued to be accorded prominent roles in regime affairs, the government moved to narrow the political opening that seemed to have begun in the late 1980s. The press bannings and the campaign against Abdurrahman Wahid were the first in these restrictive salvos. Then, in 1995, the government launched proceedings against another outspoken Muslim democrat (this one active in ICMI), Sri Bintang Pamungkas. Sri Bintang was accused of having slandered President Suharto in the course of speeches given during a visit to Germany. To its credit, the ICMI leadership resisted pressures to expel Sri Bintang from the organization. However, that leadership—including some with close personal ties to Sri Bintang—was forced to stand by in silence as the government made behind-the-scenes deals to arrange Sri Bintang's expulsion from the parliament and his conviction of the slander charges in a court of law. Though he has appealed his sentence, Sri Bintang's influence in national affairs, not to mention ICMI, has been drastically circumscribed. The government's effort to split accommodating Muslims from prodemocracy activists had taken another victim.

To their credit, several independent Muslims, such as Dawam Rahardjo and Nurcholish Madjid, have continued to make brave and principled statements on the need to tolerate opposition and effect a deeper democratization of Indonesian politics. Sadly, however, their comments have come to be treated by some realpolitik Muslims as the irrelevant musings of political idealists. Meanwhile, the government has escalated its campaign against more influential prodemocracy activists. At the time of this writing (July–August 1996), it launched a fierce assault on the the leader of the Indonesian Democratic Party, Megawati Sukarnoputri. The daughter of Indonesia's first president, Sukarno, Megawati's increasingly bold calls for democracy and justice appear to have so alarmed the regime's inner circle that they arranged her ouster from the party leadership.

All this shows that Muslims in general and ICMI members in particular operate in a political environment that is constrained to an extreme by the authoritarian nature of Indonesia's leadership. Though certain Muslim individuals have been accorded greater influence, others—those who raise more serious challenges to the structure of authority itself—have been systematically marginalized. The danger here is not merely that the mass of ordinary citizens, Muslim and non-Muslim, are being excluded from civic life. It is that, in addition, such corporatist centralization will smother what is most remarkable in Indonesian Islam, its rich tradition of independence, pluralism, and tolerance. By itself, the participation of Muslims in government says little about which Islamic principles will be implemented in policy and even less about how Islam might contribute to democratization.

The depoliticization of Islam under the New Order created challenges and opportunities for the Muslim community, a situation that favored the growth of a moderate, civil leadership. However, developments since mid-1994 make all too apparent just how difficult it will be for civic-minded Muslims to realize their ideals in practice. In the face of growing Muslim influence in society, the government may respond with concessions to a few leaders while stifling criticism and independent civic organization. In such circumstances, Muslim leaders face a painful dilemma: how to balance the interests of the religious community *(ummat)* with those of the nation as a whole. This tension has been exploited by New Order strategists in their campaign to split Muslims from secular-democratic reformers. In years to come, Muslim efforts to respond to this tension will determine which vision of Islam predominates in the Muslim community and which vision of nation.

Notes

1. From the Javanese word for "red," *abangan* refers to those Javanese less strict in their performance of Islamic devotional obligations than the so-called *santri,* practicing or "orthodox" Muslims (Geertz 1960).

2. The interviews on which the original version of this chapter was based were conducted during visits of three to four weeks over the summers from 1991 to 1995, primarily in Jakarta, with side trips to Yogyakarta and Malang. I also engaged in extended discussions with Abdurrahman Wahid in February and September of 1992, Nurcholish Madjid in March of 1992, and Aswab Mahasin during the fall term of 1992, during their visits to my home institute in Boston.

3. On the relationship of generation-of-'66 Muslim activists to the PSI and economic technocrats, see Liddle 1973 and, especially, Raillon 1984, 145–170. On the ideology of the PSI technocrats in the early New Order, see MacDougall 1975.

4. Interviews with Djohan Effendi, Dawam Rahardjo, Usep Fathudin, and Utomo Danadjaja, July 1993. Danadjaja and Fathudin were leaders of the moderate wing of the Pelajar Islam, forced from the organization in 1971 because of their public support of Nurcholish Madjid. A. Wahib, Dawam Rahardjo, and Djohan Effendi were members of the "Lingkaran Limited Discussion Group," a discussion group in Yogyakarta organized by Mutki Ali, who would become minister of religion in 1971. The role of this Yogya-based group has sometimes been neglected in outsiders' accounts of the *pembaruan* (renewal) movement. An important exception is Greg Barton's (1995) important analysis of Indonesian neomodernism.

5. See Madjid's "Modernisasi Ialah Rasionalisasi Bukan Westernisasi" (Modernization Is Rationalization, Not Westernization), "Keharusan Pemikiran Islam dan Masalah Integrasi Umat" (The Necessity of Islamic Thought and the Problem of the Integration of the Community of Believers), "Sekali Lagi Tentang Sekularisasi" (Once More on Secularization), and "Perspectif Pembaruan Pemikiran dalam Islam" (The Perspective of Intellectual Renewal in Islam), now reprinted in Madjid 1984. All four essays are available in English translation in the appendixes to Hassan 1980.

6. In his most recent writings Madjid has tended to link his ideas more explicitly to classical Islamic theology and commentary. Some observers see evidence of a greater "conservativism" in Madjid's mature writings. However, Madjid shows no reluctance to take on controversy, and this theological turn is better understood as an effort on his part to ensure the lasting influence of his work

by contextualizing it within a broader Islamic tradition. For examples of his recent writings, see Madjid 1992. For an illustration of his continuing willingness to take on controversy, see Madjid's impassioned plea for Islamic tolerance of other religions, made in the fall of 1992 in the aftermath of attacks on Christian churches in East Java and southern Sulawesi (Madjid 1993).

7. Book-length versions of these critiques can be found in Rasjidi 1972 and Saefuddin 1973.

8. In our discussion on June 19, 1993, Madjid again affirmed that he is "still quite comfortable" with his views on secularism and secularization, "though it is not economical to use these terms, inviting as they do such emotional reactions from people."

9. As Howard M. Federspiel has noted, another consequence of this change was the arrival of a new class of Muslim intellectuals on the national stage. Unlike traditional Islamic leaders, this new class had no reverential titles and had only nominal ties to the *pesantren*-based system of Islamic education. They were more likely to have been trained in Western social science than in traditional Islamic philosophy or scripture. While committed to the ideals of modernization, they rejected the idea that development could be undertaken as a mere technological process without reference to cultural and moral values. See Federspiel 1992, 7–12. These Muslim intellectuals have probably done more than secularists to popularize the methods and concerns of Western-style social science among the Indonesian public. In an important article, Dale Eickelman (1992) has analyzed a not dissimilar pattern of mass education and leadership reorganization in the Muslim Middle East.

10. Henry Munson Jr. (1988) and Olivier Roy (1994) illustrate how different the situation was in much of the Middle East; Hussin Mutalib's account (1990) shows how much the situation of Islam in Malaysia differed from that of Indonesia.

11. Bahtiar Effendy (1995) provides an excellent analysis of the career of one of the most remarkable of these leaders: Munawir Sjadzali, minister of religion during the critical transition years from 1983 to 1993.

12. Avery T. Willis (1977) provides an unusually frank Protestant assessment of this history. A minister of religious affairs before the New Order, Dr. Muhammad Rasjidi published a stinging denunciation of the government policy on Christian missions in 1978. See Rasjidi 1978, 23–28.

13. These figures are from Badan Perencanaan, 1990, 209; Kantor Statistik dan Pemerintah Daerah Jawa Timur, 1992, 72; Kantor Statistik Propinsi Jawa Timur, 1981:178; Kantor Statistik Propinsi Jawa Tengah, 1993; and Kantor Statistik Propinsi Jawa Tengah, 1984, 182.

14. See *Tempo*, December 8, 1990, 34–37. For a description of the vast scale of *dakwah* at a provincial level, see Pierre Labrousse and Farida Soemargono 1985, and in an area historically renowned as a bastion of Javanism, see Hefner 1987, 533–554.

15. Interview, June 19, 1993.

16. Compare Pranowo 1991 on the Islamic resurgence in a former Javanist stronghold in the Magelang regency of Central Java with Hefner (1990, 193–227) on a Javanist portion of Pasuruan, East Java. Evidence of the progress of Islamization can be found, however, in the most unexpected sources. Stephen C. Headley's study of the *ruwatan* tradition of exorcism in the Solo region of Central Java (forthcoming), for example, shows that this non-Islamic cult has declined drastically in recent years in the face of the Islamic advance. Paul Stange's studies of contemporary Javanist mysticism imply similar conclusions. In the mid-1980s he wrote that "even though Islam may be politically on the defensive, in the religious sphere it has been gaining ground.... Islamic discourse, I would argue, increasingly defines the context of Javanese mysticism" (1986, 79–80).

17. See Pranowo 1991; on Hindu conversion see Lyon 1977 and Hefner 1985.

18. Interviews with University of Indonesia students, July 1992, and with Imaduddin Abdulrahim, August 1992 and June 1993. Ali and Effendy place the Salman revival in the context of other developments among urban Muslims (1986, 308). Cf. Abdulaziz et al. 1991, 207–287.

19. As the Islamic revival intensified in the early 1990s, however, less tolerant movements have gained a small following. For an overview of their growth—and their rejection of the inclusivistic Islam of Abdurrahman Wahid and Nurcholish Madjid—see *Tempo* 1993, 14–21. Anti-Christian activities have not been limited to student radicals, as was illustrated in the burning of evangelical Christian churches in Pasuruan, East Java, in the fall of 1992 and in Surabaya during July–August 1996.

20. For other examples see Wahib 1981 and Mulkhan 1992; on the development of the Muslim middle class as a whole, see Mahasin 1990.

21. Interestingly, however, in its personalism and accessibility this segment of the Islamic resurgence also resembles the contemporary evangelical boom in the Americas. Compare, for example, "Dai-Dai Baru Bak Matahari Terbit," *Tempo*, April 11, 1992, pp. 14–23, with David Martin's (1990) portrayal of Latin American evangelicalism.

22. What follows draws heavily on interviews with Imaduddin Abdulrahim, Syafi'i Anwar, Dawam Rahardjo, Nurcholish Madjid, Wardiman Djojonegoro, and Aswab Mahasin in August 1992 and June–July 1993.

23. Appointed minister of education in 1993, Wardiman again proved himself a more interestingly complex and moderate figure than critics had anticipated. Among other things, during the controversy surrounding speaking permits in June of 1995, when some government officials were calling for forceful restrictions on public speech, Wardiman moved quickly to announce that no such permits were required for university functions. Similarly, during the government crackdown on left-wing opponents in July 1996, Wardiman was quick to speak out against the suggestions of several military officials that, because some of the protestors had been students, sterner security measures had to be applied on campus.

24. Interview with Sri Bintang, July 22, 1992.
25. Interview with T. Abdullah, June 24, 1993. Though concerned about the predominance of government bureaucrats in ICMI, Abdullah categorically rejected the conclusions of some Western observers that ICMI was developed merely to provide President Suharto and Minister Habibie with political support. "No," he said, "there's been a real change in the religiosity of the government elite, real Islamization." In addition, he noted that "there are pockets of independent activity in ICMI where people are bravely raising new questions, about human rights and economic equalization."
26. Interview with D. Effendi, July 1993.
27. Interviews with Ridwan Saidi, July 1992, Abdurrahman Wahid, July 1992, 1993, and June 1, 1995. Both men also commented that they felt that ICMI suf-fered from a peculiarly bureaucratic vision of Islam. The same theme ran through Nahdlatul Ulama press commentaries released shortly after ICMI's founding.
28. See *Tempo* 1992a, 21–31. On the Forum Demokrasi's founding, see "Demokrasi Kita," in *Tempo* 1991, 17–27.
29. Interview with Wardiman Djojonegoro, August 9, 1992. Since the field research conducted for this article, Wardiman's national role has been enhanced with his appointment in March of 1993 to the influential position of minister of education and culture. The appointment was widely regarded as strong evidence of the Habibie group's broad influence in the new cabinet. The portfolios of trade, transport, and health also went to Habibie affiliates from his technology agency. More surprising, Habibie supporters were also posted to the influential national planning agency BAPPENAS. See *DeTik* 1993, 4–5. Though not specifically identified as Habibie supporters, the minister of finance, Drs. Mar'ie Muhammad, and the minister for the environment, Sarwono Kusumaatmadja, are also regarded as ICMI supporters, both having backgrounds as Islamic student activists.
30. Interviews 1993 and 1995; see also Dawam Rahardjo's brief but intelligent account of these events (1995, 29).
31. Publicly, however, the military press remained cautious, urging the organization to stick to its goals of national unity and development. See, for example, the editorial in the military newspaper *Angkatan Bersenjata*, "ICMI, Selamat Datang" (ICMI Welcome), December 10, 1990. Behind-the-scenes military criticism continued, prompting Dr. Habibie to make a much-publicized visit to the offices of the chief of staff, Try Sutrisno, on February 22, 1992, in an effort to dispel rumors that the military opposed ICMI. The armed forces commander subsequently released the text of his statement to Habibie. The document's twenty-five short paragraphs make no fewer than twenty references to the Pancasila, religious pluralism, and the need for vigilance against those who would undermine national unity.
32. See *Kompas*, June 18, 1993, p. 1.
33. Another illustration of ICMI's ability to provide a forum for previously mar-

ginalized intellectuals is the case of Adi Sasono. Sasono has a reputation as a progressive, though ambitious, Muslim with strong ties to the NGO community. During most of the 1980s he was well known for his democratic socialist, "dependency theory" views on development. In the early 1980s he, along with Aswab Mahasin and a number of other liberal Muslim intellectuals, established a foundation to help former communist political prisoners integrate back into society, an initiative that excited strong disapproval in certain government circles. From this background as a Muslim outsider, Sasono has risen to the position of close advisor to Minister Habibie; in December 1995 he became the ICMI secretary-general.

34. ICMI's national newspaper, *Republika,* was launched on January 3, 1993, and immediately given high marks for the quality of its reporting. Its circulation has grown from 45,000 in January 1993 to 120,000 in July 1994. See "Islam Kosmopolitan dalam Berita" (Cosmopolitan Islam in the News), *Tempo,* January 9, 1993, p. 33. On the founding of the government-supported Islamic Bank, Bank Muamalat Indonesia (BMI), see *Prospek,* November 2, 1991, "Mengapa Baru Sekarang BMI Berdiri" (Why the Islamic Bank Has Only Now Been Established). See also Hefner 1996.

35. See "Belum Saatnya Proyek Untung" (Not Yet Time for the Project to Earn a Profit), *Tempo,* October 31, 1992, pp. 27–29. See also "Engineering the Future," *The Economist,* April 17, 1993 (special supplement), pp. 12–13.

36. See Rahardjo's outspoken comments in *Berita Buana,* January 14, 1991. Other Muslim independents voiced similar concerns about the subordination of ICMI to bureaucratic power during the weeks preceding Habibie's announcement on February 14. See, for example, *Suara Karya,* January 31, 1991, p. 1, and *Pelita,* January 31, 1991, p. 1.

37. Based on interviews with junior ICMI staff involved in the conference preparations, July 1992. Though reporters from several news organizations were present at the human rights conference, the police closure was mentioned in only one press report, "ICMI pun Kena Semprit," *Tempo,* May 9, 1992.

38. An article on the president's pilgrimage in *Tempo* (July 6, 1991), "Bukan Haji Politik" (Not a Political Pilgrimage), provides (despite its title) an unusually frank assessment of the political considerations that influenced Suharto's trip. At the same time, the report emphasizes that the president's profession of Muslim devotion has a deeper precedent than the early 1990s. Among other things, it notes that the president reads Arabic script and received a portion of his education in Muhammadiyah schools. While many Indonesianists in the West speak as if Suharto's religious ideas remain unchanged, there is ample evidence that he began to adjust his views in the early 1980s. For example, around that time the president hired a well-known Islamic preacher, Kyai Haji Qosim Nursekha, to train his family in Islamic devotion. The president's interest in mysticism continued through this period, but it is interesting to note that one of his most influential mystical counselors, H. Zahid Husein, is

said to have played a role in the 1980s encouraging Javanist mystical sects to identify with Islam and distance themselves from Christianity.

39. The most heated incident was the "Monitor Case," in which the government demanded and won a prison term of five years against Arswendo Atmowiloto, a popular journalist at the Christian-owned tabloid *Monitor*. Arswendo was responsible for a poll in which readers listed the Prophet Muhammad as eleventh among the individuals they most admired. This may not be an inaccurate measure of the views of *Monitor*'s heavily Christian and Chinese readership, but the inclusion of the Prophet alongside ordinary individuals was seen by militant Muslims as blasphemous and excited violent street protests. In response to these actions, the government moved to secure Arswendo's conviction. Critics saw the move as a blatant effort to court Muslim support before the presidential elections. The government's handling of the incident caused concern among Western observers and a fair number of Muslims, who saw it as an example of the way in which the symbols of Islamic solidarity can be abused by those seeking political advantage. See *News from Asia Watch*, April 10, 1991. More recent prosecutions for slandering Islam have included two cases against student-artists who have mimicked Islamic devotion during their performances, in June 1992 and January 1993.

40. This is, for example, the concept of religion that underlies Robert Bellah's (1975) discussion of civil religion in America. On the intellectual development in the early modern era of this idea of religion's limited involvement in government, see Oakley 1991.

References Cited

Abdulaziz, Imam Tholkhah, and Soetarman. 1991. *Gerakan Islam Kontemporer di Indonesia* (Islamic Movements in Contemporary Indonesia). Jakarta: Pustaka Firdaus.

Adnan, Zifirdaus. 1990. "Islamic Religion: Yes, Islamic Ideology: No! Islam and State in Indonesia." In Arief Budiman, ed., *State and Civil Society in Indonesia*, pp. 441–478. Clayton, Victoria (Australia): Centre of Southeast Asian Studies, Monash University.

Ali, Fachry, and Bahtiar Effendy. 1986. *Merambah Jalan Baru Islam: Rekonstruksi Pemikiran Islam Indonesia Masa Orde Baru* (To Blaze a New Path for Islam: The Reconstruction of Indonesian Islamic Thought in the New Order). Bandung: Mizan.

Anderson, Benedict R. O'G. 1977. "Religion and Politics in Indonesia since Independence." In Benedict R. O'G. Anderson, Mitsuo Nakamura, and Mohammad Slamet, eds., *Religion and Social Ethos in Indonesia*, pp. 21–32. Clayton, Australia: Centre of Southeast Asian Studies, Monash University.

———. 1978. "Cartoons and Monuments: The Evolution of Political Communication under the New Order." In Karl D. Jackson and Lucian W. Pye, eds., *Political Power and Communications in Indonesia*, pp. 282–321. Berkeley and Los Angeles: University of California Press.

———. 1983. "Old State, New Society: Indonesia's New Order in Comparative Historical Perspective." *Journal of Asian Studies* 42:477–496.

———. 1989. "Current Data on the Indonesian Military Elite." *Indonesia* 48:65–96.

Badan Perencanaan Pembangunan Daerah. 1990. *Dokumentasi Hasil Pelaksanaan Pembangunan Tahun 1984, 1988, dan 1989* (Documentation of Development Results for 1984, 1988, and 1989). Surabaya: Regional Planning Board.

Barton, Greg. 1995. "Neo-Modernism: A Vital Synthesis of Traditionalist and Modernist Islamic Thought in Indonesia." *Studie Islamika: Indonesian Journal for Islamic Studies* 2 (3): 1–75.

Bellah, Robert. 1975. *The Broken Covenant: American Civil Religion in Time of Trial*. Chicago: University of Chicago Press.

Boland, B. J. 1982. *The Struggle of Islam in Modern Indonesia*. The Hague: Martinus Nijhoff.

Bowen, John R. 1993. *Muslims through Discourse: Religion and Ritual in Gayo Society*. Princeton: Princeton University Press.

Casanova, Jose. 1994. *Public Religions in the Modern World*. Chicago: University of Chicago Press.

Cohen, Jean, and Andrew Arato. 1992. *Civil Society and Political Theory*. Cambridge: MIT Press.

Crouch, Harold. 1988. *The Army and Politics in Indonesia*, Revised edition. Ithaca: Cornell University Press.

DeTik. 1993. "Mafia Berkeley, Habibie, Atau Konglomerat" (The Berkeley Mafia, Habibie, or Conglomerates). April 9–17, pp. 4–5.

Dick, Howard W. 1985. "The Rise of a Middle Class and the Changing Concept of Equity in Indonesia: An Interpretation." *Indonesia* 39:71–92.

———. 1990. "Further Reflections on the Middle Class." In Richard Tanter and Kenneth Young, *The Politics of Middle Class Indonesia*, pp. 63–70. Clayton, Australia: Centre of Southeast Asian Studies, Monash University.

Dijk, Cees van. 1985. "Survey of Political Developments in Indonesia in the Second Half of 1984: The National Congress of the PPP and the Pancasila Principle." *Review of Indonesian and Malaysian Affairs* 19 (1): 177–202.

Dunn, John. 1969. "The Creation of the Legitimate Polity." In Dunn, *The Political Thought of John Locke*, pp. 120–147. Cambridge: Cambridge University Press.

Editor. 1993. "Kritik Bintang untuk Bintang" (Bintang's Criticism for the [Party of the] Star). January, pp.74–75.

Effendy, Bahtiar. 1995. "Islam and the State in Indonesia: Munawir Sjadzali and the Development of a New Theological Underpinning of Political Islam." *Studia Islamika: Indonesian Journal for Islamic Studies* 2 (2): 97–121.

Eickelman, Dale F. 1992. "Mass Education and the Religious Imagination in Contemporary Arab Societies." *American Ethnologist* 19 (4): 643–655.

Eickelman, Dale F., and James Piscatori. 1996. *Muslim Politics*. Princeton: Princeton University Press.

Emmerson, Donald K. 1978. "The Bureaucracy in Political Context: Weakness in Strength." In Karl D. Jackson and Lucian W. Pye, eds., *Political Power and Communications in Indonesia*, pp. 82–136. Berkeley and Los Angeles: University of California Press.

Esposito, John L., and John O. Voll. 1996. *Islam and Democracy*. New York: Oxford University Press.

Federspiel, Howard M. 1992. *Muslim Intellectuals and National Development in Indonesia*. New York: Nova Science Publishers.

Geertz, Clifford. 1960. *The Religion of Java*. New York: Free Press.

Gellner, Ernest. 1981. "Flux and Reflux in the Faith of Men." In Gellner, *Muslim Society*, pp. 1–85. Cambridge: Cambridge University Press.

———. 1983. *Nations and Nationalism*. Ithaca: Cornell University Press.

Habermas, Jurgen. 1989. *The Structural Transformation of the Public Sphere: An Inquiry into a Category of Bourgeois Society*. Translated by Thomas Burger. Cambridge, Mass.: MIT Press.

Habibie, B. J. 1991. "Peranan Ilmu Pengetahuan dan Teknologi dalam Proses Transformasi Masyarakat" (The Role of Science and Technology in the Process of Societal Transformation). In ICMI (no author), *Membangun Masyarakat Indonesia Abad XXI*, pp. 1–17. Jakarta: ICMI National Office.

Hall, John A. 1986. *Powers and Liberties: The Causes and Consequences of the Rise of the West*. Berkeley and Los Angeles: University of California Press.

Hari, Syamsuddin. 1990. "PPP and Politics under the New Order." *Prisma* 49:31–51.

Hassan, Muhammad Kamal. 1980. *Muslim Intellectual Responses to "New Order" Indonesia*. Kuala Lumpur: Dewan Bahasa dan Pustaka.

Headley, Stephen C. Forthcoming. *The Murwa Kala: A Southeast Asian Cosmogony*.

Hefner, Robert W. 1985. *Hindu Javanese: Tengger Tradition and Islam*. Princeton: Princeton University Press.

———. 1987. "Islamizing Java? Religion and Politics in Rural East Java." *Journal of Asian Studies* 46 (3): 533–554.

———. 1990. *The Political Economy of Mountain Java: An Interpretive History*. Berkeley and Los Angeles: University of California Press.

———, ed. 1993. *Conversion to Christianity: Historical and Anthropological Perspectives on a Great Transformation*. Berkeley and Los Angeles: University of California Press.

———. 1996. "Islamizing Capitalism: On the Founding of Indonesia's First Islamic Bank." In Mark R. Woodward and James Rush, eds., *Intellectual Renewal in Indonesian Islam*, pp. 67–92. Tempe: Center for Southeast Asian Studies, Arizona State University.

Hodgson, Marshall G. S. 1974. *The Venture of Islam: Conscience and History in a World Civilization*. 3 vols. Chicago: University of Chicago Press.

ICMI (no author). 1991. *Membangun Masyarakat Indonesia Abad XXI: Prosiding Simposium Nasional Cendekiawan Muslim, 1991* (To Build a Twenty-First

Century Indonesian People: Proceedings of the 1991 National Symposium of Muslim Intellectuals). Jakarta: ICMI National Office.

Indonesia. 1992. "Current Data on the Indonesian Military Elite: July 1–January 1, 1992." 53:93–136.

Kantor Statistik dan Pemerintah Daerah Jawa Timur. 1992. *Jawa Timur dalam Angka, 1990* (East Java in Statistics, 1990). Surabaya: East Java Government Statistical Office.

Kantor Statistik Propinsi Jawa Tengah. 1984. *Jawa Tengah dalam Angka, 1983.* (Central Java in Statistics). Semarang: Central Java Government Statistical Office.

———. 1993. *Jawa Tengah dalam Angka, 1992.* Semarang: Central Java Government Statistical Office.

Kantor Statistik Propinsi Jawa Timur. 1981. *Statistik Jawa Timur, 1980* (East Java Statistics, 1980). Surabaya: East Java Government Statistical Office.

Kompas. 1990. "ICMI Jaring Cendekiawan Konsep Minimal" (ICMI: The Minimal Concept of an Intellectual Network). December 5.

Kuntowijoyo. 1991. *Paradigma Islam: Interpretasi Untuk Aksi* (Islamic Paradigms: Interpretation for Action). Bandung: Mizan.

Labrousse, Pierre, and Farida Soemargono. 1985. "De l'Islam comme morale du développement: L'action des bureaux de propagation de la fois (Lembaga Dakwah) vue de Surabaya." In M. Bonneff, H. Chambert-Loir, Denys Lombard, and Christian Pelras, eds., *L'Islam en Indonésie,* pp. 219–228. Special edition of *Archipel,* no. 30. Paris: Association Archipel.

Lev, Daniel S. 1990. "Intermediate Classes and Change in Indonesia: Some Initial Reflections." In Richard Tanter and Kenneth Young, eds., *The Politics of Middle Class Indonesia,* pp. 25–43. Clayton, Australia: Centre of Southeast Asian Studies, Monash University.

Liddle, R. William. 1973. "Modernizing Indonesian Politics." In Liddle, ed., *Political Participation in Modern Indonesia,* pp. 177–206. Monograph Series No. 19. New Haven: Southeast Asia Studies, Yale University.

Lombard, Denys. 1990. *Le carrefour javanais: Essai d'histoire globale.* 3 vols. Paris: EHESS.

Lyon, M. L. 1977. "Politics and Religious Identity: Genesis of a Javanese-Hindu Movement in Rural Central Java." Ph.D. dissertation, Department of Anthropology, University of California, Berkeley.

MacDougall, John James. 1975. "Technocrats as Modernizers: The Economists of Indonesia's New Order." Ph.D. dissertation, Department of Political Science, University of Michigan.

Mackie, Jamie. 1990. "Money and the Middle Class." In Richard Tanter and Kenneth Young, eds., *The Politics of Middle Class Indonesia,* pp. 96–122. Clayton, Australia: Centre of Southeast Asian Studies, Monash University.

Madjid, Nurcholish. 1984. *Islam Kemodernan dan Ke-Indonesiaan* (Islam, Modernity, and Indonesianness). Bandung: Mizan.

————. 1992. *Islam, Doktrin, dan Peradaban* (Islam, Doctrine, and Civilization). Jakarta: Paramadina.

————. 1993. "Mengkaji Ulang Pembaruan Pemikiran Islam" (Rethinking the Renewal of Islamic Thought). *Ulumul Qur'an* 4 (1): 1–23.

Mahasin, Aswab. 1990. "The Santri Middle Class: An Insider's View." In Richard Tanter and Kenneth Young, eds., *The Politics of Middle Class Indonesia*, pp. 138–144. Clayton, Australia: Centre of Southeast Asian Studies, Monash University.

Martin, David. 1990. *Tongues of Fire: The Explosion of Protestantism in Latin America*. Oxford: Blackwell.

Mulkhan, Abdul Munir. 1992. *Runtuhnya Mitos Politik Santri* (The Collapse of the Myth of *Santri* Politics). Yogyakarta: SIPress.

Munson, Henry. 1988. *Islam and Revolution in the Middle East*. New Haven: Yale University Press.

Mutalib, Hussin. 1990. *Islam and Ethnicity in Malay Politics*. Singapore: Oxford University Press.

Noer, Deliar. 1987. *Partai Islam di Pentas Nasional* (Muslim Parties on the National Stage). Jakarta: Grafiti Pers.

Oakley, Francis. 1991. "Christian Obedience and Authority: 1520–1550." In J. H. Burns, ed., *The Cambridge History of Political Thought, 1450–1700*, pp. 159–192. Cambridge: Cambridge University Press.

Pelita. 1990. "Hari Ini President Soeharto Buka Simposium Cendekiawan" (Today President Suharto Opens an Intellectual Symposium). December 6.

Pranowo, Bambang. 1990. "Which Islam and Which Pancasila? Islam and State in Indonesia: A Comment." In Arief Budiman, ed., *State and Civil Society in Indonesia*, pp. 479–502. Clayton, Australia: Centre of Southeast Asian Studies, Monash University.

————. 1991. "Creating Islamic Tradition in Rural Java." Ph.D. dissertation, Department of Anthropology, Monash University.

Putnam, Robert D. 1993. *Making Democracy Work: Civic Traditions in Modern Italy*. Princeton: Princeton University Press.

Rahardjo, M. Dawam. 1995. "Visi Dan Misi Kehadiran ICMI: Sebuah Pengantar" (The Vision and Mission of ICMI: An Introduction). In Rahardjo, ed., *ICMI: Antara Status Quo dan Demokratisasi* [ICMI: Between the Status Quo and Democratization], pp. 25–43. Bandung: Mizan.

Raillon, Francois. 1984. *Les étudiants indonésiens et l'Ordre Nouveau: Politique et idéologie du Mahasiswa Indonesia (1966–1974)*. Paris: Éditions de la Maison des Sciences de l'Homme.

Rasjidi, Muhammad. 1972. *Koreksi Terhadap Drs. Nurcholish Madjid Tentang Sekularisasi* (A Correction to Nurcholish Madjid on Secularization). Jakarta: Bulan Bintang.

————. 1978. "Role of Christian Mission: The Indonesian Experience." *Readings in Islam* 2 (2): 23–28.

Reeve, David. 1985. *Golkar of Indonesia: An Alternative to the Party System.* Singapore: Oxford University Press.

Robison, Richard. 1986. *Indonesia: The Rise of Capital.* ASAA Publication 13. Sydney: Allen & Unwin.

Roy, Olivier. 1994. *The Failure of Political Islam.* Translated by Carol Volk. Cambridge, Mass.: Harvard University Press.

Saefuddin Anshary, Endang. 1973. *Kritik atas Faham dan Gerakan "Pembaruan" Drs. Nurcholish Madjid* (A Criticism of the Concept and Movement for "Renewal" of Nurcholish Madjid). Bandung: Bulan Sabit.

Samson, Allan A. 1971–1972. "Army and Islam in Indonesia." *Pacific Affairs* 44 (4): 545–565.

———. 1973. "Religious Belief and Political Action in Indonesian Islamic Modernism." In R. William Liddle, ed., *Political Participation in Modern Indonesia,* pp. 116–142. Monograph Series No. 19. New Haven: Southeast Asia Studies, Yale University.

Seligman, Adam B. 1992. *The Idea of Civil Society.* New York: Free Press.

Selznick, Philip. 1992. *The Moral Commonwealth: Social Theory and the Promise of Community.* Berkeley and Los Angeles: University of California Press.

Sitompul, Agussalim. 1986. *Pemikiran HMI dan Relevansinya dengan Sejarah Perjuangan Bangsa Indonesia* (The Thought of the Association of Muslim Indonesians and Its Relevance for the History of the Struggle of the Indonesian People). Jakarta: Integrita Dinamika Press.

Sjahrir. 1993. "Habibie, Tek-Ti, dan Teknokrat" (Habibie, High Tech, and Technocrats). *Tempo,* July 3, pp. 86–87.

Stange, Paul. 1986. " 'Legitimate' Mysticism in Indonesia." *Review of Indonesian and Malaysian Affairs* 22 (2): 72–86.

Tamara, M. Nasir. 1985. "Islam as a Political Force in Indonesia: 1965–1985." Occasional paper. Cambridge, Mass.: Center for International Affairs, Harvard University.

Tanja, Victor Immanuel. 1982. *Himpunan Mahasiswa Islam* (The Association of Islamic Students). Jakarta: Sinar Harapan.

Tempo. 1986. "Islam Setelah Asas Tunggal" (Islam after the Asas Tunggal). June 14, p. 16.

Tempo. 1990. "Setelah Boom Sarjana Islam" (After the Boom in Islamic Graduates). December 8, pp. 34–47.

Tempo. 1991. "Demokrasi Kita" (Our Democracy). April 13, pp. 17–27.

Tempo. 1992a. "Beringin Makin Hijau" (The Banyan Tree Is Increasingly Green). October 23, pp. 21–31.

Tempo. 1992b. "Dai-Dai Baru Bak Matahari Terbit" (The Sun Rises on New Islamic Proselytizers). April 11, pp. 14–23.

Tempo. 1993. "Nurcholish Madjid dan Berbagai Jawaban Lain" (Nurcholish Madjid and Several Other Answers). April 3, pp. 14–21.

Wahib, Ahmad. 1981. *Pergolakan Pemikiran Islam: Catatan Harian Ahmad Wahib*

(Islamic Intellectual Turbulence: The Diaries of Ahmad Wahib). Jakarta: LP3ES.

Wahid, Abdurrahman. 1990. "Indonesia's Muslim Middle Class: An Imperative or a Choice?" In Richard Tanter and Kenneth Young, eds., *The Politics of Middle Class Indonesia,* pp. 22–24. Clayton, Australia: Centre of Southeast Asian Studies, Monash University.

Ward, Ken. 1970. *The Foundation of the Partai Muslimin Indonesia.* Ithaca: Modern Indonesia Project, Southeast Asia Program, Cornell University.

————. 1974. *The 1971 Elections in Indonesia: An East Java Case Study.* Papers on Southeast Asia, No. 2. Clayton, Australia: Centre of Southeast Asian Studies, Monash University.

Wertheim, W. F. 1986. "Indonesian Moslems under Sukarno and Suharto: Majority with a Minority Mentality." In B. B. Hering, ed., *Studies on Indonesian Islam,* pp. 15–35. Occasional Paper No. 19. Townsville: Centre for Southeast Asian Studies, James Cook University.

Willis, Avery T. 1977. *Indonesian Revival: Why Two Million Came to Christ.* Pasadena: William Carey.

Woodward, Mark. 1989. *Islam in Java: Normative Piety and Mysticism in the Sultanate of Yogyakarta.* Tucson: University of Arizona Press.

Chapter 4

Traditionalist Islam and the State in Indonesia
THE ROAD TO LEGITIMACY AND RENEWAL

Andrée Feillard

Since the 1980s one of Indonesia's oldest and largest Islamic organizations, Nahdlatul Ulama (NU), has attracted increasing attention. Nahdlatul Ulama (Ar., "Rise of Muslim Scholars") was created in 1926 as a reaction against Muslim reformists who opposed the *ulama*'s authority in the interpretation of religious texts and law, and who condemned popular Islamic practices such as saint worship. Representing economic as well as religious interests, Nahdlatul Ulama soon became an important organization comprising peasants, petty traders, professional religious officials, and politicians from diverse backgrounds. Though support for NU is still primarily rural, Indonesia's recent urban growth has resulted in the organization's absorption of a new urban membership. Since 1984 the NU has been under the leadership of an alliance of *ulama* and intellectuals, including the sons and grandsons of the movement's founders.

The importance of the Nahdlatul Ulama comes from the fact that it has long played a major role in Indonesian politics. When then-president Sukarno banned the party of Muslim reformists, Masyumi, in 1960, the NU was left at the center stage of Indonesian politics as the largest of Muslim parties. Shortly thereafter, the nation witnessed the transfer of power from the communist-friendly Sukarno regime to the staunchly anticommunist regime of General Suharto, who came to power after the destruction of the Indonesian Communist Party (PKI) in 1965–1966 (see Hefner, Chapter 3, this volume). At first Nahdlatul Ulama cooperated with the military and the government in the repression of the PKI. To its disappointment, however, it soon found that its collaboration did not bring the political influence for which party leaders had hoped. A few years into Suharto's "New Order" regime, NU was forced to join forces with its modernist Muslim rivals and become a subordinate component in a unified and politically ineffectual Islamic party, the Partai Persatuan dan Pembangunan (PPP). NU continued to defend its right to play an autonomous role in politics, however, resulting in increased tensions with the government. In 1984, uneasy with this confrontation with the Suharto regime, the NU separated from the PPP and officially withdrew from national politics entirely. NU's withdrawal was seen by many observers as a major victory for the government's "secularization" efforts. Without NU, the PPP, Indonesia's only Islamic party, could no longer claim the *ulama*'s backing, with the result that its support in the Muslim community declined.

In this Chapter I analyze NU's unusual relationship with the state up to the period of its withdrawal from party politics. The NU's cooperation with the Sukarno and then Suharto regimes has not been purely "opportunistic," as some Western scholars have suggested. Instead, it should be seen as the result of both the Sunni tradition of legitimating governmental authority and, equally important, the NU leadership's deep commitment to nationalist ideals. I will also suggest that it was the leadership's inability to maintain cohesion among its membership that prompted them to withdraw from the PPP. I thus disagree with Anderson's conclusion that the NU was "extremely successful" in defending "their own inner core" in the 1970s despite government efforts to depoliticize Muslim organizations (1977, 24). Only as a result of its defensive initiatives has the NU been able slowly to regain the hold it risked losing in the 1980s (Jones 1984).

I also describe the impact of these events on Indonesian religious life in general. Consistent with the observations of certain authors concerning the deepening Islamization of Indonesian society (Abdullah 1987; Hefner 1985, 1987; Pranowo 1991), Islam as a cultural and spiritual activity seems to be prospering more than ever. At the same time, the map of Indonesian Islam has recently been altered with the creation of a government-backed "Association of Indonesian Muslim Intellectuals" (ICMI, see Hefner, Chapter 3, this volume). This new organization has contributed to a blurring of the boundary between traditionalist and reformist Islam, and posed new challenges to independent Muslim organizations like Nahdlatul Ulama.

Nahdlatul Ulama and the State through 1965

Primary concern for religious affairs, the Sunni tradition's characteristic fear of chaos, a fierce defense of Islamic law *(shari'ah)*, together with a readiness to compromise for the sake of national unity—these have been the constant themes of NU's political thinking since its founding. The two proclaimed aims of the NU at the time of its formation in 1926 were to create links among *ulama* and to defend religious life against reformism.

Charity, education, and the promotion of agriculture and commerce were also among its stated objectives. Although nationalism was not mentioned explicitly as one of the aims of the NU, it is clear that already at this time nationalist sentiments were strong among some Muslim scholars. History shows, however, that NU officials acted cautiously throughout this period, intervening in the political arena only when the organization's interests were at stake. Indeed, in 1938 NU provided the colonial government with a rather remarkable measure of legitimation by proclaiming the Netherlands Indies to be an "Islamic realm" *(dar al-Islam)*. They did so on the grounds that Muslims were ministered to by government-sanctioned Islamic officials *(penghulu)* who applied the *shari'ah* (Haidar 1991, 156).

Nationalist rather than purely religious considerations also seem to have influenced NU's alliance with Indonesian political leaders in the final years of the colonial era. In June 1940, for example, at a secret meeting during its fifteenth congress, eleven leading *ulama* agreed to support the nationalist leader Sukarno as president of the future Indonesian state. The other candidate under discussion was Mohammad Hatta, a devout Muslim from Sumatra; he received just one of the eleven votes initially cast (Anam 1985, 112). This support for Sukarno is all the more remarkable because at the time he was publicly expressing sympathy for Islamic reformism and, somewhat paradoxically, for the secular modernization undertaken by the Turkish leader Kemal Atatürk. Sukarno advocated a separation of religion and state, and a Western-style democracy where Muslims would defend their interests through parliament (Noer 1980, 301–304). Though in its newspapers and public statements NU expressed shock and disappointment with Sukarno's secularizing ideas, at no point did it reconsider its June decision to support Sukarno.

Despite its increased self-confidence after it was given a national role during the Japanese occupation, NU's intervention in independence debates in 1945 was marked by a continued willingness to accommodate nationalist values. There are few testimonies to NU's role in the formulation of the constitution and the Pancasila ideology (the state ideology originally formulated under Sukarno's leadership), but a recent oral account of Kyai Masykur, who participated in the preparatory committees, sheds light on the role of some NU leaders. According to Masykur, Sukarno asked the opinion of several Islamic leaders on the principles to be included in the national ideology just before he announced the formulation of the Pancasila on June 1, 1945. Masykur relates how he told Sukarno: "I agree with the principle of humanity, but it has to be just; it should not be allowed to favor one's child while taking action toward others. Because the Prophet said: 'If Fatima steals, I will cut her hand.' And Siti Fatima was the daughter of the Prophet." I have found no evidence to confirm the authenticity of the exchange, but if it is true, we can say there was some collaboration by NU officials in the elaboration of the Pancasila.

Despite its collaboration with nationalist leaders, NU did continue to fight for the principle that *shari'ah* should be the ultimate basis of government. For example, NU leaders strenuously insisted that the "Jakarta Charter" be included in the constitution. The Charter stated that the future republic was to be based on the principle of "Belief in God with the obligation for Muslim believers to follow the *shari'ah* in accordance with the principles of a just and civilized humanity." NU leaders also proposed that the president and vice-president be obliged to be Muslims. Wahid Hasyim showed characteristic flexibility, however, when, one day after the declaration of independence on August 17, 1945, he agreed to drop the Charter from the constitution in the face of continuing objections from Christians in eastern Indonesia, who refused to join a republic based on such explicitly Islamic ideals. Four Muslim leaders, including Wahid, agreed to the compromise. In place of the Charter, Hasyim proposed that the first principle of the Pancasila ideology, which concerns belief in God *(ketuhanan),* be changed by the addition of the words *yang maha esa* ("one and only"). This small adjustment, with its clear sense of monotheistic divinity, brought the principle of belief in God into line with Muslim understandings of *tauhid,* belief in the unity and oneness of God, one of the most central of values for Muslims (Noer 1990, 255).

Wahid Hasyim is reported to have justified his liberal compromise in the following way. First, he said, the circumstances of national struggle required unity in the face of Dutch efforts to reclaim their colony. Second, he believed that "the obligation for Muslims to follow the *shari'ah* would find its place in the honest application of paragraph 29 of the Constitution, which guaranteed every citizen the freedom to profess and practice his religion" (Zuhri 1987, 302). By being satisfied with a paragraph mentioning "freedom" even though the Jakarta Charter mentioned an "obligation," it would appear that Wahid Hasyim had a flexible understanding of the vaguely worded charter, not the strict one feared by some secular and Christian politicians.

Hasyim's position does not seem to have been contested within NU, and the organization reaffirmed its support for the monotheistic republic several times afterwards. At the end of 1953, for example, the *ulama* decided that Sukarno's government would be named *"walliyy'l Amri Dharuri bi'Syaukah,"* a title giving legitimacy to a government in a not-fully-Islamic state. This title provided the Ministry of Religion with the authority it required to handle religious court cases according to *fiqh* (jurisprudential) rules (Haidar 1992, 364–377; Zuhri 1987, 426). The decision was condemned by some Islamic groups because it was seen as hampering efforts to establish an Islamic state in the Constituent Assembly (Lev 1972, 50; Geertz 1960, 212).

Nahdlatul Ulama's continuing cooperation with nationalists was reinforced by its conflict with Muslim reformists in the early 1950s. The decisive moment in the shift occurred shortly after the election in 1950 of Kyai Wahab Hasbullah, a man of great dynamism, to the position of NU's *rois aam* (president-general), after the death of Kyai Hasyim Asy'ari. In his inaugural speech, the outspoken leader from Jombang (in East Java) spoke of NU's power as that of a "cannon" and touched on political matters in an unusually explicit manner (Zuhri 1987, 390). Two years later in 1952, the NU took the bold step of quitting what was then the major Islamic party, Masyumi, an organization that had been established during the Japanese occupation in an effort to unite traditionalists and reformists. NU's action was prompted by its perception that reformists had come to dominate the party (Noer 1987, 101; Abubakar 1957, 478). NU was now determined to work hard to respond to the challenge of the more cosmopolitan and better-educated modernists. The organization recruited to its ranks economists, jurists, and businessmen, many of whom had no previous links with NU (Anam 1985, 197). At the same time and with Sukarno's support, NU secured for itself a comfortable position on the political scene and maintained control of the Ministry of Religion. Created on January 3, 1946, the Ministry would remain a pillar of NU strength and a precious source of patronage until the early 1970s.

There were, however, basic differences between the nationalists and NU, most notably with regard to NU's demand for a "national state based on Islam." In practical terms, this formula implied that, except for "administrators," who could be non-Muslims, the head of state and cabinet ministers had to be Muslims. At the same time, religious education would be obligatory, but non-Muslim religions would be respected. A certain degree of autonomy could be given to regions with non-Muslim majorities, NU officials said, "as long as this would not be detrimental to general interest." In defending the Islamic state during debates at the Constituent Assembly, NU remained faithful to its Islamic principles. The debates about Islam versus Pancasila were very tense. Kyai Wahab Hasbullah on occasion even referred to the situation as one of *jahiliya,* a Qur'anic term standing for the state of ignorance before the divine revelation to the Prophet (Bonneff et al. 1980, 133).

In the end, Islam failed to obtain the two-thirds majority required to change the constitution, and in 1959 NU leaders accepted a presidential decree in favor of a return to the 1945 non-Islamic constitution with vague concessions to the Jakarta Charter. In explaining this pragmatism, Greg Fealey has pointed to the application of the *fiqh* rule that avoidance of harm *(mafsadah)* must take precedence over the seeking of benefit *(masla-hat)* (1992, 8). Indeed, in the Sunni tradition of legitimation, political chaos must in general be avoided. In this instance, Kyai Wahab was convinced that the *ummat* (the Muslim community) was not ready for a confrontation with the government. NU did not want to miss the opportunity to carry out its function of *"amar ma'ruf nahi munkar,"* which is to say, "to work for good and combat evil" (Zuhri 1987, 484).

The question arises, however, as to why NU had become so wary of Pancasila fourteen years after having accepted it as the national ideology. It seems that, besides NU's understandable preference for a state based on Islam, many Muslims had come to see the Pancasila as an ideology whose real intent was to defend Javanese mysticism, which most pious Muslims condemned as *shirk* or polytheistic associationism. In addition, despite its emphasis on belief in God, the Pancasila had not proved to be as effective a shield as Muslims had hoped against the Communist Party, which had showed astounding strength in the 1955 elections, winning 16.4 percent of the votes as opposed to NU's 18.4 percent.

The years following the 1955 elections brought Nahdlatul Ulama closer to Sukarno. The abolition of parliamentary democracy and the turn to an executive-dominated "Guided Democracy" in the late 1950s was not opposed by many NU politicians. Thus, NU chairman Idham Chalid explained that one had to understand that democracy was not "a target in itself" and could have limits "for the sake of the people's well-being." There were also patronage ties binding Sukarno to Kyai Wahab. This close cooperation was evident when Sukarno dropped corruption charges against Wahib Wahab, minister of religion and Kyai Wahab's son, in exchange for a personal favor—namely, that the new minister of religion, a member of NU, should sanction the president's marriage to a third wife, Haryati, despite strong public disapproval (Zuhri 1987, 531). After the disastrous events of 1965–1966 and the transfer of emergency powers from Sukarno to General Suharto, as late as June 1966, Kyai Wahab declared that NU would continue to support Sukarno as its candidate for president in all future elections.

NU *and the "New Order": 1965 to the 1980s*

The attempted coup of September 1965 was the climax of mounting tensions between the Communist Party and pro-Western generals, but it came as a shock nonetheless to Nahdlatul Ulama. Despite its active participation in the violent anticommunist repression that left half a million people dead, the NU reacted ambiguously to the political rearrangements that resulted from the coup. Whereas some older NU leaders remained loyal to Sukarno, younger leaders in parliament helped General Suharto's rise to power by providing him with support in the parliament (DPR) and the People's Consultative Assembly (MPR). Despite this critical assistance, the new regime imposed greater controls on NU than the "Old Order" had ever attempted. Tensions with the authorities ran high over the establishment of a new political system and an army-backed political party, Golkar, which proved to be a powerful rival in the following legislative elections held in 1971 (see Hefner, Chapter 3, this volume). The same year, for the first time since 1952, the key position of minister of religion was not given to an NU official. In addition, in 1973, NU was forced to merge with other Islamic parties into a single party, the PPP. Thoughout all these developments, NU was torn between obvious frustration and the awareness that it could not afford to antagonize the government.

Nonetheless, NU did challenge the government on several occasions: in 1974, when it opposed civil marriage for Muslims and restrictions on polygamy; in 1978, with its rejection of government attempts to give mystical groups equal standing with officially recognized religions; and in 1980, when it demanded participation in elections control and the maintenance of the *ka'bah* as the PPP's party logo. As a result of such initiatives, radical NU politicians were barred from the 1982 legislative elections. Shortly thereafter, other NU politicians were excluded from the PPP board.

This tense relationship underwent dramatic changes after 1983–1984. At that time NU withdrew its formal support for the PPP, freed its followers from any obligation to support the Muslim party, and issued a regulation banning NU executives from holding executive positions in the PPP (this last regulation, however, was not vigorously enforced). As a result of these policies, the PPP's monopoly on Islamic support was broken, giving the government-supported party, Golkar, a greater chance to woo Muslim supporters. This withdrawal of NU from party politics was popularly referred to as a return to the *khittah* (spirit) of 1926. One proponent of the move was NU's foremost intellectual, the grandson of NU's founding father Hasyim Asy'ari and son of Wahid Hasyim, Abdurrahman Wahid. In 1984, he was elected president of NU's executive body, the Tanfidziyah.

The *khittah* was basically a return to moderation. In a well-publicized speech in 1982, Kyai Ali Ma'sum, NU's president-general, had asked government officials why relations between the government and the NU were so bad at the national level, yet the NU had never rebelled and had always supported development in the villages. According to my own interviews with

NU officials, the organization received some four hundred letters in 1983 alone asking why relations with the government had been allowed to worsen. Interviews reveal that one of the main reasons for the reorientation away from the PPP was to reduce tensions with the government and create a more peaceful environment in which the organization's social and religious activities could operate unencumbered. The growing tensions with the authorities and the NU leadership's neglect of social activities had seriously weakened the organization's mass base, creating, among other things, a widening gap between the older leadership and the younger membership. As Kyai Machrus Ali said, the NU had "given in to its thirst for power" while neglecting its social programs (Yusuf et al. 1983, 122–125).

This new spirit of pragmatism was dramatically demonstrated when, in 1983, President Suharto requested that all mass organizations in Indonesia formally accept the Pancasila ideology into their statutes as their "sole principle" *(asas tunggal)*. Before this time the Pancasila had been regarded as Indonesia's national ideology, but independent social organizations were not required to endorse it. Despite widespread Christian and Muslim opposition to the government scheme, the initiative came at a time when the NU was deeply divided regarding its political options, and it had the unintended effect of strengthening the hand of moderates in the organization. The moderates were unhappy with the leadership of the putatively Islamic political party, the PPP, and saw the government scheme as a means to withdraw support from the PPP with government support. A formula was elaborated and justified with *fiqh* (Islamic jurisprudence) rules by Kyai Achmad Siddiq, a senior *ulama* from Jember in East Java, who was elected *rois aam* in 1984. Interviews indicate that Kyai Siddiq acted with the support of other senior *ulama,* such as Kyai As'ad of Situbondo, Kyai Machrus Ali of Kediri, Kyai Masykur of Jakarta, and Kyai Ali Ma'sum of Yogyakarta. In NU's new statutes, the Pancasila was cited as a principle *(asas),* while Islam was cited as a faith *(aqidah)*. The formula cleverly accepted the government ideology while clothing its precise relationship to Islam in an aura of vagueness.

NU's willingness to cooperate with the government now went even further, to include the organization's dramatic endorsement of the idea that Indonesia was, and should remain, a non-Islamic state. In its 1983 national conference, NU officials proclaimed that the "values which have become the foundation of the Indonesian republic have been finalized with the Constitution of the 18th of August 1945." Although it escaped the attention of the national press, this sentence was basically a reiteration of the August 18, 1945, abandonment of the Jakarta Charter. Kyai Siddiq, it now seemed, was intent on returning traditionalist Islam to its role as the "people of the middle," a people of moderation (Siddiq 1985, 14).

Kyai Siddiq was preoccupied with perfecting NU's integration into the Indonesian nation, pushing the *ummat* to come to terms with the meanings of the modern state and nationalism, and reconciling faith with modernity. He thought of NU as a "pioneer" that was to integrate the Muslim community into the Indonesian nation-state once and for all (Siddiq 1985, 27). To perfect this ideal unitary state, Siddiq advocated fraternity *(ukhuwah)* both within the Muslim *ummat* and with the non-Muslim community (p. 25). This was, one should note, a daring stance at the time. Many Muslims were deeply resentful of the government's efforts to impose the Pancasila, and general tensions between the government and Muslims had exploded in several incidents, such as the bloody Tanjung Priok riots in Jakarta three months before the 1984 NU congress.

In all these initiatives NU demonstrated a remarkable inventiveness and flexibility with regard to Islamic political ideals. Though it did not abandon *shari'ah* outright, neither did it mention it explicitly. However, the 1984 reorientation was entirely consistent with NU's 1945 vision of an independent unitary Indonesia that should include non-Muslims as well as Muslims. The Indonesian *ulama* were once again demonstrating their independence of thought in adapting to political realities.

The political consequences of the 1984 reorientation became clearer in 1987, with the astounding electoral defeat of the nominally Islamic political party, the PPP, in large part as a result of the loss of NU's backing. From a total of 27.8 percent of the vote in the previous election, the PPP obtained only 16 percent of the vote (a 27.5 percent drop compared to the Muslim vote in 1955). The fact that Muslim regions with small NU memberships also provided only weak support for the PPP (in West Sumatra the PPP lost 19 percent of the vote; in Aceh, it lost 15.71 percent) indicates that the NU was not the only factor in the party's defeat. One can also cite the disenchantment with the PPP chief's authoritarian style, the PPP's loss of Muslim identity after its acceptance of the *asas tunggal,* and the impressive election efforts of Golkar's powerful chairman Sudharmono.

As for NU, it was left with only twenty-two seats scattered among several political parties in parliament. Not surprisingly, NU politicians who regretted the loss of political influence and benefits launched stern attacks against Wahid in 1987. He survived their onslaught at the November 1987 Cilacap conference. As an example of how the conference atmosphere favored the nonpolitical orientation, let me relate a small incident. When an older activist, Professor Ali Hassan Achmad Addary, bluntly expressed his angry disappointment with the government and spoke in a nostalgic tone of the golden age when NU members were also government officials, there was an embarrassing silence in the conference hall. Ali Hassan was allowed to continue his diatribe, but afterward there was not so much as a single comment on it. There was, it seems, good reason for this lack of support. Overall, the benefits of the reorientation seemed thus far to outweigh its losses.

Gains and Losses: The Impact of the Reorientation

Nahdlatul Ulama suffered in many ways during the first years of the New Order. A 1970 ban on civil servants' association with any political party other than Golkar and the formation of a corps of civil servants (Korps Karyawan Pegawai Republik Indonesia) had the combined effect of depriving the NU of its influential backbone in the bureaucracy (Ward 1974, 109). An unknown number of activists in the women's group (Muslimat), the youth group Ansor, and other NU affiliates started to give back their membership cards. Furthermore, strict surveillance by the authorities dissuaded less militant members from pursuing organizational involvements. In Surabaya, recalls one local leader, "when fifteen activists were invited to NU meetings, five would show up besides seven policemen in plain clothes." Later, the fusion of Muslim parties into the government-organized PPP had the additional effect of discouraging militants primarily supportive of NU but not the PPP. Although activities picked up slightly after 1979, they were often still hampered by bad relations with the authorities. For example, before 1984, NU's women's association, the Muslimat, was not given the official green light for cooperation with the government's education program for family welfare (Pendidikan Kesejahteraan Keluarga).

As a result of such exclusion and pressure by the government, local representation bureaus within NU were reduced to ceremonial activities without recruitment of a younger generation of cadres. Many bureaus had functioned unchanged for nine years. Within NU's youth organization, Ansor, only twelve of the twenty-five provincial bureaus showed signs of activity (Nahdlatul Ulama 1987, 100). At a conference in 1991, my conference notes indicate, one delegate complained that Ansor had been "sleeping" for too many years, at which another delegate joked that it had not only been sleeping, but it had been "dead."

The most remarkable consequence of the new relationship with the authorities after 1984 has been a return to the organization of civil servants, who were among the first to have left in the 1970s. Now, civil servants participate in the organization not only as members but as cadres. In 1992 many provincial bureaus were controlled by membership recruited from the civil service. In Bengkulu, 60 percent of the provincial bureau was made up of civil servants; the figure was 75 percent in East Java, 70 percent in South Sulawesi, and 60 percent in Central Sulawesi. In West Nusatenggara in 1991, the NU executive chairman was first assistant to the governor. The same trend exists within the Muslimat, where more activists are now civil servants or wives of civil servants. While some civil servants dare to affiliate with the organization, others only reveal their former affiliation to it. Thus, Buchori Masruri, head of the NU executive board in Central Java, commented to me, "Now, the district chief *(camat)* tells us: 'My father was NU, so, I am also part of NU.' People come out and say they used to belong to us."

Better relations with the authorities have also translated into a greater readiness from officials at both national and local levels to attend NU-organized ceremonies. During the Fatayat (NU's organization of young girls) congress in 1986, six ministers attended the inauguration ceremony. Most important, permits for all kinds of activities have become easier to acquire. Zainut Tauhid, chairman of NU's young men's association (Ikatan Pemuda Nahdlatul Ulama), said that in the past permits had to be requested four weeks in advance of meetings; nowadays, a week is sufficient. In almost all provinces, the NU cooperates with the authorities on various development projects. In Bengkulu, for example, the governor has made available 350 hectares for ginger plantations. In South Kalimantan, the governor has promised a fifty million rupiah (U.S.$23,000) donation for the construction of a mosque in Banjarmasin. Besides cooperation in economic matters and donation for religious purposes, cooperation has started for the training of NU militia (Banzer Ansor) by the army. This kind of cooperation is much sought after, but a lack of funds, says the military, hampers more training. Ansor has also signed a memorandum of understanding with the powerful "youth movement of the children of armed forces personnel" (Forum Komunikasi Putra-Putri Purnawirawan Abri). Plans have been readied for joint management courses, cooperative courses, and music festivals. (My interviews indicate, however, that thus far little appears to have been done to realize these goals). NU officials are also regularly consulted on religious matters. For example, before spreading more toward East Java, the Mathahil Anwar, a government-led *pesantren* (Islamic boarding school) association, inquired about NU sensitivities.

The honeymoon between NU and the government seems, however, to have limits. While relations with the authorities have improved significantly, local authorities in some regions keep a close watch on NU officials; it is also clear that the relationship can be reevaluated at almost any time. Thus, in Bali, the new bureau failed to be recognized by the local military authorities in 1991. In North Sulawesi, the provincial administration "advised" NU to hold its regional conference after the 1992 elections. The West Kalimantan branch failed to obtain the promised construction of a bridge leading to a *pesantren* in an isolated area, in part, it seems, because the local NU leadership still supported the PPP. Neither the regent nor the governor came to inaugurate their regional conference in 1991. In general, however, local NU leaders have been eager to improve relations with the government. In Linggarjati and in Lampung, many delegates asked that Abdurrahman Wahid come to their province to smooth relations with the local authorities.

The slow but constant recovery of NU's membership following the 1984 political reorientation is difficult to assess statistically. In 1971, the NU won 10.2 million votes, or 18.67 percent of the Indonesian electorate. After its (government-mandated) fusion with the PPP, there was no way of directly assessing the traditionalist movement's electoral strength. NU officials have no precise registration data: Idham Chalid rightly compared the NU to a *pesantren salaf,* an old-style Qur'anic school where students would come and go without any registration. A recent registration drive has, as yet, also produced no figures. The man in charge, Chafidz Usman, estimates the NU has forty million sympathizers. A look at the temporary registration figures available in the provinces seems to indicate that this figure may be over-blown. Certain regions are doing well in their registration, such as East Java, a long time NU stronghold, where as of 1991 1.2 million members had been registered, for an estimated total of seven million supporters. The figure may seem low, but a distinction must be made between active members and people indirectly associated with the movement, through family ties or reverence for religious leaders. Other regions, however, lag behind the East Java rebound. An extreme example is Aceh, where twenty *pesantren* are identified as "potential NU affiliates." The local leader reported to me in January of 1992 that he no longer dares to approach these *pesantren,* since they "have survived by their own means for too long without NU help."

Comparison can be made with NU's women's organization, the Muslimat, the best-organized of NU affiliates. This organization had already registered 1.2 million members in East and Central Java by 1991, compared to the 3.5 million members it had for the whole of Indonesia before 1971. Even though the number of members is still low compared to the earlier period, the recovery seems substantial. Indeed the Muslimat is today considered one of the most influential women's organizations in Indonesia and, as such, has been asked to participate in childcare programs by UNICEF. The organization in charge of NU's *pesantren,* the Robithotul Maahidil

Islamiyah (RMI), is also slowly regaining strength. At a national meeting of *pesantren* in early 1991, 120 *pesantren* participated, although few came from outside Java. Conversely, however, by 1987, the mosques' organization Hai'ah Ta'miril Masajid Indonesia (HTMI), had only succeeded in setting up two bureaus in Java. Its leaders complained that many mosques were still afraid to display the NU symbol "in this still uncertain environment."

NU is thus recovering its organizational strength, but at a pace that varies widely depending on region and the strength of local affiliates. Many obstacles remain. Some older religious leaders blame the slowness of the recovery on a diminution of the social pressures that, in the first half of the twentieth century, motivated people to join the organization. For example, in earlier times a Muslim had to have his NU membership card to be sure to benefit from the *tahlil* prayers recited at his funeral. In East Java, an NU membership card was regarded as the equivalent of a national ID or could even replace a driver's license, says Kyai Safeii Sulaiman. Today, however, many younger activists believe that the image of NU as part of the "opposition" is a major handicap. A Jambi delegate commented to me, "People keep considering us part of PPP, and civil servants are still hesitant to join us."

The Impact on Education

One of the New Order's most enduring priorities has been the development of a modern educational system. Given the large number of school children and limited national resources, government policy has sought to coordinate governmental activities with those of private schools, including Islamic ones. The share of the private sector in Islamic education decreases with the age of the children and their weight in society. In 1988, out of the three million primary school children going to Islamic schools *(madrasah ibtidaiyah)* (another 25.5 million went to non-Islamic schools), only 6 percent went to state-supported Islamic schools. However, according to 1991 figures, the government provides support for 29 percent of public Islamic junior high schools *(madrasah tsanawiyah)*, 46 percent for public Islamic senior high schools *(madrasah aliyah)*, and 74.6 percent for public Islamic universities (IAIN).

While the government's share in Islamic education has increased, NU's share seems to have suffered. NU officials estimate that 85 percent of all private *madrasah*s have some kind of ties to their organization. Nonetheless, in 1991, only some five thousand *madrasah*s, or 16.8 percent of the total, were registered with NU's educational institute, the Lembaga Pendidikan Maarif. It appears that in the early 1970s local government pressures led many schools to drop their identification panels, no longer showing their affiliation with the NU. Certain schools chose names only indirectly identifiable as associated with the NU, like Wahid Hasyim school, named after the former NU leader and minister of religion. For similar reasons, the NU University renamed itself Universitas Sunan Giri in 1972.

It would be wrong, however, to attribute NU's weakened position to administrative pressures alone; neglect among militants, more and more interested in politics rather than education, also played a role. Hasyim Latief, a leading NU activist in East Java, worried about the decline of NU's educational institute as early as the 1970s. According to him, 30 percent of the *madrasah*s had already left the LP Maarif at that time. After 1984, the institute issued a new regulation asking its former *madrasah*s to show their NU identity and to register with NU's education body. There has been a response, but so far it is only a small one. This reluctance seems related to several factors: the traditional independence of rural religious leaders, the lack of organization of the LP Maarif, and, most important, the latter organization's lack of funds. Indeed, schools formerly tied to the NU cannot expect much financially from the old organization; more often they turn for funds to the Ministry of Religion.

Nahdlatul Ulama's *pesantren* association, the RMI, has faced another type of obstacle in its efforts to revive its national organization: Saudi Arabian influence. Islamic schools established by graduates of Saudi schools are sometimes suspicious of Nahdlatul Ulama. In addition to doctrinal differences, tensions arise because of NU's willingness to accept Western aid. Since more and more young Islamic scholars now study in Saudi Arabia, this problem may well get worse. In an effort to deal with the problem, NU officials would like to arrange studies in Saudi Arabia on their own and maintain better contact with students during their residence there. It should be noted, however, that Saudi influence is not always detrimental to NU interests. Several young scholars who studied in the holy land remain active in the organization.

In financial terms, NU schools have benefited significantly from their new relationship with government authorities. Subsidies going directly to religious schools have increased. According to Muzlih, an executive of NU's *pesantren* board in East Java, subsidies to NU schools in that province were four times greater in 1990 than they were before 1984. The Ministry of Religion has also indicated that it plans to embark upon a major renovation of Islamic primary schools worth U.S.$20 million from 1991 through 1995. Twenty-five percent of Islamic junior high schools *(tsanawiyah)* should receive six million rupiah (about $1,800) each for building renovations. *Pesantren* have also received new aid: sixty recently received 600,000 rupiah each ($275). During my field observation in East and Central Java, I visited two new *pesantren* (al-Azhar in Bangil and al-Muhsin in Yogyakarkta), whose initial capital had come from government subsidies. Government assistance to other *pesantren* I visited included everything from medical equipment to the awarding of medals of honor. Acceptance of this assistance is indicative of the more relaxed relationship between the government and religious scholars.

Naturally, with the greater government funds, the potential exists for government interference in educational affairs. The government's share in Islamic education may well increase in coming years, as more and more religious schools with troubled finances ask for state aid in the form of takeovers. Already by 1991, for example, the Ministry of Religion had received some one thousand letters from *madrasah*s asking for such intervention. In 1991 alone, according to Zamakhsyari Dhofier, director for the development of Islamic institutions in the Ministry of Religion, 120 *madrasah*s became public schools; another hundred are likely to follow suit in 1992. Both the state and private education profit from the situation: the latter gets a new vigor, while the former has more leeway to interfere in private religious education.

After NU leaders were no longer awarded leadership of the Ministry of Religion in 1971, the organization's influence over the thousands of religious teachers in state-supported religious schools (*madrasah*s) also diminished. One consequence was that many teachers began to provide religious instruction closer in substance to reformist than traditionalist views. The same tendency was evident in religious textbooks published by the Ministry of Religion. Some of these textbooks are simply put aside by the local religious teachers, who regard them as too sympathetic to the reformist doctrine.

A new measure of government control is also evident in the Ministry of Religion's nomination of *madrasah* directors. In 1991, 30 percent of NU schools already had government-appointed directors. NU has asked its *madrasah*s to resist the trend, but dependence on government subsidies has had more weight than the recommendations of NU leaders. Another development, considered an annoyance by some NU militants, is the holding of more exams by the ministry, under a program that began at the end of the 1980s. East Java was still resisting the trend in 1991. Some NU schools have also sought to escape the Ministry of Religion's hold by declaring themselves nonreligious schools and thus falling under the competence of the Ministry of Education. Thirty schools, mostly in East Java, have already taken such a tack, though most maintain a religious "supplement" to preserve a religious character. Militants in NU who complain about government intervention, interestingly, do so largely for reasons of doctrine (defense of rituals, and schools of law or *madzhab*) and institutional autonomy rather than politics alone.

Overall, however, the new relationship with the authorities has created an atmosphere of openness that both sides see as beneficial. Young religious leaders are happy to see that the *pesantren* curriculum is modernizing, thus opening them to socioeconomic progress. More nonreligious subjects are being taught in religious schools (Thomas 1988, 903). To improve the curriculum, other programs have been established with the ministries of Industry, Labor, Education, and Religion. A few pioneer *pesantren* even provide courses on family planning, family welfare, and reproductive health.

There is a growing willingness among teachers in Islamic schools to accept the state-recommended curriculum, and thus the state exams that students are eager to take (these are necessary for later enrollment in universities). Already in the 1970s, the Ministry of Religion offered state recognition to those *madrasah*s ready to increase the content of their general curriculum and to reduce religion courses to 30 percent of the total. This increase in general subjects was designed to facilitate the later enrollment of *pesantren* students in schools of higher education. In an interview in 1992, Zamakhsyari Dhofier indicated that the government plans to reduce to 22 percent the religious education content in 90 percent of all *madrasah*s. To counterbalance this reduction, the ministry intends to have a few of the best religious schools specialize in and improve religious education; for example, it has encouraged five *madrasah aliyah* (senior high schools) to offer a 70 percent religion curriculum. In Bangil, a region in East Java known for its religious conservatism, seven of thirteen NU-affiliated *pesantren* prepared state exams in 1991, including two who had done so only in the past year. Some, however, like the *pesantren* Salafiyyah, still dare not take this step for fear of breaking with tradition. Paradoxically, however, this last *pesantren* offers courses in English and journalism, and also an intensive eight-month course for girls who want to try to take state exams.

With this cooperation between NU and the government, state officials also find it easier to promote two of their most important initiatives, family planning and the Pancasila ideology. During my visits to Bangil, East Java, for example, I found that the majority of the *pesantren* had recently established Pancasila civic education courses (P4); only two schools in the area still refused the courses. K.H. Siraji of the *pesantren* Nurud Dlolam welcomed official visits to his *pesantren* but explained his unwillingness to sponsor Pancasila courses in the following terms: "When one knows religion, one can apply the P4. Everything is already in the religion." At the *pesantren* Salafiyyahal-Fatah, Malang, the response was similar: "Everything is already there in Islam, and our founding fathers did participate in the definition of Pancasila." Neither of the two seemed to suffer from strained relations or reprisals from the authorities for this stance. Outside the *pesantren*, NU activists also appear eager to participate in P4 training; some have even begun to serve as instructors and teaching cadre *(mandala)*. Ansor has begun to send more and more of its members to participate in the longest and most advanced P4 course, which requires 145 hours of classroom study. Every year, eight Ansor people attend these "super-P4" courses, whereas formerly the government limited the number to two people. Saifullah Maksum, Ansor secretary-general, says that NU activists who have followed these courses have become "true national leaders because their horizons have widened." With their ascension into these cadre positions, the NU has come closer to the symbolic core of the New Order.

Overall, NU's response to efforts to promote the national ideology has been positive. In 1991 the *pesantren* association (RMI) decided to introduce civic education *(wawasan kebangsaan)* into the *pesantren* curriculum. No objection was raised at the RMI national conference in Gresik in 1991, when the proposal was made. For its part, the government has shown some sensitivity to Muslim concerns about the content of the Pancasila courses. Recently, the director of P4 education (Prajitno) told me that the government intended to develop a "Pancasila course according to Islam." He also noted that, as of 1991, some 64 million of Indonesia's 185 million people had followed some kind of Pancasila course.

The Impact on Religious Predication

Significant changes have also taken place in the field of Islamic predication or *dakwah*. This field has always been susceptible to extensive government interference because of official concerns about the content of public speeches. NU preachers have long complained about restrictions on their freedom of speech; according to NU reports, some 10 percent of NU preachers indicate that they once had regular difficulties with authorities. Now, however, especially since 1987, NU officials have noticed that the religious conferences *(pengajian umum)* that used to require permits require only a note of information to the Office for Religious Affairs in a district or no notification at all. In years past, conferences held without prior permit might result in arrests. Nowadays there is also a freer circulation of preachers throughout the country: permits to move within a regency *(kabupaten)* are no longer necessary. In the early 1980s, a Yogyakarta activist would have to make several trips to Jakarta to get a permit to invite a preacher—a costly affair. For the Muslimat, only if fifty or more people are to be present must they give advance notice of a gathering to the authorities. Even during the general election campaign of 1987, according to one Muslimat activist, public recitations of the Qur'an *(pengajian)* could be held, a remarkable departure from earlier times. One notable leftover from the earlier system, however, is that, when a preacher goes to speak in another province, the text of the speech is still required in advance of the meeting.

One middle-aged religious leader from Lampung summarized the situation to me in the following words: "We are not yet very close to the government—this is all new for us—but we feel some relaxation as far as *dakwah* is concerned. Permits are easier to get. Often, we no longer need them. Now the people are calm, they no longer feel that they are distrusted, they are no longer afraid." According to a delegate from Tasikmalaya, there are now five times more *dakwah* activities in his region. In Bengkulu, as long as one is part of the *dakwah* group headed by the military (Korem), one can travel throughout the entire province to preach. In Yogyakarta, a young *dakwah* group, the Kodama, says the local authorities recently entrusted them with the administration of a *musholla* (prayer house) and a rehabilitation center for the blind and invalid. K.H. Fuad Hasyim, of the *pesantren* Buntet Cirebon, commented to me that the 1984 reversal is very profitable from the point of view of predication, though he conceded restrictions remain in place for the "hardliners who have not endorsed the *khittah* spirit" of moderation.

Preachers and religious teachers *(kyai)* appear pleased that NU has gained a new legitimacy through its cooperation with authorities. This legitimacy is expressed by the presence of officials at NU ceremonies, by the lending of government buildings for religious meetings and by the government's allowing NU officials to lead official ceremonies. In 1989 a major *semaan* (recitation of the Qur'an by heart by a young man while the audience follows the text in the holy book) was organized at the sultan's palace in Yogyakarta. In 1991 another *semaan* took place in the headquarters of the military command in Surabaya (Kodam) for the inauguration of the extension of a mosque in the complex.

With this new public legitimacy, NU audience has also widened. Now, civil servants dare to come to Qur'anic recitations. As Buchori Masruri of Central Java explained: "Before Situbondo, civil servants liked to listen to our preachers, but they did not dare do so. Only PPP supporters listened to us. Now even Golkar listens and top officials too." Indeed, in general religious ceremonies have become more fashionable in Indonesian society. Saiful Mujab, a leader in Yogyakarta, commented that "people feel obliged to join Golkar/NU *pengajian* because it is the *lurah* (village chief) who invites them. All who say they are Muslims feel obliged to come. There are

50 percent more people who come, not only NU people but also the *aban-gan* [nonpracticing or mystically inclined Muslims], those who do not pray but who want to learn the texts."

NU's audience has also broadened because the organization's appeals are no longer as political as they used to be. Some preachers have also stopped revealing their affiliation with NU, a strategy that seems especially popular in urban areas, where NU's image is not as prestigious as in rural areas. Zuhdi Mukhdlor of the Kodama commented to me, "When we do not identify ourselves as NU, we feel freer in our mission and we are better accepted." Even the president of NU's predication institute (Lembaga Dak-wah NU), K.H. Syukron Makmun, a popular orator even in Malaysia and Brunei, observed: "Since Situbondo, we no longer proclaim our NU identity in our sermons. In the past, this was a 'must' for electoral purposes. Now I know that those who come to listen to me at the mosque are not always from NU. If I say I am NU, I know the others will go away." In August 1991 K.H. Syukron told me that as a result of these changes he now senses a stronger sense of Islamic fraternity across doctrinal divides, as evidenced in the fact that he is often invited to Muhammadiyah meetings. It appears that the most popular preachers nowadays have NU origins or education but make a point of not revealing that background to the public. Thus, for example, few people know that Zainuddin MZ, the Muslim "superstar" preacher who gives as many as four sermons a day and has a huge organization in sixteen provinces, has strong NU ties: He was a pupil of K.H. Idham Chalid. Although this strategy of not highlighting one's ties to NU is of little benefit to the organization, it is very beneficial for the wider Islamization of the country.

NU's own *dakwah* activities have not been extensively coordinated by the organization leadership. Indeed, in recent years the NU leadership seems to have been more concerned with economic assistance and community development than with predication per se. Abdurrahman Wahid has commented that he wants to emphasize the quality rather than the quantity of Indonesian Muslims. There have been sporadic complaints that the NU preachers were less organized than their counterparts from the modernist Muhammadiyah. NU's Predication Institute, the LDNU, reported in 1987 that only one province had responded to its appeal to create a representative organization. Since then, LDNU's chairman, K.H. Syukron Makmun, has intensified his efforts. The greatest response has come from Indonesia's outer islands. Since 1989 a fifteen-day course for seventy-five to one hundred people has been organized every three months to improve the general and religious knowledge of preachers. In 1990 NU sent twenty-five preachers to transmigration regions, part of a government plan to send one thousand such preachers to remote areas. There is already a considerable improvement over the 1960s and 1970s when NU's predication institution Missi Islam sent out only one or two preachers.

Women too have been prominent in *dakwah* activities. The Muslimat and Fatayat (NU's girls association) say they now feel they are taken more seriously by the government. It has asked their support in disseminating the government's message in matters of education and family planning, the environment, and economic cooperatives. The Fatayat also has many active female preachers; in fact, each branch usually has ten or more. The Fatayat organizes predication courses every week.

Student groups like Kodama have also been quite active. The group now has 180 preachers working in forty-eight regions. They say they have noticed the impact of their work in the multiplication of mosques in their region and the disappearance of dogs (prohibited by the Shafi'i school of law). Moreover, ordinary citizens have become active in *majelis ta'lim,* spontaneous *dakwah* groups organized in neighborhoods. Two hundred neighbors are enough to create a *majelis ta'lim.* They are multiplying everywhere in Indonesia. In Yogyakarta, says Saiful Mujab, "there used to be two or three such groups ten years ago, but now there are hundreds of them." The *majelis ta'lim,* sometimes developing outside the NU structure, can keep in touch with the *pesantren* by asking the advice of *ulama* on controversial religious issues. Young Ansor activists have commented that they fear that the *majelis ta'lim,* which increasingly take the initiative in *dakwah,* may finally outrace the NU itself.

Overall, however, NU officials concur that their organization has profited from the 1984 reorientation. The legitimacy it has gained has increased its hold on the *ummat.* Although cooperation with the government means sermons have become largely of moral content, NU's orators have continued to criticize corruption, injustice, the national lottery, excessive luxury, and such "Western-imported" problems as alcoholism, narcotics, and sexual freedom. A delegate from Central Java spoke of recent developments in the following way: "Things have changed. Now, we have the same country, the same government. All this belongs to us in common. Before, we had the impression the government was there and we here. You know, the noncooperation with the Netherlands.... It was the same with the New Order."

NU's most acute problem now is to fix the limits of state authority so that religious leaders can maintain a measure of autonomy and play the mediating role they play so well: representing their organization's interests with the authorities, while at the same time relaying the government's message to the Muslim community. The Indonesian Muslim press has spoken of a "crisis of confidence in Islamic organizations because they are too close to the government and have too conciliatory a tone " (*Pelita* 1991, 22:4). Indeed, some religious leaders complain that the relationship with Golkar has had a negative effect on attendance in their *pesantren*. Other rural religious leaders, however, have found the relationship profitable.

Conclusion

At a national conference in 1987, Nahdlatul Ulama officials explained that they wanted to become more than "the man at the roadside who is asked to push the car and should be happy to receive a thank you." They meant that NU officials aspire to regain the respect and prestige they feel their organization deserves. It seems that NU is heading in the right direction toward achieving this aim. Civil servants are coming back, meetings are easier to organize, schools are better subsidized, and *dakwah* is prospering. NU has achieved its success while continuing to push back the limits of state authority, as is particularly evident in the field of education.

In effect, NU is participating in the Islamization of the country in cooperation with a government often described by Western (and some Indonesian) scholars as "secular" or "anti-Islamic." In fact, the NU 1984 reversal has been a fresh start in what is in fact an old and mutually beneficial *entente* between Indonesian nationalists and traditionalist Muslims. As we have seen, the *ulama* supported Sukarno as president in 1940, 1945, and 1959, despite visible differences on the question of religion and state. The Sunni tradition of legitimating government authority was in this case reinforced by the strength of nationalist sentiments among NU officials. Under the New Order, confrontation with the state created a deep malaise and a loss of membership in the ranks of the organization. Thus, the 1984 reversal was not so much opportunism in the national political arena as an urgent strategy for survival.

The change in NU attitude found its clearest expression in the organization's acceptance of *asas tunggal,* the government policy requiring all organizations to accept the Pancasila as their sole ideological basis. With its acceptance, NU dared to draw a line between ideology and religion, and openly embraced nationalist ideals. The example of the Indian Muslim scholars who chose to participate in the secular and democratic Republic of India comes to mind as a parallel. Christian Troll has spoken of their "remarkable flexibility, independence of mind and creativeness . . . in the effort to come to terms with a situation that is challenging not only on the practical but also on the ideological level" (1993, 84). In the words of the anthropologist Mitsuo Nakamura, this "liberation of Islam from political stigma and constraints" has resulted in a "reduction of suspicion" on the part of the government and the initiation of programs designed to increase Islamic influence in national culture (Nakamura 1993). Thus, for example, a bill on Islamic courts, prepared in the early 1980s, was passed in 1989, returning jurisdiction over inheritance and donation to Islamic courts in Java, Madura, and South Kalimantan. A drive to rationalize Islamic law was initiated at the same time with the compilation of Islamic jurisprudence drawing mostly on the Shafi'i school of law.

The new relationship between the Indonesian government and Muslims has brought about increased cooperation with other Islamic groups, including the radical reformist Dewan Dakwah Islamiyah Indonesia (DDII). In 1991 the minister of religion, Munawir Sjadzali, told me that the DDII has come closer to the government. A supreme court high official, Busthanul Arifin, was invited to speak in front of one hundred DDII preachers in 1991. A UNICEF health education project is being organized under the auspices of the DDII on the recommendation of the Ministry of Religion. In 1990 the young editors of a DDII information magazine, *Prospek,* were invited to friendly discussions with local military officials in a Central Javanese town. DDII's magazine *Serial Media Dakwah* has also been freer in its polemics against inroads made by Christian missions in the Indonesian archipelago. Besides the DDII, the reformist Muhammadiyah organization has also experienced an improved atmosphere for its activities. In a 1991 interview with a high-ranking Muhammadiyah official (Ramli Thaha), for example, I was told that in 1985 the organization had just three branches in the predominantly Christian eastern province of Nusa Tenggara Timur; by 1991 it had seventeen.

These concessions to varied Muslim groups have reinforced the impression that government policy has changed from one of containment to an ardent embrace of the once-marginalized Muslim community. There is some debate over whether this shift should be ascribed to the recent estrangement of the president from a part of the armed forces, a rift that became public in 1988, when the army opposed Suharto's choice for vice-president, Sudharmono. I see this latter event as the catalyst for a process already begun on a more modest scale in the early 1980s. Developments such as the growth of an Islamic middle class, mass education, and compulsory religious education (imposed as an antidote to communism after 1966) were the longer-term influences on the government.

Whatever the precise reasons, the creation of ICMI (see Hefner, Chapter 3, this volume) has changed the map of Islam in Indonesia, contributing to a blurring of boundaries between traditionalist and reformist Islam. Rather than a matter of ritual, the dividing line is now a matter of how much stress should be placed on Muslim identity and how much on pluralism and religious tolerance. As Robert Hefner notes in this volume, the important debate of the early 1990s has been the choice between a "national" or an "Islamic society." The NU chairman, Abdurrahman Wahid, has committed himself to the "national" ideal, leaving Islam to exert a moral influence rather than imposing a totalistic program. Although ICMI has among its members intellectuals deemed "fundamentalist" by the government, it has so far not embraced a totalistic program but is rather, as Hefner notes, a political response on the part of the Muslim middle class to what is perceived as the continuing social and economic marginalization of Muslims. Unfortunately perhaps, the defense of these interests may be hard to reconcile with the ideal of pluralism and tolerance preached by Muslim intellectuals like Nurcholish Madjid and promoted by the Suharto regime for more than twenty years.

ICMI's impact on NU should be noted without being exaggerated. Some NU intellectuals have chosen to join ICMI, while Wahid has rejected it as sectarian. It may be too early or too simple to speak of a rift, since some NU intellectuals who have joined ICMI have evident sympathy for Wahid's arguments against sectarianism. Thus, to return to a theme that runs through several essays in the present volume, we could say that higher education and the emergence of an educated middle class are indirectly responsible for the challenge to NU and Wahid. It is precisely these same developments, however, that have facilitated NU's recent recovery and allowed Wahid to survive the "rift" so far.

References Cited

Abdullah, Taufik. 1987. "Pandangan Hidup Ulama Indonesia: Ikhtisar Laporan Umum Sebuah Penelitian" (The World View of Indonesian *Ulama*: A Summary Report on Research). *Masyarakat Indonesia* 14 (3): 181–221.

Abubakar. 1957. *Sejarah Hidup KH A Wahid Hasyim dan Karangan Tersiar* (A Biograpy of K.H. A. Wahid Hasyim and His Writings). Jakarta: Panitya Buku Peringatan Alm. K.H. A. Wahid Hasyim.

Anam, Choirul. 1985. *Pertumbuhan dan Perkembangan Nahdlatul Ulama* (The Growth and Development of Nahdlatul Ulama). Surabaya: Jatayu Sala.

Anderson, Benedict R. O'G. 1977. "Religion and Politics in Indonesia since Independence." In Benedict R. O'G. Anderson, Mitsuo Nakamura, and Mohammad Slamet, eds., *Religion and Social Ethos in Indonesia*, pp. 21–32. Clayton, Australia: Monash University.

Anshari, H. Endang Saifuddin. 1981. *Piagam Jakarta 22 Juni 1945 dan Sejarah Konsensus Nasional Antara Nasionalis Islami dan Nasionalis Sekular Tentang dasar Negara Republik Indonesia*. Bandung: Perpustakaan Salman ITB, Lembaga Studi Islam.

Bonneff, Marcel. 1980. *Pantjasila: Trente années de débats politiques en Indonésie*. Paris: Éditions de la Maison des Sciences de l'Homme.

Eickelman, Dale F. 1987. "Changing Interpretations of Islamic Movements." In William Roff, ed., *Islam and the Political Economy of Meaning: Comparative Studies of Muslim Discourse*, pp. 13–29. Berkeley and Los Angeles: University of California Press.

Fealey, Greg. 1992. "Rowing in a Typhoon: Nahdlatul Ulama and the Decline of Constitutional Democracy." Paper given at the conference on "Democracy in Indonesia: 1950s–1990s," December 1992, Monash University, Clayton, Australia.

Gaborieau, Marc. 1989. "Les oulémas/soufis dans l'Inde Moghole: Anthropologie historique de religieux musulmans." Paris. *Annales ESC*, Sept.–Oct., pp. 1185–1204.

Geertz, Clifford. 1960. *The Religion of Java*. Chicago: University of Chicago Press.

Haidar, Ali. 1991. "Nahdatul Ulama dan Islam di Indonesia: Pendekatan Fikih dalam Politik" (Nahdlatul Ulama and Indonesian Islam: A Political and Jurisprudential Analysis). Doctoral dissertation in Islamic Studies, IAIN Syarif Hidayatullah, Jakarta.

Hefner, Robert W. 1985. *Hindu Javanese: Tengger Tradition and Islam*. Princeton: Princeton University Press.

———. 1987. "Islamizing Java? Religion and Politics in Rural East Java." *Journal of Asian Studies* 46 (3): 533–554.

Jones, Sydney. 1984. "The Contraction and Expansion of the *Umat* and the Role of the Nahdatul Ulama in Indonesia." *Indonesia* 38:1–20.

Lev, Daniel. 1966. *The Transition to Guided Democracy: Indonesian Politics, 1957–1959*. Ithaca, N.Y.: Modern Indonesia Project, Southeast Asia Program Cornell University.

———. 1972. *Islamic Courts in Indonesia: A Study in the Political Bases of Legal Institutions*. Berkeley and Los Angeles: University of California Press.

Nahdlatul Ulama. 1987. "Bahan Konperensi Besar NU" (Materials from NU's National Conference). November 17–18, Panitia Penyelenggara Munas dan Konbes NU, Jakarta.

Nakamura, Mitsuo. 1981. "The Radical Traditionalism of the *Nadlatul Ulama* in Indonesia: A Personal Account of Its Twenty-Sixth National Congress, June 1979, Semarang." *Journal of Southeast Asian Studies*, 19:187–204.

———. 1993. "To Be Proud of Being a Muslim: The Formation of the Indonesian Association of Muslim Intellectuals (ICMI)." Paper Presented at Conference on "Islam and The Social Construction of Identities: Comparative Perspectives on Southeast Asian Muslims." School of Hawaiian, Asian and Pacific Studies, University of Hawai'i at Mānoa, August 4–6, 1993.

Noer, Deliar. 1980. *Gerakan Modern Islam di Indonesia, 1900–1942* (Modern Islamic Movements in Indonesia). Jakarta: LP3ES.

———. 1987. *Partai Islam di Pentas Nasional* (Muslim Parties on the National Stage). Jakarta: PT. Pustaka Utama Grafiti.

_____. 1990. *Mohammad Hatta Biografi Politik* (Mohammad Hatta, a Political Biography). Jakarta: LP3ES.

Pranowo, Bambang. 1991. "Islam and Party Politics in Rural Java." Paper presented at ASEAN Moslem Social Scientists: The Fourth Forum in Indonesia, August 21–24, Lembang, West Java.

Siddiq, K.H. Achmad. 1985. *Islam, Pancasila dan Ukhuwah Islamiyah* (Islam, Pancasila, and Islamic Organizations). Jakarta: Lajnah Ta'lif wan Nasyur PBNU, Sumber Barokah.

Thomas, R. Murray. 1988. "The Islamic Revival and Indonesian Education." *Asian Survey* 28 (9): 897–915.

Troll, Christian W. 1993. "Sharing Islamically in the Pluralistic Nation State of India: The Views of Some Recent and Contemporary Indian Muslim Leaders and Thinkers." *La transmission du savoir dans le monde musulman périphérique*, pp. 63–86. Lettre d'Information No. 13. Paris: Centre National de Recherche Scientifique.

Ward, Kenneth. 1974. *The 1971 Election in Indonesia. An East Java Case Study*. Victoria, Australia: Monash Papers on Southeast Asia.

Watt, Montgomery W. 1968. *Islamic Political Thought: The Basic Concepts*. Edinburgh: Edinburgh University Press.

Yusuf, Slamet Effendy, Ichwan Syam, and Masdar Farid Mas'udi. 1983. *Dinamika Kaum Santri: Menelusuri Jejak dan Pergolakan Internal NU* (Santri Dynamics: Investigating the Trail and Internal Turmoil of NU). Jakarta: CV Rajawali.

Zuhri, Saifuddin. 1987. *Berangkat dari Pesantren*. Jakarta: Gunung Agung.

Part II
Reformers and Reformism

Chapter 5

Modern Intentions
RESHAPING SUBJECTIVITIES IN AN INDONESIAN MUSLIM SOCIETY

John R. Bowen

In the aftermath of the cold war, some in North America have found their next enemy in Islam, an Islam construed to be monolithic and antimodern. Replacing the clash of economies is a clash of civilizations: the secularized West versus overreligious Islam. This dichotomy rests on a particular construction of what it is to be modern, a construction that arose from the European Enlightenment and that celebrates the ideal of a secular public sphere of deliberative discourse. A modern society, in this view, must draw a sharp boundary between the religious values of the individual and the political values of the public.[1]

From this perspective, social movements that urge people to become more steadfastly religious in order to become more modern are internally contradictory, if not outright threatening to modernity itself. Secularizing states throughout the world have taken this view seriously, arrogating to themselves the right to define the modes and manners of public behavior, and to view religious-based public norms (of dress, legal standing, or education) as anathema. Here, post-Enlightenment political theory converges conveniently with the interests of those in power.

Ironically, these state actions have made all religious movements "modern" by dictating the terms by which they must operate. In shaping their activities, religious movements must take account of modern state structures, ideologies, and forces, as well as international economic exchanges and transnational communication flows.[2] Culturally, as well, religious movements have redefined their own ideas in engagement with European modernity and in particular with ideas of agency, individual responsibility, and subjectivity. As Charles Taylor has argued (1989), European modernity has historically entailed a radical detachment of subjectivity from the outer world, including the social world, and a consequent refocusing inward. This process of fashioning a cultural model of individualized subjectivity has been religious as well as political in the Euro-American world.

Taylor's analysis leads us to ask what kinds of cultural subjectivities modernity-making may have engendered elsewhere in the world. Such an inquiry builds on the long-standing concern of cultural anthropologists with local ideas of self and subjectivity but asks what challenges to these ideas are posed in the name of a "modernity" that is also religious.

I examine here one such confrontation between older and newer religious practices where notions of subjectivity became central. The broader context for the case is the set of movements for religious reform that animated many Muslims throughout the Dutch and British East Indies (and elsewhere), beginning early in the twentieth century. I consider what has been at stake in Gayo society in the highlands of Sumatra, where, beginning in the 1930s, heated disputes arose over whether a worshiper should recite a statement of intent before worship. The debates implicated ideas about subjectivity, persons, and actions, and contained a strong critique of local thinking about religion. The dispute was carried out along many channels; I examine here the religious poetry created to disseminate the reformers' views. Finally, I consider what other courses the reform movement might have taken, drawing on materials from neighboring societies to do so. I use this case to suggest strategies for proceeding beyond the single ethnographic study to a comparative study of Muslim modernist projects.

Through this case study I wish to underline the importance of strategy, beliefs, and rhetorics to *religious* phenomena, religious in the narrowest sense of matters of worship and liturgy.[3] These strategies, beliefs, and rhetorics are highly responsive to social and cultural features and processes. Religious actors select from a variety of ideas and emphasize those that offer the best chances of success in a particular social environment, or so I argue. Such a claim is commonplace in studies of the social and political aspects of Islamic movements.[4] But debates about worship or liturgy have generally been left to the text-based Islamicist, whose training leads him or her to focus on the origins of particular ideas in normative texts. This unfortunate division of labor has at times led scholars of religion to respond to field studies of religious ideas with some hostility.[5] My own assumption, one shared by most anthropologists, is that we do wish to understand how people have interpreted and debated particular religious issues, and why they have emphasized some matters over others. This kind of knowledge allows us to understand why transnational movements (such as Islamic reformist movements) catch on at some times and places and not at others; local studies give us a window onto the rhetorics and forms that mediate between "local" and "translocal" phenomena. Indeed, the more we (quite rightly) turn our anthropological attentions to "transnational" phenomena —whether religion, migration, or music—the harder we must work to retain the particularities and diversities in our analytic frame, lest all blur into generalized World Culture.

In what follows I seek to explain the particular set of religion-oriented acts taken by specific individuals and groups by identifying the social frameworks in which they acted, their own intentions and interests, and their sense of the relative cultural force of various alternative ways of discussing religious matters. An account of a set of actions thus derived may in turn be made more plausible by contrasting them with other sets, chosen to be as controlled as possible, that is, as close to the original set in terms of period and cultural features—the old anthropological strategy of "controlled comparison."

Disputes over Intent

When I first heard about the religious controversies that had animated many Gayo earlier in this century, I found it difficult to understand why these disputes had been so prominent and why, in the 1980s, they continued to occasion discussion and debate. Beginning in the mid-1930s, a group of Gayo religious teachers who had recently returned to their Sumatran homeland from schooling elsewhere in the Dutch East Indies began to urge their fellow men and women to purify their religious activities of non-Islamic elements. These teachers emphasized the unique authority of the Qur'an and *hadith*, and associated themselves with the general movement for religious reform called the "young group" *(kaum muda)*. The *kaum muda* drew extensively from the Salafi movement in the Middle East, inspired by the Egyptian scholar Muhammad Abduh. Other Gayo teachers resisted the "young group" position, affirming long-standing religious practices and the authority of prominent religious scholars of the past. These scholars increasingly identified with the general Indies-wide "old group" *(kaum tua)* position. These two labels were of general archipelagic currency and are usually glossed as "modernist" and "traditionalist."[6]

In the main Gayo town of Takèngën, these teachers engaged in public and private debates over such liturgical matters as how many times to bend down in worship, whether or not to offer a distinct prayer at morning worship, or whether to remind a just-buried corpse of the main tenets of Islam. But no debate occasioned as much hurt and discord as that concerning the statement of intent to worship.[7] Many Gayo (and other Muslims), just before beginning to worship (proclaiming *Allahu akbar*), state to themselves their intent to worship, usually reciting a one-sentence formula (in

Gayo, Indonesian, or, for the more learned, Arabic), such as: "I worship at daybreak with two cycles on account of God, may He be exhalted." Those who do pronounce the formula consider it to be an aid to worship; most modernists see it as an illegitimate addition to the actions dictated by scripture. The opening pronouncement "I worship" in Arabic is "*ushalli,*" and the dispute has been called the "*ushalli* controversy."[8]

One traditionalist scholar in Takèngën recalled the disputes over the *ushalli* that began in the 1930s. "They [modernists] kept telling us we were wrong, and the disputes led to some divorces. Some people moved from Takèngën to Bireuën [on the northern coast] because they were ashamed at all the disputes." These early debates over the *ushalli* made it emblematic of the traditionalist position, as in the following couplet linking the *ushalli* to the holding of ritual meals (also critized by modernists):

| semiyang berushalli | At worship, say the *ushalli;* |
| Molut berkenduri | On the Prophet's Birthday, hold a ritual meal. |

Of all the issues that increasingly embroiled traditionalists and modernists in Takèngën, "it was the *ushalli* that caused the most turmoil," he said. Such was the degree of local antagonism that the principal imam of the mosque in Kota Raja (today Banda Aceh) intervened in the mid-1930s, instructing scholars on both sides to quell their enthusiasm. But the disputes continued, and the *ushalli* question was central in a public debate held in 1941 between the chief spokesmen for the two camps.

Why was the controvery over the *ushalli* the hardest felt of these disputes? What was it about a preliminary pronouncement of intent that was so objectionable to modernists and so important to others? It alone of the disputed aspects of worship raised the issue of subjectivity in worship, and part of the answer to this question will lie in the notions of subjectivity and action that underlie ideas of religious modernism. But not all Indonesian societies were as touched by this particular controversy; another part of the answer thus must lie in the specific history of Gayo modernists' efforts at persuasion.[9]

Now, having the right intent when engaged in ritual activity is generally important to Muslims. Specifically, most Muslims, whether Gayo, Egyptian, or British, would agree that one must form the correct intent before beginning ritual worship (Wensinck 1953; cf. Fischer 1980, 63–64). It thus seems strange that modernists, who urged Muslims to purify their religious practice by returning to the Qur'an and *hadith,* would argue that one should not express the intent to worship. But they did so argue, on the grounds that there was insufficient textual evidence that the prophet

Muhammad himself ever stated a formula of intent to worship and that, following the general principle of strictly following Muhammad in matters of worship, we should therefore refrain from uttering such a statement.

This particular issue might have been a minor one were it not that early on it became a token of the larger controversy.[10] Modernism began to take root in the Indies in the first few years of this century, when several scholars returned from study in Mecca to their homes in West Sumatra. In 1906 one such scholar, 'Abd al-Karim, began to criticize established ritual practices, including the practices of holding an additional worship session after the Friday congregational worship and adding a separate section (the *qunut*) to morning worship, along with a long list of other matters having to do with delivering recitations to the deceased or to God on his or her behalf. 'Abd al-Karim directed his criticisms at the organized religious orders *(tarîqa)* of West Sumatra, whose members engaged in precisely these practices. These orders were important political bodies as well as associations for religious learning and worship, and these criticisms launched an extensive and hard-fought series of public debates over knowledge and authority. About this time 'Abd al-Karim asked Ahmad Khatib, his teacher in Mecca (and of Sumatran origin himself), for an opinion *(fatwa)* on the *ushalli* question. Ahmad Khatib complied, coming out in favor of the practice, but 'Abd al-Karim rejected the *fatwa,* issuing his own counter-*fatwa*. His rejection of the venerated Meccan stirred up a storm of protest in West Sumatra and generated a great deal of hostility toward him.

Thereafter, the practice of saying the *ushalli* came to index one's acceptance of a larger package of positions; it thus became quite salient among the disputed practices. But in most Sumatran societies it did not become the main issue. The rhetorics adopted by modernists varied. In much of lowland Aceh, for example, reform-oriented groups underscored the importance of the individual's rationality as a weapon against the passions (Siegel 1969). In West Sumatra itself, ideas of socially liberating modernity permeate much influential writing by Muslim reformers (Abdullah 1971; Hamka 1958). But in the Gayo highlands it *was* the *ushalli* that provided the encompassing framework for critiques and replies on a wide variety of topics. Why this issue in this place? It is not enough to identify the general Muslim sources or the general archipelagowide currency of the *ushalli*; the long-lasting importance of the *ushalli* and of the issue of intent in Gayo religious rhetoric requires a local explanation.

The Social Frameworks for the Disputes

One place to begin is with the social history of religious life in the highlands.[11] Although Gayo probably converted to Islam during the expansion of the Acehnese kingdom in the sixteenth and seventeenth centuries, little is known about religious ideas and institutions in the highlands before 1900. Dutch forces invaded the area during the period from 1901 to 1904 as part of their effort to occupy Aceh. By the 1920s they had turned their attention from pacifying the countryside to encouraging export agriculture, and the town of Takèngën in northern Gayoland soon became a center for trade, government, and education. The town took on a marked multicultural character, as traders and teachers from elsewhere in the Dutch East Indies came there to settle. Many of them came from West Sumatra, where they had studied in the new style of religious school. In Takèngën they were joined by a new class of Gayo merchants and civil servants, who had to learn what was beginning to be called Indonesian in order to speak with them.

By the mid-1930s, Gayo and other Sumatran teachers of both modernist and traditionalist persuasions had established their own religious associations and schools in or near Takèngën. Their emerging doctrinal differences attracted widespread public attention, and their spokesmen engaged in public debates, particularly over the correct ways to worship and whether to speak with the dead. Friday preachers took sides on these issues, and disagreements among preachers led to the building of new mosques. People carried the arguments away from the mosques into town coffee shops and village prayer houses.

Out of these developments emerged a new public sphere of Islamic discourse in Takèngën. This sphere was defined by religion *(agama;* Ar. *dîn)* and religious practice *(ibëdët;* Ar. *'ibâdât)* as warranted by explicit prescriptions in the Qur'an and *hadith.* The participants in this sphere included Gayo, Acehnese, and other Sumatrans who shared a set of religious ideas and practices detached from any particular place. Indeed, to retain their legitimacy as properly religious, these practices needed to be explicitly distinguished from purely local forms of ritual. The immigrant character of the town contributed to its flavor: the people who arrived there brought forms of social, religious, and economic life that could exist apart from a village base. Moreover, the two largest groups of Muslim immigrants, the West Sumatran Minangkabau and the Acehnese, both came from cultures where circular migration was part of the life course. Men in both regions typically spent years away from their homelands (Kato 1982; Siegel 1969). These migratory traditions probably accentuated the sense of detachment from place that characterized the new socioreligious ideas.[12]

But if many Gayo modernists participated in town life, they also maintained ties to the surrounding villages. Many continued to live in the villages and work in the town; others visited their natal villages frequently for feasts and celebrations. No migratory culture emerged here.

This particular combination of networks and allegiances has given a distinctive stamp to highlands modernist culture. Gayo modernists participate in a supraethnic, pronationalist, Arabic-language-based religious culture, but they also aim at reforming established rural social practices from within. Their specific social orientation has led Gayo modernists to carve out a distinct religious sphere of activity, in which people of diverse backgrounds could participate (in town life) but that would also allow for the continuation of older cultural activities and social ties (largely in the villages).

Gayo modernists thus have underscored the contrast between matters of religion, where one must follow scriptural norms, and all other matters, where, in the words of Muhammad, "you know best your affairs." This position has allowed them to urge practicable reforms in village religious life without calling for the abandonment of other social practices, something neither they nor their audience would have welcomed. Their stance has led them to accent certain features of the general modernist position over other features (see Hourani 1983). They have emphasized the scriptural constraints on interpretation rather than the process of independent reasoning *(ijtihad),* usually claiming that there is one correct interpretation of scripture and vehemently denouncing all innovation *(bid'a)* in ritual affairs. By stressing the boundary between religious ritual *(ibadat)* and the rest of life, they have played down claims that a particular set of religious orientations should guide all activities (such as reason [aqal], so prominent in the modernist discourses of Aceh, Malaysia, and North Africa).

Within the religious domain, Gayo have emphasized the direct, unavoidable link between the subjectivity of the individual worshiper and the reception of the ritual act by God. The intent associated with an act defines it: an act of sacrifice, worship, or pilgrimage to Mecca counts as such only if one undertakes it for the sake of God (rather than in hope of gaining wealth or prestige). The degree of concentration during the act also gives it more or less value: the individual thus must strive in a mental battle against distraction and the Devil. The merit that results from religious practice accrues only to the actor, and so all claims that actions can create merit for others are illegitimate.

As I often heard modernist friends declare: "Everything depends on intent." Now, the term "intent" (Gayo *niët;* Ind. *niat;* < Ar. *niyyâ)* has a broad range of meaning in Gayo life, much broader than what is meant by the modernists. It refers to a general sphere of communication: for example, a vow that one will sacrifice an animal or offer a meal to a spirit in return for the spirit's help in healing a child or securing a bountiful harvest. Or it can refer in negative fashion to the "hidden intentions" behind an ostensibly good act.[13]

In modernist usage, however, "intent" is intended to define the subjective component of a more narrow view of religion and ritual. Against older notions of ritual as a wide field of powerful *communication,* modernists assert a conception of ritual as the tightly defined range of ways in which an individual can fulfill God's commands, and thus as *obedience.* This shift can be seen in Weberian typological terms as a shift away from instrumental rationality toward value rationality. It reaches widely into domains of agricultural ritual, liturgical form, and treatment of the dead (Bowen 1993a, 315–330).[14] Emphasizing the importance of intent in itself does not constitute a critical intervention into preexisting religious discourse. What is specific to the Gayo case is how the emphasis on intent can be used as a foundation for a sweeping modernist critique of ritual practices.

If ritual is primarily about communicating with God, then anything that serves to clear the way and the mind must be in God's service and thus properly part of worship. If, however, ritual is primarily about obeying God's commands, then two objections to the *ushalli* follow. First, because scripture does not explicitly order worshipers to pronounce the *ushalli,* we should not pronounce it. In religious matters we must strictly follow scripture, using our powers to reason but not adding or subtracting one iota of information. (Modernists emphasize the religious importance of translating scripture into vernaculars not so that people can judge and interpret freely on their own—for that you need specialists—but so that they will know what they say in worship and thus have the correct intent.) Altering what scripture says is improper "innovation" *(bid'a).*

Secondly (and here is what is especially stressed in Gayo society), adding the *ushalli* to the prescribed ritual pattern implies that intent is not already part of every ritual act, that it is something extraneous to religious action (as in certain social science circles "ideas" are seen as detached from "behavior"). Because you must perform all your religious acts with the correct intent (in order to serve God), intent should suffuse all acts. As several Gayo modernist scholars put it, we express the intent to worship by preparing for worship: by walking to the mosque, by performing ablutions, and so forth, even before we begin to worship. If one's subjective formation of intent defines and constitutes an act as a religious act of a particular nature, then the notion that one can have action apart from intent is false and misleading. Including the *ushalli* in worship may dangerously weaken the principle that actions have built-in intentions precisely because it implies that such a statement is needed.

The *ushalli* controversy thus provided the Takèngën modernists a chance to stress that intent is a quality that accompanies all actions and renders them valid or invalid. But why did traditionalists feel compelled to defend the *ushalli?* At first glance it seems odd that the couplet quoted earlier included the *ushalli* as one of two practices that defined the traditionalist position. Part of the answer is undoubtedly historical. Because modernists criticized traditionalists for the *ushalli* relatively early in the history of highlands debates, the practice became a traditionalist emblem. Traditionalists also see that a broader issue is at stake here. The *ushalli* represents clearly the central idea that worship is communication with God and that a separate act of stating intention is necessary to effect that communication. Traditionalist scholars criticize a broad array of modernist ideas about ritual on this general point. For example, modernists speak too quickly, so that their half-intoned words run together and they end up saying ridiculous things to God. Communication needs to have a channel opened for it, and the *ushalli* does just that, directing worship to God. In their view, modernists seek to deny them a way of creating this personal pathway.

Rhetorics of Persuasion

I have said that my task is to try and account for the particular shape of modernist interventions and the responses to those interventions. But this accounting should include, at least to the anthropological way of thinking, not just what issues arose, but *how* modernists set out to persuade people to change what they did. The history of persuasion is not simply the reflection or translation of high-level scholarly disputes; it also involves the strategic creation of rhetorical forms by those seeking to persuade.

In order to change the ways the less educated among the Gayo understood religious ritual, modernists created an entirely new genre of poetry, which in its formal features as well as its content underscored the separateness of religious matters from secular ones. The poetry, called *saèr* (from Malay *sha'ir* [Bowen 1991, 242–243]), embodies the particular highlands mixture of socioreligious emphases. Most poems feature one or more lines of Arabic scripture, followed by an elaboration of the scriptural message in Gayo verse. This juxtaposing of languages and styles may be unique in the Islamic world. It underlines the scriptural dependence of religious understanding and addresses a Gayo-speaking audience. The poetry was generally sung by local poets, some of whom were also popular singers in other genres. It soon became a highly popular performance genre.[15]

In these poems modernists stress the importance of forming and holding the correct intent, a task that requires remaining attentive, having faith, and correctly formulating, to oneself, the act's religious purpose. They argue that intent is necessary to create any religious merit and that, therefore, one cannot create merit for others. Based on this proposition, they eliminate from the sphere of religious activity *(ibadat)* practices that were (and still are) important to many Gayo, including reciting verses for the benefit of the deceased (Bowen n.d.).

Once they have narrowed the field of permissible ritual action to exclude certain older practices, modernists then ask: What are the conditions for worship to be effective? Here modernists refocus the question of efficacy on the worshiper's subjectivity rather than on the social conditions surrounding the event. The poems attack three specific elements of an older subjective stance toward worship: ignorance, blindly following others people's teachings, and following Gayo norms rather than religious ones. Following others people's teachings without thinking through the matter yourself is usually referred to as *taqlid,* a term that can otherwise be used to convey the more neutral idea that one follows established teachings, usually of a particular religious legal tradition. Sometimes the practice is attacked as *taqlid buta,* "blind obedience." Following established Gayo cultural norms or *ëdët* (Malay *adat*) is also incorrect in religious matters; one should instead think things out for oneself after consulting those with religious knowledge. Thinking for oneself is sometimes referred to as *ijtihad,* "independent legal reasoning." The poets link ignorance, blind obedience, and following *ëdët* as all signaling that the actor does not have the proper intent. Herein lies the link between religious reform and modernity: backwardness, ignorance, and traditions are all viewed as hindering the progress toward proper religious action.

Much of the religious poetry written in the 1930s and 1940s argues that knowledge is required for acceptable worship, since only with knowledge can one formulate the correct intent for each act of worship. The first poem in a handwritten manuscript dating from about 1950 (Daudy 1950), written by the foremost poet, Tengku Mudë Kala, directly addresses this multiplex problem. The poem links the problem of "blind obedience" (and the critique of *ëdët*) to the absence of intent and reminds the listener that God will not accept such worship. As with all the poems, it begins with a quotation from scripture; in this case, verse 36 of Qur'an 17, which reads: "Follow not that of which you have no knowledge. The hearing and the sight and the heart: each of these will be questioned."

The first two stanzas of the poem provide a vernacular gloss of the Arabic verse, adding the explanation that what the Qur'an condemns as mere "imitation" is carrying out worship according to past practice or the dictates of so-called teachers. The poem then returns to the original gloss to effect a persuasive closure midway through the poem.

telah berkata Allah ta'ala	So spoke God the highest,
menegah jema buët uru-uru	forbidding people to imitate.
enti itunung ko sara buët	Do not follow a practice
ikë gërë dëpët ningko ilmu	if you do not have the knowledge.
kerna penengé orum penèngon	Because about your hearing and sight
ikunëi tuhën barang ngë tentu	God will surely enquire,
demikian ku atas até	and similarly for your heart,
oyapé besé periksë mutuju	He will inspect it closely.
amal ibëdët enti menurut ëdët	Religious practice, don't [carry out] according to *ëdët*,
mungikut buët si ngë telah lalu	following practices of by-gone days:
tanih-temanih turun-temurun	handed down, passed along,
kunë perbuëtën ni muyang datu	however it was done by our ancestors.
berbuët ibëdët gelah karna Allah	Practice religion solely for God,
enti ërëp tung ijazah	not just for a diploma
ari tengku guru	from the honored teacher.
berbuët ibëdët kë malé ibuëtën	Practice religion; when ready,
dalil keterangan ikunëi	ask for justifications
ku tengku	from a teacher.
enti lagu jema ikut-ikutën	Don't be like those who just follow;
sana ibuëtën ërëp itetiru	whatever is done, they just imitate it.
olok pedi sesat taqlid bota	They are far astray, the blind imitators;
iharapé pahla nisé delé demu	they hope to get lots of merit.
padahal tuhën ngë munegah	Yet God has forbidden;
gërë iosah buët uru-uru	has not allowed us to merely imitate.

. . . .

After further elaborations of this message, the poet then introduces a second voice, that of an uninformed Gayo person who worships in an unthinking, uncaring fashion:

naku ngĕ beta iĕjĕr awan	For me, grandpa taught me just so.
pasal ipinahan sĕbĕr mi tengku	Straying [from scripture]? Don't worry so much about it, teacher.
sebĕb awanku pĕ mubaca kitĕb	For grandpa also read the book,
mungaji sirĕt munapal nahu	recited the Prophet's life, memorized Arabic.
tentang aku gĕrĕ asal menuntut	As for me, no need to learn;
melĕngkan mengikut manatni awanku	just follow grandpa's legacy.
ɔowa ni sembahyangku pĕ jaɔi konot-konot	The worship prayers I just keep short;
jaɔi singkĕt-singkĕt enti mi naru	keep brief, never long.
kuatas kutuyuh kubaca Fatihah	Up and down, I recite the Fatihah;[16]
ngĕ meta kutamah tikik mi Qul hu	finished, I add a bit of "Qul hu"[17]
kĕ iterimĕĕ keta terimĕĕ	If it's accepted, then it's accepted;
ikĕ gĕrĕ pĕ sana kenĕ aku	if not, what can I say about it?

. . . .

These passages use the notion of blind obedience *(taqlid buta)* to link following tradition to not forming the correct intent during ritual: absence of intent signals the twinned negative characteristics of merely following others *(taqlid;* Gayo *uru-uru)* and being blind or without knowledge. The willingness to renounce past practices and detach oneself from past authority becomes the necessary condition for authentic religious practice.

The requirements of intent in worship also include attentiveness, the subject of a number of poems. Poem number 45 in Mudë Kala's 1950 collection is one of several making the further claim that those who worship without proper intent will find that their worship does not count. The poem begins with a *hadith:* "Be informed that God does not respond to a prayer from an inadvertent and oblivious heart." Mudë Kala then depicts the unthinking way in which many people just run through their worship, with their minds floating off elsewhere, for example, to the state of their ricefields. I give the complete poem here, beginning with stanzas 1 to 7:

berkata nabi Muhammaɔ	Said the Prophet Muhammad,
munerangan ku umĕt	explaining to his people [about]
ɔo'a gĕrĕ makbul	prayers that are not received.
ara-kĕ ibetĕhko bĕwĕnĕ jema	Do you all know
tentang ni ɔo'a si gĕrĕ makul	about prayers that are ineffective?

gërë iterimë tuhën ɖo'a ni jema · God does not accept people's prayers
   keɖikën ara ɖo'a iapal ·   if prayers are learned;

awah berɖo'a atëwé lalé · the mouth prays; the heart is lazy
   lagu si lengé peningëté muraul ·   as if it is weak; thoughts wander.
gërë sunguh até muniro ɖo'a · Beseeching is not done earnestly,
   ërëp ngë ara gërë ɖalih betul ·   just so that there is [a prayer],
      it does not have to be straight.
keɖikën até ngë mujejawang · If the heart is roaming,
   biër sembahyang ngë wët kunul ·   even though worship has begun.
awah mubaca até berkekirë · The mouth is reciting, the heart
   is figuring
   bëwëh si rikë ngë telam-timul ·   all sorts of matters, up and down.

tengah ibëɖët pikirné terbang · In the middle of worship,
   thoughts are flying
   lagu lelayang si gërë berkampul ·   like a kite no longer held down.
isoné até ngë mutetayang · So the heart is long gone:
   isi kin pematang ngë teriɖah ·   "there are the hills, the knoll
   buntul ·   is in view,

isi kin sagi méh jëjëp lengkëk · there is the field's edge, with every
   little row;
   isi kin relët ngë teriɖah arul ·   there is the corner, the stream's
   come into view."
enta isihën tekebir isihën wajah · Who knows where is the *takbîr*
   or the *wajah*;
   enta isihën Fatiha orum atahyatul ·   who knows where is al-Fâtiha
   or the *atahyatul*.

gërë ibetëh arti ni baca · He does not know the meaning
   of what is read;
   sana ɖië makna iprinné kul ·   whatever its meaning, he says
   it's deep.

enta isihën ujung enta isihën raliq · Who knows where is the end
   or the beginning,
   ngë mubabalik ngë ɖabuh kancul ·   turning all around, becoming all
   confused.
cubë itimang orum pikirën · Try and weigh it yourself;
   mera-kë memangan ikë parang ·   does a dull knife ever bite?
   tumpul

The poet then draws a sharp contrast to the intense way in which these same people would utter *doa* intended as spells. He draws the picture in such a way as to clarify the result people intend spells to have, without claiming either that they do have that result or that it is appropriate to say such spells (stanzas 8–11):

ɔup ɔo'a kebël mera menjaɔi	Whereas an invulnerability spell would work
karna sunguh ate iopul-opul	because earnestly the head shakes back and forth,
karna perasane ara berpa'eɔah	because it's felt to be worthwhile,
waktu bertengkah mera wë semul	that when fighting, knives won't cut.
ɔo'a pengokop orum pegempar	Spells to unnerve or create confusion,
ɔo'a tegër orum penimul	to make tough and strong;
tape tekebir sawah ku salam	but from the *takbîr* all the way to the *salam,*
ate we belayar ngë mugerupul	his heart flies and shakes.
ngë mari sembahyang ɔabuh berɔo'a	After worshiping, he sets in to pray,
ikecëpën mata lagu jema sugul	closing the eyes like someone meditating.
ngë mungë gernang ibubuh geritik	The drum has sounded, now he shakes;
ngë lepas ɔepik itama cangkul	the fish are gone, now he sets the net.
apabilë sembahyang si mengoh n'oya	If worship is done in that way,
nabi berkata mana bisa makul	the Prophet said: How can it be effective?
kitë muniro numë ku jema kucak	We make requests not to a little guy;
kitë bercerak orum jema kul	we speak with a big guy.

While in the midst of worship, "from the *takbîr* all the way to the *salam,*" his heart is still in his fields, but the minute worship ends and he has a chance to ask for a favor from God through petitionary prayer, he instantly becomes intensely focused on what he is doing. Not that this is proper—Mudë Kala ridicules the shaking and eye shutting to underscore the person's intensity while not making it seem as if the prayers will be effective. God is not receiving these prayers: "the fish are gone, now he sets the net."

This sort of criticism offended many Gayo, some of whom indeed knew little more Qur'an than the short verses mentioned here. But such was the intent of the poems: to shake people up, so that they would realize their errors and "come to *tauhid*" (God's essential oneness), as one poet put it. Even the manner and vocal timbre of some modernist teachers was grating—famously so in the case of Tengku Jali, the modernist teacher who initiated public debates on ritual matters in the late 1930s and founded the leading modernist school in the Takèngën area, called Islamic Education. Even modernist-leaning Gayo men and women remember his loud manner, his shrill voice, and his punishment, generously meted out to lazy students. I knew one of his successors, Tengku Mukhlis, and found him a man of generous heart and deep religious devotion, but irritating in his unwillingness to let a matter drop and his quickness to anger when someone failed to follow what he considered to be correct religious procedure. "That is not religion!" was his frequent cry. Such direct challenges to others were (and are) quite contrary to the general Gayo tendency to avoid public confrontations or accusations and, I am convinced, were made with that sense of purposive transgression very much in mind.

The sarcasm, shrillness, and confrontational style were all, I believe, aimed at shaking up ideas taken for granted about the world, at interrupting the normal social fabric and etiquette, so that it could be replaced by something else. Gayo modernists did not seek to construct a city on a hill, but to reform the behavior of villagers and townspeople without removing them from their social context. They did so by insistently drawing them back to scripture, underlining both the Arabic source and the vernacular gloss, and on the basis of these truths assaying villagers' behavior in the religious sphere.

In its tone and specific textual links, Gayo modernist rhetoric links following scripture to throwing off the past. In this it echoes the broad thrust of Indonesianist modernist writing during the first half of the twentieth century, from the shrill blasts aimed at other religious scholars by Ahmad Hassan (1968) of the Persis movement (Federspiel 1970) to the novels of the religious scholar Hamka and other, principally West Sumatran, authors who celebrate the release that Islam provides from the constraints of tradition.

But traditionalist scholars have been able to reinterpret the implications of intent for ritual criticism. Indeed, they have used the modernist emphasis on intent as the basis for a counterreformation within traditionalist practice and commentary. Granted, they say, that intent determines what a practice is and thus whether or not it is acceptable. But we cannot know the intent of another, so we should not be quick to criticize the practice of another person. Here the scholars draw on a general Gayo tendency to acknowledge the possibility that intent is other than what one sees in behavior.[18] As Tengku Ali Salwany, a noted traditionalist scholar in Takèngën, explained to me, when people hold ritual meals with special foods and incense, they may conceive of these objects as objects of devotion or they may understand them as ways of bringing people together to worship God. The only difference between the two possibilities is the (unobservable) intent of the actors. The former intent is incorrect from a religious point of view, but the latter is perfectly acceptable to God. Incense, for example, is fine if it is intended as a way of making things fragrant (Muhammad himself used it for this purpose), but not as a way of calling a person's soul or making requests to angels.

Not only has this line of reasoning enabled traditionalist scholars to defend older practices, both in private and in public meetings of the district Council of Ulama, it also enables some modernist-leaning individuals to attend controversial ritual events and interpret their own participation as consistent with their general religious principles. This possibility of multiple interpretations is facilitated by the general tendency to minimize public exegesis of rituals or to offer only the most general account of what the ritual is all about (Bowen 1993a, 315–318).

In the village of Isak, for example, nearly all residents attend the recitations for the dead described earlier. Sometimes no public speech is given about the ritual (other than formulaic speeches of welcome). When such speeches are given, they usually simply say that the chanting "helps the spirit of the deceased." The explanation allows each individual to figure out just how this help reaches its destination. Some think that the food eaten and the words recited travel straight to the spirit of the deceased, who enjoys their benefit. Others reject emphatically such an idea but believe that the words reach God, who then relieves the burdens on the deceased because he is pleased by the recitations. Still others participate in the recitations on the assumption that they are simply recitations for the glory of God and that it is entirely up to God, whose will is unfathomable, what he does about the deceased. Such, for example, is roughly the position held by one modernist teacher who does attend these sessions. Other modernists, however, find no possible interpretation acceptable and avoid these events. These ambiguities of exegesis allow people to resist, or at least to deflect, demands that they turn away from older ritual practices. The very focus on intent in Gayo modernist discourse may have contributed to the maintaining of liturgical pluralism within villages and neighborhoods.

Explanations and Comparisons

My argument so far has stayed within the confines of Gayo history. I have indicated how the concept of intent has been invoked in Gayo religious debates and with what effects. I have also argued that Gayo modernists focused on narrow religious reform rather than broader societal issues at least in part because they retained a strong identification with their villages even as they became actors in a new religious sphere. The town of Takèngën became a multiethnic center for modernist thinking and thus encouraged both the development of a transethnic formulation of religious concerns and early alliances with nationalism. Yet because Gayo reformers continued to be deeply involved in village affairs, they focused on transforming village religious life. This set of social commitments led them to carve out a distinct religious sphere for reform, and this sphere defined the limits of public debate.

This line of argument emphasizes the role of social ties in channeling religious reform strategies in one direction rather than another. An alternative, ultimately complementary line of reasoning would have begun from cultural features rather than social relations. I might have argued as follows: Gayo generally emphasize the power of internal, unobservable events, and so a reformist emphasis on the problem of intent enjoyed a good cultural fit. Gayo practices of healing and sorcery, for example, rest on the possibility of effecting bodily transformations entirely through powerful depictive imagination, with no public activity. This intensely private sort of healing contrasts with very public practices found elsewhere in the region; the theories behind it ensure that one cannot reach any conclusions about someone's activities from his or her observable characteristics or actions (Bowen 1993a, 106–171).

These social or cultural arguments ought to lead me (and all other analysts of such things) to make comparisons with other cases. In saying that Gayo did such and such because of certain social or cultural features, I am also, at least implicitly, stating that in the absence of those features things would have gone otherwise. Cultural arguments, for example, require us to consider the ways that other cultural frameworks might have shaped religious discourse. For example, the Gayo cultural view contrasts with that described for Morocco by Lawrence Rosen (1984, 47–59), in which one can read from social characteristics of persons to the attendant mental states. The Moroccan view asserts that persons have essential differences in their mental characteristics, depending on such critical social differences as gender and place of origin. Where Gayo culture emphasizes practices and allows for a great deal of circumstantial variability and contingency in intent, Moroccan culture emphasizes the social construction of persons and a lesser degree of variability. Consistent with this difference is the importance of gender-based contrasts of (male) reason versus (female) passion in Moroccan religious discourse vis-à-vis the virtual absence of such contrasts in Gayo discourse.

This sort of comparison—in which different cultural patterns explain, by contextualizing, different religious histories—is that usually followed in cultural accounts. For the study of Islam the best known of such pattern-comparisons is Clifford Geertz' *Islam Observed* (1968), which, however right or wrong it might be (see Munson 1993), set out a cultural contrast in style and focus between North African and Javanese ways of being Muslims.

My starting point has, however, been less the styles and patterns characteristic of a society or region than the particular intentions, strategies, and rhetoric of actors, the issues they chose to emphasize, and the ways they formulated and expressed their ideas so as to influence various audiences. Comparisons might, then, emphasize differences in projects and strategies. Such comparisons could be broad in scope, as when William Roff (1987) depicts the contrasting ways that movements adapted "Wahhabi" ideas to particular circumstances in the nineteenth century. But one can also look at controlled comparisons, where microvariation in social conditions, conversion strategies, and cultural forms emerge within a more specific region. I can only suggest the lines of such a comparative analysis here, working outward from the Gayo case to that of lowland Aceh (and suggesting a potential contrast with the earlier reformist struggles in West Sumatra). When more fully fleshed out, such comparisons may illuminate both the highly differentiated projects of modernist persuasion and the relations among social structures, religious change, and cultural forms.

The contrast with Aceh is particularly telling for the frequent cultural contacts between the two peoples, especially in religious affairs, and the development in both societies of a modernist Islamic consciousness in the 1920s and 1930s (Siegel 1969). The social context for religious modernism in lowland, northern Aceh differed from that in the highlands in two major ways. First, the context was all-Acehnese. The most important organization was not the pan-Indonesian Muhammadiyah but the Aceh-specific association of religious teachers called PUSA (Persatuan Ulama Seluruh Aceh), All-Aceh Association of Religious Scholars, led by a future governor of Aceh, Daud Beureueh. Modernist imaginings thus primarily concerned a new Aceh rather than Aceh's place in a new Indonesia.

Second, modernists developed their social critique in terms of the opposition of village life and the world beyond, the *rantau*. "They appealed to men to act not as villagers but as Muslims; to the *ulama*, this meant forgetting traditional social identities" (Siegel 1969, 74). This opposition was also strongly linked to oppositions of gender and religious values. Most Acehnese men spent years away from their village at study or work, in all-male settings. Women, by contrast, were at the center of village life, remaining in their natal villages after marriage, receiving houses from their fathers, and managing ricefields. Men felt they were treated as children by their wives when at home; the high divorce rates of the area followed from these tensions. Male religious spokesmen identified women with emotions and desires, *hawa nafsu,* which the properly religious (male) individual must transcend through the strengthening of reason, *aqal.* Men could best develop reason and control passions away from the village, on the *rantau.*

The Acehnese social fabric in which modernism developed was thus one of a male/female opposition within an ethnically specific framework. Acehnese modernists sought to transcend village life rather than, as in the Gayo highlands, reforming it. They did so in the idiom of struggle: for self-mastery through worship and for economic success through individual labor, both in some sense a continuation of the earlier struggle against the Dutch through war. These struggles involved individuals, joined in "mechanical solidarity." A powerful image of the properly religious society was found in congregational worship, where all Acehnese worshiped side by side and in precisely the same way (Siegel 1969, 262–275). The social and political importance of this image led provincial leaders to feel particularly threatened by particularistic, inward-looking, local forms of worship (Bowen 1989).

The earlier struggles as conceptualized by *ulama* were embodied in the poetry of holy war. The epic of the Acehnese war, the Hikayat Prang Sabi (Story of the Holy War), relates the journey from this world to the next (Siegel 1969, 74–77; 1979, 229–265). Arabic scripture also appears here, and, as in Gayo poetry, it is foregrounded against the background metrical scheme (Siegel 1979, 261). Here, too, scripture has an "unvarying message" to convey (p. 263). But scripture serves not as a source of correction for wayward villagers, as in highlands verse, but as a source of promise, of the reward that awaits the fighter in paradise.

From the 1930s on, Acehnese religious forms looked at the possibility for creating a new society on earth rather than in paradise. These new forms of religious persuasion include sermons and newspaper articles. They emphasize not the reform of village life in a strictly demarcated religious sphere, but the building of a new society on socioreligious principles. If Gayo modernists stress the boundary of religion and the rest of society, their Acehnese counterparts emphasize "the idea of society as a manifestation of *ibadah* (religious duty)" (Siegel 1969, 116). Acehnese modernist writings point to the tone that worship gives to all of life, not the reform of specific acts (as in the Gayo poetry). They portray Aceh as a once and future glorious nation, in which struggle strengthens reason and reason orders men in their actions (Siegel 1969, 119–133).

The tone of the earlier poetry and the later sermons and articles is redemptive, future-looking. These forms take men out of their current social surrounds and turn them toward a future promised society. The dominant metaphor is an awakening from sleep, not the interruption of current social practices. And it is a message that is directed at men, not women. Thus Gayo modernists urge their fellow men and women to transcend ethnic identity in favor of a scripture-based life in their village surrounds; Acehnese modernists urge their fellow men to transcend village identity in favor of an ideal Acehnese unity of supralocal male individuals.

A third, geographically close contrast is in Minangkabau society, where men have lived on the margins of the village, rather than fully in it, as in Gayo, or apart from it, as in Aceh. Christine Dobbin (1983) has shown how, in the early nineteenth century, the combination of a growth in coffee cropping and a new, highly reformist Muslim ideology led to sharp attacks on village practices by these marginal men *and* to attempts to establish new, purified communities. In the early twentieth century, modernist teachers created distinct school communities in greater tension with the villages than was the case in Aceh. One might argue that these marginal schools continued the social heritage of the earlier reformist movement, in contrast to Acehnese ideals of total separation and Gayo direct involvement in village reform.

These brief remarks point toward an ethnological, comparative study of religious modernisms that would underscore the local particulars of putatively universalistic projects. It also might lay the groundwork for a general framework of comparison. For one can discern other emphases in Gayo modernism that, given different social conditions, could emerge as dominant and that indeed in other parts of the world have become *the* dominant form of modernist intervention. Let me suggest three specific associations between social situations and religious emphases:

First, certain struggles revolve around efforts by a reforming group to distinguish itself from others, either from other religious streams within Islam or from other groups in a broader, non-Islamic cultural framework. In such cases Muslims may emphasize public self-definition, especially through congregational worship but also, potentially, through fasting, the keeping of rules regarding purity, and so forth. An early phase of Gayo modernism was, indeed, characterized by reformers' concern with establishing separate mosques as signs of their distinction from the older tradition. Muslims in similar situations in West Africa (Launay 1992) and China (Gladney 1991) have played up worship or ritual purity as markers of social (including ethnic) distinction.

Second, other reformers place at the forefront the struggle against pre-existing socioreligious hierarchies and thus underscore the egalitarian (and possibly also the latitudinarian) messages of "scripturalism." In such cases, such as the South Asian movements studied by Barbara Metcalf (1982), one would expect to find an emphasis on *tafsir* (interpretation) and *ijtihad* (independent reflection) and the antielite values they can be seen as promoting. And, in those Gayo places where traditional rulers sought to suppress modernist teachers, it was indeed the right to appeal directly to scripture that was stressed; this emphasis was absent in those places where such teachers obtained rulers' backing or achieved power themselves. The specific effects of colonial rule must be factored into these accounts: for example, British and Dutch colonial suppression of social reform discourse may have pushed reformists to emphasize the reform of individual religious practice.

Finally, with the Gayo/Aceh and Gayo/Morocco contrasts in mind, one might expect that broad differences in the cultural construction of personhood would shape religious reform movements and that, in particular, a strong male-female ideological contrast might support movements for the wholesale reworking of society (in order to change individuals) rather than the reform of specific liturgical practices.

Why Emphasize Diversity?

I have argued that comparing religious histories allows us to study specific ideas, practices, and strategies in a way that avoids two common reductionisms: the normative essentialism that reduces religious phenomena to the elements that fit the Great Tradition and the ethnographic particularism that reduces them to the elements that fit the local cultural logic. Both kinds of reductionism continue to plague the study of Islam and other "world religions"; both are understandable outgrowths of disciplinary training. Textually trained historians of religion find it natural to look for text-based similarities across societies, while field-trained anthropologists find it equally natural to highlight the differential patterning of religious cultures.

Neither approach, taken by itself, can make much sense of movements —religious or otherwise—that appeal to members of diverse societies precisely because of their rhetorics of transcending cultural differences. Rather, because such movements themselves strategically incorporate both local and translocal ideas, so should their analyses. Comparisons involve, or should involve, paying attention to the multiple social levels at which religious phenomena exist: from norms and practices found in nearly all Muslim societies (worshiping, even if the forms vary, or avoiding pork, even if not all comply), through the texts and histories that characterize regions, to the ways specific individuals and groups select from the broader-scale phenomena those that fit their own ideas, intentions, and interests.

Keeping these levels distinct and tracing the myriad choices and reasons of distinct groups of Muslims will, I trust, make difficult the labeling and lumping of movements that appears to characterize current popular studies of religious movements and especially studies of so-called fundamentalisms. The problem is not just the social-scientific one, that this labeling obscures much more than it discloses about Muslim and other reform movements. The problem is also political and moral, because, as I think most of us would admit, the more we can consider others to partake of an undifferentiated Other (whether communism, terrorism, or Islam), the less we feel obliged to treat them as morally equivalent to ourselves. We, of course, are composed of complex, intersecting motives; they do everything out of their singular Otherness.

It thus becomes especially incumbent upon those of us who write about current Others to stress their particularity of ideas, their complexity of motives, and their general humanity. And herein lies a possible contribution of comparative studies, even studies of small and far-off places, to social life. It only makes sense if there is some relationship between social science writing and political acting, if the more particularity that bleeds through portraits of current political Others, the greater the humanity that will surface in foreign (or domestic) policy. This hope may be naive, but it has the advantage of being hope.

Notes

1. The now-classic statement of this perspective is Jurgen Habermas' (1989 [1962]) historical treatise on the European bourgeois public sphere. A recent collection of essays edited by Craig Calhoun (1992) provides useful critiques of Habermas' argument; notable in both works, however, is the absence of attention to the possibility that religious movements can be modernizing.

2. As much recent work in the anthropology of religion has shown, attempts to define a religion in terms offered (or commanded) by the state end up radically transforming the nature of religious thought and activity. For a classic statement of this idea, see Smith 1963; for recent examples from Indonesia, see Atkinson 1983; Steedly 1993. See also Talal Asad's remark that Saudia Arabian *ulama* are, in their calls for the public accountability of the king and their engagement with modern state institutions, "*part* of modernity and not a *reaction* to it" (1993, 226).

3. Compare Talal Asad's (1993) effort to place the study of power and discipline at the center of the anthropology of religion.

4. For examples from the study of Islamic movements, see the essays in Burke and Lapidus 1988; for Southeast Asian cases, see Hefner 1987; Kessler 1978; and the essays by Horvatich and McKenna in this volume.

5. I discuss this problem more generally in Bowen 1993a, 3–11. As a case in point: at the conference where this essay was presented, the distinguished scholar of Arabic and Islam Anthony Johns objected strongly to my contextualizing reading of the "intent" debate, arguing that the matter was general to Islam and could not be reduced to matters of Gayo history and thinking. I have profited from our exchange and cite some of his remarks below, but the objections assumed that the only interesting question one can pose of religious phenomena is a philological one: Where did the idea come from? and not: How is it locally understood, and why?

6. On the development of Islamic institutions in the highlands during this period, see Bowen 1991, 93–118; 1993a, 39–73. On modernist Muslim developments in West Sumatra, see Noer 1973 and Abdullah 1971.

7. I use "worship" to refer to the ritual referred to in Arabic as *salât,* in Gayo as *semiyang,* and in Indonesian as *sembahyang,* reserving "prayer" for the petitionary prayers known as *doa.*

8. Some Muslims stressing the spirituality of worship have represented this pronouncement as the instant of turning away from the world toward God (Schimmel 1975, 149).

9. My own curiosity was initially ignited by the historian Taufik Abdullah's remarks that the Gayo had made much more of these matters than had the people of his own birthplace in West Sumatra, which itself was a center for liturgical controversy in the 1920s and 1930s.

10. For this account of developments in West Sumatra I follow the account in Johns 1993.

11. For a fuller account of this history, see Bowen 1993a, 30–38.

12. On comparable European ideas, see Taylor 1989, 37–39).

13. Compare the range of meanings of *niyyâ* found in Morocco, including "desire," "sincere," and "faith" (Eickelman 1976, 163; Rosen 1984, 49–56).

14. It also can be compared to what Taylor describes as the shift from seeing the universe through the lens of an "ontic logos," thus as enspirited, to a sharply dualistic view of mind and body, in which previous interlocutors in the natural world are voided of their communicative potential (1989, 185–192).

15. See Bowen 1993b for an extended account of this genre.

16. The first verse of the Qur'an, with which one begins the recitation portion of each ritual unit of worship.

17. Qur'an 112, al-Ikhlâs, referred to here by its opening phrase; Gayo scholars dislike this informal way of designating it.

18. Contrast the greater Moroccan assuredness on this score (Rosen 1984: 49–55).

References Cited

Abdullah, Taufik 1971. *Schools and Politics: The Kaum Muda Movement in West Sumatra (1927–1933)*. Ithaca: Cornell University Modern Indonesia Project.

Asad, Talal. 1993. *Genealogies of Religion*. Baltimore: Johns Hopkins University Press.

Atkinson, Jane Monnig. 1983. "Religions in Dialogue: The Construction of an Indonesian Minority Religion." *American Ethnologist* 10:684–696.

Bowen, John R. 1989. "Salat in Indonesia: The Social Meanings of an Islamic Ritual." *Man* (n.s.), 24:299–318.

———. 1991. *Sumatran Politics and Poetics: Gayo History, 1900–1989*. New Haven: Yale University Press.

———. 1993a. *Muslims through Discourse: Religion and Ritual in Gayo Society*. Princeton: Princeton University Press.

———. 1993b. "A Modernist Muslim Poetic: Irony and Social Critique in Islamic Verse." *Journal of Asian Studies* 45:629–646.

———. n.d. "Interruptive Rhetorics: On the Persuasiveness of Religious Modernism in Sumatra." To appear in a volume on language and authority in South and Southeast Asia.

Burke, Edmund, III, and Ira M. Lapidus, eds. 1988. *Islam, Politics, and Social Movements*. Berkeley and Los Angeles: University of California Press.

Calhoun, Craig, ed. 1992. *Habermas and the Public Sphere*. Cambridge: MIT Press.

Daudy, Abdurrahman. 1950. Untitled manuscript.

Dobbin, Christine. 1983. *Islamic Revivalism in a Changing Peasant Economy: Central Sumatra, 1784–1847*. London: Curzon Press.

Eickelman, Dale F. 1976. *Moroccan Islam*. Austin: University of Texas.

Federspiel, Howard M. 1970. *Persatuan Islam: Islamic Reform in Twentieth-Century Indonesia*. Ithaca: Cornell University Modern Indonesia Project.

Fischer, Michael. 1980. *Iran: From Religious Dispute to Revolution*. Cambridge: Harvard University Press.

Geertz, Clifford. 1968. *Islam Observed*. New Haven: Yale University Press.

Gladney, Dru C. 1991. *Muslim Chinese: Ethnic Nationalism in the People's Republic*. Cambridge, Mass.: Council on East Asian Studies, Harvard University.

Habermas, Jurgen. 1989. *The Structural Transformation of the Public Sphere: An Inquiry into a Category of Bourgeois Society*. Translated by Thomas Burger. 1962. Reprint, Cambridge: MIT Press.

Hamka [Haji Abdul Malik Karim Amrullah]. 1958. *Ajahku* (My Father). Jakarta: Widjaja.

Hassan, Ahmad. 1968 *Soal-Jawab Tentang Berbagai Masalah Agama* (Questions and Answers on Various Religious Issues). Bandung: Diponegoro.

Hefner, Robert W. 1987. "Islamizing Java? Religion and Politics in Rural East Java." *Journal of Asian Studies* 46:533–554.

Hourani, Albert. 1983. *Arabic Thought in the Liberal Age, 1798–1939*. 1962. Reprint, Cambridge: Cambridge University Press.

Johns, Anthony. 1993. "Responses, Reflections, and Memories." Paper presented at the conference on "Islam and the Social Construction of Identities: Comparative Perspectives on Southeast Asian Muslims," School of Hawaiian, Asian and Pacific Studies, University of Hawai'i at Manoa, Honolulu, August 4–6.

Kato, Tsuyoshi. 1982. *Matriliny and Migration: Evolving Minangkabau Traditions in Indonesia*. Ithaca: Cornell University Press.

Kessler, Clive S. 1978. *Islam and Politics in a Malay State: Kelantan, 1838–1969*. Ithaca: Cornell University Press.

Launay, Robert. 1992. *Beyond the Stream: Islam and Society in a West African Town*. Berkeley and Los Angeles: University of California Press.

Metcalf, Barbara Daly. 1982. *Islamic Revival in British India: Deoband, 1860–1900*. Princeton: Princeton University Press.

Munson, Henry. 1993. *Religion and Politics in North Africa*. New Haven: Yale University Press.

Nakamura, Mitsuo. 1983. *The Crescent Arises over the Banyan Tree*. Yogyakarta: Gajah Mada University Press.

Noer, Deliar. 1973. *The Modernist Muslim Movement in Indonesia, 1900–1942*. Kuala Lumpur: Oxford University Press.

Roff, William R. 1987. "Islamic Movements: One or Many?" In William R. Roff, ed. *Islam and the Political Economy of Meaning*, pp. 31–52. Berkeley and Los Angeles: University of California Press.

Rosen, Lawrence. 1984. *Bargaining for Reality: The Construction of Social Relations in a Muslim Community*. Chicago: University of Chicago Press.

Schimmel, Annemarie. 1975. *Mystical Dimensions of Islam*. Chapel Hill: University of North Carolina Press.

Siegel, James T. 1969. *The Rope of God*. Berkeley and Los Angeles: University of California Press.

———. 1979. *Shadow and Sound: The Historical Thought of a Sumatran People*. Chicago: University of Chicago Press.

Smith, Wilfred Cantwell. 1963. *The Meaning and End of Religion*. New York: Macmillan.

Steedly, Mary Margaret. 1993. *Hanging without a Rope*. Princeton: Princeton University Press.

Taylor, Charles. 1989. *Sources of the Self: The Making of the Modern Identity*. Cambridge, Mass.: Harvard University Press.

Wensinck, A. J. 1953. "Nîya." In H. A. R. Gibb and J. H. Kramers, eds., *The Shorter Encyclopedia of Islam*, pp. 449–450. Ithaca: Cornell University Press.

Chapter 6

The Ahmadiyya Movement in Simunul

ISLAMIC REFORM IN ONE REMOTE AND UNLIKELY PLACE

Patricia Horvatich

A century ago, Christiaan Snouck Hurgronje, a student of Islam, warned his colleagues in the Netherlands East Indies Civil Service that Islam in Indonesia, "which seemed so static, so sunk in a torpid medievalism, was actually changing in fundamental ways, but these changes were so gradual, so subtle, so concentrated in remote, and, to non-Islamic minds, unlikely places that although they take place before our very eyes, they are hidden from those who do not make a careful study of the subject" (Snouck Hurgronje 1906, 280 as quoted in Geertz 1963, 16). Islam *is* changing in Southeast Asia. Indeed, events associated with Islamic reform in Southeast Asia have been hard to miss. Unlike the subtle and gradual changes Snouck Hurgronje observed in the nineteenth century, major changes associated with Islamic reform have been very public, occasionally violent, and sudden. Although scholars recognize that Islam is changing in Southeast Asia, few have attended to Snouck Hurgronje's observation that Islamic change is occurring in remote and unlikely places. The focus of most scholars has rarely strayed to rural areas. Studies such as those by Alfian (1989), Howard Federspiel (1970), Judith Nagata (1984), Mitsuo Nakamura (1984), and James Peacock (1978) have concentrated on regional centers such as Yogyakarta, Padang, Bandung, and Kuala Lumpur, where the major movements of Islamic reform have been organized.

As I will show in this chapter, and as Michael Peletz and Martin Rössler demonstrate in theirs, Islamic reform is not exclusively an urban phenomenon. Indeed, as Peletz argues, processes and effects of Islamic reform in rural areas among ordinary Muslims merit far more attention from scholars than they have received in the past. Such attention to Islamic reform in "remote" and "unlikely" places challenges widely accepted conclusions that modernism is a movement of urban intellectuals and that villagers are in no danger of losing their faith because their spiritual life is cared for by the imam of the local mosque (see Gibb 1947, 69). To assume that modernism is an urban movement of intellectuals or to claim as Ernest Gellner does that "Sufism is the opium of the tribesmen, reformism of the townsmen" (1981, 160) is to perceive villages as closed communities.

Rural villages in Southeast Asia are *not* encapsulated enclaves of tradition. Not only are most villages in Southeast Asia incorporated within the world market, they are also very much involved in an international exchange of ideas. To a great degree, this exchange has been made possible by public mass education.

This chapter will show that mass education in the Philippines is shaping modern discourses of Islamic reform by prompting college-educated Sama to criticize traditional practitioners of Islam. Specifically, I examine the ways the Ahmadiyya movement, an international movement of Islamic reform, was introduced to the people of a rural Philippine community. I explore the reasons some individuals in Simunul, Tawi-Tawi, find truth in Ahmadi teachings, while others reject them as heretical. I also examine the ways people have come to interpret the teachings of the Ahmadi and what the term *ahmadi* has come to mean to them. As Sama of Simunul Island appropriate new terms and concepts, they give them new meanings, thus changing standard interpretations of Ahmadi teachings. In such a way Islamic reform has come about in this small island community in the Sulu Archipelago.

Like other authors in this volume, I examine the process of Islamic reform with attention to ways individuals strategize to effect and resist change in their communities. I focus on the beliefs and actions of "ordinary" Muslims: not intellectuals, politicians, or religious leaders, but residents of a rural Philippine community. I pay particular attention to the college-educated members of this community, because it is these individuals who advocate the need to reform Islam. Following Dale Eickelman (1992) and Barbara Metcalf (this volume), I argue that there is a significant relation between mass education and Islamic reform by showing that mass education has prepared the ground for the development of alternative Islamic discourses and activism in Simunul, Tawi-Tawi.

The Sama of Simunul Island
Tawi-Tawi lies in the southwesternmost corner of the Philippines, only miles from Sabah, Malaysia. Over three hundred islands are located in this province, most of them small and uninhabited. The island of Tawi-Tawi is

the largest of these islands. The Sama are the predominant ethnic group of Tawi-Tawi Province and live along the coast of Tawi-Tawi Island and on the shores of the many small islands that surround it.[1] The island of Bongao (pronounced "Bunggau"), located on the western tip of Tawi-Tawi Island, is the provincial capital and regional center of trade.

Simunul Island is seven miles south of Bongao. The island is only fifteen square miles in size, but it contains fifteen *barangay* (communities) and is home to over 25,000 people. With its swaying palm trees and turquoise-colored sea, Simunul is picture perfect. There were moments during my fieldwork there when, watching the sun set over the sea and listening to the call to prayer, I believed that Simunul was a timeless, distant place. As a coup was attempted in Manila, as Iraq invaded Kuwait and the Gulf War ensued, and as the Soviet Union collapsed, life went on as usual in Simunul.

Or, I should say, life went on as usual for me. People of Simunul were aware of these world events and understood that they would soon experience the ripples of their effects. After the coup attempt in Manila, more people planted cassava because they realized that political instability in the capital would result in inflated food prices. Likewise, the situation in the Middle East caused the price of gasoline to rise, requiring people to pay another five pesos to travel to Bongao.

The Sama of Simunul, concerned about their kin who work in Middle East, closely followed the events of the war announced over the radio. One man was convinced that if a world war ensued, Simunul would be one of the first places to be bombed, as a result of its strategic importance. This conviction is less absurd when one considers that the Japanese invaded Simunul during the Second World War, that Simunul was the training ground for President Marcos' covert Operation Merdeka in 1967,[2] that the people of West Simunul participated in the Moro National Liberation Front from 1972 to 1974, and that the Philippine Navy shelled West Simunul because of this MNLF activity.[3] The people of Simunul do not "go off to war" in foreign lands. Unfortunately, national and international violence has a way of coming to their small island.

While I could thus pretend to be on a remote and isolated island, the Sama with whom I lived could not afford the luxury of such an illusion. The seas I perceived as clear, tranquil, and little-trafficked were actually swirling ocean currents that for centuries have been drawing the Sama into contact with a succession of outside powers. Simunul is not and has never been an isolated enclave.

For centuries the Sama of Simunul Island were subjects of the Sulu Sultanate. This sultanate emerged in the fourteenth century and was dominated by the Tausug people of the island of Jolo (pronounced "holo"). The

Sultan of Sulu administered the Tausug, Sama, and Bajau people of the Sulu Archipelago by assigning *datu,* traditional regional leaders, to specific regions. These *datu* were usually Tausug men who were subordinate, loyal, and accountable to the sultan.

The Sama also have ties to the Malays of Sabah, Malaysia, with whom they have a lively and profitable trading relationship. This relationship continues today in spite of the national boundaries that separate Malaysia and the Philippines, and the laws that define their trade as smuggling. Currently, almost half of the Simunul population lives and works in Sabah, where they easily find jobs in lumber mills, restaurants, and shops. The wages are quite high in Sabah, and consumer goods are much cheaper than in Tawi-Tawi. When the Malaysian government cracks down on illegal aliens, the Sama are shipped back to Tawi-Tawi, only to return days later aboard the boats of traders/smugglers. There is thus a steady traffic of people and goods between Sabah and Simunul.

The Sama are also oriented toward Mecca. Mecca is the *ponsot dunia,* or navel of the world, for these Muslims. People pray toward Mecca, sacrifice to travel to Mecca as pilgrims, and, when they die, are buried with their bodies facing Mecca. The Middle East is not only a center of Islam, however. It is also a center of employment. The Sama began sending people abroad in 1975. In 1990 about 14 percent of women from Simunul between the ages of twenty and forty worked in the Middle East as domestic helpers, midwives, and nurses. Seven percent of men of the same age group worked in the Middle East as laborers.

The people of Simunul are oriented toward the United States as well. After the Spanish-American War of 1898, the United States took possession of the Philippines. After many violent military acts, the Americans "subdued" the Muslims of Mindanao and Sulu, a feat the Spanish had failed to accomplish during their three-hundred-year reign in the Philippines. Employing a policy of attraction, the American government instituted public schools throughout the Philippines. In 1918 the United States built an elementary school in Simunul. Shortly thereafter, children continued their studies in a high school located in Jolo. By the 1930s the Sama themselves were becoming teachers and replacing the Americans and Christian Filipinos who taught them. Today, about 30 percent of the adult population of Simunul has had some college education, and half of this number are college graduates.[4] Their ability to speak English fosters an awareness of and participation in world events and discourses.

These seas of strong currents carried Tausug *datu* to Simunul and brought American teachers and administrators to Bongao. These seas carried furtive traders and workers to Malaysia and brought pilgrims to the

Persian Gulf. These seas also brought foreign Muslims, carrying the Word of Islam, to the people of Simunul.

One of the first of these foreign Muslims was a man the *sarsila* (local histories) identify as Sheik Makhdum. According to the *sarsila*, Sheik Makhdum arrived in Simunul aboard an iron ship but, once in sight of the island, walked the remaining distance on the water. He taught the people of Simunul about Islam and impressed them with his supernatural abilities. Sheik Makhdum built a mosque for his followers, carrying tree trunks from the jungle to the seashore as if they weighed no more than matchsticks. The pillars of this mosque still stand today, serving as a testament to the presence and the power of Sheik Makhdum. These pillars have been dated to the fourteenth century and support the claim that this is the oldest known mosque in the Philippines.

Many Muslim traders and missionaries followed Sheik Makhdum to Simunul, some of them spending their lives on the island. The descendants of these missionaries have a special status in the community and are believed to be direct descendants of the Prophet Muhammad.

After the Second World War, many Muslim Filipinos were educated in *madrasah* (schools of Islamic learning) in Jolo and Basilan. These learned men became missionaries and traveled throughout Mindanao and Sulu to teach people about Islam. Four of these missionaries found their way to Simunul and spent years living with and teaching the Sama.

The Introduction of the Ahmadi Teachings

In 1957 a man known as Haji Hussein brought a new Muslim discourse to Simunul: the Ahmadi teachings.[5] The Ahmadiyya movement was founded by Mirza Ghulam Ahmad in India during the late nineteenth century. Like leaders of other movements of Islamic reform, Ghulam Ahmad was convinced that Islam had sunk to unprecedented depths owing to corruption, innovation, tomb worship, worship of Sufi shaikhs, and even polytheism. On the whole the teachings of Ghulam Ahmad agree with Islam, especially modern interpretations of Islam that call for the removal of non-Islamic beliefs and practices. The teachings differ, however, in two significant respects. First, Ghulam Ahmad claimed to be a *mujaddid,* a renewer or reformer of Islam, and then later to be a *nabi,* a prophet. And second, he claimed to be the *mahdi,* the messiah expected to appear on the day of resurrection.

Of these claims the first is the most heretical according to mainstream Sunni Islam. Belief in the prophethood of Muhammad is central to the Muslim faith, and the recognition of Muhammad as the *last* prophet is, to most, a cardinal article of Islam. The Ahmadi are able to claim that

Ghulam Ahmad was a prophet by reinterpreting a verse in the Qur'an, in al-Ahzab (The Clans) 33:40, that states, "Muhammad was not the father of any man among you, but the messenger of Allah and Khatam al-Nabiyyin." "Khatam al-Nabiyyin" literally means the *seal* of the prophets, but Sunni Muslims have interpreted this to mean the *last* of the prophets. Ahmadi, in contrast, argue that "Khatam al-Nabiyyin" means that Muhammad was not the *last*, but the *best* prophet. Because the Ahmadi allow for prophets after Muhammad, Mirza Ghulam Ahmad was able to claim that *he* was one such prophet whose mission was not to change Islam or to introduce new tenets of the faith, but to reform Islam in accordance with that which was set down by Muhammad (Friedmann 1987, 50–57).

In 1914 the Ahmadi split into two factions: the Qadiyani and the Lahori. The Qadiyani group is the original group founded by Ghulam Ahmad, and the Lahori group is a splinter group that is more conciliatory toward mainstream Sunni Muslims. The Lahori group watered down the notion of Ghulam Ahmad's claim to prophethood by arguing that his prophethood is so identical with that of Muhammad that it has no existence of its own; it is shadowy or manifestational. This interpretation of the Lahori faction is consistent with the earlier claim of Ghulam Ahmad, according to which he was a *mujaddid,* a renewer of religion (Friedmann 1987, 150–151).

Ghulam Ahmad also claimed that he was the *mahdi,* the messiah. Traditionally, Sunni Muslims believe that this role is reserved for Isa (Jesus). They believe that in the final days Isa will play a role in resurrecting the dead. Ghulam Ahmad claimed this position for himself. He argued that Isa did not die on the cross nor does he now wait in heaven in his earthly form, but he was taken down from the cross and healed of his wounds. Ghulam Ahmad argued that Isa migrated to India, where he preached the gospel until his natural death at the age of one hundred twenty years (Friedmann 1987, 112–115).

Sunni Muslims in Pakistan have called the Ahmadi heretics and have persecuted them. In 1984 the government passed an ordinance forbidding Ahmadi from calling their faith Islam, preaching or propagating the teachings of Ghulam Ahmad, calling for prayer in the usual Muslim way, and using Islamic titles for their leaders. Similarly, the Kingdom of Saudi Arabia has forbidden the Ahmadi from performing the *hajj,* the pilgrimage to Mecca, one of the five pillars of Islam. Ahmadi have been imprisoned, tortured, and killed throughout the Muslim world (Friedmann 1987, 46).

Despite this persecution, the Ahmadi have done more for the world-wide propagation of Islam than many other Muslim groups. They have missionaries throughout the world, and their literature is rich and extensive. Ghulam Ahmad alone wrote eighty-eight books, over 15,000 pages, in Urdu, Arabic, and Persian. The movement has also published journals, newsletters, pamphlets, books, and translations of the Qur'an in many languages (Friedmann 1987, xi, 10).

There were Ahmadi in Southeast Asia as early as the mid 1920s, but aside from a few references in English works,[6] the presence and influence of Ahmadi teachings go unnoted in the literature. I suspect that there are many people who call themselves Ahmadi in Indonesia and Malaysia, and I know that there is a sizable group in Sabah. My informants believe there are members of the Ahmadiyya movement in Lanao and Magindanao and know there are many followers in Jolo and Zamboanga. In Tawi-Tawi there are just two places in which the Ahmadi teachings have a significant number of followers: Kagayan Tawi-Tawi and Simunul.

Haji Hussein, originally from Kagayan Tawi-Tawi, was the district supervisor of schools assigned by the government to work in Simunul in the late 1950s. During the month of Ramadan in 1957, Haji Hussein invited an Ahmadi missionary from India to visit Simunul to share the teachings of Ghulam Ahmad. This man, Dr. Gulam Yasin, stayed in Simunul for one month. Every evening men, many of them teachers (because of the influence of Haji Hussein and because they could understand English), gathered to discuss Islam. New Ahmadi-published English translations of the Qur'an were given to men who took an interest in the teachings of the Ahmadi. These were the first English-translated Qur'ans that the members of the community had ever possessed, and they were treasured.

By the time Dr. Yasin had left the community, some twenty to thirty men, all of them teachers, had become members of the movement. By "members" I mean that these men had formally registered with the movement and were official supporters. Though affiliated with the Ahmadiyya, these men did nothing to organize or institutionalize a local chapter in the district. They did not meet on a regular basis and did not even know who else had signed the membership list.

As the years passed, no other missionaries came to Simunul, and no new literature was brought to the community. Haji Hussein was replaced by another district supervisor and interest in the Ahmadi teachings waned. A few people came across the literature and became interested in the movement, but few others showed any interest in the teachings between 1957 and 1990.

Then, while I was in Simunul in August of 1990, another Ahmadi missionary from Pakistan came to the island. A man from the community, Haji Quezon, had met Mansul Ahmad Khan in Manila, where Ahmad Khan was involved in a project translating the Qur'an into Pilipino. Haji Quezon invited Ahmad Khan to Simunul as Haji Hussein had invited Dr. Yasin over thirty years ago. The missionary agreed to stay in Simunul for three days.

I attended the discussion groups held by Ahmad Khan and was surprised when my research assistant informed me that most of the crowded room of forty to fifty men and women were Ahmadi. The discussion was fascinating. It was conducted in English, and the questions asked by people of Simunul were well-informed. People were obviously familiar with the Ahmadi literature and understood the basic Ahmadi teachings. The main topic of discussion concerned Ghulam Ahmad's claim to prophethood. People wanted to understand the nature of his prophethood so that they might respond to those who dismiss his claims. Prophethood was discussed in the terms set out by the Qadiyani school; that is, Ghulam Ahmad was a prophet and not merely a reformer.

The following day the discussion group addressed administrative issues. The missionary explained to people how they should organize meetings, how much money they should donate to the movement, and how they should increase their membership. In the general discussion that followed, the missionary argued that certain calendrical and life-cycle rituals that were practiced by the community were innovations to Islam and should no longer be performed.[7]

The official president of the Ahmadiyya movement in Simunul, a man I will call Haji Ali Bima, informed me that after this discussion Ahmad Khan made many promises to him. Ahmad Khan promised to send a teacher to Simunul to teach people about Islam and promised that, if he could secure the necessary funds, the organization would start a program in which young boys between the ages of seven and ten would be sent to London to learn from Ahmadi there.

During the three-day visit of the Ahmadi missionary, fifteen men registered as members of the movement. This increased the total membership in Simunul from thirty-five to fifty people, an increase of 40 percent. I noticed the new Qur'ans brought by the missionary in the homes of the new members, and stacks of pamphlets were left with Haji Ali Bima to be loaned to interested individuals.

Sama Interest in the Ahmadi Teachings

Many Sama individuals are interested in the Ahmadiyya movement because its teachings are delivered by prestigious, powerful, and charismatic individuals. In 1957 these people were Haji Hussein, the district supervisor of schools, and the Indian missionary Dr. Gulam Yasin. In 1990, these men were Haji Quezon, a former teacher and politician, Haji Ali Bima, an articulate and charismatic school teacher, and the Ahmadi from Pakistan, Mansul Ahmad Khan.

In Simunul, as elsewhere in Muslim Southeast Asia, prestigious people include teachers and Muslims from the Middle East, South Asia, and other parts of Southeast Asia. Arabs are particularly revered, because people believe that they carried Islam and civilization to their communities centuries ago. Because of their proximity to the *ponsot dunia,* the center of the Muslim world, people believe that Arabs are blessed with *barakah,* God-given powers. Teachers are also persons of high status. A college education is highly valued, and, as wage earners, teachers can purchase prestige items and host lavish rituals, further enhancing their status in the community. Therefore, when high-status individuals bring the Ahmadi teachings to the community, people are interested in learning about them. As I explained earlier, in the thirty-year interval between 1957 and 1990, few people registered as members with the Ahmadiyya movement. Thus, without the mediation of certain individuals, the movement lacked the ability to attract the interest of most people.

People become interested in signing the membership lists for a second reason: because of the prestige it bestows upon them as members of an international movement headed by an educated elite who are closer to the center of Islam. People repeatedly emphasized to me that the Ahmadiyya movement is a movement of intellectuals. People are impressed by the credentials of the authors of the literature they read and have come to believe that the Ahmadi are the most highly educated Muslims in the world. There are several books in the community that contain testimonials from people who have joined the movement. These testimonials are from American engineers, Australian physicians, and Swiss journalists. Many times I heard people say that if, for example, an American engineer joined the movement, then there must be some truth in the teachings. As Haji Ali Bima, the president of the local Ahmadiyya movement, stated to me (in English):

> The Ahmadiyya movement is so progressive. In one hundred years it grew from just a few followers to now about twenty million. Out of these members, if there are a thousand members, you won't find one or two who is not educated. In other Muslim sects, very few are educated. Very few can understand what they are hearing. They just believe without understanding.
>
> We have limited education and understanding of English, we followers of Ahmadiyya. But what about those Ahmadi in America or Spain or Australia or London who are doctors, professors, and scientists? Why do

they accept Ahmadi? That is my question. They were not Muslim before, and now they embrace Ahmadiyya. Do you think these people would merely accept this religion if they can't find the truth in it? They are not ordinary people. They are writers and scholars. If there is nothing to be found in the Ahmadiyya movement, do you think these people will join this religion? They will not.

The third reason people are interested in the Ahmadi teachings is that the teachings coincide with their understandings and goals. The people who are interested in the teachings have come into contact with ideas of Islamic reform and have found them acceptable. The goal of the reformers is to teach their community to practice Islam as they believe it was practiced in early Muslim history. Their goal is eventually to rid the beliefs and practices of their community of the compendia of additions that have become attached to Islam. These goals require challenging the power and authority of traditional *imam*,[8] and persuading the community to bring their beliefs and practices into accordance with the teachings in the Qur'an and *hadith* (traditions concerning the life and works of the Prophet Muhammad). Reformers need the literature, the arguments, and the support of an international Muslim organization to accomplish these goals. By providing people with Qur'ans translated into English, by giving people the prestige of belonging to an international Islamic movement, and by supporting their struggles to effect change in their community, the Ahmadiyya movement provides reformers the tools they require.

The fourth reason the Ahmadi teachings are supported in Simunul is that these teachings find an acceptable medium in which to set down their roots. "Truth" is no longer assumed by the educated to be in the possession of imam. Rather, many people believe that truth is to be found in texts. The Ahmadi literature provides rational, abstract arguments college-educated Sama find convincing. The arguments in this literature are well constructed and supported by evidence. Thus the presentation and form of these teachings are familiar to and accepted as superior by some of the educated members of the community. Consider, for example, this portion of an interview I conducted (in English) with Haji Ali Bima:

> You must have observed that we have only a few educated people in our community. If [people have not] gone to school, they are not as informed and matured as the people who have gone on to college. I was not an Ahmadi before. [I cannot simply accept] a teaching that would not challenge my intelligence, my thinking. I cannot easily accept. It's like being influenced by a speaker or a singer or whatever. If it doesn't touch

your heart, your emotion, your intellect, you won't be convinced. But if things are given to you, if you listen to it, and it comes into your heart and you accept it wholeheartedly according to your interpretation, according to your intellect . . . I think that is the highest part of a human being that if you accept it and believe that there is truth in it. Because, for example, who can tell us where is God? The questions Why do we pray? Why do we believe in God? Why do we have the Islamic religion? Do we just merely believe in God, in the Islam religion, without investigating what it is for? Most if not all of our people just merely believe in it without wondering. They do not understand. You believe me! They just merely follow. . . . [Ahmadi] books and pamphlets are everywhere. They give a reading and then show you the reference so everything can be verified. . . . And within their books they say if you disagree, you can write us and can communicate with us, and we will answer you. They can say that. They are willing to answer any criticism. No other Muslim sect can say that. It's as if the other sects are making us blind. Just to accept and say yes. With the Ahmadi, no. Before you join, you give us your commentary, you give us your criticism. Write and we will answer you. I found something very Islamic in the Ahmadiyya movement. They say God will curse us if we add, subtract, or change anything in the Qur'an. The only thing that people will not accept is that Ahmad was a prophet.

Who is a Muslim? Who is the true, sincere, faithful follower of the Prophet Muhammad? One who is innovating? One who is changing? One who is blindly following? Or one who is not blind, one who doesn't change, and one who sticks to the teaching of the Prophet Muhammad? Simple as that. Very simple.

Note the way that Haji Ali Bima distinguishes between the people who are college-educated and those who are not. To Haji Ali Bima, it makes sense that college-educated people are interested in the Ahmadi teachings because these teachings appeal to their *intellect*. The Ahmadi do not follow their imam blindly. They want to understand the meaning and purpose of Islam. They are attracted to the teachings of the Ahmadi because the Ahmadi literature provides the rationalized, abstracted literature that they appreciate. All Ahmadi statements are supported by references to the Qur'an and *hadith*, and this impresses those who are familiar with this form of discourse.

The Ahmadi teachings are also popular because the Ahmadi encourage dialogue with other Muslims. For example, Haji Ali Bima believes that if he has a question or if he disagrees with a point in the Ahmadi literature, he can address a letter to the organization in Pakistan. Because Ahmadi members in Simunul can read and write English, they can engage in an international exchange of ideas. Knowledge of English and access to a somewhat reliable international postal system thus enable this remote community to communicate with Muslim centers of knowledge.

These are some of the reasons why many people are interested in the Ahmadi teachings and why some fifty people in Simunul have registered as members. The Ahmadiyya movement did not "come" to Simunul and "effect" certain changes in practice and belief. Rather, teachings were brought by important men at significant historical moments in which these teachings were likely to be considered. People joined because the teachings appealed to their intellect, they accepted the teachings as truth, and they enjoyed the prestige of belonging to an international Muslim organization.

Resistance to the Ahmadi Teachings

Most people of the community reject the teachings of the Ahmadi. These individuals reject the teachings for the same reason they resist all new Muslim discourses: because they find satisfaction in following the ways of their ancestors *(sara' mattoa)* and in continuing the customs and traditions *(adat)* of the past. Perhaps "reject" is too strong a word. I believe these individuals simply ignore the reformist impulse; the teachings hold no appeal for them, and the arguments of the reformers are easily dismissed.

There are also a significant number of people who criticize the traditional ways but are also critical of Ahmadi teachings. When asked why they are not interested in becoming members of the movement, people shrug and explain that they do not believe there was a prophet after Muhammad. Though this is the only reason people have ever offered me, I suspect there are other reasons as well. One reason is the persecution of the Ahmadi followers in Malaysia. Another reason is that people do not want to commit themselves to any one system of belief.

In Malaysia there is an active campaign against Ahmadi teachings. Members of the movement who live in Sabah report that the government keeps them under surveillance and that they are harassed by government officials. One man told me that while he was waiting for his papers to be processed for entry into Sabah, he was reading a pamphlet published by the Ahmadi. An official approached him and demanded to know if he was a follower of the Ahmadiyya movement. The man explained that he was not; he was merely reading the pamphlet to compare the Ahmadi teachings with his own understanding of Islam. The official snatched the pamphlet from his hands and tore it to shreds.

Ustadh (teachers and scholars of Islam) also appear on Malaysian television broadcasts to argue that the teachings of the Ahmadi are false. The *ustadh* instruct people to avoid living with known Ahmadi, shaking their hands, and sharing their food. In other words, the *ustadh* instruct people to ostracize the Ahmadi.

People exposed to this persecution of Ahmadi in Sabah are understandably wary of the movement, even though Malaysian television broadcasts do not reach Simunul, and there is no organized action to repress Ahmadi teachings in the southern Philippines. Because many Sama have lived in Sabah, they are quite aware of and many have witnessed this persecution of Ahmadi.

Many of the people who are critical of the traditional ways but who do not support the Ahmadi teachings fail to do so, I would argue, to keep all their bases covered. One teacher, for example, claims that the Ahmadi teachings are good and that Islam should be reformed along the lines the Ahmadi propose. This teacher charges that the older *imam* know better than to perform traditional rituals, but that they continue these practices because it is the way they earn money. Even as she offers these criticisms, however, this teacher continues to invite the *imam* to say the *duwa'a salamat* (prayer of thanksgiving) for her family every Friday. This teacher also asks the *imam* and the *pandei* (female ritual specialists) to perform traditional rituals for her family on every occasion. Her practices suggest that this teacher is not entirely convinced the Ahmadi teachings are true, even though she agrees with them on some level. By agreeing with the Ahmadi teachings and continuing the traditional practices, it is as if this teacher hopes that God will reward her for at least some of her practices.

Along the same lines, I often asked the woman with whom I lived, Haja Buangcan Calbit, what she thought of the Ahmadi teachings. Haja Buangcan accompanied me to the meetings held by Ahmad Khan and told me that she agreed with everything the Ahmadi missionary said. When I asked her if she was going to become an Ahmadi, she just laughed. She was less patient with Haji Ali Bima's wife, Sitti Mariam. On our way to the discussion group, Haja Buangcan jokingly declared to the people we passed that "I'm an Ahmadi now!" Sitti Mariam interpreted Haja Buangcan's flippancy as derision and told Haja Buangcan that she should not condemn the Ahmadi without a trial. Haja Buangcan replied angrily, "Well, why are you trying to convince me! I have a mind. I can read and come to my own conclusions!"

Or not come to any conclusion at all. Many people do not want to commit themselves to one discourse or another. They may not even see these discourses as separate and competing, as I do, but may hold them in some harmony, drawing upon them in different situations.

This ambivalence about reformist ideas appears very similar to that described in this volume by Michael Peletz with regard to rural Malays. The difference between Malays and Sama is the fields in which they operate. In Malaysia, on the one hand, Muslims must act within a politically and religiously charged arena in which ambivalence about Islamic reform is often perceived as resistance to Islam or Muslim identity itself. On the other hand, in Tawi-Tawi (and Cotabato—see McKenna, this volume) Muslims have the space to express their uncertainty and dissent without the fear of reprisal that Malays experience. There is thus room for the contradiction and ambivalence I describe here. There are also opportunities for alternative discourses, like the Ahmadi teachings, to develop and thrive.

In a society in which almost all organizations and group action are based on kinship, it seems odd that the Ahmadi membership is composed of individuals and not families. People will always support their kin in times of dispute and conflict. The cause of the dispute is irrelevant; it does not matter if the one involved is right or wrong. The Sama of Simunul claim that they will always support their kin, because to come to the aid of kin affirms their relationships. But in this view I am assuming that there is a bounded group of Ahmadi that should be based on kinship and that there is a dispute or conflict in which people should become involved to support their kin. Only when I forgo these assumptions am I able to understand the reason that people do not sign the membership list out of loyalty to their kin and spouses. Simply put, there is no bounded group, and there is no open conflict that compels people to choose sides. This situation will become more clear in a moment, as I discuss the ways the Ahmadi are viewed, the ways the Ahmadi act, and what the term *ahmadi* has come to mean in Simunul.

Local Constructions of Ahmadi

As I indicated above, there are no factions in Simunul based on interpretations of Islam. A single household may contain individuals who hold widely divergent beliefs. For example, the mother of my language helper is a traditional *pandei* and her mother's brother, an unmarried school teacher, follows the Ahmadi teachings. My language helper and her sisters, all college-educated, agree with the teachings of the Ahmadi but would never call themselves Ahmadi. The family of Haji Ibrahim is similarly diverse. Haji Ibrahim, a head *imam,* follows the traditional ways, but his brother Haji Pillak, a school teacher, signed the Ahmadi membership list over thirty years ago. A third brother is also a school teacher but he, like Haji Ibrahim, is more traditional. Haji Ibrahim's son-in-law, Haji Omar, is a reformer but not an Ahmadi. Haji Omar's father, however, is a new member of the movement, and his father's brother has been a member since 1957.

These examples show that many kinds of interpretations of Islam may exist within families; there are no factions composed of people who follow particular interpretations. It is thus very important that an outside observer resist labeling people and reducing this very fluid and situational phenomenon to categories. People in Simunul simply cannot be placed along a continuum opposing tradition to reform. Likewise, it is not possible to assert that there are certain numbers of *ahmadi* and non-*ahmadi* in the community.

To make matters more complex, though there are no factions, there are names for them. In the past people used the term *"anak baha'u"* (the younger people/generation) when referring to the critics of the traditional ways and used *"mma'-mma' "* (the fathers or old men/older generation) as the oppositional term. This distinction corresponds with the categories *kaum muda* and *kaum tua* used in Malaysia and parts of Indonesia (see Bowen, this volume). It is significant that people in Simunul use the term *"mma'-mma',"* which means older men, instead of a term that means older people. The Sama of Simunul use this term because it is believed that the people who present the most serious challenge to the reformers, the people who are seen as reinforcing and clinging to traditional ways, are the older *imam.*

Though the terms used in the past, *"anak baha'u"* and *"mma'-mma',"* imply that there are fundamental differences between younger people and older men, not all younger people were critics and not all older men were conservative. These terms are still in use today but are misleading descriptors, because members of the older generation are just as likely to be reformers. Again, the people who first became interested in the Ahmadi teachings did so over thirty years ago. These people are now in their sixties, seventies, and eighties.

The terms that have replaced the younger and older generation are *"ahmadi"* (here I do not capitalize *"ahmadi"* since I am not referring to members of the Ahmadiyya movement) and *"orthodox."* People use the term *"ahmadi"* for *anyone* who criticizes the traditional ways. So-called *ahmadi* do not have to agree with the Ahmadi teachings or have any relationship with the Ahmadiyya movement. Indeed, I have heard *"ahmadi"* used for people I know to be opposed to the Ahmadi teachings. I do not know where the term *"orthodox"* originated. The term is loosely applied to all of those who support traditional practices but usually refers to the more outspoken and visible imam.

The terms *"ahmadi"* and *"orthodox"* gloss over significant differences among people within a group and are rarely self-referential. People never refer to themselves as *orthodox* and only in some contexts would refer to themselves as *ahmadi.*

Beliefs and Practices of the Ahmadi

How do people of the community think about the *ahmadi*? And how do people, who in certain situations call themselves Ahmadi, act in various situations? The answers to these questions show that the boundaries around the Ahmadiyya movement are very fluid, that this movement is by no means monolithic, and that being Ahmadi is not an essential identity—that is, who *ahmadi* are and what *ahmadi* means depends very much on context.

While I was living in Simunul, I noticed that there was a wide gap between professed belief and practice of those who claimed to be Ahmadi. People did not always embody or enact the Ahmadi teachings they supported. For example, before Maulud, a day that commemorates the birth of the Prophet Muhammad, two members of the Ahmadiyya movement told me that the rituals practiced have no basis in the Qur'an and *hadith* and, therefore, should not be performed by a Muslim community. Since these men were quite adamant about this issue, I was surprised to find them in the midst of these celebrations performing leading roles in these rituals. When I asked one of these men why he took part in Maulud, he shrugged and replied that as a member of the community he must act as one. He explained that if he refused to attend and practice these rituals, his family and the *orthodox* would be upset with him.

People who follow the Ahmadi teachings also do not pray in a separate mosque. All members of the community continue to pray together in the same mosques to avoid expressing overt conflict. The missionary Mansul Ahmad Khan was indeed surprised to learn that Ahmadi and non-Ahmadi pray together in the community mosques, because Ghulam Ahmad enjoined his followers not to pray behind a non-Ahmadi imam. According to his teachings, non-Ahmadi are infidels and Ahmadi are instructed to worship within their own mosques or in their own homes (Friedmann 1987, 155).

Members of the Ahmadiyya movement also continue to go on the *hajj*. To make the pilgrimage to Mecca is one of the five pillars of Islam, and becoming a *haji* is one of the most prestigious goals one can accomplish in one's lifetime. Though one may claim to be an Ahmadi in certain situations, this admission is never made when one is about to embark on the pilgrimage, because the Kingdom of Saudi Arabia does not permit Ahmadi to perform the *hajj*.

Thus, members of the Ahmadiyya movement may decline to act as Ahmadi to avoid conflict in the community, and they may decline to identify themselves as Ahmadi when this admission prevents them from performing important and prestigious activities. In everyday and ritual practice, then, there is little distinction between those who follow the teachings of Ghulam Ahmad and those who do not.

Ahmadi members also reconsider and reinterpret the basic tenets of Ahmadi teachings. Specifically, Ahmadi do not accept Ghulam Ahmad's claim to prophethood and continue to assert that Muhammad was the last prophet. According to these individuals, Mirza Ghulam Ahmad was a reformer, or an imam, who tried to reform Islam according to the tenets set down by Muhammad. Virtually every Ahmadi in Simunul with whom I spoke stated that Ghulam Ahmad was not a prophet. Even Haji Ali Bima, the local president of the Ahmadiyya movement in Simunul, indicated his uncertainty about the issue of Ghulam Ahmad's prophethood. Haji Ali Bima explained to me, "You see we do not know. We don't know the term. We are not Arabs. We do not know Khatam al-Nabiyyin." Because the proof of whether Ghulam Ahmad was a prophet rests on the interpretation of this one Arabic phrase, a phrase that no one in the community can understand, Haji Ali Bima cannot be entirely sure that Ghulam Ahmad was a prophet.

This interpretation remains within the range of the Ahmadi teachings. As I explained earlier, there are two schools of thought within the Ahmadiyya movement: one that declares that Ghulam Ahmad was a prophet (nabi) and one that declares he is a renewer of religion, a reformer (mujaddid). Mansul Ahmad Khan, the Ahmadi missionary who came to Simunul in 1990, was clearly a follower of the first school. As he explained the nature of prophethood and the claims of Ghulam Ahmad in the discussion group, Ahmad Khan made it quite clear that Ghulam Ahmad was a prophet, not merely a reformer. However, the people of Simunul do not accept this claim.

Understanding how a Muslim discourse such as the Ahmadiyya movement is experienced and understood by people, why people are attracted to the teachings, why they resist them, and how change comes about requires challenging our assumptions about social movements. The Ahmadiyya movement in Simunul is not rigidly bounded. It is a fluid phenomenon, a discourse upon which people may draw in specific situations. An Ahmadi cannot be identified with the movement at all times. Rather, *ahmadi* refers to a situational state of being. Also, the label *"ahmadi"* has come to have a wide application independent of its original referent.

Conclusions

The relation between mass education and Islamic reform would have surprised American administrators of the Philippines who instituted compulsory public education to promote a secular, national culture. American officials in the Philippines emphasized education above all else and made attendance at public schools compulsory by 1906. These administrators intended public schools to be the means by which Muslims would be brought into Philippine political and social life, made into good citizens, and integrated into the future Republic of the Philippines (Thomas 1971, 55, 60). Through education, American officials sought to instill modern American ways of thinking and behaving in the citizens of a future independent state.

To accomplish American goals, the influence of Islam had to be reduced. In a 1903 report, General Samuel Sumner, the military commander of the Department of Mindanao, argued that

> If it is contemplated to change the customs and habits of these people and bring them to an intelligent understanding and appreciation of our methods of government, it will be necessary to eradicate about all the customs that have heretofore governed their habits of life. They are an essentially different people from us in thought, word and action and their religion will be a serious bar to any efforts towards Christian civilization. So long as Mohammedanism prevails, Anglo-Saxon civilization will make slow headway." (cited in Bentley 1989, 76)

Ten years later, John Pershing, the governor of Moro Province, argued that Muslim teachers and missionaries had "cursed" Moro Province and that their presence was detrimental to good government. Pershing went on to state that there was little doubt that the "occult inspiration" of these men was responsible for much of the resistance to the American administration (Report of the Governor of the Moro Province 1913, 33, as quoted by Gowing 1983, 217).

Readers will note that my portrayal of American strategies and objectives in the Philippines directly contradicts that of Thomas McKenna, presented in this volume. According to McKenna, powerful and influential Americans like Najeeb Saleeby and Edward M. Kuder strove to promote Islam for the benefit of the American government and the good of the Moro people. It is important to recognize, however, that American policies in the Philippines were far from consistent and mutually reinforcing. American administrators were anything but like-minded ideologues. Support for both our positions can easily be found in historical documents: for every Najeeb Saleeby there is a Samuel Sumner; for every Edward M. Kuder there is a John Pershing. While some Americans recognized that a Muslim identity that transcended ethnolinguistic and geographical boundaries could serve as the basis of modern citizenship, most, I would argue, believed that only the complete elimination of religious and cultural differences between peoples of the Philippines could serve to integrate them within a single nation (see also Bentley 1989).

Christian Filipinos most clearly used modern secular education to subdue Muslim resistance and create modern Filipino citizens when they assumed control of the government in 1935. Believing themselves to be free of religious malevolence in their new secular government, Christian Filipino leaders dismissed the significance of Islam and Muslim identity. According to President Quezon and other political leaders, it was not religion but simple backwardness that separated Muslims from Christians—a problem to be overcome with policies that promoted education and modernization (George 1980, 87).

In 1957 the Philippine government created the Commission on National Integration (CNI) to bring about "the moral, material, economic, social and political advancement of the National Cultural Minorities" and to make "real, complete and permanent the integration of all the National Cultural Minorities into the body politic" (Tamano 1974, 263). Education was a major part of the CNI and was recognized by the Philippine government, as by the American government before it, as an effective instrument of nation building. Indeed, some educators recommended that Muslim children start school as early as five years old to "break the mores of traditional society faster" (Isidro 1968, 65).

Like American and Christian Filipino political leaders, many scholars have also assumed that Western education would reduce the significance and influence of Islam in Muslim societies. For example, Harry J. Benda, a historian of Southeast Asia, stated that "Western education was the surest means of reducing and ultimately defeating the influence of Islam" (1972 [1958], 89). Modernization theorists have proposed that education is an effective tool to create citizens equipped to participate in the economic development of their societies and have argued that schools are the means by which dominant elites inculcate ideologies that buttress the orders they control.[9]

Contrary to these expectations, mass education in Muslim societies has not succeeded in stripping Islam from the fabric of Muslim lives. Far from reducing the influence of Islam in the lives of Muslims, mass education often supports Islamic activism (see Eickelman 1992). Education has certainly played an important role in shaping modern Islamic discourses in the Sama community in which I worked. As I have shown, college-educated Sama are not only literate in English, but have developed a method of learning and thinking that prompts many of them to conceive of knowledge as abstract and unlimited. Many college-educated Sama learn to think critically and believe that knowledge is truth and that truth can be discovered through rational means. No longer willing to accept traditional *imams*' esoteric knowledge and their "unscientific" claims to supernatural abilities, many college-educated Sama are advancing modern ways of knowing Islam and being a Muslim. Thus, in spite of the efforts of the American and Philippine governments to diminish the place of Islam in the lives of its Muslims, college-educated Sama are among those most interested in Islam and those most likely to be reformers and teachers of Islam. It is this college-educated group of men and women who use the Ahmadiyya movement, its teachings, and its literature to criticize traditional Islamic practices.[10]

Many of the authors in this volume have made a deliberate attempt to shift the focus of study to encompass ways that "ordinary" Muslims living in rural places are dealing with issues of Islamic reform. We have also struggled to emphasize processes instead of structures, actors instead of institutions. From our essays there emerges a picture of movements being forged in politically charged fields by actors inspired by diverse and often contradictory objectives. All of these essays demonstrate that the study of a social movement as an object and an abstraction makes far less sense than to examine the ways a discourse of often inchoate ideas is understood by individuals and used in their everyday lives.

Wilfred Cantwell Smith, a renowned scholar of religion, once stated that the study of religion is the study of persons (1980, 503). Smith meant that doctrine and meaning come to life when interpreted by people. For those of us who seek to understand the meaning Islam has for people, it is to these interpretations that we must turn. Studying the meaning Islam has for Muslims requires a focus on how people relate to doctrine in practical ways. It requires a focus on the actions and interactions of individuals in specific situations. From the impoverished Hasan of Martin Rössler's chapter who struggles to make the *hajj* to improve his social status to the masterminds of NU and ICMI discussed by Andrée Feillard and Robert Hefner, all people must consider the worlds of meaning in which they find themselves and strategize to effect change in their communities. The means by which they do this offer insight into the importance of reformist debates and the ways in which change is occurring in Muslim societies throughout the world.

Notes

I conducted fieldwork in the province of Tawi-Tawi, Philippines, from September 1989 to January 1991. During this time I received financial support from two agencies: the National Science Foundation (grant number BNS-

8913070), and the Joint Committee on Southeast Asia of the Social Science Research Council and the American Council of Learned Societies. I am very grateful for these funds. I also appreciate the sponsorship of the Institute of Islamic Studies at the University of the Philippines. This study would not have been possible without the understanding, graciousness, and hospitality of my friends in Tawi-Tawi.

1. Though most Sama identify themselves as "Sama" and claim that "Samal" is a derogatory exonym, there are ethnic groups that prefer the name "Samal." These Samal live in parts of Palawan occupied by migrants from eastern Tawi-Tawi (Lanfranco Blanchetti-Revelli, personal communication) and Sibutu (Allison 1976–1979). Unfortunately, within academic and national discourses, "Samal" has become the popular name for the Sama.

2. Operation Jabidah was a secret plan of the Marcos government to train Muslims of the Sulu Archipelago to infiltrate and seize Sabah, Malaysia. After training in Simunul, the soldiers went to the island of Corregidor, where a group of them were massacred when they threatened to abandon the operation. One witness to this massacre survived to reveal the existence of this aborted plan. Top leaders of Operation Jabidah (or Operation Merdeka, as it was named by these leaders) claimed that this plan was to *prevent* private armies of the Tausug and the Sama from invading Sabah (Kurais 1979, 113; Majul 1985, 42–43; de Manila 1989).

3. The Moro National Liberation Front (MNLF) is a militant separatist organization that has struggled for the political autonomy of Muslims in the Philippines. The MNLF dates its beginning from the Corregidor massacre in 1968 and continues to be a political force. The majority of young men of Simunul followed the lead of local MNLF commanders and became "Blackshirts" between 1972 and 1974.

4. These rates are higher than the provincial average. According to the data provided by the National Census and Statistics Office (1980), only 16 percent of adults in Tawi-Tawi have some college education and only 2 percent are degree holders. The Sama of Simunul are known throughout the province as highly educated and progressive people.

5. Haji Hussein is a pseudonym. I identify no Sama follower of the Ahmadiyya movement by name.

6. For references to the Ahmadiyya movement in Southeast Asia, see Benda 1958, 50–54; Casino 1973, 383; Federspiel 1970, 99–104; van Nieuwenhuijze 1958, 58–59; Roff 1967, 80; and Wertheim 1959, 213.

7. An innovation (Ar. *bid'a*) is a practice or belief that was not revealed in the Qur'an and established by the Sunnah on the basis of Prophetic traditions. Innovations are, therefore, possibly contrary to Islam or un-Islamic.

8. In Sama communities men who have achieved superior knowledge of Islam, take an interest in Islamic rituals, and display piety and the possession of certain abilities are formally appointed as imam. Imam lead the *sambahayang* (Ar. *salat*), congregational prayers, and also serve as mediators between indi-

viduals and God by performing special prayers, healing, and conducting certain rituals. Each mosque has a head *imam* who appoints other imam and *pandei. Pandei* are female ritual specialists. *Pandei,* like *imam,* know how to heal, curse, and remove curses but also serve as midwives and perform life-cycle rituals for girls and women.

9. See Althusser 1971, Gramsci 1971, Inkeles 1969, 1974, Inkeles and Smith 1974, and Poulantzas 1978. See also Carnoy 1982 and Keyes 1991 for reviews of these theories.

10. See Eickelman 1992 and Horvatich 1994 for more on the relation of Islamic reform to mass education and modern political institutions.

References Cited

Alfian. 1989. *Muhammadiyah: The Political Behavior of a Muslim Modernist Organization under Dutch Colonialism.* Yogyakarta: Gajah Mada University Press.

Allison, Karen. 1976–1979. Unpublished field notes on Sama society and culture.

Althusser, Louis. 1971. *Lenin and Philosophy and Other Essays.* New York: Monthly Review Press.

Benda, Harry J. 1958. *The Crescent and the Rising Sun: Indonesian Islam under the Japanese Occupation, 1942–1945.* The Hague: Van Hoeve.

_____. 1972. "Christiaan Snouck Hurgronje and the Foundations of Dutch Islamic Policy in Indonesia." 1958. In *Continuity and Change in Southeast Asia: Collected Journal Articles of Harry J. Benda,* pp. 83–92. Southeast Asia Studies Monograph Series no. 18. New Haven: Yale University.

Bentley, G. Carter. 1989. "Implicit Evangelism: American Education among the Muslim Maranao. *Pilipinas* 12:73–96.

Carnoy, Martin. 1982. "Education, Economy, and the State." In Michael W. Apple, ed., *Cultural and Economic Reproduction in Education,* pp. 79–126. London: Routledge and Kegan Paul.

Casino, Eric S. 1973. "The Jama Maupun: A Study of Social Change." Ph.D. dissertation, Department of Anthropology, University of Sydney.

Eickelman, Dale F. 1992. "Mass Higher Education and the Religious Imagination in Contemporary Arab Societies." *American Ethnologist* 19 (4): 643–655.

Federspiel, Howard M. 1970. *Persatuan Islam: Islamic Reform in Twentieth-Century Indonesia.* Ithaca: Cornell University Press.

Friedmann, Yohanan. 1987. *Prophecy Continuous: Aspects of Ahmadi Religious Thought and Its Medieval Background.* Berkeley and Los Angeles: University of California Press.

Geertz, Clifford. 1963. "Modernisation in a Moslem Society: The Indonesian Case." *Quest* 39:9–7.

Gellner, Ernest. 1981. *Muslim Society.* Cambridge: Cambridge University Press.

George, T. J. S. 1980. *Revolt in Mindanao: The Rise of Islam in Philippine Politics.* Kuala Lumpur: Oxford University Press.

Gibb, H. A. R. 1947. *Modern Trends in Islam*. Chicago: Chicago University Press.

Gowing, Peter G. 1983. *Mandate in Moroland: The American Government of Muslim Filipinos, 1899–1920*. 1977. Reprint, Quezon City: New Day Publishers.

Gramsci, Antonio. 1971. *Selections from Prison Notebooks*. New York: International Publishers.

Horvatich, Patricia. 1994. "Ways of Knowing Islam." *American Ethnologist* 21 (4): 807–820.

Inkeles, Alex. 1969. "Making Man Modern: On the Causes and Consequences of Individual Change in Six Developing Countries." *American Journal of Sociology* 75:208–225.

———. 1974. "The School as a Context for Modernization." In Alex Inkeles and Donald B. Holsinger, *Education and Individual Modernity in Developing Countries*, pp, 7–23. Leiden: Brill.

Inkeles, Alex, and D. H. Smith. 1974. *Becoming Modern*. Cambridge, Mass.: Harvard University Press.

Isidro, Antonio y Santos. 1968. *The Moro Problem: An Approach through Education*. Marawi City: Mindanao State University, University Research Center.

Keyes, Charles F. 1991. "State Schools in Rural Communities: Reflections on Rural Education and Cultural Change in Southeast Asia." In Charles F. Keyes, ed., *Reshaping Local Worlds: Formal Education and Cultural Change in Rural Southeast Asia*, pp. 1–18. New Haven: Yale University Southeast Asian Studies.

Kurais, Muhammad. 1979. *The History of Tawi-Tawi and Its People*. Bonggao: Mindanao State University, Sulu College of Technology and Oceanography.

Majul, Cesar A. 1985. *The Contemporary Movement in the Philippines*. Berkeley and Los Angeles: University of California Press.

Manila, Quijano de. 1989. "The Philippine Invasion of Sabah: A Tragic Tale of Patriotism and Incompetence." *Moro Kurier* 4 (1/2): 4–11.

Nagata, Judith. 1984. *The Reflowering of Islam in Malaysia*. Vancouver: University of British Columbia Press.

Nakamura, Mitsuo. 1984. *The Crescent Arises over the Banyan Tree: A Study of the Muhammadiyah Movement in a Central Javanese Town*. Yogyakarta: Gajah Mada University Press.

National Census and Statistics Office. 1980. *Census of Population and Housing, Tawi-Tawi*. Manila: National Economic and Development Authority, Republic of the Philippines.

Nieuwenhuijze, C. A. O. van. 1958. *Aspects of Islam in Post-Colonial Indonesia*. The Hague: Van Hoeve.

Peacock, James L. 1978. *Purifying the Faith: The Muhammadiyah Movement in Indonesian Islam*. Menlo Park: The Benjamin/Cummings Publishing Company.

Poulantzas, Nicos. 1978. *L'état, le pouvoir, le socialisme*. Paris: Presses Universitaires de France.

Roff, William R. 1967. *The Origins of Malay Nationalism*. New Haven: Yale University Press.

Smith, Wilfred Cantwell. 1980. "The True Meaning of Scripture: An Empirical Historian's Nonreductionist Interpretation of the Qur'an." *International Journal of Middle East Studies* 11 (4): 487–505.

Snouck Hurgronje, Christiaan. 1906. *The Achenese*. Leiden: Brill.

Tamano, Mamintal A. J. 1974. "Problem of the Muslims: A National Concern." In Peter G. Gowing and Robert D. McAmis, eds., *The Muslim Filipinos*, pp. 13–23. Manila: Solidaridad Publishing House.

Thomas, Ralph B. 1971. "Muslim but Filipino: The Integration of Philippine Muslims, 1917–1946." Ph.D. dissertation, University of Pennsylvania.

Wertheim, W. F. 1959. *Indonesian Society in Transition*. The Hague: Van Hoeve.

Chapter 7

Identity Construction, Nation Formation, and Islamic Revivalism in Malaysia

Shamsul A. B.

One of the most perceptive recent observations on the relationship between religion and the modern nation-states in East and Southeast Asia appeared in an essay by Keyes, Hardacre, and Kendall (1994). The authors observed that the complex relationship between religion and nation formation has often engendered what they called a "crisis of authority." In their words,

> The process of creating modern nation states has . . . entailed two rather contradictory stances towards religion. While the modernizing stance leads to a deemphasis of ritual practices, the nation-building one leads to the promotion of selected practices and even the invention of new rites. Modernization emphasizes rational action; nation-building insists on a commitment of faith. The tension between these two stances as well as that between each of them and those of religious practices that derive their authority from other than the state have contributed to the crisis of authority. (Keyes, Hardacre, and Kendall 1994, 5–6)

Building on this argument, I would add that the contradiction underlying the "crisis of authority" is often the result of a contestation of faiths, in particular, faith in the religion versus faith in the nation. We have ample evidence from world history that multitudes of people have died or are willing to die, rightly or wrongly, for the sake of the "nation" or "religion." In this essay, however, I examine an instance in which religion and nation have overlapped or fused, so that religious identity has become part and parcel of national identity; there seem to be similar cases in many countries around the world (Weisbrod 1983). An interesting feature of this process is that the concept of national identity itself is often a contested one, especially where the concept is developed in a multiethnic and secular society.

What interests me in such cases is how, in its effort to construct a national identity based on a particular religion, the state sometimes ends up confronting the very religious revival it had earlier sought to promote. Although, as in Malaysia, the challenge is often perceived by the state as an internal one, its transnational or global nature cannot be dismissed lightly. In the Malaysian case, the revival's impact on domestic interethnic relations has to be considered as well. In light of all these issues, the Malaysian experience provides a worthy case for examining the contestation between the state and Islamic revivalism.

Before I proceed with this analysis, let me make a few remarks on the analytical approach I adopt here. I contend that, like most social phenomena, identity construction and nation formation take place within two levels of social reality. The first is the official or "authority-defined" social reality, created by people who are part of the dominant power structure; the second is the "everyday-defined" social reality, experienced by the people in the course of their everyday lives (Shamsul n.d.*b*). At any given time, these two social realities exist side by side. Although intricately linked and mutually influential, they are in fact rarely identical. Both are mediated through the social class position of those who experience and interpret social reality. Both are also embedded in relationships of social power.

In this chapter I wish therefore to locate the discourse, ruptures, and tensions that have characterized the contestation between the state and the Islamic revivalist *(dakwah)* movement in Malaysia over the past twenty-five years. Elsewhere I have dealt with microsociological aspects of this contest (Shamsul 1995), examining the lives of individual activists in an Islamic revivalist group; these individuals have largely escaped the attention of Malaysianists writing on the revivalist movement since the mid-1970s (Shamsul 1983). Most analysts have focused on the movement as a group or organization, outlining its origin, leadership, and overall impact on society (Muhammad Abu Bakar 1989; Chandra Muzaffar 1984; Nagata 1984; Zainah Anwar 1987; Husin Mutalib 1990). My present contribution, a macrosociological one, is meant, first, to complement my recent microsociological study and, second, to frame the study of Islamic revivalism in Malaysia within the broader study of identity and nation formation (see Shamsul n.d.*b*).

Ethnicity, Identity, and Religion: Malay, Malayness and Islam

The social categories of "race" and "nation" entered into the indigenous world view in Malaysia through European colonization. Their introduction had a humble and unnoticed beginning. What seemed to be harmless bureaucratic practices of census taking actually helped to introduce and consolidate the racial categories of Malay, Chinese, and Indian (Hirschman 1985, 1986; Milner 1994; Shamsul n.d.*a*). The introduction of legislative measures such as the Malay Reservation Act, the establishment of a Department of Chinese Affairs, and the founding of government-approved toddy shops for Indians all further drove home the point. The racial categories of Malay, Indian, and Chinese came to be vital for anyone who wished to take advantage of the colonial bureaucracy or avoid its wrath.

The evolution and consolidation of these racial categories was further promoted through the vernacular education system. In such contexts racial categories developed into racially based understandings of nation. Ethnic difference came to be the defining mode of everyday social reality. The idea of Malayness and, eventually, the aspiration for a "Malay nation" were thus deeply affected by the circumstances of British rule (Roff 1967; Ariffin Omar 1993). Although the British never established a unified Malay nation as such (instead endorsing a union of Malay principalities [*kerajaan*]), the concept of "Malayness" came to be accepted as an official feature of colonial and native politics.

"Malayness" came to be defined in terms of the three pillars of *agama, bahasa dan raja,* i.e., Muslim religion, Malay language, and the aristocratic government of the sultans. These pillars were then written into the constitution of postcolonial Malaysia. Thus, for example, the constitution requires that Malays be Muslims. In other words, by definition, Malays cannot but be Muslims in Malaysia. A Chinese or an Indian who marries a Malay has to agree to convert to Islam as a precondition of the marriage; in so doing he or she is assimilated into the Malay community, a process popularly known as *masuk Melayu* (lit. "become a Malay"). Their offspring are subsequently categorized as Malays.

Having one's identity officially designated as Malay is, of course, not a matter of free choice; nonetheless it has its benefits. For instance, as a Malay, one is entitled to numerous benefits under the terms of the the pro-Malay affirmative action policy known as the New Economic policy (NEP), launched in 1971 and completed in 1990. In fact, ethnic Malays enjoy other privileges under the terms of the national constitution. However, not every Malay succeeds in acquiring access to these benefits because policies like the NEP are based on, to borrow W. Wertheim's famous phrase "betting on the strong few and not on the weak many." Elsewhere I have examined this problem of access to official benefits in a rural community where I conducted research in the early 1980s, a decade after the NEP was implemented (Shamsul 1986).

Both from the authority-defined as well as the everyday-defined perspective, to be Malay in Malaysia is to be Muslim. However, the relationship has by no means been a static or an uncontested one. It is constantly being redefined by new influences and events. This dynamic was keenly illustrated with the emergence in the 1970s of the Islamic revivalist movement, popularly known as the *dakwah* (lit. "to summon or call") movement. One consequence of the *dakwah* movement's development was that Islam came to be highlighted as the pillar of Malay identity. Through its ruling elite and political party UMNO (United Malays National Organization), the state was forced to respond to this revivalist movement. This response led to the state's increased attention to Islam and its subsequent adoption of an Islamization strategy of its own (Mauzy and Milne 1983/1984).

Though Nagata perceives, rather simplistically, that the contestation between the state and the Islamic revivalism involves competing "models of development" (1995), I believe that the contest involves considerably more than that. Among other things, it involves the general effort to redefine Malayness in the aftermath of the May 1969 racial riots and to improve the generally unfavorable economic situation of Malays. As undertaken by the state, the effort to redefine Malayness led to the mainstreaming of Islam into all domains of Malaysian social life. If previously Islam was mainly expressed in symbolic terms, especially in relation to the institution of the royalty and popular Malay culture, the government's efforts drew Islam into the heart of all economic and noneconomic life. By implication, the government's effort also means that Muslim Malays have now entered the mainstream of the economy as full participants in the corporate world. This perception is neatly captured in the now popular phrase *"Melayu baru"* (lit. "new Malay"). This notion implies that the Malay community has itself been thoroughly transformed, with a new identity, a high economic profile, and an increased sense of religiosity (Shamsul n.d.c).

It should also be noted that the role of Islam as a pillar of Malay identity is today especially critical because the other two original pillars of Malayness, royalty and language, have come to be seen by the Malay elite as problematic. After independence, the Malay ruling elite came to view the native Malay royalty as serious competitors rather than as corulers. The situation of the royalty was further undermined by a series of scandals and corruption charges publicized in government-controlled dailies during 1992. A similar downgrading of importance in Malay identity has occurred with the Malay language. While recognizing the political importance of the Malay language, the government elite has come to view the economic and technological utility of Malay as limited in an era of globalization. In 1994 the prime minister, Dr. Mahathir Mohamed, thus suggested that technical subjects be taught in English in Malaysia's colleges.

In the following pages, I shall present a description and an analysis of the government's mainstreaming effort, whereby it sought to respond to the revivalist movement by developing religious programs of its own. I shall divide the history into four stages over a twenty-five-year period. In doing so, I also want to examine the two major wings of the revivalist movement, namely the radicals and the moderates, paying particular attention to how each asserts its ideological positions and identity based on its particular way of claiming truth. The radicals, we shall see, demand a total and uncompromising response to the revivalist appeal, while the moderates are more tolerant of heterogeneity. I shall also examine the reasons for the government's preference for the moderate revivalist approach, with particular reference to the government's political goals and the global development of Islam.

Phases of the Dakwah Movement

As the term is used throughout this essay, "revivalism" refers to the attempt to restructure the past in a form relevant to contemporary social interests. Terms used interchangeably with "revivalism" are "resurgence," "rediscovery," "rebirth," "reassertion," "renewal," and "reformulation," to name but a few. In my opinion, Islamic revivalism in Malaysia has been motivated by at least six major intentions, some of which have motivated revivalism elsewhere in Southeast Asia (Evers and Siddique 1993). Not in any order of importance, they are as follows: (1) to overcome the pressures of or construct a reply to modernization; (2) to express anti-imperialist or antihegemonical sentiments; (3) to promote spiritual renewal from within a given religion, such as the move to "re-Islamize knowledge"; (4) to counter the influences of societal rationalization; (5) to resolve how to live in a world of radical doubt through the reformulation of traditional symbols and systems of meaning; and (6) to reinvent and reconstruct tradition, thus allowing a redefinition or reassertion of ethnoreligious identities in a plural society.

In practice these intentions often overlap; rarely does any one of them dominate the *dakwah* movement at a given moment. The Malaysian *dakwah* movement was never a really homogenous one, even in its initial stages when it was dominated by university students. The best way to determine how these varied motives interact is to construct a periodization of the movement to date. I have identified four phases of Islamic revivalism in Malaysia over the past twenty-five years: the "reawakening period" (1969–1974), the "forward movement period" (1975–1979), the "mainstreaming period" (1980–1990), and the "*dakwah* and industrialized Malaysia period" (1991 onwards).

Phase 1: The Reawakening Period (1969–1974)

On May 13, 1969, a racial clash between Chinese and Malays took place in Kuala Lumpur, Malaysia's capital. It has been argued that Islamic revivalism in Malaysia emerged in the aftermath of this riot, a crisis that generated a sense of failure among young Malaysian Muslims, especially university students. From this perspective, the riot could be seen as a catalyst for the turn to Islam among Malay youths attempting to resolve how to live in a world of radical doubt. However, this was not the first or the biggest Sino-Malay racial clash in Malaysian history. A bloodier and more extensive conflict occurred during the interregnum of 1945 (Cheah Boon Keng 1983), in which religion and millenarianism were also central to the Malay response to the violent attack by Chinese. During the war, the Chinese had been abused politically by the Japanese; in several infamous incidents many Chinese were mercilessly massacred and buried in unmarked mass graves. Malay nationalists tended to support the Japanese during the occupation, however, since both groups shared certain nationalist ideals.

In the aftermath of the 1969 riot, there was a reemergence of Islamic-oriented, millenarian-inclined, martial art *(silat)* cult groups. These groups traced their origins back to the armed Sabilillah movement that attacked rural Chinese settlements in revenge and self-defense during the Sino-Malay clashes in late 1945, almost immediately after the Japanese surrendered to the British. Most of these "reborn" groups were based in Malay settlements on the outskirts of the national capital, Kuala Lumpur, where most university students lived because of the Malay social environment and inexpensive housing. Many of these students were caught in the crisis mood of the time because of sheer proximity to centers of violence. Some went on to become members or supporters of *silat* cult groups. In an atmosphere of millenarian expectation, it was not suprising that their ethnic and religious consciousness was heightened to a level where they "awoke" to Islam and turned to mysticism and magic to resolve their spiritual and material problems.

The pivotal moment in the institutionalization of the revivalist movement took place in August of 1969 on the campus of the University of

Malaya, the only university in Malaysia at the time, when the National Association of Muslim Students decided to establish a Muslim youth organization named Angkatan Belia Islam Malaysia (ABIM), or the Malaysian Muslim Youth Movement. Designed to operate off campus, ABIM was to serve as an organizational platform for young Muslim graduates to continue their *dakwah* activities in the broader public sphere after leaving the university.

ABIM was officially registered in 1971 and grew to a position of strength by the mid-1970s. The organization's motto was to strive "toward building a society that is based on the principles of Islam." It had an educational wing, the activities of which center around a private school, Yayasan Anda (lit. "Your Institute"). The school played multiple roles, providing cheap education for the poor, financing for ABIM, a recruitment office for new cadres, a publicity organization, a think tank for the forward movement, and a headquarters for the coordination of *dakwah* projects among various Muslim youth organizations.

The situation on the local campus also influenced the birth of the *dakwah* movement. It is not an exaggeration to describe the atmosphere at the University of Malaya in the 1960s and 1970s as an open, liberal, and exciting one, at least until the introduction of the Universities and the University College Act, 1971, which imposed draconian restrictions on student activities. University life remained intellectually vibrant, however, and by 1971 Malaysia had established three other universities, Universiti Kebangsaan Malaysia (UKM), Universiti Pertanian Malaysia (UPM), and Universiti Sains Malaysia (USM). The resulting expansion of the student population provided additional opportunities for the recruitment of *dakwah* supporters.

The sense of political crisis, doubts about their future after graduation, and the exhilarating freedom of campus life encouraged students to turn to Islam. In doing so, however, they quickly discovered that, beyond the daily rituals, they knew very little about intellectual aspects of Islam. Students thus awoke to their personal religious deficiency as they joined the appeal for "Muslims to be better Muslims."

There was another form of revivalism in Malaysian society that resulted from the 1969 race riot. Between May 1969 and February 1971, parliament was suspended and the country came under emergency rule. This became a period of serious rethinking, bargaining, reconstructing, and reconciliation at all levels of the society. New ideas, strategies, and institutions emerged; some were rediscovered, others were modifications of previous ones. All were related to attempts to recreate the racial harmony that had existed before the riots. The pro-Malay Muslim affirmative New Economic Policy (NEP) was one especially important creation of this rethinking process. The Islamic revivalist movement must be examined in this wider social context.

Most analyses of the revivalist movement overlook the importance of the link between the Malaysian *dakwah* activists and their Indonesian counterparts, especially Muslim student associations, during this formative stage from 1969 to 1972 (see, for instance, Nagata 1984). As the movement's first influential international contact, the Indonesians provided an important stimulus to Islamic revivalism in Malaysia. This is perhaps not surprising, as it is a well-established tradition for Malaysian Muslims to look toward Indonesian Muslims for spiritual inspiration, intellectual guidance, and practical help. The two regions share many cultural and linguistics traits, and Indonesia was the main route through which Islam came to Malaysia some five centuries ago. By the mid-1970s, Indonesian contacts and influence had declined as the *dakwah* movement became more pluralistic and internationalized, owing to developments in the Middle East, Pakistan, and other parts of the Islamic world.

The single most important event that gave the *dakwah* movement, particularly ABIM, its much needed political credentials in the eyes of the Malaysian public took place in December 1974, when thousands of students demonstrated in the streets of Kuala Lumpur to protest against peasant hunger and poverty. The event was organized by *dakwah* leaders within the student organization. The government reacted to the demonstration by arresting 1,200 of the protesters and treating the protest as a student problem rather than an Islamic challenge to its legitimacy and authority. It would take the federal government another five years to recognize that the protest was motivated by Islamic objectives and to take appropriate counteraction. At the time the government was preoccupied with other matters, trying to settle a series of internal leadership crises, mainly in the Malay ruling party, UMNO (see Shamsul 1988). In the same year Partai Islam, a Malay-based opposition party, joined the ruling coalition, which until then had been dominated by UMNO. This created a political vacuum into which ABIM comfortably positioned itself, with considerable support and sympathy from disappointed supporters of Partai Islam.

Thus it could be said that in its first phase the *dakwah* movement moved from a limited concern with Muslim consciousness raising to a broader concern with controlling national politics through student activism. This transiton in just five years from the personal to the national-political was indeed a great achievement for the *dakwah* movement. It made Malaysia more Islamically inclined and enabled the movement to address Islamic issues more positively.

Phase 2: The Forward Movement Period (1975–1979)

The second phase of Malaysian *dakwah* can be regarded as the "forward movement" phase in two senses. First, the movement had consolidated itself and found its niche in the Malaysian sociopolitical sphere. Hence it was ready to proceed with its religious agenda and political strategies. Second, during this period the government and the ruling coalition suffered from unprecedented internal strife, with bitter battles among the top leaders of UMNO. The fact that the battles were about "money politics" and the "siphoning of party election funds"—in a word, about corruption among top party leaders—helped to make ABIM, with its progressive approach, a credible political opposition. Part of ABIM's appeal lay in the fact that it did not see Islam in black and white, as a choice between good and evil, or right and wrong, and did not believe in imposing Islam on non-Muslims.

From 1969 until about 1976 or 1977, ABIM and the National Association of Muslim Students were dominated by liberal arts students with only a small number of science students. The reason was simple: Most of the Malay Muslim students were in the arts faculties, and they had primary responsibility for running student organizations. Some time later, however, ABIM's influence declined, at least on local campuses. The National Association of Muslim Students and student unions in local universities were taken over by a new *dakwah* student group, dominated this time not by the arts but by the science students. By this time the number of science students in Malaysian universities had increased dramatically with the expansion of Malaysia's science faculties. Despite the popularity of the new *dakwah* organization, most arts students continued to support the ABIM approach to *dakwah*.

The new *dakwah* group was known on campus as the IRC (Islamic Representative Council). It had originated overseas among Malay Muslim science undergraduates whose study was sponsored by the Malaysian government. Because this organization was born outside the Malaysian sociopolitical milieu and was informed mainly by sectarian Islamic groups based in the Middle East and South Asia, its focus was more religion for religion's sake rather than religion for society's sake. The IRC saw ABIM's Islam as too spicy and impure (read: tolerant of heterogeneity), unlike theirs, which was more true to the original and pure (read: demanding total response).

The IRC and similar groups adopted a covert, guerrillalike style of organization. They established secret cells to spread their Islamic message and infiltrated existing organizations to try to initiate change from within. The group adopted the "education" approach or *tarbiyah,* through the formation and spread of small secret cells among the students. It denounced the Malaysian government as un-Islamic and accused it of upholding a secular and infidel system of rule.

Recruiting from among the science students, the IRC adopted what could be seen as a black and white approach to Islam. In their view, one either practices Islam in a complete way or is an infidel; one either fights for Islam or is irreligious; if a member of an Islamic group, one must be a full-time *dakwah* activist, not merely a sympathizer. One incident drew the attention of the entire country to the new *dakwah* movement. One day the daughter of then–prime minister Hussein Onn arrived home veiled and announced that she had married a fellow student without her father's consent or knowledge. From this, it was obvious to everyone that Islamic revivalism had touched not only alienated overseas students, most of whom came from poor or ordinary rural families, but also children of the urban middle and upper class, brought up in a Westernized way.

Thus, by the end of the 1970s, the *dakwah* movement in Malaysia had been pluralized and radicalized. As a result, ABIM's dominance was reduced substantially. On campuses, there was a sharp divide between ABIM and IRC supporters, who looked down on each other with a holier than thou attitude. By this time, too, the government had devised a response to the Islamic challenge. The option for the government was not so much to dismantle the *dakwah* movement—by then it was almost impossible to do so —but to coopt or mainstream it so that it could serve government interests. The 1980s were a period during which the government was preoccupied with just this struggle.

Phase 3: The Mainstreaming Period (1979–1990)
A combination of international and domestic factors influenced the government's renewed focus on Islam. Government initiatives were notable in the late 1970s and increased to unprecedented levels in the 1980s with the appearance in 1981 of a new prime minister, Dr. Mahathir Mohamed. Mahathir had earlier been influential in the drafting and implementation of policies as the acting prime minister when Prime Minister Hussein Onn had fallen seriously ill in 1978. One of Mahathir's chief policy concerns was the position of Islam in Malaysia and Malaysia's position as an Islamic nation in the Muslim world.

At the international level, too, a number of events influenced internal Islamic affairs: the oil crisis of 1973 and the Arab-Israeli war in the same year; the rise of Middle Eastern Islamic states as "Islamic financiers"; the strengthening of the Organization of the Islamic Conference (OIC) as a basis for the formation of a so-called Muslim Bloc; the Palestinian issue and the

PLO's rise to prominence; the perceived Libyan dominance in the international politics of violence; the Russian occupation of Afghanistan; and, most important of all, the Islamic revolution in Iran. All these events not only transformed the perception and position of Islam in global politics but also heightened Islam's domestic role in Islamic countries like Malaysia.

During these years, there was a visible increase in Malaysian participation in the Muslim Bloc as a result of its pro-Muslim foreign policy. Malaysia's unqualified support for the PLO struggle, for instance, prompted Arafat to make the comment that "Malaysia is even closer to us than some of the Arab nations." Relations with Muslim countries provided excellent political capital for the government in its attempt to prove its Islamic credentials to Malaysian Muslim voters. Malaysia also profited substantially in its trade relations with the petro-dollar rich Islamic nations in the Middle East.

The most immediate challenge shaping the government's policies on Islam was the domestic *dakwah* movement. The movement not only had achieved a formidable position in the political sphere but also had transformed Malay thinking and culture. The most obvious illustration of this influence was the widespread use of *mini-telekung,* a head cloth that covers not only the neck and hair but the chest as well, now worn by growing numbers of Muslim women. The challenge to the government increased when Partai Islam left the ruling coalition and resumed its role as the Malay Muslim opposition. Its new leadership jettisoned its Malay nationalist orientation in favor of a more universalistic Islamic focus, similar to the one adopted by the IRC group of the student *dakwah*. In the government's estimation, the combination of the student-based *dakwah* movement and Partai Islam was politically explosive.

To defuse the situation, the government chose to adopt a "mainstreaming" rather than a confrontational approach to this perceived threat. First and foremost, the government had to accept the increased importance of Islam globally. It did this by approaching any Islamic issue in a positive manner, politically and economically. Domestically, the government attempted to coopt groups and offered its own version of *dakwah,* one more moderate, tolerant, and suitable to Malaysian society, with its multiple ethnic groups and almost equal proportion of Muslims and non-Muslims.

To demonstrate the sincerity of its Muslim-oriented foreign policy, the government introduced a series of policies designed to demonstrate its commitment to developing Islamic institutions among Malays, spending millions of dollars on these projects between 1979 and 1982. The projects included a pledge of MRY$26 million toward the establishment of the Southeast Asian Islamic Research Center, based in Malaysia; the introduction of Islamic religious knowledge as a subject in national education examinations; the official launching of the National *Dakwah* Month; the plan to remodel the Malaysian economic system into an Islamic one, beginning with the establishment of Islamic banks, pawnshops, insurance, and an Islamic Economic Foundation; the formation of Islamic think tanks, such as the Islamic Resources Group and a Special Islamic Enforcement Group; and the commitment to establish an International Islamic University in Kuala Lumpur.

These policies and programs were enough to convince Anwar Ibrahim, the internationally respected and locally popular ABIM leader, to join UMNO and the government in 1982. Soon thereafter he was appointed deputy minister of religious affairs in Mahathir's cabinet. Later he assumed full and more powerful ministerial positions. Other Islamic-oriented programs were introduced after Anwar Ibrahim joined UMNO, including the establishment of the Islamic Medical Center, the founding of International Islamic University in 1983, and the upgrading of the Islamic Center as the nerve center of the government's Islamic bureaucracy.

Officially, Islam is the prerogative of the state governments within the Federation of Malaysia. In the face of these federal efforts, many states began to introduce their own Islamization programs, especially as regarded issues of public morality. Thus many states banned alcohol consumption by Muslims in public. In this manner, the momentum of *dakwah*ism at the federal level spread to state governments, affecting not only urban but rural areas, where Islam has been practiced for generations in a manner different from the overt and self-righteous "*dakwah* way." The overall impact was the heightening of Islamic consciousness nationwide. By the end of the 1980s, the once-urban phenomenon of *dakwah* had migrated to rural areas. The wearing of *mini-telekung* by women became a common sight in the countryside, largely as a result of government efforts.

By the end of the 1980s, more and more of the government policies became "ABIMized," in a fashion that paralleled Anwar Ibrahim's ascendancy from deputy minister (in charge of Islamic affairs) to minister of agriculture and then education and finance. In early 1994 Anwar became Malaysia's deputy prime minister. In this context, *dakwah* groups that had not been mainstreamed became targets of government surveillance and dismantlement. The banning of Darul Arqam, a well-known economically oriented *dakwah* group, in 1994, was one such example. However, such efforts were not always successful, as evidenced in the government's limited success against the IRC in local universities. In general, university campuses resisted government mainstreaming and remained bastions of nongovernmental *dakwah*.

Nationally, however, the *dakwah* movement as a whole has demonstrated considerable ideological flexibility. The movement today is quite pluralized and appeals to a wider spectrum of Malays than it did in the late 1960s. This diversity allows the movement to accommodate political dissidents as well as those seeking spiritual salvation as an alternative to modernization.

The main attraction of the *dakwah* movement, however, was its ability, however limited, to combine theory and practice by attempting to implement the doctrinal precepts of fundamentalist Islamic ideology in the context of Malay Muslims living in a multiethnic country. The movement succeeded in exploiting numerous doctrinal and programmatic emphases: the sense of brotherhood in a community of believers, the relative autonomy of individual Muslims in practicing their religion and preserving their dignity, the encouragement of communally oriented social and welfare activities, and the "religious" obligation to be "political" so as to change a bad society into a good one consistent with the precepts of Islam.

In the public sphere, the impact of *dakwah* on the social fabric of Malaysian life is widespread and felt not only by Muslims but also by non-Muslims of Chinese and Indian descent. Consequently, relations between Muslims and non-Muslims (read: Malay and non-Malay) have become tense and awkward at times because of the influence of strict Islamic codes of behavior promoted by the *dakwah* movement (Zainah 1987; Ackerman and Lee 1988; Shamsul 1994). One example that demonstrates how the *dakwah* ethos has permeated every layer of society and affected everyday forms of social interaction at the grassroots level can be seen in Malay Muslim dietary rules or food taboos. Many Muslims now will not eat food brought by non-Muslim colleagues to social gatherings, be they at the workplace or at the homes of non-Muslim colleagues. In the past such food, as long as it was not pork, was eaten without fuss. Now, however, food taboos extend to anything cooked by non-Muslims, because they have not cleansed their cooking utensils in the Islamic way. Fast-food restaurants have to observe Muslim rules very strictly or their licenses can be revoked. Even in five-star hotels there are now separate Muslim and non-Muslim kitchens. Non-Muslims see this as evidence of increasing Muslim intolerance of non-Malays and non-Muslims.

Phase 4: *Dakwah* and Industrialized Malaysia (1991 Onwards)
One must not forget the wider social context within which the *dakwah* movement in Malaysia has flourished, especially in terms of Malaysia's economic performance. The 1990s and the twenty-first century hold great promise for Malaysia's economic future, as the nation moves into a differ-

ent phase of its existence. Without doubt the *dakwah* movement too will be affected by this transformation. In this context, one could ask, what is the future of the *dakwah* movement as a whole, and what actions will the government take in relation to the movement?

It is not difficult to find evidence that the government has responded successfully to the challenge of the *dakwah* movement. It has managed to keep the radical movements at bay while coopting moderate elements, avoiding serious confrontation over the past decade. It achieved this by introducing its own version of *dakwah*, one palatable both internationally and locally. The success of this effort can be attributed to several things, the most important being the government's willingness to embrace the cause for reasons neither purely religious nor political.

One must not underestimate the contribution of the mastermind himself, Malaysia's prime minister, Dr. Mahathir Mohamed, whose personal interest in matters relating to student politics and *dakwah* goes back to the days of the 1974 student uprising when he was the minister of education. With his intimate knowledge of student politics and the evolution of the *dakwah* movement, he was in the best position to observe what was going on in both domains. With the whole machinery of government at his disposal, he was also able to reshape aspects of the sociopolitical landscape of the country to the government's advantage in responding to the challenges of Islam in general and the *dakwah* movement in particular (Khoo Boo Teik 1995). Malaysia's spectacular economic success, achieving some of the highest growth rates in the world, has also made it possible for the government not only to finance its *dakwah* programs lavishly but also to initiate special Islamic-oriented policies in the economy. To observers in the industrialized nations, Malaysia is one of the "mini-tigers" in the making. To the developing world, Malaysia is a success story and a model of Third World development. To the Muslim Bloc, Malaysia is a successful Islamic nation and one that is rich and kind enough to assist other struggling Muslim nations.

The economic and political confidence that Malaysia has gained at home and abroad has made it more ambitious, though cautiously so. It is ambitious in that it aspires to be a developed industrial nation by 2020. It is cautious because it understands that realization of this vision is contingent upon the nation's ability to maintain not only economic growth but also, more importantly, political and social stability. Thus, in early 1991, Dr. Mahathir announced that Malaysia shall not follow the same route the West took in its journey to industrialization and modernization (Mahathir 1991). He has said that Malaysia's path to 2020 shall be guided by spiritual, religious, and moral consciousness of the highest level. This is a tall order indeed. The issue here is what shall be the source of this guidance.

Such a pronouncement could be dismissed as merely rhetorical. But it is significant in the context of this essay that the propagation of such religious values and the confidence with which these values are now being proclaimed by the government can be attributed to the government's success in dealing with the Islamic and *dakwah* challenge. Because the whole issue of Islam and *dakwah* is so intricately linked to issues of ethnic identity (Shamsul 1994) and the political survival of the nation, it is no surprise that the government has taken the matter seriously. Seen from this perspective, *dakwah* has an important role in the government's vision of a developed and industrialized Malaysian nation.

At the international level, Malaysia's successful response to the *dakwah* challenge contributed tremendously toward enhancing Malaysia's image as a successful nation within the Muslim Bloc. This image has resulted in a manifold increase over the past five years in Malaysia's trade relations with oil-rich Islamic nations in the Middle East and even Central Asia. In the first half of 1993 alone, Malaysia has concluded business agreements worth more than U.S.$5 billion with Iran and another U.S.$2 billion with Kuwait, Uzbekistan, and Saudi Arabia. Only Japan has been able to make comparably sized deals with the Middle Eastern nations in the past. This is just the beginning of Malaysia's large-scale trade with other Muslim countries, which is projected to increase twofold in the next ten years.

It seems likely that in the next century we will see the development of a "two-tier" *dakwah* in Malaysia. On one level will be the government version of *dakwah,* with its wider network of subscribers involved in the everyday practice of governance and social interaction. Because the government has a large bureaucratic machine and almost unlimited funds at its disposal, its particular version of *dakwah* will be continuously maintained, supported, and propagated for domestic and international consumption.

On the second level will be the *dakwah* groups created outside the structure of government. The government will no doubt persist in its struggle to dismantle these groups, no matter how large their organization. Over the past two years this is exactly what the government has done to Darul Arqam, the best-known noncampus *dakwah* organization in Malaysia, which was established shortly after the May 1969 racial riot. Groups like the Darul Arqam are basically small-scale in terms of organization and funding, but compact and solid enough to resist being dismantled for a while by outsiders, including the government. But in 1994, Darul Arqam was disbanded after being banned by the government for its alleged "deviationist" activities. However, most of the non-ABIM *dakwah* organizations are found in the universities and are particularly strong in the natural sciences faculties. They are perceived by university authorities in Malaysia as "social irritants." They have survived in the universities, because forming an association or club in a university is much easier than establishing a nongovernmental organization outside the campus.

The *dakwah* movement is here to stay in Malaysia. It has now moved from a peripheral position, when it first appeared in 1969, to a central position in the social life of Malaysians. It has also spread from urban to rural areas and extended its influence from the middle class, where its founders were located, to both upper and lower classes. It has become ideologically pluralized, so that individuals drawn to the movement have the ability to choose extremist or moderate *dakwah* as they please. In daily interaction, to be *"dakwah"* can mean merely being relatively more strict in one's observance of Muslim codes or it can mean committed activism.

Conclusion

It is difficult to separate the birth of the Malaysian *dakwah* movement from the aftermath of the race riots of 1969. The riots were a significant watershed in Malaysia's postcolonial politics, economy, and society. As with the bloodier racial clashes of 1946 after the Japanese surrender, religious elements, Islamic and non-Islamic, became the natural refuge with which Malays coped with intense disorientation and social turmoil. In 1946 the social context within which the religious elements appeared was dictated by the need to survive a violent and vengeful attack, mainly by the Chinese. In 1969 religious elements reappeared, but this time as a response to the pressures of modernization and the need to maintain the ethnic boundaries required for political hegemony. The Islamic revivalist movement emerged from these circumstances and, once established, began to function with its own logic, albeit not unrelated to the rise of Islamic influence globally.

Equally important, the movement's emergence also redefined Malay identity. Islam as a pillar of Malayness was pushed to center stage in politics and society. In its initial stages, the *dakwah* movement was inward-looking and primarily concerned with reeducating the Muslim self. Its political attitude was moderate and integrated into Malaysian student politics, demanding social and economic justice for the weak in a multiethnic society. Its mission, however, was clearly Islamic, emphasizing the need for the Muslim-dominated government to return to the teachings of the Qur'an and to try to turn to Islam as a panacea for the ills besetting society. The orientation was clearly one of "Islamism," conceiving of Islam as a political ideology (Roy 1994). It has been informed by the so-called Islamic political imagination, dominated by the paradigmatic ideal "of the first community of believers at the time of the Prophet and of the first four caliphs" (p. 12).

This Islamism was the main feature of the first phase (1969–1974) of Malaysia's *dakwah* movement, shaped by the students' experience in organizations in the arts faculty. This arts-based tradition of *dakwah* continues to this day. In the second phase (1975–1979), however, this moderate *dakwah* lost ground to a more radical version of *dakwah*, brought home from abroad by government-sponsored science graduates. As part of the same policy, the government also created a number of fully residential junior science colleges for Malay students selected on the basis of their excellent performance in national examinations. Radical *dakwah* found its way into these colleges as a result of the patient and dedicated campaigning of *dakwah* teachers who had trained abroad and then been posted to these colleges. *Dakwah* thus migrated from the university level to the secondary schools and was dominated in the science colleges by the radical group. In the ordinary secondary schools the moderate *dakwah* was also influential, but only among the arts-stream students (see Shamsul 1995).

Radical *dakwah* finally found its way into the campuses through students from the junior science colleges. The influence of radical *dakwah* grew as the number of science students in the universities increased. By the end of the 1970s, *dakwah* activists had a strong grip on national student politics, controlling all the student unions in the country. At the same time the government began to respond to the Islamic challenge. Previously it had been unable to do so because of internal leadership crises and its error in mistaking the *dakwah* movement for mere student politics.

The third phase of the *dakwah* movement (1979–1990) was dominated by the government's effort to mainstream *dakwah* groups by implementing Islamic-oriented programs, funding local and foreign Islamic organizations, establishing Islamic economic institutions, promulgating a pro-Muslim foreign policy, and becoming active in Muslim Bloc politics. It emphasized the need for a moderate approach toward Islam in a multiethnic society like Malaysia. These actions convinced arts-based *dakwah* groups like ABIM to join the government, thereby providing the bulk of the ideas and practical projects for the government's *dakwah* programs. While the machinery of government embraced a moderate *dakwah* approach, however, the student unions in government-funded universities did not. They remained in the hands of the radical *dakwah* from science faculties. University authorities were unable to dismantle this movement because of the weakness of university bureaucracies and the *dakwah* groups' resilience.

Events during these phases of Malaysian *dakwah* largely support Dale Eickelman's (1992) argument that mass education and mass communication facilitate awareness among the Muslim majority of a "plurality of traditions" within Islam; they thus expand "the style and scale of possible discourse, reconfigure the nature of religious thought and action, and encourage explicit debate over meaning" (p. 644). Such has been the case in Malaysia (see also Hefner, Horvatich, and Metcalf, this volume).

In the early 1990s the government prepared the nation to move into the next century, guided by the vision that Malaysia should be an industrialized nation by the year 2020. The moderate *dakwah* emphasis on the spiritual and moral foundations required for such an effort became national policy. Meanwhile, the government's efforts to mainstream and moderate the *dakwah* movement continues. This attempt at "*dakwah* cleansing" will likely fail, however, because the government itself indirectly nurtures radical *dakwah* through its system of junior science colleges. Students at these colleges became *dakwah* at an early age through systematic *tarbiyah* (education) used by the radical *dakwah* group to recruit new members in secondary school. The positivistic scientific paradigms of the West have provided these students with the analytic tools for the reinterpretation of Islam in a narrow, legalistic way.

The arts students continue to propagate moderate *dakwah* and dominate the government's efforts to "Islamize" Malaysian society. The government's effort to dismantle radical *dakwah,* therefore, has been initiated by moderate *dakwah* elements in the government itself. In one sense, the contest seems like a continuation of the rivarly between science and arts students. As one of my arts informants remarked, "Being clever and brilliant like the science students is not good enough in this country. Being powerful is most important, and power is what the arts students have controlled in this country for so long" (Shamsul 1995, 131).

In this sense, what we see in Malaysia today is the ongoing interaction of global knowledge, both Western and Islamic, and local knowledge, both indigenous and indigenized. The interaction hardly provides a fixed point of reference for the society, because it keeps on shifting as historical and other circumstances shape its form and content. Among the crucial questions being asked is "Is Western social knowledge the only source of social knowledge? What is the role of revealed knowledge?" The science students have reeducated themselves about Islam in a detailed and systematic manner not by using any method borrowed from famous Islamic Sufis or Ayatollah Khomeini, but according to the positivistic canons of the natural sciences. By using the approach that they know best, that is, the Western, rational, positivistic method, they have, in fact, adopted a narrowly legalistic, black-and-white, conservative position regarding Islam. They see "Islamic knowledge" or theology in terms of rules, formulae, and equations, a way of categorizing and perceiving the world they have learned from their study of the natural sciences.

Sociologically speaking, this contest is a classic example of a struggle over the definition of tradition, particularly "authentic" tradition. The contest to define what is and what is not authentic inevitably takes on a confrontational form, as different versions of "tradition" compete with one another. One could thus argue that one of the most important elements in Islamic fundamentalism is precisely this struggle over the definition of what is an authentic Islamic tradition—a tradition with which the believers are to confront the forces of unbelief, corruption, and oppression (see Gilsenan 1982, 15).

Malaysian *dakwah* has demonstrated the intensity and complexity of this struggle to define the authentic Islamic tradition. Seen from the perspective of a multiethnic and multireligious Malaysian society, this internal process involves a struggle to define and maintain an authentic Malay Muslim tradition and identity relative to non-Malays and non-Muslims (Shamsul 1994), while also confronting the centrifugal pressures of a market economy, affluence, and growth of a middle class. However, the interesting twist to this search for authenticity is that during the process Malayness itself came to be redefined and reconstituted. This profound social transformation will continue to play a significant role in the shaping of Malaysia's future.

References Cited

Ackerman, S. E., and R. L. M. Lee. 1988. *Heaven in Transition: Non-Muslim Religious Innovation and Ethnic Identity in Malaysia*. Honolulu: University of Hawai'i Press.

Ariffin Omar. 1993. *Bangsa Melayu: Malay Concepts of Democracy and Community, 1945–1950*. Kuala Lumpur: Oxford University Press.

Chandra Muzaffar. 1987. *Islamic Resurgence in Malaysia*. Petaling Jaya: Fajar Bakti.

Cheah Boon Kheng. 1983. *Red Star over Malaya: Resistance and Social Conflict during and after the Japanese Occupation, 1941–1946*. Singapore: Singapore University Press.

Eickelman, Dale. 1985. *Knowledge and Power in Morocco*. Princeton, N.J.: Princeton University Press.

———. 1992. "Mass Higher Education and the Religious Imagination in Contemporary Arab Societies." *American Ethnologist*, 19 (4): 643–655.

Evers, H. D., and Sharon Siddique. 1993. "Religious Revivalism in Southeast Asia: An Introduction". *Sojourn* 8 (3): 1–27.

Gilsenan, Michael. 1973. *Saint and Sufi in Modern Egypt*. Oxford: Clarendon Press.

———. 1982. *Recognizing Islam: An Anthropological Introduction*. London: Croom Helm.

Hirschman, Charles. 1985. "The Meaning and Measurement of Ethnicity in Malaysia." *Journal of Asian Studies* 46 (3): 555–582.

———. 1986. "The Making of Race in Colonial Malaya: Political Economy and Racial Ideology." *Sociological Forum* 2 (1): 330–361.

Husin Mutalib. 1990. *Islam and Ethnicity in Malay Politics.* Singapore: Oxford University Press.

Kessler, C. S. 1978. *Islam and Politics in a Malay State: Kelantan, 1838–1969.* Ithaca: Cornell University Press.

Keyes, Charles, Helen Hardacre, and Laurel Kendall. 1994. "Introduction: Contested Visions of Community in East and Southeast Asia". In Charles Keyes, Laurel Kendall and Helen Hardacre, eds., *Asian Visions of Authority: Religion and the Modern States in East and Southeast Asia,* pp. 1–16. Honolulu: University of Hawai'i Press.

Khoo Boo Teik. 1995. *Paradoxes of Mahathirism: An Intellectual Biography of Mahathir Mohamed.* Kuala Lumpur: Oxford University Press.

Mahathir Mohamed. 1991. "Malaysia: The Way Forward." Keynote paper for the Inaugural Meeting of the Malaysian Business Council, Kuala Lumpur, February 28.

Mauzy, Diane, and R. S. Milne. 1983/1984. "The Mahathir Administration in Malaysia: Discipline through Islam." *Pacific Affairs* 56 (4): 617–648.

Milner, Anthony. 1994. *The Invention of Politics in Colonial Malaya.* Melbourne: Cambridge University Press.

Muhammad Abu Bakar. 1989. *Penghayatan Sebuah Ideal* (The Comprehension of an Ideal). Kuala Lumpur: Dewan Bahasa dan Pustaka.

Nagata, J. 1984. *The Reflowering of Malaysian Islam.* Vancouver: University of British Columbia Press.

———. 1995. "How to Be Islamic without Being an Islamic State: Contested Models of Development in Malaysia." In Akbar S. Ahmed and Hastings Donnan, eds., *Islam, Globalization and Postmodernity,* pp. 63–90. London: Routledge.

Roff, William. 1967. *The Origins of Malay Nationalism.* Kuala Lumpur: University of Malaya Press.

Roy, Olivier. 1994. *The Failure of Political Islam.* London: I. B. Tauris.

Shamsul A. B. 1983. "A Revival in the Study of Islam in Malaysia." *Man* (n.s.), 18 (2): 399–404.

———. 1986. *From British to Bumiputera Rule: Local Politics and Rural Development in Peninsular Malaysia.* Singapore: Institute of Southeast Asian Studies.

———. 1988. "The Battle Royal: The UMNO Elections of 1987." In Mohamed Ayoob and Ng Chee Yuen, eds., *Southeast Asian Affairs, 1988,* pp. 170–188. Singapore: Institute of Southeast Asian Studies.

———. 1989. "From Urban to Rural: The 'Migration' of the Islamic Revival Phenomenon in Malaysia." In *Proceedings of the Congress on Urbanism and Islam,* vol. 4, pp. 1–34. Tokyo: Institute of Oriental Culture, University of Tokyo.

———. 1994. "Religion and Ethnic Politics in Malaysia: The Significance of the Islamic Revivalist Movement." In Charles Keyes, L. Kendall, and H. Hardacre, eds., *Asian Visions of Authority,* pp. 99–116. Honolulu: University of Hawai'i Press.

———. 1995. "Inventing Certainties: The Dakwah Persona in Malaysia." In Wendy James, ed., *The Pursuit of Certainty: Religious and Cultural Formulations,* pp. 112–133. London: Routledge.

———. 1996. "Nation-of-Intents in Malaysia." In Stein Tonnesson and Hans Antloev, eds., *Asian Forms of the Nation,* pp. 426–456. London: Curzon Press.

———. n.d.*a.* "The Bureaucratic Management of Identity in a Modern Nation-State: The Malaysian Way." In Dru Gladney, ed., *Making Majority, Composing Nation.* Stanford: Stanford University Press, in press.

———. n.d.*b.* "Debating about Identity in Malaysia: A Discourse Analysis." In Zawawi Ibrahim, ed., *Negotiating Identities in a Changing Malaysia.* Special issue of the journal *Tōnan Ajia Kenkyū.* Center for Southeast Asian Studies, Kyoto University, Japan, forthcoming.

———. n.d.*c.* "Orang Kaya Baru: The Cultural Construction of the Malay 'New Rich.' " In Michael Pinches, ed., *The Cultural Construction of the New Rich in Asia.* London: Routledge, forthcoming.

Weisbrod, Lilly. 1983. "Religion as National Identity in a Secular Society." *Review of Religious Research* 24 (3): 188–205.

Zainah Anwar. 1987. *Islamic Revivalism in Malaysia: Dakwah among the Students.* Petaling Jaya: Pelanduk.

Part III
Ordinary Muslims

Chapter 8

"Ordinary Muslims" and Muslim Resurgents in Contemporary Malaysia
NOTES ON AN AMBIVALENT RELATIONSHIP

Michael G. Peletz

Recent scholarship on Islam in Malaysia has focused on Malaysia's Islamic resurgence and the ways in which Malay Muslim reformers and modernists conceptualize their moral communities and visions of and for the future (see, for example, Kessler 1980; Shamsul A. B. 1983; Nagata 1984; Chandra Muzaffar 1987; Muhammad Abu Bakar 1987; Zainah Anwar 1987; Banks 1990; Nash 1991; Jomo and Shabery Cheek 1992; and Husin Mutalib 1993). Such scholarship has clearly enriched our understanding of the theology of the resurgence. It has also shed light on the organizational activities, cultural identities, and life experiences of the resurgents—the vast majority of whom are associated with the urban middle class—as well as their doctrinal and ideological stances vis-à-vis state policies bearing on national development and Malaysia's ethnic mosaic. Unfortunately, however, recent scholarship on Malaysian Islam has largely ignored the experiences and voices of "ordinary Muslims" (or "ordinary Malays" —the two terms are used here interchangeably),[1] who are not in the forefront of contemporary religious or political developments and who are in many cases far more ambivalent about the resurgence than we have been led to believe. As a consequence of the neglect of what K. S. Jomo and Ahmad Shabery Cheek have recently dubbed the "silent constituency" (1992, 104–105), the existing literature provides limited and ultimately skewed perspectives on the religious and political landscapes of contemporary Malaysia, and we are left with the impression that the entire Muslim community in Malaysia is either centrally involved in the resurgence or at least squarely behind it. Such triumphalist impressions are strengthened both by media coverage of Islam in Malaysia, especially that afforded by international media, and by the accounts of celebrated novelists (for example, Naipaul 1981). More generally, the available literature provides little sense of the range of variation within the Malay community as regards what it means to be a (Malay) Muslim in present-day Malaysia and certainly does not address the comparative and theoretical implications of such variation.

This essay deals with the experiences, voices, and cultural identities of Malaysia's ordinary Muslims—the majority of whom are Malays living in rural areas—particularly as they relate to the discourses of Islamic resurgence. Drawing on data from different regions of the Malay peninsula, I examine rural Malays' styles of religiosity, and I investigate their perceptions of and attitudes toward the resurgence and the various organizations, state policies, and agents centrally involved in its spread (and containment). I am especially interested in the implications of the variable and at times contradictory ways in which symbols and idioms of moral community, modernity, and progress are invoked in the discourses of activists and their ordinary Muslim counterparts. Of equal concern, however, are issues and arguments that are not voiced publicly and that are in many cases "unthinkable" for political or moral reasons. One such issue is that, while processes involving the reformulation of some traditions and the suppression or elimination of others may well be a prerequisite for modernization and religious development, they also entail a certain deracination or cultural impoverishment for local communities and the "Malay race" in its entirety. A central objective of the essay is thus to examine the production and consumption of contrasting discourses on Islam and Malay cultural identity in contemporary Malaysia. The broader goals of the essay are to further our understanding of Islamic constructions of identity in Southeast Asia and to contribute to the comparative and theoretical literature on the political economy of contested symbols and meanings.

The material presented here is organized into four sections. The first provides background information on some of the political, economic, and religious variables that have given rise to the resurgence as well as some of the legal and other initiatives associated with it. The second deals with the religious climate (including manifestations of and reactions to the resurgence) in rural areas and among ordinary Muslims generally. The third expands the scope of inquiry by examining some recent dynamics and dilemmas related to the institution of feasting, an institution that is held in low regard by resurgents but is nonetheless of central importance as far as most ordinary Malays are concerned. This part of the essay includes a discussion of a hastily arranged—and heavily stigmatized—"shotgun wedding," the ritual streamlining of which corresponds in many respects to the resurgents' views of how all weddings should be. The case study and commentary included here indicate that the resurgents advocate a type of ritual purification and "cultural cleansing" that strike at the heart of ordinary Malays' basic values. The fourth (and final) section of the essay addresses rural Malays' ambivalence and hostility toward the resurgence, the focus being on the reason why such sentiments are not usually realized either in practice (as the latter term is generally understood) or even in what James C. Scott (1990) refers to as "hidden transcripts." At the risk of oversimplification, I argue that strategies of resistance and oppositional ideologies are relatively unelaborated not only because of censorship and fears of political reprisals (variables typically cited in the cross-cultural literature as *the* primary impediments to resistance), but also—and more importantly— because of the existential and moral constraints entailed in the construction of ordinary Malays' cultural identities. Using recent work by Scott (1985; 1990) as an example of the burgeoning genre of resistance studies, I contend that such studies need to devote greater attention to moral variables generally and to the political economy and cultural psychology of ambivalence ("the experience of comingled contradictory emotions" [Weigert 1991]) in particular.

One final introductory comment concerns terminology. Terms such as "ordinary Muslims" (and "ordinary Malays"), on the one hand, and "Muslim resurgents" ("*dakwah* adherents," "*dakwah* supporters," and so forth), on the other, are defined largely through contrast and are employed to refer to "religious orientations or modes of piety rather than fixed sociological categories" (Woodward 1989, 8). There are potential problems with the use of such terms, but they are, to my mind, less pronounced than the dilemmas associated with other terms that might be employed in their place. A more fine-grained terminological distinction than the one used here would be more consistent with the nuances of the data presented in the following pages, but I assume the reader will keep in mind that there is considerable variation in religious orientations among ordinary Muslims and Muslim resurgents alike.

Islamic Resurgence in Contemporary Malaysia: An Introductory Sketch

Malaysia's Islamic resurgence is known as the *dakwah* movement. The term *dakwah* means "to call," or to respond to the call (see Shamsul and Feillard, this volume), hence missionary work, including making Muslims better Muslims. The resurgence is usually said to date from the late 1960s or early 1970s, even though it is most appropriately viewed as an outgrowth of earlier developments in Islamic nationalism and reform, such as those associated with the Kaum Muda ("Young Group") movement of the 1920s and 1930s (see Bowen, this volume; Roff 1967). The Kaum Muda movement was thoroughly home-grown, but it was animated and sustained in part by the activities and organizations of Muslims in Indonesia, Singapore, and elsewhere. The same is true of *dakwah*. More generally, developments such as *dakwah* have tended to be cyclical in nature, as illustrated by Barbara Andaya and Yoneo Ishii's (1992) study of religious dynamics in Southeast Asia during the period between 1600 and 1800 (see also Johns 1980, 164) and by Ernest Gellner's (1981) work on historical trends in other parts of the Muslim world.

Most scholars approach the resurgence as a response—indeed, a form of resistance—to one or more of the following analytically related and culturally interlocked sets of developments. The first development concerns the postcolonial state's Western-oriented development policies, which entail a heavily interventionist role for the state with respect to economic planning, distribution, and capitalist processes as a whole. These policies are widely seen as contributing to Malaysia's overdependence on foreign (particularly Western) capital; to the economic success of Chinese and Indians relative to Malays, who comprise roughly half of the country's total population; and to upper-class corruption as well as deracination and moral and spiritual bankruptcy throughout the Malay community. The second development involves the simultaneous shifting and hardening of class interests and animosities, especially between the newly emerged middle class and an entrenched (aristocratic) ruling class. The third development is the tightening of ethnic boundaries, particularly those separating Malays and Chinese. These boundaries have become increasingly salient in recent decades, owing in no small measure to the New Economic Policy (NEP). Implemented in 1971, the NEP was geared toward helping Malays "catch up" economically with Chinese and Indians, and placed tremendous emphasis on "race"—being a Malay or a non-Malay—as a criterion in the allocation of scarce and highly prized government resources (scholarships and loans, contractor's licenses, business permits, and so forth). The NEP is commonly regarded as having encouraged a certain cultural assertiveness—some would say chauvinism—among Malays (see Chandra Muzaffar 1987; Zainah Anwar 1987). This cultural assertiveness is especially pronounced as regards Islam, the practice of which, along with speaking the Malay language (Bahasa Melayu) and observing Malay "custom" *(adat),* is a defining feature, and increasingly *the* key symbol, of Malayness. More broadly, whatever else the *dakwah* movement is, scholars generally view it as a powerful vehicle for the articulation of moral opposition to government development policies, traditional as well as emergent class structures, and other ethnic groups.

Dakwah organizations are highly diverse and their objectives are in certain respects mutually incompatible. However, they all share an overriding concern to revitalize or reactualize (local) Islam and the (local) Muslim community by encouraging stronger commitment to the teachings of the Qur'an and the Hadith, in order to effect a more Islamic way of life. The main organizations include the following: (1) Darul Arqam, a communal, land-based organization that enjoins its members to emulate the life of the Prophet and that strives for economic self-sufficiency; (2) ABIM (Angkatan Belia Islam Malaysia, the Malaysian Islamic Youth Organization), which emphasizes formal education and is extremely popular among university students and youth generally, and encourages lobbying efforts, active participation in party politics, and otherwise "working within the system" (though it is also suspected by the government of "socialist leanings"; Kessler 1980, 9); and (3) PERKIM (Pertubuhan Kebajikan Islam Malaysia, the Malaysian Islamic Welfare and Missionary Association), a moderate if not conservative charitable organization, sponsored by the government, which is geared toward assisting recent converts to Islam. Also worthy of mention here is PAS (Parti Islam Se-Malaysia, the Pan-Malayan Islamic Party), the major (Malay) opposition party, which has a decidely populist orientation (see Kessler 1978). Strictly speaking, PAS is not part of the *dakwah* movement, though many of its objectives are espoused by some segments of the movement. The most basic of these objectives is the creation of an Islamic state with the Qur'an and the Sunnah as its constitution.[2]

Most *dakwah* adherents are members of the urban midsle class, but we can be more specific. As Wazir Jahan Karim puts it, *dakwah* supporters "are mainly middle-level urban workers, student groups or professionals without social status or power, who are marginally involved with modern development processes and generally incapable of acquiring an important platform in decision-making concerned with the government machinery or economy" (1992, 175). *Dakwah* followers are especially visible in university settings and are easily identified by the distinctive dress that many of them wear (long, loose-fitting robes [*hijab*] as well as veils and other headgear in the case of women; long, flowing robes [*jubah*] and in some instances turbans in the case of men) as well as their active participation in religious study groups *(usrah)*. Their overall numbers, however, are difficult to gauge. Some observers have estimated that 60 to 70 percent of Malay university women don the costume of *dakwah* adherents and otherwise ally themselves with the resurgence and that the figure for university men is comparable (Chandra Muzaffar 1987, 3; Zainah Anwar 1987, 33; Nash 1991, 710). Whatever the figures, the more relevant and uncontested point is that *dakwah* adherents actually constitute a minority—though a vociferous and powerful minority—of urban Malays as a whole (see Karim 1992, 176).

The relationships between the various segments of the movement and the state merit careful consideration, for they have fueled many of the political and religious dynamics characteristic of contemporary Malaysia. For the most part, Darul Arqam and PERKIM are not much of a threat to the state, but ABIM and PAS clearly are, particularly since their leaders have on numerous occasions publicly charged that the ruling party (UMNO, the United Malays National Organization) has failed to safeguard the interests and well-being of the Malay community, especially with regard to Islam. In order to undercut the opposition, the ruling party has had to work overtime to validate its Islamic credentials by going forward with its own far-reaching, though ultimately moderate, Islamization program. This program to "out-Islamicize" the opposition, which does at times have those qualities of an arms race that Gregory Bateson (in a very different context) referred to as "schismogenesis" (Bateson 1936), has included the building and refurbishing of prayer houses and mosques, the creation of an Islamic university and an Islamic system of banking and finance, the sponsoring of a plethora of Islamic seminars and conferences, and, last but not least, the passage of myriad legislative measures bearing on Islam. While these moves have succeeded in undercutting PAS and ABIM, and in retaining the support of urban middle-class Malays who constitute that segment of the population most responsive to *dakwah* appeals, they have also seriously alienated non-Malays, who make up roughly half of Malaysia's multiethnic population. More important, these measures have also clearly alienated significant numbers of ordinary, especially rural, Malays, who perceive them as direct attacks on their basic values and key features of their cultural identities. To appreciate the political and religious dynamics at issue here we need only consider some recent developments in Malaysia's Islamic legal system, such as stepped-up efforts to rationalize the operation of the Islamic courts and expand their jurisdiction, and more vigorous attempts to stamp out "deviationist teaching."

Expanding and Rationalizing the Islamic Legal System

Efforts to upgrade the administration of Islam have taken various forms over the past few decades. Most obvious are legislative and other measures to centralize, standardize, and otherwise rationalize the operation of the Islamic courts so that they will be more compatible with—and thus in a better position to assume critical functions of—the secular courts, which were established by the British during the colonial era (1874–1957) and continue to handle most of the civil and criminal offenses of Muslims and non-Muslims alike. These measures have included stiffer sanctions for violations of Islamic law; provisions for better educating Islamic judges; and proposals to transfer authority from district judges to their state-level counterparts, which will involve (among other things) stripping district judges of their long-standing authority to handle various aspects of marriage and divorce.

For a number of reasons, the centralization, standardization, and overall rationalization of the Islamic legal system will further burden litigants and others who must deal with the courts. The most readily apparent reason is that, in order to conduct their business, they will have to travel farther (to the state capital, rather than the district capital) and will thus be further inconvenienced and incur greater expense. It is fair to assume, too, that the atmosphere in the state-level courts will be more formal, more foreign, and otherwise more intimidating than the atmosphere of district-level courts and that some such differences will have a greater negative impact on women than on men.

Having said this, I should emphasize that while much of the impetus for the reformulation and more strict administration of Islamic "family law" derives from concerns with the implications of high rates of divorce and abandonment, a good number of the specific legislative proposals aimed at addressing such concerns are grounded in the belief that a significant range of the problems in marriage and much of the "fault" in divorce is due to the inappropriate behavior of men (cf. Ong 1990a, 453–454n.3). Note, for example, that one of the key pieces of legislation proposed in some states in recent years forbids men to repudiate their wives outside of the courtroom. The implementation of this legislation will involve a dramatic break with established practice, insofar as men have always been able to repudiate their wives wherever—and whenever (and on whatever grounds) —they want. Such repudiation, unless revoked by the husband within one hundred days, constitutes a legally binding divorce. (Husbands are required by the state to register all such repudiations and divorces with an Islamic magistrate, but failure to do so does not render them invalid.) The idea behind the new legislation is to cut down on the number of repudiations issued in the "heat of the moment" and thus to lower the divorce rate and help insure the stability and durability of marriage and family units generally; but it will clearly restrict the autonomy and social control exercised by men in their roles as husbands. So, too, will legislation making it more difficult for men to enter into polygynous unions. Such points are important to bear in mind lest we mistakenly assume, as many are wont to do, that the legislative and other measures associated with the resurgence invariably proceed at the expense of the (considerable) autonomy and social control traditionally enjoyed by women, and entail few, if any, restrictions with respect to the autonomy and social control exercised by men.

Recent years have also seen the establishment of academic journals dealing with Islamic law, such as *Jernal Hukum* (The Law Journal), which set out in writing and thus make widely available for comparison and analysis judicial decisions that may be used in the future as judicial precedents of one sort or another, although, strictly speaking, Islamic religious law operates without the benefit of judicial precedent. This may result, as M. B. Hooker suggests, in the imposition of "an English law form" (1989, 228), though it is more likely that the codified judicial decisions will serve instead as general guidelines, analogous in some ways to the *amal* literature in Morocco (Rosen 1989).

Cracking Down on "Deviationist Teaching" and "Religious Extremism"

Legislative and police moves to curtail what is referred to as "deviationist teaching" and "religious extremism" have received much press in Malaysia over the past few decades, but curiously they have not attracted much scholarly interest. Scott, for example, devotes minimal attention to such phenomena, even though he acknowledges that "rarely a month goes by without a newspaper account of the prosecution of a religious teacher accused of the propagation of false doctrines" (Scott 1985, 335n.67). Significantly, the latter admission is relegated to a footnote, just as the "flying letter" *(surat layang)* containing subversive religious/political prophecies that circulated in Kedah in the course of his fieldwork is presented, unanalyzed, in an appendix.[3]

The media are in fact full of accounts of various types of ritual specialists *(dukun/bomoh)* and religious scholars *(ulama)* who are charged with possessing prohibited pamphlets and prayer mats, or misusing Qur'anic verses for the purpose of multiplying money or predicting lottery results. Legal and political initiatives in this area are an index of the state's longstanding concern to homogenize and otherwise tidy up Malay "folk religion" by cleansing it of what the state defines as "pre-Islamic accretions." These measures are also aimed at curbing the introduction and spread of Shi'ite, especially Iranian, teachings and stifling all dissent cast in religious terms. The state has increasingly reserved and exercised the right to define all alternative religious discourse as counterhegemonic and subversive, and thus not only an affront to the dignity of Malays, Islam, or both, but also likely to engender religious or ethnic tension, thereby threatening communal harmony and national security.

Efforts to better insulate Muslims from the machinations of Christian and other non-Muslim missionaries are another dominant theme in the media and in national political discourse. While it has long been a criminal offense in Malaysia to attempt to convert Muslims to any non-Muslim religion, state vigilance toward Christian missionaries has been stepped up in the wake of fears that Chinese, Indian, and other non-Malay Christians will use Christianity to galvanize support for multiethnic political alliances capable of challenging the political supremacy of Malays vis-à-vis non-Malay Others (see Lee 1988; Peletz 1993b). Recent years have thus witnessed the passage of legislation making it a criminal offense for non-Muslims to use words and phrases seen by authorities as specifically Islamic, such as "assalamualaikum" ("peace be with you"), lest they "confuse" local Muslims. Since I discuss these matters elsewhere (Peletz 1993b), I need only mention here that measures such as these are a part of concerted efforts to tighten, render less permeable, and redefine boundaries separating Malays and Muslims generally from Chinese and Indians (and non-Muslims as a whole). So, too, are the heated debates in legislative and other circles about the appropriateness of the death penalty for the crime of apostasy and about the wisdom and constitutionality of recent laws that allow non-Muslim minors to convert to Islam without parental consent (see Seda-Poulin 1993).

Policing Bodies and Sexualities

Attempts to improve policing of the Muslim community have also entailed a good deal of legislation and controversy concerning the body and sexuality, particularly the ritual appropriateness of various types of food products and cosmetics, and of blood transfusions between Muslims and non-Muslims. Similarly, state policies have extolled the virtues of Muslim women wearing veils and other types of headgear, and observing one or another form of purdah (female seclusion), at least in certain contexts. These initiatives reflect heightened concern with the integrity of the Malay social body and the stability of the Malaysian body politic as well as recent trends toward a more pronounced segregation and dichotomization of male and female spheres (see Ong 1988; 1990a; 1990b; Peletz 1996).

The past few years have also seen concerted efforts by Islamic reformers and various state governments to crack down on and ultimately eliminate transsexuals, transvestites, and all other types of gender crossers (pondan). These efforts include both legislation and scholarly conferences, one of which was held at the University of Malaya while I was in the field in 1987. A spokesman at the conference went on record as saying that transsexualism (being a mak nyah) is an act of God and that transsexuals should be accepted by the Muslim community, especially since "they don't have any control over their situations." He added, however, that the Islamic stand on the *mak nyah* question is clear—Islam divides humans into two categories, male and female—and that problems arise when a transsexual tries to behave or dress like a woman or take hormone pills, actions that, according to him, are forbidden in Islam. Thus, while "these people require ... sympathy and fair treatment from all quarters," "efforts should be made to bring them to the right path" (i.e., "they should be convinced that they are men").[4]

As for the legislative measures in question, the state of Kelantan recently passed laws making it an offense for Muslim men to dress or act like women in public. The state of Penang was seeking to enact similar laws during 1987 and 1988, so as to broaden its ability to act against transvestites. Legislative changes such as these will in all likelihood be introduced in other states as well. It seems reasonable to assume that the next few years will also see an increase in federal provisions geared toward better regulating and perhaps eliminating all types of gender crossing, such as the 1983 ruling that forbade sex change operations among all Muslims in the country.

Recent moves against *mak nyah* and *pondan* are profitably viewed alongside contemporary legislative and other initiatives aimed at exercising greater control over the body and the bodies of women in particular. Ong provides incisive analyses of some of these issues (1988; 1990a; 1990b), so I need not elaborate here. I would simply underscore the point, effectively glossed over in the literature, that we need to keep squarely within our analytic gaze the ways in which state policies and discourses affect the bodies and sexualities of both women *and* men. It is important to bear in mind, too, that the legislative and other recent trends at issue here have antecedents that date back many centuries. While women and transvestites (the majority of whom seem to have been male) were highly regarded as ritual specialists throughout much of Southeast Asia during the early part of the period between 1400 and 1680, they experienced a marked decline in status and prestige during the latter part of this period, owing to the development of Islam and other Great Religions (Reid 1988; Andaya and Ishii 1992). For the most part, this decline in status did not entail actual stigma, at least in the case of transvestites and other varieties of gender crossers. It is nonetheless true that, at present, the sole ritual activity specifically linked with gender crossing is that of the bridal attendant *(mak andam)*. Legislative and other measures of the sort discussed earlier will probably eliminate this link in the not too distant future and thus contribute to a further secularization of the role—resulting in its redefinition as a contaminating, as opposed to sacred, mediator "perversely muddling and enmiring the [increasingly] polar terms of the classical [gender] system" (Stallybrass and White 1986, 110). More generally, such measures will contribute to a heightened dichotomization of gender, especially since they seem to have as their central goals the elimination of all mediating categories such as *pondan* and *mak nyah,* and the simultaneous cleansing ("defeminization") of locally defined masculinities (see Peletz 1996).

The Religious Climate in Rural Areas and among Ordinary Muslims Generally

A crucial question is how the legal and other initiatives outlined here have been received by ordinary Muslims. Before turning to this question, however, it will be useful to consider recent historical transformations in rural areas and among ordinary Muslims as a whole.[5]

For example, I noted various changes in the fieldwork site of Bogang (Negeri Sembilan) between my first period of research, from 1978 to 1980, and my second, from 1987 to 1988.[6] First, the public address system housed in the village mosque and used to call people to prayer was always operational (and set at a higher volume) during the second period, in sharp contrast to the situation during my first fieldwork, when it was typically out of order. Second, the quintessentially Islamic salutation *"assalamualaikum"* was far more frequently used (see Milner 1986, 60; see also Peletz 1993b), and other Islamic symbols and idioms permeated local discourse. Third, young male *dakwah* adherents now appeared in the village on a fairly regular basis to "spread the word." And fourth, the dress of girls and young women had become much more modest, and some of them had taken to wearing the long skirts, *mini-telekung* (head coverings, like those worn by Catholic nuns in the United States), and other headgear donned by female *dakwah* adherents in the cities.

Transformations such as these are in some respects superficial, but they are important public markers of the shifting religious climate in villages like Bogang. Other, less "tangible" changes include the further delegitimization of spirit cults, shamanism, and other ritual practices subsumed under the rubric of *adat;* the development of non- or arelational forms of individualism, realized by conceptualizing serious wrongdoing (such as the harboring of spirit familiars [*pelisit*]) in terms of "sin" *(dosa)* rather than "taboo" *(pantang [larang]);* the emergence of a more pronounced pan-Islamic consciousness, a key feature of which is greater awareness of current trends elsewhere in the Muslim world, where Islamic resurgence, efforts to forge worldwide Islamic solidarity, and radical separation between Muslims and non-Muslims is the order of the day; heightened concern with demarcating local (i.e., intra-Malaysian) boundaries between Muslims and non-Muslims;

and, related to this last point, greater suspicions of all non-Muslims, as expressed in the intensified bodily vigilance of males and females alike.[7]

While many of these shifts are broadly compatible with the stated objectives and overall agendas of *dakwah* leaders, we should not jump to the conclusion that ordinary Muslims are firmly behind or centrally involved in the resurgence. Indeed, we should start with a clean slate and the most basic questions: How are the legal and other initiatives cited earlier being received by ordinary, especially rural, Malays? And, more broadly: What is the nature of ordinary, particularly rural, Malays' perceptions of and attitudes toward the resurgence? The answers to these questions are elusive for two reasons. First, some of the legal and other initiatives noted earlier are of very recent origin and have yet to have their full impact in rural areas. And second, such questions have been largely ignored in the literature, even though most observers are well aware that Malaysia's Islamic resurgence is a predominantly urban, middle-class phenomenon.[8]

The short, admittedly imprecise, answer to the question regarding ordinary, especially rural, Malays' perceptions of and attitudes toward the resurgence is that, while some of them support it, many, perhaps most, are clearly hostile both to various elements of the movement and to the state agents and others who endorse it. This hostility exists even though ordinary Malays experience Islam as central to their daily lives and cultural identities, and embrace in principle most, if not all, efforts to accord Islam greater primacy among Malays and in Malaysia generally. In Bogang, for example, many elders lament that those who have sought to sanitize local religion by cleansing it of its "parochial accretions" are ignorant not only of the true teachings of Islam, but also of the ways of local spirits *(jinn)*; these elders hasten to add that the neglect of spirits due to the nonperformance of rituals such as *berpuar* and *bayar niat* has led to repeated crop failure and, in some cases, the demise of rice production altogether.[9]

Others speak scornfully of the fact that members of certain *dakwah* groups (for example, Darul Arqam) have thrown their televisions, radios, furniture, and other household commodities into local rivers to dramatize their disdain of the polluting influences of Western materialism and to underscore their commitment to returning to the pristine simplicity of the lifestyle of the Prophet. These dramatic gestures were highly publicized— and undoubtedly exaggerated—in the government-controlled national press at a time when the government was actively attempting to discredit the more radical elements of the movement. Though practices such as these are not typical of the *dakwah* movement as a whole, they loom large in some villagers' perceptions of the resurgence in its entirety.[10] More to the point, they fly directly in the face of the most pressing concerns of rural Malays, especially the poorest among them, who seek to improve their standards of living—ideally to attain middle-class status through the acquisition of more land and other wealth-generating resources—and who struggle desperately to avoid further impoverishment and proletarianization (see also Karim 1992, 167, 175, 184–185).

Other residents of Bogang talk about the sexual inappropriateness and hypocrisy of the members of some *dakwah* groups (Darul Arqam?) who, according to villagers' understandings of accounts in the local media, allegedly engage in "group sex" while enjoining fellow Muslims to observe strict sexual segregation. Still others feel that the *dakwah* emphasis on sexual segregation is largely redundant, since sexual segregation has long been a feature of rural Malay society. Perhaps more important, they feel that it represents a glaring example of the resurgents' ignorance of rural Malay culture and yet another indication of their profound hostility to it (cf. MacAllister 1992, 475).

Bogang villagers' reactions to recent trends involving women donning veils and other headgear are also ambivalent at best. My (adoptive) mother once remarked to me that women wearing *dakwah* headgear look "like ghosts" and "must surely stink since they are all covered up." She later recounted with laughter that her adolescent son had informed her (apparently half jokingly) that if she ever wore such clothing he would "yank it off and throw it into the fire." More generally, when I asked female elders why village girls had begun wearing *dakwah* attire, I was told on more than one occasion that they do so only "because their teachers would drive them out of school if they didn't." Comments such as these contain much hyperbole and both oversimplify and distort the motivations of those who wear veils; note, however that the underlying sentiments have also been reported for other regions of Negeri Sembilan and for other parts of the peninsula (see, for example, Karim 1992, 185–187; cf. Scott 1985, 196n.19).

Bogang residents' negative perceptions of and oppositional stances toward the local Islamic magistrate (or *kadi;* Ar. *qadi*) are of interest here, for the *kadi,* a graduate of the prestigious al-Azhar University in Cairo, is both a key symbol and a primary agent of the resurgence. The former headman *(ketua kampung)* of Bogang feels that the *kadi* is a "playboy," who is taken to swaggering about and being arrogant *(sombong)*. Another village elder complained bitterly of the *kadi*'s injustice for having publicly slandered and otherwise embarrassed him at the local mosque, assuring me as he did so that he was not afraid of "people in turbans" (a shorthand reference to pilgrims [*haji*] and male *dakwah* alike). Both sets of comments are deeply allegorical. Far from being merely narratives of the self encountering an Other, they constitute highly condensed symbolic statements of the ways in which ordinary Malays as a collectivity represent the Islamic resurgents (and vice versa). That such allegorical comments depict the resurgents as arrogant or *sombong* is quite revealing insofar as *sombong* is perhaps best translated as "unresponsive to social expectation." The perception that the resurgents are unresponsive to social expectation and to ordinary Malays' concerns with reciprocity and reproduction in particular lies at the heart of ordinary Malays' negative or at least highly ambivalent assessments of the *dakwah* movement.

Bear in mind that many villagers from Bogang and neighboring communities resist the *kadi*'s efforts to obtain complete information about their marriages and divorces. This resistance commonly involves noncompliance in accurately or completely filling out the standardized forms that the state requires of all individuals entering into marriage. (These forms request information bearing on past marital experience and current marital status, the value of marriage payments, and so forth.) Some such resistance is abetted by the *kadi*'s staff, who tend to empathize with villagers' status concerns, especially the loss of face and the shame *(malu)* experienced by those who give or receive marriage payments of relatively low value, and who would rather not add insult to injury by making a formal record of such payments. They are willing to condone this resistance even though the forms in question provide the only written record of marriage payments and are thus essential for negotiations and financial settlements associated with the dissolution of marriage through certain types of divorce.

More broadly, Malays throughout the peninsula are apprehensive that the merging of secular and religious law will result in the imposition of harsher *shari'ah* penalties for crimes currently handled by the secular legal system.[11] Such concerns warrant brief comment, for they point up both the conundrums of ordinary Malays who raise questions about the resurgents and their agendas, and the types of discursive responses articulated by *dakwah* adherents when confronted with such concerns. Consider the introduction of legislation (brought into force in 1986) allowing the Islamic courts in Kelantan to impose corporal punishment (caning) on those guilty of certain offenses, such as the consumption of alcohol. The introduction of this legislation met with strong disfavor from some Malay jurists and from various other quarters of the Malay population, on the grounds that punishments such as caning were retrograde, or draconian, or out of keeping with Islam. This criticism, in turn, led supporters of the legislation to respond by equating opponents of the new laws with the "colonial masters" whose policies severely constrained the operations and overall development of the Islamic courts. Such equations are explicit in the concluding remarks of an article on the "caning controversy," written by the eminent Ahmad Ibrahim, professor emeritus and shaikh, Kulliyyah of Laws, International Islamic University:

> During the colonial period it was the policy of the colonial rulers to restrict the powers and jurisdiction of the Shari'ah courts. The Shari'ah courts have suffered from this policy of restriction and neglect. Recently efforts have been made to raise their status and powers and to improve the position and status of the Shari'ah courts and their judges. It is a pity that these efforts, instead of getting the support of those who should be interested in a better system of justice for the Muslims in Malaysia, are constantly being attacked and criticized by some Muslim leaders. It seems that they, like the Colonial masters in the past, would like to see the Shari'ah courts forever restricted and neglected. (Ahmad Ibrahim 1987, 105)

Ordinary Malays, for their part, perceive the actions and pronouncements of the resurgents as involving a direct attack on sanctified elements of their basic values and cultural identities. The value conflicts at issue are especially pronounced in the realm of feasting. This will be apparent from material presented in the following section, which includes brief comments on three different wedding feasts, along with a more in-depth discussion of a "shotgun" wedding and the feast associated with it. The latter wedding is of interest not only because it represented the culmination of a social drama that was a disturbing sign of the times, but also because it was a hastily arranged and ritually streamlined affair that corresponds in numerous ways to the type of ceremonial that the resurgents propose for *all* weddings. It brings up a larger issue, addressed primarily in the concluding section of the essay. Ordinary Malays are in many respects strongly opposed to the ritual purification and cultural cleansing advocated by the resurgents, but the cultural identities of ordinary Malays offer little if any moral space for the elaboration of strategies of resistance or oppositional ideologies that have the capacity to critique the resurgence in religious or other terms or to otherwise construct alternative moral visions of or for the future.

Dilemmas of Feasting

The resurgents' pointed criticisms of "wasteful feasts" and of the feasting (*kenduri*) complex in its entirety pose serious dilemmas for ordinary Malays. The criticisms index searing condemnations of ordinary Malays' basic values (including many values that they construe as thoroughly Islamic) but are made in the name of Islam, on the grounds that feasts incorporate animistic and Hindu-Buddhist—hence pagan—elements and are, in a good many cases, sinfully wasteful (*maksiat*; cf. MacAllister 1987, 442–443). These quandaries are readily apparent when one stops to consider that the hosting of feasts in connection with weddings, funerals, circumcisions, and so forth, continues to be one of the main avenues through which ordinary Malays advance their claims to status and prestige. (Bear in mind, too, that the legitimacy of such claims increasingly requires demonstrating one's familiarity with things "modern" [Western].) The sponsoring of feasts is of further importance in that it enables sponsors both to reciprocate the generosity of friends, relatives, and political allies whose feasts they have attended in the past and to create ritual and other debts in others, especially potential allies. There are other benefits of feasting, such as the feelings of harmony, well-being, and safety *(slamet)* that feasts ideally engender among hosts and guests alike and the fact that they bring pleasure to the spirits of the deceased ancestors *(roh arwah)* and other local spirit beings *(jinn)*, and otherwise serve to reciprocate the assistance of all such spirits and thus help insure social and cultural reproduction.

All things being equal, the rough gauge of a feast's relative success is, first, the number of guests in attendance (though the more luminaries among them the better); and second, the amount and quality of meat and other food served, along with the elaborateness (and presumed cost) of the ritual displays that accompany the feast. Highly successful feasts, on the one hand, are frequently the subject of nostalgic reminiscing for months, even years, after they have occurred. "Minimalist" feasts, on the other hand, tend to be forgotten quickly or at least pushed into the collective unconscious, for they are often a source of deep embarrassment and shame for sponsors, their kin, and the community at large.

The most spectacular series of feasts I attended during my first period of fieldwork was a four-day affair held in a neighboring village (in December 1979) in connection with the wedding of a young couple, both of whom earned their living tapping rubber. Well over a thousand guests attended the celebrations, and, judging from the comments I heard, the majority of them were deeply impressed by the fact that two or three large water buffaloes had been slaughtered along with a number of goats and dozens of chickens. Equally striking, the four-day celebration included some of the most sanctified ritual components of times past. A shamanic specialist *(pawang)*, for example, came out of retirement to oversee the opening ceremonies, which involved the beating of a large gong and the ritual blessing of royal regalia, some of which had been borrowed from the *undang* (supreme lord and lawgiver), the traditional chief of the district. The regalia, which included daggers *(kris)*, flags, and royal streamers, were blessed first by the *pawang* and then by various clan chiefs in attendance so as to ward off evil spirits and misfortune. This ritual was observed with considerable interest and intensity, partly because such regalia are believed to partake of the *daulat* (royal majesty) of the *undang,* but also because a good many people at the wedding, indeed most of those under forty years of age, had never seen such ceremonies.

The elaborate ritual treatment of royal regalia, to say nothing of the inclusion in the ceremonies of a shamanic specialist, sets this wedding apart from all others I attended or heard about in the course of my fieldwork. So, too, does the fact that the ceremonies were effectively concluded on the fourth day by a ritual blessing of the bride and groom, which was overseen by a bridal attendant *(mak andam)* who instructed the couple to drink— and later showered them with—the juice of fresh coconuts and also encircled them with live chickens that were subsequently set free (much to the amusement and glee of all present), presumably to ensure their fertility.

It was not simply the inclusion of long-abandoned ritual elements that made this wedding truly awesome and glorious as far as many, perhaps most, villagers were concerned. Also impressive was the scale and lavishness of ritual practices that are still commonly found in weddings but are in many cases attenuated or streamlined. I refer specifically to the Indic-origin "royal" treatment afforded the bridal couple, both as they were carried about in sedan chairs in a raucous procession that circumambulated the bride's house and in the context of the subsequent "sitting in state" *(bersanding),* during which time the bride and the groom were entertained by young men performing stylized "plate dances" *(tarian piring)* and martial arts *(silat).* Worthy of remark too was the bride's (and, to a lesser extent, the groom's) regal attire. The bride's outfit included a richly decorated, highly ornate Minangkabau-style headdress of gold and silver that was among the finest I have ever seen.

Note, finally, that this wedding boasted the performance of three different types of music. The first was a lively gong and *rebana*-drum genre performed by the troupe of musicians whose task it was to provide musical accompaniment to the circumambulatory (and other) processions around the bride's house. (Musical troupes such as these are a standard feature of weddings.) Second, there was a more measured gong and drum genre, like that which often accompanies the performance of *dikir,* Sufi-origin chanting of the name of God in a highly stylized fashion, sometimes resulting in a kind of frenzied ecstasy. And third, there was modern "rock-and-roll" music played by a teen band also hired for the occasion, which belted out highly amplified tunes on their electric guitars and drums until well past midnight on the first night of festivities.[12] The rock musicians provided the appropriate musical backdrop to the "rock dancing" that was a major draw of the wedding, at least (or especially) for local youth. Their female companions, moreover, tirelessly honored most invitations to dance, thus providing an excellent negative example of femininity, as far as most elders were concerned. Coincidentally or otherwise, on many occasions the rock band struck up its music just after male elders had begun their Sufistic chanting and drumming, creating a "battle of the bands." The rock band won out in more ways than one: not only did they have the advantage in terms of sheer volume; many youths were thoroughly versed in their tunes but altogether unfamiliar with the *dikir* music.

I did not attend or hear of any local wedding feasts as ritually lavish as the four-day affair described here during my second period of fieldwork (the overall cost of the wedding was probably between eight thousand and ten thousand ringgit; U.S.$3,700–4,600), although feasting has clearly become more competitive in recent years (MacAllister 1987, 406, 439–440). The most imposing local feast of which I have knowledge was the one sponsored by my (adoptive) parents in connection with the (December 1987) marriage of their second son. My father is the former headman of the village and is also a traditional healer *(dukun)* of considerable renown, who continues to ply his specialized trade, the ritual treatment of victims of poisoning and sorcery. Despite his strong identification with the ritual practices of *dukun* and *pawang,* his son's wedding did not include any such ritual experts. In fact, while it did boast relatively elaborate "sitting in state," it had a decidedly more "modern" flavor than the wedding described earlier, consistent with the fact that both bride and groom were currently residing in Kuala Lumpur, where they held low-level office jobs, and were in these and other ways influenced by and self-identified with things modern and Western. The modern elements of the ritual display included the Western-style wedding outfits worn by the bride and groom after they removed their traditional attire (a handsome, finely tailored business suit in the case of the groom, a stunning white wedding gown in the case of the bride) and the gifts from the bride to the groom, which included a long-sleeve button-down Yves St. Laurent shirt, a set of toilet articles (after-shave, powder, soap), and, for the bride, high-heel shoes, a purse, makeup, and various designer items. Perhaps most emblematic of the couple's commitment to modernity, however, was their hiring of a video crew from Kuala Lumpur to make a permanent video record, complete with sound track, of the entire wedding.

Interestingly, while these highly festive and self-consciously modern wedding celebrations were in full swing, a far more attenuated—and self-consciously "Islamic"—wedding was also under way, just across the railroad tracks. The latter wedding, which underscores the religious and social diversity of communities like Bogang, involved a young woman whose father had died in the mid-1980s and who clearly identified with numerous aspects of the Islamic resurgence. Not surprisingly, she would not countenance any type of "sitting in state" and refused to wear traditional wedding attire—much to the dismay of her mother, a devout woman who had undertaken the pilgrimage to Mecca a few years earlier. Instead of wearing conventional wedding garb, the bride donned white *baju kurung* (tunic) and white *kain tedung* (head scarf), thus identifying herself with *dakwah* adherents. (The groom, for his part, was attired in "Malay shirt" [*baju Melayu*] and waist skirt, but none of the rest of the conventional costume.) The wedding included few traditional elements of the sort that are subsumed under the rubric of *adat* and few if any modern additions (such as rock bands or video teams). As such, it necessarily focused on those ritual elements most clearly defined as Islamic, such as the *akad nikah* and the Islamic prayers that follow the recitation of the marriage service *(khutbah nikah)*. The bride's "stubbornness" in refusing to wear traditional wedding clothes and participate in any form of "sitting in state" prompted comments from some villagers that she was an "extremist" (cf. Karim 1992, 212), though the remarks of others focused mainly on how few people attended the wedding.

The poor turnout was due partly to "bad timing": this was one of two wedding celebrations occurring simultaneously, and many people were drawn to the other wedding. Also relevant is that the bride's family was held in low esteem: both parents were of Minangkabau, hence foreign, birth and were thus viewed as "outsiders," a fact reinforced by their formal affiliation with the "outsider" clan (Biduanda Dagang). The father (Pak Hassan), moreover, had been widely envied, owing to his status as a former civil servant; he had also been roundly disliked because of his penchant for gambling and alcohol and his frequent attempts to borrow money from fellow villagers.[13] It is of interest that, in my many conversations with Pak Hassan before he died, he made frequent reference to the fact that "most villagers" knew next to nothing about Malay *adat* or Islam. Indeed, he often remarked of my father that his curing practices were "un-Islamic," hence seriously sinful. (My parents, for their part, voiced their criticisms of Pak Hassan in Islamic terms: that he was stingy, violated basic Islamic proscriptions on gambling, the consumption of alcohol, and so on. I return to such matters later on.) In these and other ways Pak Hassan made clear that, with respect to his own cultural identity, his primary frame of reference was the larger imagined/national community of Malays and, beyond that, the *ummat,* not simply the local village community. His daughter made much the same statement through the attenuated and otherwise self-consciously Islamic ritual design of her wedding.

This was by no means the most scaled-down wedding feast that occurred during my fieldwork, however. The most bare-bones of all wedding feasts was one held in connection with a "shotgun marriage" *(bidan terjun)* in September 1979.[14]

Rubiah and Nordin's Shotgun Marriage

The social drama began to unfold when Rubiah, a shapely and otherwise striking fifteen-year-old schoolgirl who was about to sit for her LCE (Lower Certificate Examination), acknowledged that she had had sexual relations with Nordin, a young man who had long lived behind her house. There was no universally acceptable solution to the problems posed by this transgression, particularly since there was bad blood between Rubiah's (adoptive) parents and Nordin's relatives.[15] There were, however, three courses of action that emerged as possibilities, each of which received backing from different members of the community.

First, village elders could lodge a complaint against the young man with the police and have him thrown in jail, presumably on charges of *zina* (illicit fornication), which is a clearly demarcated and very serious offense both in religious law and in local custom *(adat)*. This was the harshest course of action and the one favored by Rubiah's father (Abang [Samad]), his mother, and his other (matrilineal) relatives. Second, they could see if Rubiah and Nordin "wanted to get married" and, assuming that they did, make immediate arrangements for a wedding feast sponsored by Rubiah's parents. This was the most conciliatory course of action and the alternative favored by Rubiah's mother, Kakak (Rozita). And third, they could arrange for a simple marriage ceremony at the village mosque and forgo the feast. This was a compromise between the first and second options that would bestow a modicum of Islamic legitimacy on the union but would nonetheless render the marriage more or less illegitimate, or at least heavily stigmatized, from the point of view of local custom. This was the alternative favored by Abang's (adoptive) father, Pak Daud, who was also the village headman.[16]

The second option won out, much to the dismay of Abang, his relatives, and many others. Rubiah and Nordin claimed that they did indeed "want to get married," so preparations began almost immediately for the marriage ceremony and feasts that were to be held on the following day.

The main feast, which began around 8:00 P.M., was very sparsely attended. There was enough to eat, but it was clearly an extremely low-budget affair, and little care had gone into the preparation of the meal. Thus there was no tea, the dishes weren't sufficiently spiced—spiciness of dishes being an index of the sponsors' expenditure and prestige—and there were no desserts or garnishings to speak of. No one commented publicly on such things, however, since to have done so would have been highly inappropriate.

Abang's mother and some of the young girls present served the food and watched to see when the plates needed refilling; but this was done in a perfunctory fashion, with very little talk. More generally, the air was thick with gloom and despair, and the overall atmosphere was even more depressing than it had been during the funeral feast for Abang's father-in-law that I had attended there some months earlier. For that matter, Abang's father left right after he finished eating, thus registering his disgust with the whole affair. So, too, did many of the other males who arrived later, although a few them returned toward the end of the evening, when Nordin and his entourage appeared at Abang's house for the marriage ceremony.

Rubiah made a brief appearance around 10:30, dressed in the same casual clothes she had been wearing earlier that day. She had done little if anything to prepare herself for the wedding, which meant that the celebration, such as it was, would go on for another couple of hours at the least.

When Rubiah came back and entered the bridal chamber, she was helped into her clothes by a group of women, who worked as fast as they could to coif her hair and apply makeup. This was a slow and laborious process, particularly since the electricity had gone out earlier and there were too few kerosene lanterns to go around. Because of the delays and the poor lighting (many people sat in the dark), at least half of those present had fallen asleep and were lying about on the floor or propped up in one or another corner.

Around 1:00 A.M., after the women served another round of food, Nordin and his contingent were sighted coming from the house next door, where they had just eaten. As they took their place on the verandah, there was considerable noise, but the air of excitement and suspense, not to mention joy, that usually accompanies weddings was clearly lacking. One of Nordin's representatives then gave M$30 to Abang's aunt, Mak Lang. Of this sum, M$20 was the *mas kawin* ("marriage gold"). Under normal circumstances, the other M$10 would have been given to the *adat* leader of the village, but in this case there were no *adat* officials in attendance, let alone involved in the ceremony, and I'm not sure what happened to the money. In any event, there were no gifts present and there was no display or talk of the larger sums of money *(hantaran, belanja hangus)* that are usually given to the bride's relatives by the groom's kin. Similarly, no rings were produced or exchanged, as usually happens in a "regular" marriage. Nor, to my knowledge, did representatives of the two sides share any betel, "long the essence of courtesy and hospitality" among Malays and other Southeast Asians (Reid 1988, 44). And, needless to say, there was no music or dancing of any sort.

The ceremony was extremely attenuated but had to conform to the minimum requirements of state-sanctioned Islamic law. Thus it necessarily focused on what are regarded by locals and by secular and religious authorities alike as "the most Islamic" elements of weddings, namely, (1) the *akad nikah*, which centers on the *imam*'s recitation of the "marriage service" *(khutbah nikah)* and the groom's repetition of a formulaic phrase recited by the *imam*; and (2) the Islamic prayers that effectively conclude the *akad nikah*. These are among the few ritual features of weddings that are sanctioned by the resurgents. These types of rituals were also highly prominent in the wedding of Pak Hassan's daughter mentioned earlier, which was also ritually streamlined and otherwise highly attenuated, albeit for quite different reasons.

After the completion of the *akad nikah*, Rubiah was led out of the bridal chamber by Mak Lang, who had arranged two plain chairs in the interior room for the newlyweds to sit on. Rubiah took her place on one of the chairs, but since the electricity was out, both she and her chair were pushed about for roughly ten minutes so that those outside would be able to see her in the light of the pressure lamp that had been borrowed from a neighbor. The commotion was greeted with much nervous and embarrassed laughter. Finally, after the agonizing delay, Nordin was invited into the room to take his place at Rubiah's side. This he did with a great deal of nervousness, looking as if he would burst out crying, or laughing, at any minute. Rubiah and Nordin sat stiffly for a few moments, facing the group of women and children who had assembled in the interior room. They were then led into the bridal chamber, where they spent the night, which was, I would guess, rather tense.

Commentary

The social drama sparked by Rubiah's confession of sex with Nordin raises a number of issues that warrant detailed analysis, but I will confine my comments to a few of the more salient themes.[17] My main concerns are to explain why the transgression engendered such a crisis (and why Rubiah's parents in particular were so distressed by the whole affair) and to point up some of the similarities between shotgun weddings of the sort described here and the types of weddings advocated by Islamic resurgents.

There are at least five reasons why Rubiah's parents (and others) were so upset that Rubiah had sex with the boy next door. First, Rubiah violated fundamental sexual and moral codes. To appreciate the gravity of Rubiah's offense, one needs to bear in mind that pre- and extramarital sex of all varieties are both morally reprehensible and severely sanctioned, as are all forms of "illicit proximity" *(khalwat)*.[18]

Second, Rubiah "ruined her life" by getting pregnant and quitting school shortly before an important exam (the LCE). Students must pass this exam if they want to go on to the next grade or be considered for various types of urban employment, including factory work. Failing the exam or not sitting for it thus precludes meaningful employment outside the village.

Third, Rubiah's actions rendered impossible a proper, let alone a lavish, wedding and thus prevented her parents from realizing what could well have been one of the most socially significant and joyous occasions of their lives. Rubiah was Abang and Kakak's only daughter (Kakak had another daughter, but this was by a former marriage), which meant that she spoiled a once-in-a-lifetime opportunity for Abang and Kakak. Weddings are usually planned many months, and in some cases years, in advance and are finely orchestrated affairs calculated not only to bring the maximum status and prestige to the sponsors of the event and their relatives and supporters, but also to insure that sponsors fully reciprocate the generosity of friends and relatives whose feasts they have attended in the past. The advance planning is necessary both to accumulate the capital to finance the wedding and to help guarantee that everything goes well. Ideally, preparations include the staining of the bride's and groom's hands and feet with henna in the ritually prescribed fashion; making sure that the bride and groom are attired in dazzling finery (and that the bride is adorned with an elaborate headdress of gold and silver); and seeing to it that the Indic-origin "sitting in state" *(bersanding)* of the bride and groom and their circumambulation of their respective households are carried out with maximum attention to detail, decorum, and dramatic flair. Sadly, however, most such ritual elements were absent from Rubiah and Nordin's wedding, as were the troupes that provide musical accompaniment to various phases of wedding ceremonies, the stylized dancing that young men perform for bridal couples, and the Sufistic chanting *(dikir)* that sometimes occurs at the beginning of weddings. Absent as well were all of the modern additions to weddings, including, most notably, teen rock bands, which are hired to attract and entertain guests and to impress upon them the sponsors' familiarity with things modern (Western).

Fourth, both the circumstances leading up to the wedding and the wedding itself brought shame and disgrace to relatives and neighbors. They were all the more upsetting since Kakak's other daughter (by a previous union) was married in distressingly similar circumstances, and there had yet to be (and never would be) an acceptable marriage within Kakak's household.

And fifth, Nordin was a highly undesirable marriage partner for Rubiah, especially as far as her parents were concerned. This was so not only because of the bad blood between the two households, but also because Nordin, though a member of a gentry clan, came from a poor household and was, in addition, "merely a laborer." The fact that he was of such a lowly and ill-paying occupation meant that Rubiah's parents could not expect to attain much if any prestige or material benefit from his future earnings.

Let us turn now to a brief consideration of some of the formal similarities between shotgun weddings and the types of marriage ceremonies and festivities advocated by Islamic resurgents. Resurgents, bear in mind, are opposed to all features of "traditional" marriages that strike them as pre-, hence, un-Islamic: circumambulatory processions, "sitting in state" ceremonies, offerings to spirits, elaborate bridal costumes, the staining of the bridal couple's hands and feet with henna, and lavish, costly feasting. In addition, they object to recent additions to weddings such as rock-and-roll bands and video crews, which are, among other things, potent symbols of things Western. Resurgents would also like to see weddings held in local mosques (and have in fact sponsored legislation with this goal in mind), their more general aim being to reorient weddings so that they focus on the *akad nikah* and other "specifically Islamic" components of traditional marriage ceremonies such as the prayers that typically follow the *imam*'s recitation of the *khutbah nikah*.

Rubiah and Nordin's wedding was held at Rubiah's home, rather than in the village mosque (though some villagers wanted the ceremonies performed in the mosque, without the benefit of a feast). This exception—and the air of urgency, gloom, and despair—aside, the overall ritual design of Rubiah's and Nordin's bare-bones wedding corresponds in many respects to the type of ceremonial the resurgents propose for all Muslim weddings. In drawing attention to this important similarity in overall ritual design, I am not suggesting that resurgents favor weddings shrouded in shame or that the meanings and feelings associated with the types of weddings they encourage are the same as those associated with a wedding like Rubiah and Nordin's. The point is simply that, for all intents and purposes, resurgents advocate a type of ceremonial that has thus far been reserved for those guilty of transgressing some of the most sacrosanct norms of Malay culture. Note, too, that such breaches tend to be more common among low-income and otherwise low-status households, as are shotgun weddings (see Peletz 1988a, 248). In a word, the type of marriage ceremonies proposed by resurgents are doubly stigmatized so far as ordinary Malays are concerned.

I should underscore, finally, that, for the most part, Malaysia's Islamic resurgents have not suggested the inclusion of new or different ritual elements to replace those they would eliminate. They have been primarily concerned with targeting objectionable elements of marriage ceremonies and are thus advocating a type of ritual purification through elimination. While this process has as its objective a heightened valorization of all things that the resurgents define as Islamic, it is geared toward the denigration and ultimate elimination of all things they construe as non-Islamic—including many rituals seen by ordinary Malays as central to their cultural identities and to their most basic concerns with reciprocity and social and cultural reproduction.

Discussion: Comparative and Theoretical Implications

The native of the [Malay] Peninsula is becoming less of a Malay and more of a Mussulman [sic]; his national ceremonies are being discarded, his racial laws are being set aside, and his inherited superstitions are opposed to Moslem belief as much as to Western science. His allegiance is being gradually transferred from national to Pan-Islamic ideals and from the local Sultans, whose fettered dignity he compares to that of "a ship in the tow of a dinghy," to the Sultan Al-Muadzam, or Sultan par excellence, the now acknowledged head of one hundred millions of Moslems. (Wilkinson 1906, 80)

These words, penned some ninety years ago by one of the most insightful of scholar-officials dealing with Malay culture, will strike anthropologically up-to-date scholars of Islam as rather dissonant.[19] I would nonetheless contend that in formulating these thoughts Wilkinson accurately prophesied key dynamics of the historical experiences of the Malay community since the beginning of the twentieth century. Most contemporary observers, myself included, would phrase the cultural and historical dynamics at issue in terms that are less value-laden and otherwise less simplistic. Specifically, contemporary observers might well—indeed, should—object to the explicit opposition between what Wilkinson refers to as "inherited superstitions," on the one hand, and what he glosses as "Moslem belief," on the other. Scholars familiar with and sympathetic to Woodward's (1988; 1989) rereading of Javanese religion are excellently positioned to delineate the problems with such perspectives, as are those who have registered dissent with Dutch structuralist traditions entailing dichotomous treatments of the relationship between *adat* and Islam in Malay and Southeast Asian Muslim culture generally (see, for example, Roff 1985; Ellen 1983; see also Peletz 1988a, esp. chap. 3). On closer analysis, many features of Javanese and Malayan religion that earlier observers (see, for example, Wilkinson 1906; Geertz 1960) interpreted as "pre-Islamic" appear to be deeply grounded in or at least highly resonant with Sufi mysticism and other Middle Eastern and South Asian Islamic traditions, and thus appropriately included within the domain of "normative Islam" or "normative piety."

Revisionist contentions concerning the Islamic status of defining features of Javanese and Malayan ritual complexes such as *slametan* or *kenduri*, shadow puppet theater, and traditional healing are based on painstaking scholarly studies of Islamic texts (including both the Qur'an and the Hadith as well as chronicles such as *Babad Tanah Jawa*) and extensive work with mystics residing in and around royal centers like Yogyakarta. These contentions along with the more encompassing debates concerning "syncretism" have encouraged a radical rethinking of our entire approach to Javanese and Malayan Islam that is highly salutary. It is important to recognize, however, that such claims and debates do not necessarily figure into the discourses of the majority of Muslims in Java or Malaysia. Javanese reformists and modernists, for example, typically appear to have little (if any) interest in the truth value of these types of claims,[20] and the Javanist majority lacks access to the relevant texts and ritual specialists necessary to make such claims a foundational part of their cultural repertoire or symbolic capital (see Woodward 1989, 149–150, 237–238). The distinction drawn here is essential to bear in mind, for the scholarly debates in question are in many respects cast in "etic" terms (however much they may build upon "emic" categories) and appear to have little direct relevance to the "emic" experiences of the majority of the population.

This is especially so in Malaysia. Since the late nineteenth century and during the past few decades in particular, core symbols of Malayness long subsumed under the rubric of *adat*—and in some cases that of Islam as well —have been denigrated by Islamic resurgents on the grounds that they are pre- or simply un-Islamic and, as a result, have had their legitimacy undermined. In some cases, moreover, the psychological and sociological scope and force of such symbols have been drastically undercut, and the ritual and other practices associated with them have ceased to exist. At the same time, there has been a dialectically related process entailing the development and expansion of Islamic institutions and the heightened scope and force of Islamic symbols and idioms, a process that has clearly advanced (though it need not do so) at the direct expense of *adat* both as an institutional framework and a system of symbols and meanings.

Various aspects of this process are clear in Kelantan. Throughout the peninsula, many urban and rural Malays who no longer adhere to rural customs not only perceive Kelantanese Malays as the most traditional of all

Malays, but also regard Kelantanese *adat* as the richest and most impressive of all Malay *adat*. Kelantanese, for their part, view the puppeteers *(dalang)* of the renowned shadow puppet theater *(wayang Siam)* as the embodiment of "tradition" (Wright 1986). And yet, religious authorities and others of a reformist bent, including most supporters of the Islamic political party, PAS (Sweeney 1972, 35), maintain that all traditional performing arts, and the shadow puppet theater in particular, are contrary to the teachings of Islam and constitute a clear threat to the public's morality and spiritual well-being. The imam of Kota Baru (Kelantan's capital) bases his opposition to *wayang Siam* and related genres on the unrestricted mingling of men and women in the audience and of male and female puppets on screen; others object on the grounds that Pak Dogol, the god/clown of the *wayang Siam,* not only acts as a servant to Seri Rama, the celebrated hero of the shadow play, but is also the *dewa Sang Yang Tunggal,* the highest of all (Hindu) demigods (Wright 1986, 31–32). In his capacity as the One Great One and as the Kelantanese incarnation of Semar, Pak Dogol is the object of the *pujaan* (praise, adoration, worship) that is ritually enacted by *dalang* at the start of each performance. In the eyes of reformers and modernists, the ritual veneration of Pak Dogol appears distressingly close to the heinous sin of *shirk,* which refers both to polytheism generally and to the worship of idols specifically. Because the distinction between Allah and Pak Dogol has been elided by various *dalang* in the past (Sweeney 1972, 35), many reformers and modernists find additional support for their position that *wayang Siam* performances are forbidden and sinful *(haram* and *berdosa).*[21]

As might be expected, *dalang* respond that such criticism is unfounded, that their craft is both Islamic in origin and in contemporary design, and that their invocations include Qur'anic prayers and chants. Their efforts in this regard are largely unsuccessful, especially since, unlike the situation in the Javanese royal capitals of Yogya and Solo, they lack elaborate court traditions and royal sponsorship to back them up. From some three hundred *dalang* in Kelantan in the mid-1960s, there were fewer than one hundred in the late 1970s (Sweeney 1972, 3; Wright 1986, 41n). Their numbers are in decline even though the federal government, in its efforts to showcase certain features of Malay culture and counter the deracinating effects of Western-oriented modernization, has made numerous efforts to encourage the arts of *dalang* and the cultural heritage they embody.[22]

Another key symbol of Kelantanese Malay culture and identity is Main Peteri, a genre of shamanistic performance found mainly in Kelantan and Trengganu that has much in common with *wayang kulit* shadow puppet theater and *mak yong* dance theater in its ethos, world view, language, and basic symbolism. Carol Laderman devotes the better part of a recent monograph to analyzing the transcripts of Main Peteri seances she attended and recorded, but she also notes at the outset of the monograph that "all the traditional healers mentioned in this book have ceased their practice due to death, infirmity, or religious considerations" (Laderman 1991, xvi). In later pages we learn that while death and infirmity are partly responsible for the cessation of some shamanistic performances, the chief factor in the decline of Main Peteri (the genre is currently defunct) and all other traditional theatrical performances is "religious opposition" from those alternatively referred to as "the Islamic establishment," the "Islamic hierarchy," "pious folk," or simply "religious people." They oppose the Main Peteri and related genres on the grounds that these performances are pre-Islamic and therefore sinful, especially because they attest to the continued significance in contemporary Malay culture of Hindu-Buddhist and pre-Indic (animist) motifs that stand as highly condensed symbols of "pre-Islamic days of ignorance." More specific objections are raised because shamans are seen by "pious folk" as trafficking in various Hindu, ancestral, and chthonic spirits and deities—some of whom are expressly sought out as alternatives to Allah when He fails to respond to ritual specialists' requests.[23]

Laderman's book thus presents us with something of an enigma, or at least an appreciable disjunction: On the one hand, owing largely to opposition cast in Islamic terms, certain long-established rituals are no longer performed. On the other hand, many of the sanctified beliefs and postulates encoded in such rituals retain their wide currency and are, for many villagers at least, still thoroughly compelling. The more general dilemma is that while Islamic opposition to local *adat* has intensified in recent decades, these very same *adat* (or certain features of them) still comprise important, if increasingly devalued, components of cultural identity among ordinary Malays in Kelantan, Negeri Sembilan, and elsewhere, particularly inasmuch as they help demarcate and reinforce the boundaries of local communities and differentiate locally defined groups of Malays both from one another and from outsiders as a whole. Bear in mind here that Malays in Kelantan have generally low regard for and certainly do not want to be identified with Malays in Negeri Sembilan (and vice versa), let alone Javanese, Minangkabau, or Acehnese. Kelantanese and other Malays differentiate themselves from one another on the basis of their *adat,* since Islam, in their view, is essentially the same wherever it is found. To grind down and obliterate distinctions of *adat* is to render Kelantanese Malays equivalent to Negeri Sembilan Malays, Javanese, and Minangkabau. This flattening and evisceration of locally defined *adat* and cultural identities may be the price that has to be paid for the cultural and political unification of Malays and their continued political supremacy vis-à-vis Chinese, Indians, and others. But it is not one that is embraced without ambivalence.

Ordinary and other Malays increasingly refer to themselves as "we Muslim people" *(kita orang Islam)* rather than "we Malay people" *(kita orang Melayu;* Nash 1991, 698)—thus providing additional support for Wilkinson's turn-of-the-century remarks about Malays becoming "more Muslim" and "less Malay." But ordinary Malays clearly experience profound ambivalence both about the overall trajectory and cultural cost of twentieth-century change and about the resurgents, state policies, and agencies most directly implicated in the transformations—most notably, the perceived losses—in question. This ambivalence would undoubtedly be less pronounced if the state-sponsored institutional changes associated with the resurgence responded more directly to the basic needs of rural Malays. As it stands, however, many of these measures are geared toward meeting the twin objectives of state building (centralizing and consolidating state power) and responding to the concerns of certain segments of an urban, middle-class constituency. Due to this orientation, one of the main effects of institutional reforms and realignments is to curb rural and other ordinary Malays' autonomy and social control and further chip away at defining features of their culture.

In light of ordinary Malays' negative perceptions of and attitudes toward the resurgence, one might reasonably expect to find some organized protest against the resurgence or at least a range of behavior that might plausibly be interpreted as overt or covert resistance to it. In the latter connection I have in mind those everyday forms of resistance that James Scott has documented for rural Malays in the Muda region of Kedah who are opposed to the Green Revolution and the New Economic Policy: character assassination, slander, back biting, gossip, shunning, foot dragging, noncompliance, and the like (Scott 1985; see also Scott 1990). Such everyday forms of resistance do exist, though, all things considered, they are not common. It is not only everyday forms of resistance that are relatively unelaborated, but also what Scott refers to in his most recent work as "the hidden transcript," that is, "the discourse that takes place 'offstage,' beyond direct observation by powerholders" (1990, 4). Why, then, despite ambivalence and hostility of the sort mentioned earlier, is there relatively little evidence either of everyday resistance to the resurgence or of an elaborated or even an incipient alternative (let alone an explicitly counterhegemonic) ideology that critiques the movement in religious or other terms?

There are at least four variables that constrain the elaboration of resistance and oppositional ideologies, including those largely confined to hidden transcripts.[24] The first two fit more or less comfortably within the scope of (can be accommodated by) contemporary resistance studies. The third and fourth do (can) not and partly for this reason will be discussed in greater detail.

First, as already noted, ordinary (and other) Malays incur potentially grave political risk if they publicly question or cast aspersions on the increasingly hegemonic discourses of the *dakwah* movement. Trafficking in alternative religious discourses, including discourses that are simply different from or largely irrelevant to the hegemonic discourses of the resurgence, is dangerous. The state not only reserves and increasingly exercises the right to define all alternative discourses as counterhegemonic and therefore an affront to the dignity of Malays and/or Islam; it also holds that such alternative religious discourses are liable to engender religious or ethnic tensions and thus threaten communal harmony and national security. In the worst-case scenario, trafficking in alternative religious discourses, even those that are not counterhegemonic, can land one in jail for an extended period, without prospects for a trial or even knowledge of one's specific offenses.

A second variable, inextricably related but not reducible to the first, has to do with the fact that village society and culture is in many respects encapsulated within a national political order in which, in the words of Bourdieu, there is "total and [in some ways] totally invisible censorship on the expression of the specific interests of the dominated . . . [such that the latter] can only choose between the sanitized words of official discourse and inarticulate grumblings" (1984, 462). In fact, such encapsulation is both incomplete and highly uneven, and, while official discourse is "highly sanitized," the alternatives are by no means invariably confined to "inarticulate grumblings". "Grumblings" bearing on class, race, ethnic, and gender relations, for example, are in many instances both highly articulate and trenchant.

The third variable that constrains the elaboration of resistance and oppositional ideologies has relatively little to do with fears of political reprisals, material losses, or censorship—concerns that relate ultimately to the inequities of power and domination and to the real or imagined experiences of discipline and punishment, and that all too often are privileged in the cross-cultural literature on resistance as *the* primary impediments to resistance. The variable to which I refer is a broadly moral or existential constraint emanating from the constitution of Malay cultural identity. To wit: ordinary Malays experience profoundly disconcerting moral and existential dilemmas if they register any form of dissent with the movement insofar as it claims as its primary objective the spiritual and material betterment of all Malays (Muslims), and likewise appears to be the only vehicle capable of protecting Malays from Chinese and Indian infidels and from the ravages and vicissitudes of government policies, state-sponsored capitalism, and the global economy (cf. MacAllister 1987, 476).

Put simply, albeit in a mixed metaphor, it is not kosher—and is in many contexts a morally treasonous offense akin to incest and cannibalism—for Malays to come out publicly against the Islamic resurgence, particularly inasmuch as doing so is tantamount to "letting down the side" if not actually renouncing one's identity as a Malay (see Jomo and Shabery Cheek 1992, 104–105). This is especially true because many of the rituals and symbols that long constituted Malay cultural identity have been eviscerated by nationalist and transnationalist discourses emphasizing Islamic nationalism and reform as well as "science," "progress," and "secular education." At this point in history, in other words, the rituals and symbols that constitute Malay cultural identity are so thoroughly enmeshed in a translocally and transnationally defined Islam that there is little if any space for the development of a moral vocabulary that allows Malays to resist the resurgence or construct an alternative vision of or for the future. Exacerbating the situation is the absence of meaningful secular movements, of the sort found in Indonesia and other countries with Muslim majorities, with the capacity to serve as alternative vehicles for the realization and canalization of reformist sentiments conducive to redemptive change. In the absence of such movements, there is hardly any room for "fence sitting," and very little middle ground generally, in the increasingly politicized religious and other social arenas in which Malays act out and create meaning and order in their lives. In this respect the situation in contemporary Malaysia differs in significant ways both from what one finds in much of Indonesia and many other countries with sizable Muslim populations (see Horvatich and McKenna, this volume) and from the situation in Malaysia (Malaya) during the heyday of the Kaum Muda movement in the early twentieth century.

The moral constraints at issue here are of comparative and theoretical interest, particularly since moral variables are typically given insufficient analytic attention in the literature on resistance. In this connection we might consider Scott's (1985) incisive analysis of everyday forms of peasant resistance in Kedah, which is in many respects the locus classicus of contemporary resistance studies. Scott does make provision for moral variables such as ties of kinship, friendship, patronage, and ritual commensality that impede poor Malays' resistance to the Green Revolution and the New Economic Policy. In Scott's view (and that of many other students of resistance, such as Taussig [1980]), however, such variables are relevant only insofar as they "muddy the 'class waters' " or otherwise impinge on relations of power and domination that obtain between major status groups (landlords and tenants, rich and poor, and so forth). Conversely, moral variables that do not impinge on relations of the latter sort are largely overlooked by Scott and many other students of resistance. Thus, while scholars like Scott distance themselves from Marxist theories of exploitation and class, they often preserve one of Marxism's hidden premises: the tendency to see class as somehow the most "essential," natural, or unfetishized of all social groupings and thus to see class interests as the most important or rational of all social interests.[25]

Of broader concern, as Ortner (1995) points out, is that scholars such as Scott give short shrift to religiosity and culture as a whole.[26] Even though Scott, especially in his 1990 work, discusses various culturally specific forms of personal humiliation and degradation that are associated with domination and are on occasion resisted on religious grounds or in religious terms, these instances of personal submission and humiliation are linked with what are ultimately narrowly defined variants of political, economic, or racial domination and exploitation. Scott makes no provision for instances of cultural domination or cultural disenfranchisement that are not part of relatively fixed forms of domination tied to class-based or feudal hierarchies or to systems of caste, apartheid, slavery, and the like. (The same is true, albeit to a lesser degree, of Taussig 1980 [see Edelman 1994].) I emphasize this point partly because, in the larger scheme of things, ordinary Malays are not deeply concerned with the political and economic implications of the resurgence, though some such implications are certainly bothersome and threatening to many of them (see also Jomo and Shabery Cheek 1992, 99).[27] It is rather the symbolic and overall cultural domination—particularly the religiously cast moral critique of their cultural identities—entailed in the movement (which is supported primarily by "middle-level urban workers, student groups, and professionals without [significant] social status or power" [Karim 1992, 175]) that is most offensive and troubling for them. Note that many of the everyday forms of resistance undertaken by ordinary Malays to "fend off" the resurgence are directed primarily at institutional infringements on their autonomy and social control. The analytically and culturally distinct dimensions of the resurgence that ordinary Malays find most *morally* offensive are much more troubling for them to confront, directly or otherwise, and are, partly for this reason, all the more vexing than the institutional encroachments mentioned earlier.

A fourth variable that constrains the elaboration of resistance and oppositional ideologies has to do with the fact that most ordinary (and other) Malays feel that they live in something of a Panopticon in which all social relations are hierarchical and power-laden and all social activities are assiduously scrutinized and evaluated by intimate and not so intimate Others. This is not the famed Panopticon of Foucault (1979), where Big Brother and his agents are ubiquitous, omniscient, and all-powerful, with their unrelenting gazes and disciplinary mechanisms penetrating the most intimate recesses of personal and social space. Rather, the Panopticon to which I refer is more like what Wikan has described for rural Bali, where endemic status rivalries are matters of life and death both in the metaphorical sense discussed by Geertz in his celebrated analysis of the Balinese cockfight (1973) and in a literal sense as well. Wikan notes, for example, that Balinese "live in a world where murder or attempted murder resulting in sickness from sorcery is the order of the day" (1989, 300); that "most people have had members of their family killed by death magic" (1987, 342); and, more generally, that "around 50 percent of all deaths . . . are thought to be caused by black magic or poison" (1989, 295). Significantly, Wikan emphasizes that most of this evil and misfortune is believed to be caused not by witches, sorcerers, or other local repositories of esoteric knowledge, but by "intimate others" who are motivated by envy, jealousy, greed, or concerns to retaliate against those who have rebuffed their advances or overtures, or otherwise given offense. As they make their daily rounds, according to Wikan, Balinese live feeling "forever vulnerable," even in the the relatively "private" contexts of their yards, kitchens, and bedrooms. In contrast to the domination and powerlessness experienced by prisoners and others trapped within the Panopticons of Foucault, however, the perennial feelings of vulnerability experienced by Balinese are only minimally (if at all) related to their positions in class or other relatively fixed status hierarchies and are only minimally (if at all) keyed to the presence within their environs of Big Brother or his agents. These feelings stem instead from the hundreds if not thousands of big and little brothers and sisters peopling their social universes, good numbers of whom are assumed to be deploying all of the social and cultural resources at their disposal for the purposes of enhancing their own prestige and simultaneously undercutting the prestige claims of all others.

Most ordinary (and other) Malays appear to feel that they live in the same type of Panopticon, one in which (to paraphrase Miranda and thus overstate the case) anything they say (or do) can and will be used against them. In the Malay Panopticon, Islamic symbols and idioms are among the most strategic—and clearly the most sanctified—of the social and cultural resources available to people to articulate their claims to high status discursively and, as is more commonly done, to make direct or indirect allusions to the status inferiority of others. The symbols and idioms of *adat* and modernity are in many cases altogether irrelevant as criteria to rank oneself vis-à-vis others and, in any event, do not resonate with the shifting religiosity characteristic of rural communities or the nation as a whole. In contexts such as these, questioning anything cast in Islamic terms, like specific legislative measures or one or the other aspect of the *dakwah* movement, increases one's vulnerability both to home-grown social criticism and to loss of prestige in locally defined hierarchies of value. Put differently, even in local communities made up entirely of ordinary Malays, it is always risky to be perceived as "insufficiently Islamic" or as a "bad Muslim." Erring on the side of being "too Islamic," in contrast, generally carries little risk and does, moreover, bring many potential social and cultural rewards.

These Panopticon-like features of the social and cultural universes of ordinary Malays thus serve to constrain the elaboration of strategies and ideologies of resistance to the Islamic resurgence. More generally, they indicate that an understanding of resistance and oppositional ideologies (including hidden transcripts) requires an analysis of the political dynamics of the presentation of self in everyday life that goes far beyond investigation of the politics of the major lines of cleavage associated with the relatively fixed hierarchies of class, race, and gender.[28] In the forever shifting, highly mercurial topographies of everyday social life, all discourses have multiple uses and are, among other things, both sources of constraint (and personal, social, and cultural mooring) as well as potentially valuable resources that can be deployed in the pursuit of social actors' culturally defined interests (see Rössler, this volume). The multiple and in many cases contradictory uses and entailments of discourses, including, most notably, religious discourses, account for a good measure of the ambivalence surrounding them. Studies of culture and politics that focus on domination and resistance or accommodation need to devote greater analytic attention to the phenomenon of ambivalence. If they fail to do so, they run the risk of being both "ethnographically thin" (to borrow Ortner's term) and highly anemic with respect to their treatment of the cultural psychology of the social actors who are at the center of their inquiries.

I will conclude by emphasizing four general sets of issues.

(1) Malaysia's Islamic resurgence is a largely urban-based, middle-class phenomenon. It has been supported by legislative moves and state policies aimed partly at encouraging the movement along relatively moderate lines and otherwise controlling and coopting it in an effort to undercut religious and political opposition and shore up support for the ruling party. The effects of the resurgence in the countryside and among ordinary Malays merit far more attention than they have received thus far, especially since most Malays live in rural areas and conceptualize and enact their religiosi-

ties and cultural identities in terms that are distinct from—and in some cases mutually incompatible with—those of the resurgents.

(2) The discourses of the resurgence, though not usually represented as monolithic in the scholarly literature, are nonetheless far less hegemonic than most accounts of the resurgence suggest. Many rural and urban Malays are extremely ambivalent and hostile toward the movement, even though they do embrace and experience Islam as central to their daily lives and identities. The fact remains, however, that their ambivalence and hostility are not necessarily realized in everyday forms of resistance or even in the elaboration of "discourses that take place 'offstage,' beyond direct observation of powerholders" (Scott's hidden transcripts).

An accurate sense of the impact of the resurgence and the support it receives in rural areas and among ordinary Muslims thus requires that our investigations extend beyond clandestine sabotage, foot dragging, noncompliance, slander, character assassination, and the like, and that they focus much more closely on the sentiments and dispositions of the rural Malay populace, many of which are not realized in practice or in hidden transcripts. A given population's refusal or reluctance to engage in practices of resistance along with its failure or unwillingness to elaborate hidden transcripts does not necessarily reflect its fears of political reprisals or material losses, its befuddlement or mystification by charismatic leaders or some other form of false consciousness, or, more generally, the efficacy of one or another type of politically motivated hegemony. Such refusals, reluctance, and failures (to phrase the issue in arguably problematic negative terms) may stem instead from moral constraints and ambivalences that are both analytically and culturally distinct from variables typically highlighted in resistance studies.

(3) Neither the state nor its policies are monolithic; similarly, ideologies propagated by the state or elites of various kinds, however hegemonic, are never thoroughly dominant or absolutely controlling. For these and other reasons we need to be more attuned both to the existence and reproduction of sentiments and dispositions that are contrary to official hegemonies and to the moral and other variables that constrain (or, alternatively, promote) their elaboration in alternative (including explicitly counterhegemonic) discourses. In the latter connection in particular, moral variables merit far more attention than they have received thus far.

And (4) the phenomenon of ambivalence is a key variable both in the religious and political arenas of contemporary Malaysia and in contexts of social and cultural change generally—indeed, in all of social life (see Weigert 1991; Peletz 1993a; 1994b; 1996; Ortner 1995). Future studies of religion and social and cultural identity in Malaysia and other parts of Muslim Southeast Asia and beyond would thus do well to devote greater attention to the cultural psychology of ambivalence and its various refractions in different political economies and the myriad social contexts they comprise.

Notes

This essay is based on about two years of field research in the state of Negeri Sembilan, Malaysia, carried out from 1978 to 1980 and 1987 to 1988, and a brief trip to Kuala Lumpur in August 1993. The first period of fieldwork was supported by the National Science Foundation (grant no. BNS-7812499) and the University of Michigan (the Center for South and Southeast Asian Studies, and the Horace Rackham School of Graduate Studies); the second was funded by the Fulbright Scholars Program, the Wenner-Gren Foundation for Anthropological Research, and the Picker Fellowship Program at Colgate University. Grants from the National Endowment for the Humanities and the Social Science Research Council also facilitated work on this essay. In addition to thanking these institutions for their support, I would like to express my gratitude to Ellen Peletz, who assisted me in the field; and Robert Hefner, Patricia Horvatich, and other participants in the 1993 conference on "Islam and the Social Construction of Identities," who provided feedback on an early version of this essay. All remaining errors and other shortcomings are of course my own.

1. All Malays are Muslims, and the vast majority of the Muslims in Malaysia are Malay. (The majority of the non-Malay Muslims are of Indian ancestry.)

2. In this essay, unless noted otherwise, the ethnographic present does not extend beyond May 1988, which is when I completed my second period of fieldwork and returned to the United States. While I have not been able to follow legal and attendant developments in Malaysia since May 1988 as closely as I would like, some of the more important developments have been reported in the international media. In 1994, for example, the government banned Darul Arqam (see also Seda-Poulin 1993).

3. I am indebted to Ortner (1995) for underscoring the significance of these oversights and for delineating some of the more general problems with resistance studies of the sort undertaken by Scott (1985; 1990). See also Gal 1995 and the sources cited in note 26 below.

4. The passages in quotes (which are taken from the *Star,* August 7 and October 25, 1987, and the *New Straits Times,* October 26, 1987) entail various oversimplifications of Islamic textual perspectives on issues associated with gender crossing. For a fascinating discussion of some of the philosophical, theological, and legal complexities involved, see Sanders 1991.

5. In the pages that follow I employ pseudonyms both for the community in which I conducted fieldwork and for all individual members of that community.

6. The Malays of Negeri Sembilan are usually treated in the literature as a special class of Malays since their social structure includes descent units of matrilineal design and is thus glossed "matrilineal," whereas Malays elsewhere in the peninsula have a social structure that is usually referred to as "bilateral" (or "cognatic"). Elsewhere I have argued that the contrasts between Negeri Sembilan and other Malays are greatly overdrawn and that the underlying similarities merit far more analytic attention than they have received thus far (Peletz 1994a; 1996; cf. Peletz 1988a; Stivens 1985; 1991).

7. Some of these trends are discussed elsewhere (Peletz 1988b; 1993a; 1993b; 1996; MacAllister 1987; Ong 1988; 1990a; 1990b).

8. Nagata's recent (1987) work is a partial exception, as are some of her earlier (1982) discussions of rural *ulamas*' (religious scholars') reactions to the challenges that the resurgents have posed to the legitimacy of their positions. So, too, is Banks' (1990) study of Malay novelists, though Banks is primarily interested in the extent to which certain novelists of rural background express generally positive views of the resurgence. Banks devotes very little attention to the degree to which such views resonate with the experiences or sentiments and dispositions of the rural Malay majority, who are obviously not men (or women) of letters. In fact, to the best of my knowledge, the only published account that deals at all substantively with questions of the sort at issue here is Wazir Jahan Karim's monograph on Malay women in Penang and other parts of the peninsula *(Women and Culture: Between Malay Adat and Islam)*, which was published in 1992 and devotes the better part of two chapters to the types of questions with which we are concerned. (See also McAllister 1987, especially chap. 12.)

9. Much the same position is documented for ritual specialists and others in Kelantan and Trengganu who lament the recent passing of shamanistic performances associated with Main Peteri, a dramatic genre that has much in common with *wayang kulit* shadow puppet theater and *mak yong* dance theater (Laderman 1991). Some of the relevant issues are taken up in the text below.

10. Darul Arqam has emerged as the master trope for the resurgence, at least for ordinary Muslims. In fact, members of Darul Arqam constitute a very small minority of those who self-identify with or are otherwise involved in the *dakwah* movement.

11. For a brief discussion of some of these concerns, see the article titled "Going Back to the Book," which appears in the August 11, 1989, edition of *Asiaweek* (cited in Banks 1990, 545n.21).

12. Village elders are deeply ambivalent about including any forms of rock or other modern music, let alone dancing, in the weddings they sponsor. But they are also well aware that the inclusion of such ritual elements is among the best ways to advance one's claims to being "modern." In some cases, wedding celebrations that include rock music and dancing are followed by feasts of forgiveness (see Peletz 1988a, 249).

13. Muslims are, of course, forbidden to consume alcohol. The vast majority of Malays in Bogang and other parts of Malaysia do observe the prohibition.

14. The term *bidan terjun* (lit. "leaping midwife") calls to mind the unexpected, and hence hurried, calling of a midwife, as when a pregnant woman experiences labor contractions sooner than anticipated.

15. In the account that follows there are a good many relationships involving informal adoptions. Informal adoption is quite common in Bogang and in Malay communities generally (see Peletz 1988a; McKinley 1981).

16. Interestingly, no one appears to have suggested the imposition of a more severe "Islamic punishment" such as one hundred lashes and a year's banishment.

17. For further discussion, see Peletz 1996, chap. 3.

18. This is a specific category of criminal offense in local custom and Islamic law alike that includes being in a secluded or confined area with a person of the opposite sex whom one is not prohibited from marrying.

19. The latter clause is a paraphrase of a point made by Valeri with respect to a very different set of issues (1990, 264).

20. There are important exceptions to this generalization. A case in point is Nurcholish Madjid, who is both a former head of the Indonesian Students Association and one of the leading figures of the Association for Indonesian Muslim Intellectuals (ICMI) (see Hefner, Chapter 3, this volume). Madjid's Paramadina Institute, which is a key player in Indonesia's middle-class *dakwah* movement, includes Sufism in the evening courses that it offers. Some of the people involved in the Indonesian *dakwah* movement are also quite willing to recognize that the old *slametan* tradition had some value inasmuch as it encouraged a feeling of community and shared involvement on the part of participants. The continuing strength of Nahdlatul Ulama also helps provide a little more space than exists in Malaysia for a slightly romantic if ambivalent attitude toward traditional village Islam (Robert Hefner, personal communication; see also Feillard, this volume).

21. Others object on the grounds that the music accompanying the performance of *wayang kulit* is "mesmerizing" (Sweeney 1972, 36).

22. Not surprisingly, all the *dalang* interviewed by Sweeney in the mid-1960s opposed PAS and supported UMNO (Sweeney 1972, 35). Almost all of the *dalang* interviewed by Wright a decade later professed the same allegiances (Wright 1986, 33, 41n.33).

23. Although the texts Laderman analyzes contain numerous references to Betara Guru (Shiva of the Hindu pantheon) and characters derived from the Hindu epic the Ramayana, none of these figures are explicitly linked in local thought either to Hindu deities or to any other Indic or otherwise non-Islamic traditions.

24. Limitations of space preclude a lengthier discussion. Another variable to which I should perhaps draw attention, if only in passing, is that ordinary Malays undoubtedly find it difficult to challenge the resurgents on theological

grounds, especially since they have far less access to key religious texts and their meanings than do the resurgents.

25. See Hefner 1990 (especially chap. 7) for an insightful development of this point.

26. I realize I run the risk of essentializing studies of resistance by citing Scott's work as typical of all such studies. There are in fact important differences between the approaches and perspectives of Scott, on the one hand, and those of Jean and John Comaroff, Aihwa Ong, Gayatri Chakravorty Spivak, and Paul Willis and others associated with British cultural studies, on the other. See Ortner 1995 for an incisive discussion of some of these differences and various problems with the study of resistance generally; see also Abu-Lughod 1990, Sholle 1990, Brown 1991, Edelman 1994, and Kaplan and Kelly 1994.

27. Others are viewed in strongly positive terms.

28. Hefner (1985; 1987; 1990) emphasizes similar points in his work on the Tengger Highlands of East Java. Note also that the rich data Hefner presents point to the centrality of profound ambivalence in local experiences of twentieth-century social history both in the Tengger Highlands and in East Java generally (see especially Hefner 1990, chap. 7).

References Cited

Abu-Lughod, Lila. 1990. "The Romance of Resistance: Tracing Transformations of Power through Bedouin Women." *American Ethnologist* 17 (1): 41–55.

Ahmad Ibrahim. 1987. "Caning for Shari'ah Court Offenses." In The Law Society, International Islamic University, Malaysia, ed., *The Law Majallah,* pp. 101–105. Petaling Jaya, Selangor: The Law Society, International Islamic University.

Andaya, Barbara, and Yoneo Ishii. 1992. "Religious Developments in Southeast Asia, circa 1500–1800." In Nicholas Tarling, ed., *The Cambridge History of Southeast Asia,* pp. 508–571. Cambridge: Cambridge University Press.

Banks, David. 1990. "Resurgent Islam and Rural Malay Culture: Malay Novelists and the Invention of Culture." *American Ethnologist* 17 (3): 531–548.

Bateson, Gregory. 1936. *Naven: A Survey of the Problems Suggested by a Composite Picture of a New Guinea Tribe Drawn from Three Points of View.* Stanford: Stanford University Press.

Bourdieu, Pierre. 1984. *Outline of a Theory of Practice.* Translated by R. Nice. Cambridge: Cambridge University Press.

Brown, Michael F. 1991. "Beyond Resistance: A Comparative Study of Utopian Renewal in Amazonia." *Ethnohistory* 38 (4): 388–413.

Chandra Muzaffar. 1987. *Islamic Resurgence in Malaysia.* Kuala Lumpur: Penerbit Fajar Bakti Sdn Bhd.

Edelman, Marc. 1994. "Landlords and the Devil: Class, Ethnic, and Gender Dimensions of Central American Peasant Narratives." *Cultural Anthropology* 9 (1): 58–93.

Ellen, Roy. 1983. "Social Theory, Ethnography, and the Understanding of Practical Islam in South-East Asia". In M. B. Hooker, ed., *Islam in South-East Asia*, pp. 50–91.Leiden: Brill.

Foucault, Michel. 1979. *Discipline and Punishment*. Translated by Allan Sheridan. New York:Vintage Books.

Gal, Susan. 1995. "Language and the 'Arts of Resistance.' " *Cultural Anthropology* 10 (3): 407–424.

Geertz, Clifford. 1960. *The Religion of Java*. New York: Free Press.

———. 1973. "Deep Play: Notes on the Balinese Cockfight." In Geertz, *The Interpretation of Cultures*, pp. 412–453. New York: Basic Books.

Gellner, Ernest. 1981. "Flux and Reflux in the Faith of Men." In Gellner, *Muslim Society*, pp. 1–85.Cambridge: Cambridge University Press.

Hefner, Robert. 1985. *Hindu Javanese: Tengger Tradition and Islam*. Princeton: Princeton University Press.

———. 1987. "The Political Economy of Islamic Conversion in Modern East Java." In William Roff, ed., *Islam and the Political Economy of Meaning*, pp. 53–78. London: Croom Helm.

———. 1990. *The Political Economy of Mountain Java: An Intrepetive History*. Berkeley and Los Angeles: University of California Press.

Hooker, M. B. 1989. Review of *Malaysia's National Language Policy and the Legal System*, by Richard Mead. *Journal of Asian Studies* 48 (1): 227–228.

Husin Mutalib. 1993. *Islam in Malaysia: From Revivalism to Islamic State?* Singapore: Singapore University Press.

Johns, A. H. 1981. "From Coastal Settlement to Islamic School and City: Islamization in Sumatra, the Malay Peninsula, and Java." In James J. Fox, ed., *Indonesia: The Making of a Culture*, pp. 163–182. Canberra: Research School of Pacific Studies, Australian National University.

Jomo, Kwame Sundaram, and Ahmad Shabery Cheek. 1992. "Malaysia's Islamic Movements." In Joel S. Kahn and Francis Loh Kok Wah, eds., *Fragmented Vision: Culture and Politics in Contemporary Malaysia*, pp. 79–105. Honolulu: University of Hawai'i Press.

Kaplan, Martha, and John D. Kelly. 1994. "Rethinking Resistance: Dialogics of 'Disaffection' in Colonial Fiji." *American Ethnologist* 21 (1): 123–151.

Karim, Wazir Jahan. 1992. *Women and Culture: Between Malay Adat and Islam*. Boulder: Westview Press.

Kessler, Clive. 1978. *Islam and Politics in a Malay State: Kelantan, 1839–1969*. Ithaca. Cornell University Press.

———. 1980. "Malaysia: Islamic Revivalism and Political Disaffection in a Divided Society." *Southeast Asia Chronicle* 75:3–11.

Laderman, Carol. 1991. *Taming the Wind of Desire: Psychology, Medicine, and Aesthetics in Malay Shamanistic Performance*. Berkeley and Los Angeles: University of California Press.

Lee, Raymond. 1988. "Patterns of Religious Tension in Malaysia." *Asian Survey* 28 (4): 400–418.

MacAllister, Carol. 1987. "Matriliny, Islam, and Capitalism: Combined and Uneven Development in the Lives of Negeri Sembilan Women." Ph.D. dissertation, University of Pittsburgh.

McKinley, Robert. 1981. "Cain and Abel on the Malay Peninsula." In Mac Marshall, ed., *Siblingship in Oceania: Studies in the Meaning of Kin Relations,* pp. 335–387. Ann Arbor: University of Michigan Press.

Milner, A. C. 1986. "Rethinking Islamic Fundamentalism in Malaysia." *Review of Indonesian and Malaysian Affairs* 20 (2): 48–75.

Muhammad Abu Bakar. 1987. *Penghayatan Sebuah Ideal: Suatu Tafsiran Tentang Islam Semasa.* (The Comprehension of an Ideal: An Interpretation of Contemporary Islam). Kuala Lumpur: Dewan Bahasa dan Pustaka.

Nagata, Judith. 1982. "Islamic Revival and the Problem of Legitimacy among Rural Religious Elites in Malaysia." *Man* 17:42–57.

———. 1984. *The Reflowering of Malaysian Islam: Modern Religious Radicals and Their Roots.* Vancouver: University of British Columbia Press.

———. 1987. "One Religion, Many Forms: The Multiple Traditions in Malay Islam." Paper presented at the eighty-sixth annual meetings of the American Anthropological Association.

Naipaul, V. S. 1981. *Among the Believers: An Islamic Journey.* New York: Alfred A Knopf.

Nash, Manning. 1991. "Islamic Resurgence in Malaysia and Indonesia." In Martin E. Marty and R. Scott Appleby, eds., *Fundamentalisms Observed,* pp. 691–739. Chicago: University of Chicago Press.

Ong, Aihwa. 1988. "The Production of Possession: Spirits and the Multinational Corporation in Malaysia." *American Ethnologist* 15 (1): 28–42.

———. 1990a. "Japanese Factories, Malay Workers: Class and Sexual Metaphors in West Malaysia." In Jane Atkinson and Shelly Errington, eds., *Power and Difference: Gender in Island Southeast Asia,* pp. 385–422. Stanford: Stanford University Press.

———. 1990b. "State Versus Islam: Malay Families, Women's Bodies, and the Body Politic in Malaysia." *American Ethnologist* 17 (2): 258–276.

Ortner, Sherry. 1995. "Resistance and the Problem of Ethnographic Refusal." *Comparative Studies in Society and History* 37 (1): 173–193.

Peletz, Michael G. 1988a. *A Share of the Harvest: Kinship, Property and Social History among the Malays of Rembau.* Berkeley and Los Angeles: University of California Press.

———. 1988b. "Poisoning, Sorcery, and Healing Rituals in Negeri Sembilan." *Bijdragen Tot de Taal-, Land-, en Volkenkunde* 144 (1): 132–164.

———. 1993a. "Knowledge, Power, and Personal Misfortune in a Malay Context." In Roy F. Ellen and C. W. Watson, eds., *Understanding Witchcraft and Sorcery in Southeast Asia,* pp. 149–177. Honolulu: University of Hawai'i Press.

———. 1993b. "Sacred Texts and Dangerous Words: The Politics of Law and Cultural Rationalization in Malaysia." *Comparative Studies in Society and History* 35 (1): 66–109.

————. 1994a. "Comparative Perspectives on Kinship and Cultural Identity in Negeri Sembilan." *Sojourn: Journal of Social Issues in Southeast Asia* 9 (1): 1–53.

————. 1994b. "Ambivalent Hearts and the Arts of Well-Being in Insular Southeast Asia." *Reviews in Anthropology* 23:143–156.

————. 1996. *Reason and Passion: Representations of Gender in a Malay Society.* Berkeley and Los Angeles: University of California Press.

Reid, Anthony. 1988. *Southeast Asia in the Age of Commerce, 1450–1680,* vol. 1: *The Lands Below the Winds.* New Haven: Yale University Press.

Roff, William. 1967. *The Origins of Malay Nationalism.* Kuala Lumpur: University of Malaya Press.

————. 1985. "Islam Obscured? Some Reflections on Studies of Islam and Society in Southeast Asia." *Archipel* 29:7–34.

Rosen, Lawrence. 1989. "Islamic 'Case Law' and the Logic of Consequence." In June Starr and Jane Collier, eds., *History and Power in the Study of Law: New Directions in Legal Anthropology,* pp. 302–319. Ithaca: Cornell University Press.

Sanders, Paula. 1991. "Gendering the Ungendered Body: Hermaphrodites in Medieval Islamic Law." In Nikki Keddie and Beth Baron, eds., *Women in Middle Eastern History: Shifting Boundaries in Sex and Gender,* pp. 74–95. New Haven: Yale University Press.

Scott, James C. 1985. *Weapons of the Weak: Everyday Forms of Peasant Resistance.* New Haven: Yale University Press.

————. 1990. *Domination and the Arts of Resistance: Hidden Transcripts.* New Haven: Yale University Press.

Seda-Poulin, Maria Luisa. 1993. "Islamization and Legal Reform in Malaysia: The Hudud Controversy of 1992." In *Southeast Asian Affairs, 1993,* pp. 224–242. Singapore: Institute of Southeast Asian Studies.

Shamsul Amri Baharuddin. 1983. "A Revival in the Study of Islam in Malaysia." *Man* 18:399–404.

Sholle, David. 1990. "Resistance: Pinning Down a Wandering Concept in Cultural Studies Discourse." *Journal of Urban and Cultural Studies* 1 (1): 87–105.

Stallybrass, Peter, and Allon White. 1986. *The Politics and Poetics of Transgression.* Ithaca: Cornell University Press.

Stivens, Maila. 1985. "The Fate of Women's Land Rights: Gender, Matriliny, and Capitalism in Rembau, Negeri Sembilan, Malaysia." In Haleh Afshar, ed., *Women, Work, and Ideology in the Third World,* pp. 3–36. London: Tavistock.

————. 1991. "The Evolution of Kinship Relations in Rembau, Negeri Sembilan, Malaysia." In J. Kemp and F. Husken, eds., *Cognation and Social Organization in Southeast Asia,* pp. 71–88. Leiden: Koninklijk Instituut voor Taal-, Land-, en Volkenkunde.

Sweeney, P. L. Amin. 1972. *The Ramayana and the Malay Shadow Play.* Kuala Lumpur: National University of Malaysia Press.

Taussig, Michael. 1980. *The Devil and Commodity Fetishism in South America.* Chapel Hill: University of North Carolina Press.

Valeri, Valerio. 1990. "Both Nature and Culture: Reflections in Menstrual and Partruitional Taboos in Huaulu (Seram)." In Jane Atkinson and Shelly Errington, eds., *Power and Difference: Gender in Island Southeast Asia,* pp. 235–272. Stanford: Stanford University Press.

Weigert, Andrew. 1991. *Mixed Emotions: Certain Steps toward Understanding Ambivalence.* Albany: SUNY Press.

Wikan, Unni. 1987. "Public Grace and Private Fears: Gaiety, Offense, and Sorcery in Northern Bali." *Ethos* 15:337–365.

———. 1989. "Managing the Heart to Brighten Face and Soul: Emotions in Balinese Morality and Health Care." *American Ethnologist* 16 (2): 294–312.

Wilkinson, Richard J. 1906. *Malay Beliefs.* London: Luzac.

Woodward, Mark R. 1988. "The Slametan: Textual Knowledge and Ritual Performance in Central Javanese Islam." *History of Religions* 28 (1): 54–89.

———. 1989. *Islam in Java: Normative Piety and Mysticism in the Sultanate of Yogyakarta.* Tucson: University of Arizona Press.

Wright, Barbara. 1986. "The Role of the Dalang in Kelantanese Malay Society." In Sharon A. Carstens, ed., *Cultural Identity in Northern Peninsular Malaysia,* pp. 29–45. Athens, Ohio: Ohio University Center for International Studies, Center for Southeast Asian Studies.

Zainah Anwar. 1987. *Islamic Revivalism in Malaysia: Dakwah among the Students.* Kuala Lumpur: Pelanduk Publications.

Chapter 9

Islamization and the Reshaping of Identities in Rural South Sulawesi

Martin Rössler

Ever since the pioneering studies of Snouck Hurgronje (1893–1895), Indonesian Islam and the processes of social change with which it is connected have been recognized as topics of extraordinary complexity. Recent studies have only served to confirm this impression, revealing enormous diversity within, for example, Javanese Islam, let alone that of the various Muslim peoples throughout the whole of the archipelago (Ellen 1983; Roff 1985; Lombard 1985). In today's Indonesia, however, this socio-religious diversity has to a certain degree been counteracted by an official ideology locating Muslim identity within the framework of national development and progress (see Boland 1982, 185–196; Hefner, Chapter 3, this volume). For much of the New Order (post-1966) era, influential segments of the government and military elite have sought to separate the state's national and developmentalist ideals from Muslim identity. This political strategy has largely been based on government efforts to require all social and religious organizations to accept the state ideology known as the Pancasila, with its emphasis on the equality of the five government-recognized religions.[1] In rural areas where Islam is the dominant religion, however, the population often perceives modern development and Muslim identity as intimately related; to be "modern" is to be Muslim. There are other local communities, however, where this identification of Muslim identity and developmentalist ideology is still in a very early or unfinished state. In these regions, Islam and ethnic or regional identity vie for the allegiance of the local population in an often unstable way. The study of religious change within these Muslim communities provides an opportunity to investigate the individual motivations and strategies of action that influence actors' commitments to one or another of these divergent, unfinished identities.

The Rise of Islam in Gowa: A Historical Sketch

Bontolowe, the village in which I conducted my research, is a community of Makassar wet-rice cultivators located about fifty miles east of Ujung Pandang in the highlands of the regency (Ind. *kabupaten*) of Gowa,[2] within the Indonesian province of South Sulawesi. Bontolowe is a new village established in the 1960s after the original settlement, known as Bulo, was moved from the river valley up to a road on the top of a steep hill overlooking its previous site.

South Sulawesi—and in particular the kingdom of Gowa formerly located in this region—has long been regarded as one of the main centers of Islam in the Malay archipelago (see Gervaise 1701, 133; Pelras 1985, 107). The region has played a significant role in the history of Islam in Indonesia, both in earlier times and in the modern republican era (see Noorduyn 1956; 1987; Kumar 1979, 24–29).

The arrival of Islam on the peninsula is commonly dated as September 22, 1605, when the king of the empire of Tallo' converted to Islam. Since that time the Makassar people have been renowned for their strict adherence to Islamic faith. Only a few years after their king's conversion, in 1611, the Makassar are said to have spread Islam to other parts of South Sulawesi. The arrival of Islam coincided with a period of intense political turmoil on Sulawesi's southern peninsula. In addition to the long-standing conflicts between Makassar and Bugis kingdoms, in 1627 the local population came into conflict with the Dutch East Indies Company (voc). It is commonly assumed that Islam at first provided Makassar and Bugis with a sense of common (Muslim) identity in the face of the European enemy (Mattulada 1976, 52, 106; Noorduyn 1956, 250; LaSide' 1975, 167). Forty years later, however, when the war against the Dutch reached its final stage, Arung Palakka, leader of the Bugis, chose not to side with his Makassar fellow-believers but with the commander of the Dutch forces. He thereby took revenge for the compulsory Islamization his kingdom had experienced some decades earlier. In 1669, Gowa surrendered (see Pelras 1985; Andaya 1981).

From 1630 until the early twentieth century, Gowa's political leaders and Islamic functionaries were both recruited from the ranks of the nobility. The ruling nobles were explicitly concerned about preserving their power by filling Islamic offices with their own kinsfolk (Abu Hamid 1978, 27). Much later, in 1926, the Muhammadiyah, an influential Indonesian Islamic reform movement (Peacock 1978; Feillard, this volume), was brought from Java to South Sulawesi. Its activities eventually led to the development of a marked social dichotomy between the nobility and pre-Islamic religion, on one hand, and commoners and Islam, on the other.

One of the primary practices targeted by the Muhammadiyah was the veneration of sacred heirlooms. Muslim reformists criticized the practice because they saw heirlooms as the pre-Islamic basis of the nobility's power (Rössler 1996) and regarded the nobility as incompatible with Islam, which they saw as emphasizing equality among men. Conversely, the colonial government and its allies among the nobility regarded the Muslim reformists as a political threat.[3] With the outbreak of the war for independence in 1945, the Muhammadiyah became one of the main forces struggling against the Dutch administration, which was still supported by influential nobles from Gowa and neighboring kingdoms (Mattulada 1976, 69). A few years later, the Darul Islam rebellion (1950–1965) broke out and, under the leadership of the charismatic Qahar Muzakkar, challenged the region's power structure even further. The rebellion was fueled by a complex array of ethnic, regional, and religious motives (Harvey 1974; 1977; van Dijk 1981, 156–217). Significantly, however, many of Qahar's followers were associated with the Muhammadiyah, which shared the rebels' anticolonialist and antifeudal attitudes. The cumulative effect of the struggle was that the Muhammadiyah and Islamic purification generally came to be regarded by many rural people as synonymous with the Darul Islam rebellion.

Though there have been numerous studies of Islam in lowland Makassar society, the role of Islam in the mountainous area east of Ujung Pandang has only recently become the focus of systematic study (Renre 1978; Abd. Rahman 1982; Rössler 1987; 1990). Research has revealed that Islam in this region appears to differ profoundly from that commonly reported for South Sulawesi. This disparity may be explained by the fact that it was not until 1910—immediately after Gowa's surrender to the Dutch—that Islam first gained influence in the highlands of South Sulawesi.[4] The first *imam*, or leader of congregational prayer, in the region where I conducted research was Suleiman Daeng Bunding, a member of the high nobility of Gowa. He had been appointed by the Dutch colonial administration. In contrast to the situation in the western lowlands, the colonial government in this region wanted to weaken the influence of the rural nobility, whose political power was largely based on pre-Islamic religious institutions. The government and its native representatives did so by supporting the spread of Islam in these upland regions (Rössler 1987, 29–37; in press). Daeng Bunding was responsible for many conversions, using a mission strategy that, among other things, involved his marrying girls from the local nobility. He was successful in part because no Makassar family of commoner or lower noble status would refuse a man of high noble rank as their son-in-law.[5] These families in turn converted to Islam because they considered it a distinguishing feature of the high nobility.

Daeng Bunding—whose children and grandchildren dominate local political life to this day—is reported to have used a variety of equally gentle methods in spreading Islam. Nonetheless, historical evidence indicates that by the late 1940s he was openly supportive of reformist Islam and the idea of the Republic of Indonesia, and opposed to the Dutch and their indigenous noble allies. In 1949, he was murdered by loyal followers of the district head of Kasepekang, who for years had been collaborating closely with the Dutch. A few months later, the Darul Islam rebels began to roam through the highland forests of Kasepekang. Many people who had derived advantage from collaborating with the Dutch were executed, including the district head. Darul Islam rebels also used this opportunity to eliminate many of the institutions and symbols of traditional belief. By the time the Muslim rebels left the area in the late 1950s, most of the sacred places and objects of pre-Islamic religion had been destroyed.

It is difficult to assess the attitude of the local population toward the rebellion during this period. Though in the 1930s and 1940s Daeng Bunding had built the first prayer houses in a few large highlands settlements, popular knowledge of Islam at that time appears to have remained limited. Few people understood the ideological principles motivating the Darul Islam rebellion. In 1984, an eighty-year-old man from Bontolowe described the situation for me in the following way: "The only thing we saw was that these people in the name of Allah burned down our houses and killed our friends and family. These men were very dangerous. We did not understand. Some of us, including [name] went with them. I do not recall why they did so. Anyway, most people did not care." Another old man, a rebel partisan, described the events of that year in the following manner: "There was trouble everywhere. I went into the forest to join Muhammadiyah. We hid there during the daytime and by night entered the villages, burning down houses. The following day, those who had remained in the villages burned down their own houses so that we would not burn them down. Sometimes it was quite ridiculous." I asked him: Why did you do that? Did you do it for reasons of Islam? Did you become "Muhammadiyah"?

No, that's just how we called them. I don't remember much. Everything was just in a mess *(kacau)*. We knew almost nothing about Islam or politics. How could we have known? There was no school, no one could read or write, no one could speak Indonesian. Few people had ever left the village for distant places such as Makassar. Sometimes if two men quarreled, on the following day one of them went off into the forest to join Muhammadiyah, while the other one stayed with his family. It was for whatever reason. I can't tell you why. It was disorder.

In the end, the rebellion had only a limited effect on the process of Islamization in the highlands. It was not long before the sacred spots destroyed by the Darul Islam were restored.[6]

In the 1960s, however, other developments began to promote changes less compatible with indigenous ways. The first stone mosque was built in Kasepekang. This coincided with government efforts at administrative reform that transformed Kasepekang into an official administrative village *(desa)*. For the first time too a man was installed as village imam. In addition, since 1970, the government's "head of spiritual affairs" has had a direct role in the regulation of local religious affairs. The holder of the office is commonly referred to as the Daeng Imang.[7] For some fifteen years, the office has been held by Aziz Nawa, whose father and younger brother have played important roles in other developments, described below.

Islam in a Highland Region

Suleiman Daeng Bunding, the primary missionary of Islam to Kasepekang, had earlier restricted his religious appeals to the families of the lower nobility. He only occasionally visited remote villages like Bulo, the site of my research. In the village itself, Bossong, the first man to study the art of Qur'anic recitation (Ind. *mengaji*), was the brother of a man who had earlier served as a priest (Mk. *sanro ada'*) in traditional, non-Islamic ritual. Older villagers recall that there was never any conflict between these two brothers. Daeng Bunding eventually installed Bossong as the village's first religious teacher. This was not a formal office, however, and its precise purpose was not understood by villagers. Indeed, at first Bossong and the few men who joined him in Islamic study were regarded as members of some kind of religious brotherhood similar to the groups that practice black magic still today in some villages.

In 1941 Giling, a trained religious teacher from Makassar, was installed as Bunding's assistant imam in the administrative complex of Likopancing, which at that time also included the settlement of Bulo. Bossong felt slighted by this appointment and migrated to Makassar. Giling held his position until 1960, when the government decided that every larger settlement within the new *desa* Kasepekang should have its own imam. In 1945, Nawa, a peasant from Bulo, married Giling's daughter, and during the following years he learned much about Islam from his father-in-law. He was a diligent student, and, when in 1960 a village congregational leader *(imam)* was to be appointed, Nawa was chosen for the position since he was the only Bulo resident capable of reciting the Qur'an. He has held the post to this day.

Even though commoners occupied the offices of imam and head of spiritual affairs, the practice of Islam in the highlands during these years remained strongly identified with noble rank. According to local nobles, the reason had to do with familial obligations originating with Daeng Bunding's activities. The present subdistrict head of Kasepekang and the village chief of Bontolowe are Daeng Bunding's grandsons. Fatimah, a Bontolowe resident who has played a great role in local Islam (see below), is one of his granddaughters. Finally, the head of the primary school in Bontolowe is married to Daeng Bunding's youngest daughter. All of these people share two characteristics that until recently distinguished them from most commoners: their education is far above average (many had finished secondary school or even attended colleges), and they explicitly identify Islam with progress and modernity.

When I began my fieldwork in 1984, Islam was a topic that, at least in the presence of the anthropologist, was discussed almost exclusively by nobles. One day I asked the head of the village school, who was originally from Ternate (Moluccas), about the population's general attitude toward Islam. He answered in the following manner:

> You cannot compare the people here to those who live in the lowlands or in the city. The mountains provide no place for religious fanaticism *(agama fanatik)*. The only thing these people consider important is cultivating their fields to make a living. Time and again there have been people from the city who settled in the villages and made propaganda for Muslim brotherhoods. These men, as a general rule, very soon returned to where they had come from. They were told by the villagers: "You guys may have the time to practice Islam, but not we. The soil is difficult in the mountains, and we must work very hard so that we can eat rice and stay alive." I am the son-in-law of Daeng Bunding, I am a Muslim, and I am educated. But I am not a man whose roots lie here. The people here are different. In my opinion, people in this and other villages have been living in their religious community for centuries, and they simply do not care if this is a Muslim community or one of the old belief. I find this quite understandable, and I have never bothered.

Such a view of local religion and society was typical among the elite in the mid-1980s. More remarkably, it is also broadly consistent with ordinary villagers' assessment of Islam. During my fieldwork I heard many people comment that the increasing influence of Islam, which is believed to stress the separation of the secular from the sacred, would transform religion into an individual rather than a communal affair. Furthermore, it was widely felt that Islam, in contrast to the indigenous belief system, would require that much time be set aside for prayers, fasting, and reflecting on God. Villagers say such conditions are consistent with city life, but not with the life of hard-working rice farmers. In other words, many people regard Islam as a religion whose basic principles are inconsistent with indigenous patterns of social and economic organization.

Besides religious officials in the village and subdistrict, one of the few individuals dissenting from this view was the head of Kasepekang. His views are illustrated by a comment that I recorded in my notebook on the occasion of the celebration of the Prophet's Birthday (Ar. *maulid*) in 1984: "As you know, *maulid* is a matter of religion *(agama)*, isn't it? So there is a public declaration *(penerangan)* and a sermon *(khutbah)* in the mosque, and then the celebration is valid *(sah)*. But the people in the villages haven't yet understood. They would still perform *maulid* rituals in their houses, burn incense and prepare special meals, and so on. This is not religion, this is just culture and custom *(kebudayaan dan kebiasaan)*. We can only become a modern society if some day these peasants understand what religion means." In the eyes of the administration, the way to achieve this aim is religious education. Most of the local nobles, of course, have had some exposure to higher education. By contrast, the first primary school for ordinary villagers was built in Bontolowe only in the 1960s. Most of Daeng Bunding's older children had been educated at Dutch schools in Makassar before the war. Some among his descendants later went to secondary school and even college. Since, by comparison with other parts of Indonesia, the educational system in South Sulawesi was until recently poorly developed (Mattulada 1988, 281; Safwan and Kutoyo 1980–1981), higher education was limited to those of greater economic means. Only nobles, with their vast landholdings, government jobs, and trading enterprises, could afford the cost of education. In the village, there is only the most basic religious training in primary school. In addition, the imam regularly holds courses in Qur'anic recitation for children between six and ten years of age. However, neither the *imam* nor his pupils understand the literal meaning of the Arabic words they utter.[8]

Before turning to a closer examination of pre-Islamic religion in highland Gowa, let me briefly explain how its relationship with Islam is now officially viewed. Such an assessment is complicated by the fact that there are no indigenous (Makassar) terms to characterize the conceptual opposition between traditional "belief" (Ind. *kepercayaan*) and Islam as a "religion" (Ind. *agama*). Throughout Indonesia, however, this contrast between belief and religion is expressed as a relationship between a (subordinate) *kepercayaan* and a (superior) *agama*. Thus everything that is not "religion" tends to be identified as mere "superstition" *(takhayyul)*, "culture" *(kebudayaan)*, or "custom" *(kebiasaan)*. In other words, traditional culture as understood in the human sciences is in official Indonesian discourse likely to be viewed as mere folklore or, in other contexts, aestheticized as indigenous "art" (cf. Acciaioli 1985, 152; Atkinson 1983; Hefner 1985, 37; Pelras 1977, 64; Rössler 1987, 110).

This manner of categorization is not only a problem for social research but also for—and, I hasten to stress, primarily for—local people. Imam Nawa one day explained:

> I accept the old belief *(kepercayaan),* and I know how to perform the old rites. Actually it is also my belief, because I am of the same descent as all the other people here. We have common ancestors, and so we share the same belief. But I am the imam, and so I must be careful not to act in contradiction to *agama.* Once I asked a great imam how I should deal with the contrast between *agama* and *kepercayaan.* He was silent for a moment and then responded: "If they ask you for help, you may help those who do not act in accordance with Islam. But if they receive help by one of their kind, then leave them alone." I have always followed this advice, and therefore I don't have any enemies in the village.

The *imam*'s comments reveal the continuing importance of local identity and illustrate the ambivalence regarding the distinction between Islam and the old belief (see also Peletz, this volume). Nawa's attitude contrasts with that of his son Nasir, who acts as a kind of deputy imam in the village. In 1984, when he was twenty-four years old, Nasir made the following observation: "The old belief is irreconcilable with true religion *(agama).* How can we village people ever become modern when even our leaders [i.e., the holders of traditional offices] practice the old belief? They make offerings to the ancestors so that the harvest be rich. No one can hear what the priest is saying during the offerings. Why is he whispering? In Islam, it is different. Our prayers are pronounced loudly and clearly, the words are Arabic, and they are taken from the holy Qur'an." As these comments indicate, when I first began my fieldwork in Bontolowe, religious life was still to a great extent governed by pre-Islamic ritual practices; but these practices were encountering growing opposition.

My primary concern here, however, is not with an elite-sponsored Islam, but with the social practices and experiences of "ordinary" people (Ellen 1983, 54; Eickelman 1987, 19; Peletz, this volume), especially the mostly illiterate peasants who until recently had no reason to distinguish "scripturalist Islam" from their own religious practice. These people's religious experiences differ significantly from those described, for example, in contemporary Java (Geertz 1960; Peacock 1978; Woodward 1988; 1989).

The divergent nature of individual and group experience within this local context, however, can shed light on aspects of Islam and Islamization elsewhere in Southeast Asia.

Identity, Religion, and Sociopolitical Organization

Like most Indonesians, the people in Bontolowe have a national identity card with the entry "Islam" under the heading "religion." There is no one who, when questioned about his or her religious affiliation, would not speak of himself or herself as Muslim. Yet at least some people living in this region say that the majority of the population is not Muslim at all. How can we reconcile the label of Islam with individual experience and cultural meaning?

Identity in highland Makassar communities was traditionally defined in terms of several inseparable components, the most important of which were territory, religion, and membership in kin groups. Each village is located within a territory (Mk. *pa'rasangeng*), the boundaries of which are regarded as fixed by customary law (Mk. *adat*), and inhabited by the localized core of a bilateral kin group (Mk. *pammanakang*). As a general rule, in precolonial times a cluster of several such village territories, such as Kasepekang, constituted an autonomous principality ruled by a *karaeng*. Some of the highland village territories, including Bulo/Bontolowe, had been autonomous before they were incorporated (in most instances by force) into principalities or the kingdom of Gowa. According to oral tradition, this happened to Bulo in the sixteenth century. Oral traditions from Bontolowe as well as from Kajang, which is located in the southeastern corner of South Sulawesi, suggest that in both regions elite domination, titles, and stratification emerged only after their subjugation by the kingdom of Gowa.[9] Accordingly, many indigenous traditions today still reflect egalitarian ideals. Thus it is said that within the village territory, no difference between people must be displayed. Members of the high nobility from the court of Gowa must not be treated as superiors, and even the king himself will not be allowed to enter the village on horseback.

In the course of recent history, however, the precise meaning of most of these traditions was lost, and today social ranking in Kasepekang is as great a concern as in the western lowlands (see Röttger-Rössler 1989). The society as a whole is divided into nobility, commoners, and (former) slaves; each of these strata is in turn internally differentiated. In addition, evaluation of individual rank, also important among commoners, depends largely on membership in cognatic descent groups. Specific terms (Mk. *pattola*) are applied to those groups in which membership entitles one to traditional political offices, such as the community head (karaeng).[10] Marriage is the primary avenue for upward mobility. Low descent rank can also be mitigated by bravery, education, wealth, occupation, or religious knowledge.

Although after the incorporation of the interior highlands into the kingdom of Gowa the translocal notion of "Makassarness" became an important concept, social identity was, and to a great degree still is, based on more localized groups. Still today anyone who does not own village land is regarded as an outsider (tu palili'). Even someone who marries a village resident and resides for decades in the village is regarded by the "people owning land" (tu pa'butta) as "a person living here, but not one of us." Beyond the framework of the village, no overarching criteria of identity are recognized. Even the historical territory of a principality lacks such a culturally acknowledged common identity. Below its ruler, there was not a centralized government but a council composed of (in the case of Kasepekang) the heads of the twelve most important villages. In two principality-wide rituals (now rarely performed), it was not common identity but the distinguishing identities of each village within this council that were highlighted.[11] While all this might appear to be merely a matter of descent and territoriality, it also entailed a religious dimension, because descent and territoriality mark not only social divides but boundaries between religious microcosms. The influence exercised by ancestral souls, for example, was and is still today believed to be restricted to the territory inhabited by their descendants.

Despite such great historical changes as the expansion of the kingdom of Gowa, it appears that Makassar living in the central and eastern mountains remained distinct from those dwelling in the western and southern lowlands. This picture is strikingly similar to the relationship of the Tengger people of East Java to the lowland Javanese population (Hefner 1985; 1990, 3). Thus, although it is difficult to explain the distinctiveness of the highland people by reference to any sociopolitical structure, there are important differences of language, material culture, and, above all, indigenous belief.[12] Though there is no specific term for the latter as a body of religious belief, there is a word for the people who adhere to certain practices and beliefs. This term is patuntung, meaning "a person who strives to bring his or her behavior into conformity with tradition." According to oral traditions from Kajang, these norms and values above all relate to honesty and modesty (Usop 1978). But being a patuntung also means adhering to a system of belief and practice that includes religious ideas, a world view, and norms for everyday behavior (Rössler 1990). "Being patuntung" was the most important criterion of local identity before Islamization.

This earlier belief system recognized a variety of deities (Mk. rihata).

One among them, "Almighty Lord" (Karaeng Kaminang Kammaya), is thought to live in an indefinite realm between the world and nothingness, exercising supreme control over the universe. From this it seems that there was traditionally a monolatric understanding of divinity. In present-day ritual it is sometimes difficult for the outside observer to determine whether this "Almighty Lord" or Allah is being addressed. Notions of Allah (Karaeng Alata'ala) have also entered traditional ritual texts, where the Islamic term has replaced Karaeng Kaminang Kammaya (see Rössler 1987, 385). Indeed, in general traditional rituals reveal widespread Islamic terminological influences, including such terms as *malaeka'* (Ar. *mala'ika*, "angel"), and *jing* (Ar. *jinn*, "spirit"). Yet locals do not consider most such usages an effect of Islamization, but merely as an aspect of "traditional" belief.

The presence of so many religious terms of Islamic origin clearly reflects the long-standing nature of Islamic influence, related, no doubt, to the long-established dominance of the kingdom of Gowa in this region. It is reported that, even in the early seventeenth century, the king of Gowa had officially integrated elements of Islamic rites of passage (including Islamic marriage, the *nikah*) into court custom. The annexation of formerly autonomous principalities in the following two hundred years resulted in the spread of these and other rituals, such as the practice of circumcision. The latter (or some related practice; Pelras 1985, 122) may be of pre-Islamic origin (Renre 1978, 112) and was formerly accompanied by the filing of the upper incisors, a practice still important in some highland regions. According to Pénard, both rites were regarded as an initiation into the community of *patuntung* (1913, 536). Old people from Bontolowe remember that tooth filing was once practiced in Kasepekang. They were told about it when they were children, but none of them had ever seen the performance. Today, circumcision is regarded as a boy's initiation into the community of Muslim faithful *(ummat)*.

From an indigenous standpoint it is not important whether the beings toward which local people direct their offerings bear Arabic or indigenous names, or whether certain spiritual beings addressed in ritual action are of Islamic or non-Islamic origin. All beliefs and rituals, even if they have long since been modified by Islamic ideas, are regarded as part of traditional heritage. The belief system shared by *patuntung* is seen as "pre-Islamic," regardless of whether it bears Islamic elements or not (Rössler 1987). The dichotomy in terms of "Islamic" versus "non-Islamic" emerged recently, only after Islamic modernists began to label certain unfamiliar practices as "non-Islamic" and the suppression of such rites became a matter of official policy (see also Bowen and Peletz, this volume).

Of particular importance for the political and religious life of the village, principality, and kingdom were sacred heirlooms (Mk. *kalompoang*). These objects were used by noble and commoner leaders alike to legitimate their authority, by providing a means for individuals to trace their descent back to regional founders.[13] However, the traditional leadership was abolished as a result of the administrative reforms carried out around 1960, and from that point on any man could strive for political power. Descent became less important, and the office of the village chief turned into a stage for open competition, as some people saw an opportunity to improve their social position. Between 1960 and 1983 no fewer than seven men held the office in Bontolowe. In 1975, for the first time in history, an "outsider" *(tu palili')* of slave descent named Jumali became village chief (see below).

These changes also worked to create tension between the formal office of the village chief and that of the traditional leader or *karaeng*. The last *karaeng* of Bontolowe was installed in 1961 but was forced by the national government to bear the Indonesian title of "village chief" (Ind. *ketua rukun kampung*) rather than the traditional title *karaeng*. Though soon replaced as village chief, this man is regarded as the *karaeng* to this day, and he still performs traditional rituals, including those centering on the sacred heirlooms. Despite the decline of this traditional leadership role, the official village chiefs who have held power since 1960 have not tended to work as direct agents of Islamization. However, the abolition of traditional political roles has led to a situation where, even if leaders adhere to the old belief rather than Islam, they no longer have any institutionalized authority in traditional religious matters. Village officials are thus in an ambiguous position, obliged to observe instructions from the district government but still involved in social networks linked to traditional beliefs and rituals.

Recently the situation has been further complicated by efforts at religious outreach undertaken by district- and provincial-level officials as well as students from the Islamic teaching colleges (IAIN) in Ujung Pandang. In 1990, for example, IAIN students visited a number of houses doing surveys on the potentially sensitive issues of villagers' habits of prayer and fasting, and the quality of their belief in Allah. After their interviews, the students found that no family invited them for coffee, let alone a warm meal. According to local custom, to treat guests—even those whom one dislikes—in such a way is not only extremely impolite but unthinkable. But local people protested the students' actions, asking, Why do such people say that we are not good Muslims? Am I a better human being if I pray five times daily, without any particular cause? Life is good when offerings are given to the Owners of the Earth or to others Who Are Powerful. They give us rice and children, and when we die some day, we will be with them. They cannot be bad beings, but these people say so. What more can Allah do than also give us rice and children?

These discussions raise complex questions about the changing role of Islam in individual and group identity. It is not a question of whether villagers profess formal adherence to Islam; clearly they do. What is at issue is instead the relationship of individual consciousness, experience, and interpretation to some wider, collective body of action or belief linking individuals and groups (Comaroff 1987, 302–306). In the case of the world religions, ultimately in question are abstract standards of action and belief the historical complexity of which is determined by much more than local actions and meanings (cf. Eickelman 1987, 24; Bowen 1992, 656–657).

Observing and interpreting these standards of action and belief in Islam is facilitated by the fact that the framework of religious action is formulated around Islam's famous "Five Pillars." These devotional obligations are intended to bring believers nearer to God and to help them fulfill their duties toward Him (Farah 1968, 134). The Pillars consist of testifying to the unity of God (Ar. *shahâda*), worshiping five times daily (Ar. *salât*), making the annual payment of the tithe (Ar. *zakât*), engaging in the the annual fast (Ar. *saum*), and making the pilgrimage (Ar. *hajj*). Throughout the Muslim world, these Five Pillars "are practised to widely differing extents, and the importance attached to each Pillar varies from one place to another" (Ellen 1983, 57). The way in which they are practiced in different Islamic contexts helps to illuminate the processes whereby Islamic identity is often divergently constructed. This can be clearly seen here in South Sulawesi in relation to two of the most important Islamic feasts, *îd al-fitr* (Ar.) and *îd al-qurbân* or *îd al-adhâ*.

The Imam's Family and a Dispute over Prayer

In the summer of 1984, a few weeks after the end-of-the-fast celebration of *îd al-fitr*, a district military official delivered an address about nonreligious matters in the school building. Nasir, the young son of the village *imam*, then took the opportunity to accuse the villagers of too rarely joining the evening prayers. Jumali, the former village chief, was again drunk and vigorously supported him, shouting that the present village chief should prohibit primitive superstition and the veneration of "wood and stones." The meeting soon dissolved in total confusion because the official did not know how to reply. The result of the turmoil was that the mosque was locked for several days. Nasir, who controlled the key, was disappointed about his failure. Most of the village's residents, however, were deeply irritated by his behavior. How could he, a young man of low social rank, dare to make such a point in public, giving the district government probably more reason for further religious propaganda?

This event is typical of how public Islamic affairs are treated at the village level. It had only temporary consequences for evening prayers, and a few weeks later everything went back to normal. The incident revealed, however, an important point: that the social position of individuals is often a decisive influence in religious conflicts and, more specifically, that marginal individuals often have a vital interest in the promotion of reformist ideas.

To understand this point requires a closer look at the *imam*'s family. Nawa's parents ran away to get married around 1918. Contrary to most other Indonesian societies, among Makassar marriage by flight is not just a symbolic act, but often results in bloodshed. After the young couple had hidden for several years in a small settlement deep in the forest (where Nawa was born), Nawa's father was still unable to pay the bride price to his parents-in-law. If they had hid any longer, all of them would have risked discovery and death. Thus, Nawa's mother went home to her father, giving him a dagger and asking him to kill her. Though it is said that no father had ever killed his daughter in such circumstances, this conventionalized act, called "running up to the blade" *(allari matanna bassia)* has severe social consequences. The young family settled down in Bulo, but from that day on, Nawa's mother was labeled a whore.[14] The self-respect (Mk. *siri'*) of all family members was destroyed. Neither Nawa nor his siblings found a spouse in Bulo or any of the neighboring villages. Since Nawa had to cultivate the fields of his father, he could not follow his brothers and sisters and migrate to some distant place. Several older people told me that the only chance Nawa ever had to improve his deplorable position as the son of a whore occurred in 1960, when the district government was looking to appoint someone to serve as a congregational leader *(imam)* for the community.

But this avenue to upward mobility had its own pitfalls. Acting as the first village *imam* served to further isolate Nawa, since in the early 1960s, as he repeatedly told me, spreading Islam in the village was a very difficult task. Appointment of the imam was regarded as an affront to village tradition *(adat)*. In fact, to this day Nawa's family is in some sense isolated, despite the fact that Nasir's elder brother, Aziz, holds the highest Islamic role in the subdistrict *(desa)*. Though by virtue of their offices, Nawa and Aziz exercise considerable authority within the community, the whole family is nonetheless regarded as "odd" by most villagers. "They hold governmental offices, but without these, they would count for nothing," I was once told. Because descent is the most important determinant of rank,

Nasir and Nawa had no chance of improving their social position by using traditional mechanisms of status mobility such as taking a spouse from one of the *adat* descent groups.[15] Excluded from such traditional status arrangements, Nawa has succeeded in achieving some respect in the village through the warmth of his personality and his involvement in Islamic affairs.

The situation is quite different with Jumali. He is an "outsider" of slave descent—a stigma that long after the official abolition of slavery under Dutch colonial rule is still of great social significance—and is widely regarded as a man of the worst character. Though he had repeatedly been accused of theft, insulting women, embezzlement, and acts of violence, he was installed as village chief in 1975. The reason was that at that time he already held a government job in the district capital, which provided him with useful political connections. Since he is also an eloquent man with an excellent knowledge of the Indonesian language (which in the 1970s was exceptional for the local people), he was seen as the best candidate for the post.

During the weeks before the meeting mentioned above, there had been constant quarreling between the village chief and Jumali. It was the dry season, and water was in short supply. Whenever he was drunk, Jumali raged outside his house, brandishing his sword and threatening to cut the whole water pipe network into pieces (which one day he did) if that "most stupid of all village chiefs" would not remedy things quickly. In the weeks and months after the meeting, he made Islam the main topic of his accusations. He was aware that the village chief, whose father had been *karaeng* in the late 1940s, was closely tied to traditional authority and rituals. In addition, the chief repeatedly refused to speak in the mosque when requested to do so because of his poor command of the Indonesian language. Thus Jumali frequently complained to district officials that under the chief's inept guidance Islam would never be established in Bontolowe.

Until very recently, opportunities for social and political mobility in these highland communities were limited, particularly for illiterate people without the chance of obtaining employment in some small government office, as Jumali had done. Now some individuals can advance their rank on bases other than traditional descent, including the manipulation of Islamic appeals, and these strategies at times are having a significant effect on social and religious life.

The Fast and the Alms: Support for the Imam

"Fasting is an armour with which one protects oneself," states a *hadith* (Ar.) put down by Bukhârî (Muhammad Ali 1983, 223). In villages in the Makassar highlands, only a few individuals actually carry out the fast for the whole of the fasting month (Ramadan), most giving it up after a few days. At another public meeting two weeks into Ramadan in 1984, a district religious official accused the population of ignoring Islam by not faithfully keeping the fast. From that day on the mosque was empty. Indeed, in general villagers tire of listening to lectures each night of the fasting month by officials or students from Islamic colleges in Ujung Pandang. Some men made a habit of walking two hours to a small prayer house up the road every day because officials never came there to deliver addresses. In 1991 further discontent was evoked by a new regulation that denied women access to the mosque of Bontolowe; they were instead to sit outside during the evening prayer. For many villagers, Ramadan has become a month of disharmony rather than purity and devotion.

Similar tensions are evident during the last days of the fasting month, when people are obliged to give alms in the form of zakât al-fitr (Ar.), the only zakât payment made here.[16] According to a decree by the district government, every household is obliged to give zakât. In effect this regulation implies that there are no poor or needy people in the village. Therefore, the village chief and Imam Nawa are the only individuals who receive a portion of the alms. In 1991 every household was asked to give four liters of rice or 1,600 rupiah for each of its members; the figure had been 700 rupiah in 1984. Data from 1984 as well as from 1991 reveal that the alms had in fact only been rendered by about a third of the population. Many people who came with rice or money to Nawa's house asked him to keep it for himself and not to hand it over to the district officials. Although the money and proceeds from selling the rice are supposed to be used for public purposes such as repairing the school building, it is more often divided among district officials and high-status people, a fact not appreciated by most villagers.

The fasting month ends with the celebration of îd al-fitr, which in the highlands is the greatest Islamic feast. Every household prepares cakes and sweets for visitors. The strategies people follow with regard to these visits correspond closely to social and economic position. Basically, there are only two categories of households during the feast: first, the high-status and better-off, whose members stay at home to receive guests, and, second, the low-status and poorer households, whose members spend the days of the feast moving from one house to the other.[17] Social rank and relationships determine the selection of households to be visited.

The First Haji

The fifth Pillar of Islam concerns the pilgrimage (hajj) to Mecca, considered obligatory for those who can afford the journey. The pilgrimage occupies an unusual position among the highland population, quite different from its role among wealthier lowlanders. In the highlands, the pilgrimage is regarded as something extraordinary and exceptional, something one can hardly afford without risking one's very existence.[18] In 1984 a young man named Hasan became a sensation when he announced that he would perform the *hajj* as the one and only person from the whole district in that year and as the very first man from the village. This astonished most villagers, because until then only nobles were regarded as rich enough to perform the pilgrimage. Hasan, who was married to the daughter of Banci, a former traditional priest (Mk. *sanro ada'*), had sold all his possessions, including his house and all of his fields and cattle, in order to be registered as a pilgrim. This event caused great excitement, but it also divided the population. Some people simply shook their heads at such an "obscure adventure," while others regarded Hasan as a shining example of piety, whose willingness to sacrifice his existence for the sake of God would surely be rewarded some day. Nasir made the following observation in 1984: "All right, Hasan is a poor man now, as far as material wealth is concerned. But that will not last long. Once you are *haji*, you soon become rich. Allah will love you, and He will reward you. All *haji* are wealthy. And in a few months Hasan will be wealthier than ever before, believe me!" By 1991 it was clear that this prediction had not come true, and Haji Hasan was still earning his means by helping other people cultivate their ricefields.

As noted above, Hasan was the son-in-law of Banci, who had formerly held the office of priest in the traditional (non-Islamic) religion, commonly regarded as the very opposite of institutionalized Islam. After the ritual performed in 1984 on the occasion of Hasan's departure for Mecca, Imam Nawa said to me: "It is good that soon we shall have a *haji* in the village, but don't you ever trust Banci! He is as old as I am, but he does not believe in God. He does not follow the words of the Prophet; instead he only communicates with the ancestors. This is probably because he had once been *sanro*! His way is not the right one."

Seven years later, in April 1991, I found myself again talking with the *imam* about Banci, but this time his words were different: "I don't want to have anything to do with Banci, no way. He is a very pious man, perhaps he is a better Muslim than I am, even though I am the *imam*. But Banci only believes in the new Islam (Mk. *isilang beru*), which is the religion of the pious townsfolk. You know, this is a kind of Islam that forbids almost everything. I feel that it is not good for us people here in the mountains. Banci always tells me: don't do this and that, this is not in accordance with the words of the Prophet, and so on. But I cannot agree, I don't want this sort of Islam." What had happened to Banci over these years? I soon began to understand when the funeral ritual of Banci's sister brought me together with him. My earlier research on funeral rites showed them to be only superficially influenced by Islam, stressing the incorporation of the deceased person's soul into the community of the ancestors (Rössler 1987, 278–299). Yet at the funeral of Banci's sister recitations of the Qur'an on the third, seventh, and twentieth night were not accompanied by the traditional acts of sacrifice, incense burning, and purification.[19]

Banci's sister had been a high-ranking woman in the most prestigious local descent group, membership in which entitles one to the office of *karaeng*. According to local tradition, then, her death should have been accompanied by a specific sequence of ritual acts. Yet all that happened each night was the recitation of the Qur'an. I presumed that this might be related to the presence of a certain *haji* at the services each night, a man I did not know. But later I came to understand the real reason. The unfamiliar *haji* was Banci's younger brother, who lived in a distant village. He had made the pilgrimage in 1989 and, immediately after returning from Mecca, had strictly prohibited the performance of any pre-Islamic ritual in his home village. I was told that he had made that place a center of "the new Islam," a term that villagers used to refer to a strict Islam associated with the Muhammadiyah in the lowlands. He had also strongly influenced his brother Banci. To not anger him or Banci, I was informed, the family at the funeral had agreed to avoid all of the traditional activities that might be seen as contrary to the "new Islam."

What was particularly striking about this situation—aside from Banci's changed attitude and the assertion of a "new Islam," a term that I had never encountered in previous years—was the fact that a single individual, who was not socially prominent even in his own village, could exercise such influence on ritual performance. However, by rejecting someone's advice to perform a "minimalist" funeral, people would have risked being stigmatized as enemies of Islam and progress. Government authorities regard minimalist funeral rites as representative of pure Islam. As Aziz Nawa once told me: "When someone is dead, why be fussy about him? He is dead and gone, and we put him under the ground, and then it's finished. There is no need to make offerings or to put flowers on his grave at the end of Ramadan. He can neither see nor smell them any more, can he?"

I soon learned, however, that very early in the morning, when Banci and his brother were visiting other households, the sequence of ritual acts required for their deceased sister's soul was secretly carried out by other members of the family, under the leadership of the deceased woman's father-in-law, a leading traditional functionary. The rites include offerings of rice and fowl, part of which is regarded as "daily food" for the deceased's soul. According to traditional belief, during the first moments after death, the soul is frail and not able to feed itself. The soul remains in this state until the death rites end, as marked by a ritual where one traditional functionary *(baku')* hands over a fowl to another functionary *(gallarang)*.[20] The fowl in this case symbolizes the soul, and, after the *gallarang* gives it back to be slaughtered, the soul is regarded as having been moved from the community of the living into the community of the ancestors. These rites need not be performed in public. What is most remarkable here is that they were performed at all.

Hajj and Hierarchy

Because of the enormous funds required for such a journey, then, the pilgrimage is considered the ultimate attribute of Islam and the sign of a remarkable person. Some are convinced that such individuals are motivated to sacrifice all their possessions by their extraordinary devotion to God. Others, however, interpret the rite with reference to the Makassar proverb *"naiki ri butta lannyinga, ammotereki ri butta tangkasa'"*: "off he went to the holy land, home he came to a waste land."[21] This proverb is applied to people who, with the aim of achieving the high prestige of the pilgrim, sell house and home—and after their return have nothing left, except for "the most expensive cap in the world," as another popular saying goes.

In any case, is it possible to judge by scientific standards what motivates such actions as the pilgrimage or to estimate what kind of religious change they bring about? Whatever its deeply religious motives, it is clear that there are social structural influences on the decision to perform the pilgrimage. In particular, in rural Makassar communities, the pilgrimage represents a risky but ambitious strategy for achieving prestige—a dominant cultural concern in this society, perhaps more so than in any other Indonesian society (see Chabot 1950; Röttger-Rössler 1989). Although religious interests may motivate people independently, it is a fact that the pilgrimage raises one's rank faster and more markedly than any other social activity.

This perspective on the pilgrimage's status implications is, in fact, widely shared among villagers. Most comment that the pilgrimage is deeply related to aspirations for wealth and status. Yusup, a religious teacher in a neighboring primary school, explained the matter in the following blunt terms: "Why do people make the pilgrimage? Because they want to show that they have money. And most important is that, as someone who has performed the pilgrimage, you are respected. Maybe you are stupid and don't know how to read or write, but everybody will honor you. People think that you are at the top of society, even if you are an illiterate descendant of slaves. That is why Makassar like the *hajj*." Yusup stated further that the last thing he would do was to perform the pilgrimage. If he had lots of money, he averred, he would instead buy as much land as he could because that, in his eyes, was something very useful, unlike the *hajj*, which he designated as an additional "pleasure."[22] In contrast to what he said before, this sounds surprising. However, his attitude may be explained by the fact that Yusup is not only highly respected for his education at an Islamic college in Ujung Pandang and for his position as a school teacher of Islam, but also as the son of a high-ranking *karaeng* regarded as the most famous ruler in the eastern highlands since the end of the war.

Yusup's opinion is widely shared. However, as Hasan's case illustrated, this strategy of raising one's status by performing the pilgrimage is not always successful. Haji Hasan is still a person of low social rank, a man who "counts for nothing," just as he was before making the *hajj*.

The Case of Fatimah

Fatimah is a thirty-six-year-old woman of noble descent who also lives in Bontolowe. During the fasting month of 1984, she told me that she was too lazy to join the *tarâwîh*-prayers every night, though as a person who was trained as a school teacher of Islam, she was actually obliged to attend. Seven years later, she was the second person from the village to perform the *hajj*. Understanding her motivations for making the pilgrimage requires a brief look at her life history (see Röttger-Rössler 1989, 115–128; 1994).

There are now only three members of the nobility living in the village. While Fatimah's mother is of commoner background, her father was a son of the noble Imam Daeng Bunding, who, after the Dutch had gained control of the region around the year 1910, had been the main agent for spreading Islam in the highlands. A crucial event in Fatimah's life history was her marriage to an outsider, whom she subsequently discovered to be already married—a fact that nobody had known before and that was the cause of Fatimah's rapid social decline, especially among her noble kin.[23] Immediately after her marriage, she moved back to Bontolowe, where she lives with her mother. Notwithstanding this dramatic experience, in recent years she has proved to be a woman of extraordinary economic skill. Primarily by lending money to peasants at high rates of interest, Fatimah has become the wealthiest person in the village. Earlier, in 1989, her father's brother, a former district head and the highest-ranking noble in the region, had announced that in 1991 he would make the pilgrimage. The expense of such an excursion represented no problem for Fatimah, so she saw an opportunity to raise her status by joining her uncle.

Other villagers commented that Fatimah had always used Islam to mark herself off from her neighbors. Though she had long claimed noble descent, we learned shortly after meeting her that she was actually of commoner descent. Much later, in 1990, we learned that she had not in fact been trained as a school teacher of Islam, as she had earlier assured us. When we discussed this fact with some other people, they laughed, and one said: "That is typical for Fatimah. She performs the daily prayers *(salat)* regularly, and her mouth talks about Islam day and night. But inside her heart she is very different. Her heart thinks of money and status. She wants us to recognize that she is of higher standing."

There is a curious continuity to this association of Islamic piety with high status. In the kingdom of Gowa and its subordinate principalities, it should be recalled, the nobility had earlier been the primary agents for the diffusion of Islam. For centuries Islam was for the nobility a significant motivation for expanding political power. After Fatimah's grandfather had started his missionary activities at the beginning of this century, the local nobility of Kasepekang and adjacent regions adopted Islam. Islam spread through marriage alliances and other social strategies concerned with hierarchy and status mobility. However, the new faith was of only marginal significance for commoners, especially those in the highlands (Pelras 1981; Noorduyn 1956; Hamonic 1985).

These considerations also relate to the pilgrimage today. Fatimah's uncle is the son of the "founder of Islam" in the region and a man of great political influence. He is in close contact with the high nobility in Ujung Pandang, many of whom are also *haji*. The pilgrimage, then, was one of the few things still missing from this man's high-status portfolio. Status concerns seem to have influenced Fatimah's decision to make the pilgrimage as well. In 1993, whenever he visited Bontolowe, Fatimah's uncle spent the night in her house. Before their *hajj,* he would not even set foot in it.

In their efforts to mark off their superior position from commoners, it seems likely that the local nobility will continue to draw on Islamic symbols. The status of *haji* is the most effective such instrument since, for financial reasons, it is out of reach of most peasants. Traditionally Makassar nobles were distinguished by their habit of bearing two names, their clothing styles, houses, language patterns, kinship terminology, ritual celebrations, and even eating habits. Many of these features, however, no longer unambiguously mark noble status. No longer in a position simply to prohibit commoner imitations of noble symbols, the nobility cling to a cultural trait that still clearly distinguishes them from most commoners: Islam.

Though the cases presented here seem to suggest that Islam now challenges hierarchical social arrangements, I would suggest that this is not, in fact, the case. Identity is still closely tied to hierarchical thinking; only the empirical content of the ranking structure has been modified. Although it may appear that Islam and supralocal identity are changing societal structures, they apparently are not; they are only filling them with new meanings.

A final example may serve to illustrate this argument. In 1984, on the occasion of the feast of immolation *(îd al-qurbân)*, the feast requiring every pious Muslim to sacrifice an animal for the sake of God, six cows were donated for sacrifice. Since Islam demands that the meat be distributed among the poor and needy, the village chief and the imam had prepared a list of some fifty households to which meat portions should be given. However, not a single representative from these households appeared on the scene. For the leaders, the reason was evident. They knew that cultural values, in particular the concept of self-respect (Mk. *siri'*), made the distribution of the meat according to Islamic precept impossible. For a Makassar, accepting a donation of meat is to admit that one cannot afford its purchase, which is to lower one's position within the social hierarchy. Where continuous redefinitions of status constitute the most significant basis for social relations, notions deriving from an exogenous religious tradition may still seem inappropriate, despite the new religion's identification with modernity and progress. The meat was thus distributed among people whose status was not likely to be negatively affected: the wealthy, nobles, and resident anthropologists!

Conclusion

It has long been asked whether the diffusion of Islam to Southeast Asia or other parts of the world was in one way or another related to local societal structures (e.g., Ibn Khaldun 1967; Johns 1957; 1975; Robson 1981; Roff 1985, 20; cf. Turner 1974, 137–150). The arguments presented here suggest that people in the Gowa highlands were more passive "victims" than active agents in the face of Islamization. I am convinced that this is how the majority of the local population assess their recent history. With victims, social theorists expect to see evidence of some kind of resistance. Yet I am not sure whether emptying the mosque or refusing to contribute alms to officials can be labeled resistance in the strict sense of the term. People are ambivalent but rarely engage in overt resistance—much like the Malays described by Michael Peletz in this volume.

Yet, there are individuals who clearly benefit from presenting themselves as "better Muslims." Political changes during the last thirty years contributed to the increasing importance of official styles in religion. In addition, growing numbers of individuals use Islam to challenge traditional hierarchies. Typically they do so, however, without repudiating the principles underlying hierarchy itself. Such individuals are still few, but the fact that their discourse is positively sanctioned by the government gives them influence beyond their numbers.

From an analytic perspective, the process I have described here is a familiar but important one in situations of socioreligious transformation. Religious change is being determined by individual choice among divergent clusters of norms and values. That there is individual choice does not mean, of course, that the decisions individuals make are unaffected by local notions of hierarchy and social order. On the contrary, individual choice has always been deeply affected by the status order and the avenues for mobility it allows. To some degree, people could always compensate for low descent ranking through demonstrations of personal bravery, education, and religious knowledge. Now, the process of Islamization has added new norms and options, which people take into account in evaluating every individual's position within hierarchically structured networks of social relations (cf. Strathern 1985).

Certainly the assimilation of Islam into such small-scale communities affects and is affected by the complex relationships existing between the individual and his or her sociocultural environment. I argue that it takes place mainly through agents whose thoughts and actions are not only shaped by their cultural background, but who in the long run also shape and modify that wider cultural system, including local views of Islam. Such a concept of agency focuses not only on how individuals construct meanings out of specific social situations, but also on how the cultural system allocates capability for action.[24] Here in the highlands, agency is evident when an individual sees Islamic devotion as a strategy for achieving prestige or redefining his or her social position. This fact does not exclude the ability of religious ideas to motivate actors independently of social constraints; my experience with this society, however, indicates that the structural principles underlying these strategies are far more profoundly influenced by the rules and preoccupations of everyday life than by religious ideals alone.

These arguments should neither be misunderstood in the sense of postulating a generalized repertoire of communitywide shared knowledge, nor should they be seen as equating culture with clusters of norms and values. Norms and values, representing a specific, action-related aspect of culture, are primarily selected as regulative guidelines for action (cf. Schneider 1976, 202–203). They therefore represent an important feature of social life, stimulating and shaping empirical events. Aside from notions regulating action, however, culture implies above all knowledge and meaning. There is an ongoing debate about where "meaning" is to be found in culture and what it does: "Meanings represent the world, create cultural entities, direct one to do certain things, and evoke certain feelings" (D'Andrade 1984, 96). In this chapter, however, I have been particularly concerned with the constructive and the directive functions of cultural meanings. If the members of a society accept and appeal to specific meanings as directive guidelines for social action and for constructing new elements of culture, these meanings appear to be more than something static or definite that could be "simply internalized" (see Hefner 1985, 269). In the process of internalizing new cultural meanings, individual actors modify them by adding or removing something, while at the same time thinking and acting within the framework of their cultural knowledge. These considerations render labels such as "essentialist" or "universalist" Islam a fiction and instead direct attention to the strategies by which agents possessing varied interests and motivations both shape and are shaped by "received" and "local Islams" (Woodward 1988, 87–89).

Any discussion of world religion must go beyond local peculiarities, since it implies a range of concepts and meanings greater than those found in small-scale societies. I strongly agree with Dale Eickelman's proposal that the "middle ground" between the village context and that of the "Islam of all times and places" be taken as the basis for comprehending Islam as a world religious tradition. Yet it has also been stressed that the local form a world religion assumes may differ considerably from its wider normative structure (Eickelman 1982, 11; Bowen 1993, 4–8). I have tried to show that such differences result from complex constructions and transformations of meaning systems. These transformations are themselves consequences of the coincidences of cultural history, only some of which are empirically observable. I have suggested, then, that we can best understand this complex process from the perspective of the "folk tradition" in local context, even if, as we know, these constructions of local meaning systems also shape the "great tradition" of Islam or any other world religion (cf. Eickelman 1982).

In Bontolowe these individual strategies for reshaping identity have become increasingly linked to the larger society as a result of several historical processes. Incorporation into the kingdom of Gowa, colonization, administrative reforms, resettlement, and Islamization—all of these comprised an "opening" of the local social system in the face of which individual strategies were devised.

Let me provide a final illustration of this interaction of local contexts with supralocal religion. In this chapter I have for the most part avoided any direct discussion of ethnic identity because of the profound differences between the coastal Makassar and the mountain population. I noted that in this mountain region there was in premodern times no more encompassing notion of identity than that associated with small territorial units; after the incorporation of the region into the kingdom of Gowa, however, "to be a Makassar" for the local people also became significant. On the occasion of the ritual that was performed before Hasan's departure for Mecca in 1984, a *haji* originating from a village across the river valley narrated his experiences during the pilgrimage. He addressed his words to me, but the audience included many more people: "When I was in Mecca, there were many fellow Indonesians with me. One day a man from Java came up to me and said: 'You just made a mistake. What you just did was not in accordance with the precept *(aturan)* of the *hajj.'* I answered: 'Do you want to teach me Islam?' And then I thrashed him soundly. He was bleeding all over. That is how we *orang Makassar* deal with such folk. How can a Javanese *(orang Jawa)* dare to say that a Makassar *(orang Makassar)* does not know Islam?" The audience lauded his behavior. This story became extremely popular and was retold on numerous occasions during the weeks and months that followed. It was the only oral comment I ever heard linking Islamic identity to Makassar ethnicity.

Is it then possible to apply the concept of identity to a situation as complex as that I have described here? Or should we rather label the case an example of an "identity in between," an aggregate of continuously changing meaning systems on the level of both the individual and the group? Personal strategies for constructing identities are shaped by cultural meaning systems, but the latter are also primarily the products of individual thought and action. From a local social perspective, identity defined in terms of adherence to a world religion is an artifact deeply informed by local structures and opportunities. Admittedly, beyond this empirical reality, the identity of the Muslim community of the faithful *(umma)* also provides directive and evocative meanings. Below the surface, however, religious identity appears to consist of a conglomerate of meaning systems of more varied origins, continuously interpreted and reconstructed by individual agents—with much the same evocative complexity as the concept of nation (Foster 1991). It is this characteristic of cultural meaning, and in particular the complex ties linking individual action to the cultural whole, that makes identity one of the most dynamic aspects of human existence and makes processes of Islamization in contemporary Sulawesi so richly complex.

Notes

I would like to thank Robert Hefner, Patricia Horvatich, and Anthony Johns for their helpful critical comments on the original version of this chapter. I am also grateful to Cynthia Bunker for putting the text into readable English and to Birgitt Röttger-Rössler, who contributed information from her own research from 1984 until 1993. Finally, I wish to dedicate this contribution to our little daughter Maren, who (I am sure) understands much of Islam and identity in Bontolowe. Fieldwork in situ was conducted under the auspices of the Indonesian Institute of Sciences (LIPI) and in collaboration with my wife, Birgitt Röttger-Rössler, for twenty-four months between April 1984 and July 1991. It was sponsored by Universitas Hasanuddin in Ujung Pandang and (in 1990–1991) funded by the Deutsche Forschungsgemeinschaft. The names of persons and localities in the area under investigation have been replaced by pseudonyms. The following abbreviations are used for foreign languages: Ar. = Arabic; Ind. = Indonesian; Mk. = Makassar.

1. Islam is the dominant world religion (besides Catholicism, Protestanism, Hinduism, and Buddhism) in Indonesia; Indonesian Muslims are the world's largest national community of Muslims.

2. Translating the local terms for administrative units below the regency poses some difficulty, since many terminological changes have occurred since colonial times. *"Kecamatan"* is here translated by "district" and *"desa,"* which largely coincided with what were "districts" until 1960, by "subdistrict." In contrast, a "village" is what in Indonesian is referred to as *"kampung,"* a settlement or a cluster of houses.

3. See Mattulada 1976, 55. These circumstances also resulted in the fact that the Muhammadiyah's influence was not strongest in the political centers—the town of Makassar and Gowa's capital Sungguminasa—but rather in the southern lowlands of Bontonompo and Limbung. Even today these areas are considered strongholds of the Muhammadiyah.

4. In some neighboring regions, Islam was spread—often by force—some decades earlier by the king of Gowa (Pénard 1913, 517; cf. Nooteboom 1947, 91).

5. Further information on some basic principles of the local social and political organization will be given below.

6. In the southern coastal regions such as Takalar and Jeneponto, most of the sacred places were not restored, because there the Muhammadiyah continued to be influential (see Muchson 1983, 28).

7. *"Daeng"* is in this context the Makassar equivalent of Indonesian *"pak"* ("father," "Mr."). Otherwise this word (literally meaning "elder brother or sister") indicates noble rank in that it links the personal name to the second name, the *pa'daengang,* which is usually taken from an ancestor (e.g., Suleiman Daeng Bunding). According to tradition, commoners are not allowed to bear two names (see below).

8. The children are trained to read Arabic script by means of a system adopted from the Bugis language (which is said to be easier and more convenient than the Makassar system), adjusting the sounds to local phonology and learning to pronounce words by "analyzing" the Arabic letters and then combining them (see also Mattulada 1977, 31).

9. While both regions were annexed by the kingdom of Gowa in the sixteenth

century, the influence of the "palace culture" of its power center (located on the western coast of the peninsula) on the culture of Kajang was comparatively weak, since it was temporally confined to some decades (Rössler 1990).

10. The nobility as a general rule strongly oppose the use of this title among commoners.

11. It is stressed by the people of Bontolowe, for example, that during such rituals, only they are allowed to cover their dishes, which is again a symbol of high rank. Though no one could ever explain the origins of this tradition, I heard it again and again, and it was always pointed out that this was one of the most significant markers of identity for the *"tu Bulo."*

12. Pelenkahu et al. (1971), mainly on the grounds of linguistic criteria, regard mountain Makassar as something like an archaic substratum of Makassar culture. They also refer to physical differences with lowland Makassar, which they explain in terms of the long period of isolation of the groups living in the mountain regions. That the indigenous belief system in the mountain regions differed from the one prevailing among the coastal Makassar was noted decades ago by Eerdmans (1897, 33), Kruyt (1906, 401), Pénard (1913), and Cense (1931).

13. Because of lack of space, only some very short remarks on this significant aspect of sociopolitical organization can be made. For a detailed decription, see Rössler 1987 and in press.

14. The only case of "running up to the blade" I was ever told of was that of Nawa's mother. In most cases the bride price is paid after a couple of years.

15. My argument is strongly supported by the results of a card sorting test that Birgitt Röttger-Rössler administered in 1984 in order to learn about indigenous principles of social ranking. While all other informants arranged 160 cards containing the names of villagers in an identical order, Nasir's order alone was different.

16. According to the Shafi'ite school (the dominant *madhhab* [Ar.] in Indonesia; see Juynboll 1903), there is no difference with regard to the categories of people to whom *zakât al-fitr* or, respectively, *zakât* are given. While these categories are in fact formulated in great detail (see Farah 1968, 142; Rasjid 1954, 209), the villagers distinguish only between the poor and needy (Ar. *fuqarâ'*; *masâkîn*), on the one hand, and the officials who collected the *zakât al-fitr,* on the other.

17. There is no principal correlation between wealth and social rank or status (see also Röttger-Rössler 1989). What is meant here is that poorer households cannot afford to prepare enough food for many visitors, while low-status households do not expect to be visited by many people, in particular not by people of higher social status.

18. In 1991 the minimum ("low-budget") cost for the pilgrimage from Indonesia amounted to six million rupiah (about U.S.$3,200 in 1991), not including extra expenses. This sum has to be compared with the average monthly income of 114,000 rupiah per household in the village or, more appropriately,

with the average monthly "surplus" of 45,000 rupiah (about U.S.$24). These statistical data, however, disguise the fact that most households do not produce a surplus at all and that income is unevenly distributed over the year in an agricultural subsistence economy.

19. Recitations are extended to the fortieth (instead of the twentieth) night only for wealthy people, because to do otherwise would double the expenses of feeding dozens to hundreds of guests every night. A family does not even extend the recitations beyond the seventh night if the deceased person was not a member of an *adat* descent group. In this context, too, Islamic ritual is closely tied to indigenous patterns of social ranking.

20. The *gallarang* originally represented a sort of executive force of the village government, since the *karaeng* himself was not allowed to speak in public. The *baku'* is the highest authority for all that concerns organizing communitywide rituals, succession to traditional offices, and membership in the community in general.

21. Both *lannying* and *tangkasa'* (Mk.) literally mean "pure," but while the first term means "pure" in the sense of "holy," *tangkasa'* has a negative connotation: "pure because there is nothing left."

22. I obtained this information during my work on indigenous criteria for the definition of wealth, when I asked informants to rank several items such as, among others, land property, gold, motorbikes, and the *hajj* as indicators of "rich people."

23. It is considered a "wrong marriage" (Mk. *sala pa'bunting*) if a woman—in particular one of noble descent—is married to a man as his second wife. By such an affair the woman's whole family loses their self-respect (Mk. *siri'*). There are only three nobles living in Bontolowe, because in each of the former principalities most members of the nobility lived in one specific village, so that they were also spatially separated from the majority of commoners.

24. Strathern provides an overview of how the term "agency" has recently been used in anthropology (1987, 22–25).

References Cited

Abd. Rahman L. 1982. "Tinjauan Terhadap Tarekat Barakka Balassuka dan Barakka Bontolebang di Kecamatan Tinggimoncong" (An Analysis of the Barakka Balassuka and Bontolebang Tarekat Orders in the District). Sarjana thesis, IAIN, Ujung Pandang.

Abu Hamid. 1978. *Sistim Pendidikan Madrasah dan Pesantren di Sulawesi Selatan* (The *Madrasah* and *Pesantren* Educational System in South Sulawesi). Ujung Pandang: Universitas Hasanuddin.

Acciaioli, Gregory. 1985. "Culture as Art: From Practice to Spectacle in Indonesia." *Canberra Anthropology* 8: (1–2): 148–172.

Andaya, Leonard Y. 1981. *The Heritage of Arung Palakka: A History of South Sulawesi (Celebes) in the Seventeenth Century.* The Hague: Martinus Nijhoff.

Atkinson, Jane Monnig. 1983. "Religions in Dialogue: The Construction of an Indonesian Minority Religion." *American Ethnologist* 10:684–696.

Boland, B. J. 1982. *The Struggle of Islam in Modern Indonesia.* The Hague: Martinus Nijhoff.

Bowen, John R. 1989. "Salât in Indonesia: The Social Meanings of an Islamic Ritual." *Man* (n.s.), 24:600–619.

———. 1992. "On Scriptural Essentialism and Ritual Variation: Muslim Sacrifice in Sumatra and Morocco." *American Ethnologist* 19:656–671.

———. 1993. *Muslims through Discourse: Religion and Ritual in Gayo Society.* Princeton: Princeton University Press.

Cederroth, Sven. 1981. *The Spell of the Ancestors and the Power of Mekkah: A Sasak Community on Lombok.* Gothenburg: Acta Universitatis Gothoburgensis.

Cense, A. A. 1931. "De patoentoengs in het bergland van Kadjang." Unpublished manuscript, Royal Institute of Linguistics and Anthropology, Leiden.

Chabot, Hendrik Th. 1950. *Verwantschap, stand en sexe in Zuid-Celebes.* Groningen/Jakarta: Wolters.

Comaroff, John L. 1987. "Of Totemism and Ethnicity: Consciousness, Practice and the Signs of Inequality." *Ethnos* 52 (3–4): 301–323.

D'Andrade, Roy G. 1984. "Cultural Meaning Systems." In R. A. Shweder and R. A. LeVine, eds., *Culture Theory: Essays on Mind, Self, and Emotion*, pp. 88–119. Cambridge: Cambridge University Press.

Dijk, Cees van. 1981. *Rebellion under the Banner of Islam; The Darul Islam in Indonesia.* The Hague: Martinus Nijhoff.

Eerdmans, A. J. A. F. 1897. "Het landschap Gowa." *Verhandelingen van het Bataviaasch Genootschap van Kunsten en Wetenschappen* 50 (3): 1–77.

Eickelman, Dale F. 1982. "The Study of Islam in Local Contexts." *Contributions to Asian Studies* 17:1–16.

———. 1987. "Changing Interpretations of Islamic Movements." In W. R. Roff, ed., *Islam and the Political Economy of Meaning: Comparative Studies of Muslim Discourse*, pp. 13–30. Berkeley and Los Angeles: University of California Press.

Ellen, Roy F. 1983. "Social Theory, Ethnography and the Understanding of Practical Islam in South-East Asia." In M. B. Hooker, ed., *Islam in South-East Asia*, pp. 50–91. Leiden: Brill.

Farah, Caesar E. 1968. *Islam: Beliefs and Observances.* New York: Free Press.

Foster, Robert J. 1991. "Making National Cultures in the Global Ecumene." *Annual Review of Anthropology* 20:235–260.

Geertz, Clifford. 1960. *The Religion of Java.* New York: The Free Press.

Gervaise, Nicolas. 1701. *A Historical Description of the Kingdom of Macasar in the East-Indies.* London. Orig. *Description historique du royaume de Macaçar.* Paris, 1688.

Hamonic, Gilbert. 1985. "La fête du grand maulid à Cikoang: Regard sur une tarekat dite 'shi'ite' en Pays Makassar." *Archipel* 29:175–191.

Harvey, Barbara S. 1974. "Tradition, Islam, and Rebellion: South Sulawesi, 1950–1965." Ph.D. dissertation, Cornell University.

———. 1977. "Darul Islam in South Sulawesi: Hutan against Kota." *Majalah Universitas Hasanuddin* 8/18 (Jan./Feb.): 10–26.

Hefner, Robert W. 1985. *Hindu Javanese: Tengger Tradition and Islam*. Princeton: Princeton University Press.

———. 1990. *The Political Economy of Mountain Java: An Interpretive History*. Berkeley and Los Angeles: University of California Press.

Ibn Khaldûn. 1967 [1377]. *The Muqaddimah: An Introduction to History*. London: Routledge and Kegan Paul.

Johns, Anthony H. 1957. "Malay Sufism, as Illustrated in an Anonymous Collection of Seventeenth-Century Tracts." *Journal of the Malayan Branch of the Royal Asiatic Society* 3 (2): 1–110.

———. 1975. "Islam in Southeast Asia: Reflections and New Directions." *Indonesia* 19:33–55.

Juynboll, Th. W. 1903. *Handleiding tot de kennis van de Mohammedaansche wet volgens de leer der Sjafi'itische school*. Leiden: Brill.

Kruyt, Alb. C. 1906. *Het Animisme in den Indischen Archipel*. The Hague: Martinus Nijhoff.

Kumar, Ann. 1979. "Developments in Four Societies over the Sixteenth to Eighteenth Centuries." In H. Aveling, ed., *The Development of Indonesian Society: From the Coming of Islam to the Present Day*, pp. 1–44. St. Lucia: University of Queensland Press.

LaSide' Daeng Tapala. 1975. "L'expansion du royaume de Goa et sa politique maritime aux XVIè et XVIIè siècles." *Archipel* 10:159–171.

Launay, Robert. 1992. *Beyond the Stream: Islam and Society in a West African Town*. Berkeley and Los Angeles: University of California Press.

Leur, J. C. van. 1955. "On Early Asian Trade." In *Indonesian Trade and Society: Essays in Asian Social and Economic History*, pp. 1–144. The Hague: van Hoeve.

Lombard, Denys. 1985. "L'horizon insulindien et son importance pour une compréhension globale de l'Islam." *Archipel* 29 (1): 35–52.

Mattulada. 1976. *Islam di Sulawesi Selatan*. Jakarta: LEKNAS/LIPI.

———. 1977. "Pengaruh Ulama dan Sistem Pendidikan Agama (Islam) dalam Rumah-Tangga Orang Bugis-Makassar di Sulawesi Sealatan" (Ulama Influence and Islamic Education in Bugis-Makassar Households in Southern Sulawesi). Unpublished research report, Universitas Hasanuddin, Ujung Pandang.

———. 1988. "Kebudayaan Bugis-Makassar" (Bugis-Makassar Culture). In Koentjaraningrat, ed., *Manusia dan Kebudayaan di Indonesia* (Humanity and Culture in Indonesia), pp. 266–285. Jakarta: Penerbit Djambatan.

Muchson. 1983. "Madrasah: Kerakap di Atas Batu" (*Madrasah*: Betel Leaf over Rock). Unpublished research report, Pusat Latihan Ilmu-Ilmu Sosial, Ujung Pandang.

Muhammad Ali, M. 1983. *A Manual of Hadith*. London: Curzon Press.

Noorduyn, J. 1956. "De Islamisering van Makasar." *Bijdragen tot de Taal-, Land- en Volkenkunde* 112:247–266.

———. 1987. "Makasar and the Islamization of Bima." *Bijdragen tot de Taal-, Land- en Volkenkunde* 143:312–342.

Nooteboom, C. 1947. "Tondongkoera: Een bergdorp in Zuidwest-Celebes." *Bijdragen tot de Taal-, Land- en Volkenkunde* 104:89–102.

Peacock, James L. 1978. *Muslim Puritans: Reformist Psychology in Southeast Asian Islam.* Berkeley and Los Angeles: University of California Press.

Pelenkahu, R. A., et al. 1971. "Dialek Kondjo di Sulawesi Selatan" (The Kondjo Dialect in South Sulawesi). Unpublished research report, Lembaga Bahasa Nasional Tjabang III, Ujung Pandang.

Pelras, Christian. 1977. "Culture, ethnie, espace social: Quelques réflexions autour du cas Bugis." *Asie du Sud-Est et du Monde Insulindien* 8 (2): 57–79.

———. 1981. "Célèbes-Sud avant l'Islam, selon les premiers témoignages étrangers." *Archipel* 21:153–184.

———. 1985. "Religion, Tradition, and the Dynamics of Islamization in South Sulawesi." *Archipel* 29 (1): 107–135.

Pénard, W. A. 1913. "De patoentoeng." *Tijdschrift voor Indische Taal-, Land- en Volkenkunde* 55:515–543.

Prins, Jan. 1948. *Adat en Islamietische plichtenleer in Indonesië.* The Hague: van Hoeve.

Rasjid, H. Sulaiman. 1954. *Fiqh Islam: Hukum Fiqh Lengkap* (Islamic Figh: Complete Figh Law). Jakarta: Penerbit Attahiriyah.

Renre, Abdullah. 1978. "Patuntung di Kecamatan Sinjai Barat" (Patuntung in West Sinjai District). Sarjana thesis, IAIN, Ujung Pandang.

Robson, S. O. 1981. "Java at the Crossroads: Aspects of Javanese Cultural History in the 14th and 15th Centuries." *Bijdragen tot de Taal-, Land- en Volkenkunde* 137:259–292.

Rössler, Martin. 1987. *Die soziale Realität des Rituals: Kontinuität und Wandel bei den Makassar von Gowa (Süd-Sulawesi/Indonesien).* Berlin: Reimer.

———. 1990. "Striving for Modesty: Fundamentals of the Religion and Social Organization among the Makassarese Patuntung." *Bijdragen tot de Taal-, Land- en Volkenkunde* 146 (2–3): 289–324.

———. In press. "From Divine Descent to Administration: Sacred Heirlooms and Political Change in Highland Gowa." Forthcoming in G. Acciaioli and C. van Dijk, eds., *Authority and Leadership in South Sulawesi.* Leiden: KITLV Press.

Röttger-Rössler, Birgitt. 1989. *Rang und Ansehen bei den Makassar von Gowa (Süd-Sulawesi/Indonesien).* Berlin: Reimer.

———. 1994. "Fatimahs Weg nach oben: Der Prozeß vertikaler Mobilität und kulturellen Wandels am Beispiel einer Lebensgeschichte." *Zeitschrift für Ethnologie* 119:229–248.

Roff, William R. 1985. "Islam Obscured? Some Reflections on Studies of Islam and Society in Southeast Asia." *Archipel* 29:7–34.

Safwan, Mardanas, and Sutrisno Kutoyo, eds., 1980–1981. *Sejarah Pendidikan daerah Sulawesi Selatan* (A History of Education in South Sulawesi). Jakarta: Departemen Pendidikan dan Kebudayaan.

Schneider, David M. 1976. "Notes toward a Theory of Culture." In K. Basso and H. A. Selby, eds., *Meaning in Anthropology,* pp. 197–220. Albuquerque: University of New Mexico Press.

Snouck Hurgronje, C. 1893–1895. *De Atjèhers.* 3 vols. Leiden: Brill.

Strathern, Marilyn. 1985. "Knowing Power and Being Equivocal: Three Melanesian Contexts." In R. Fardon, ed., *Power and Knowledge: Anthropological and Sociological Approaches,* pp. 1–81. Edinburgh: Scottish Academic Press.

———. 1987. "Introduction." In M. Strathern, ed., *Dealing with Inequality: Analysing Gender Relations in Melanesia and Beyond,* pp. 1–32. Cambridge: Cambridge University Press.

Turner, Bryan S. 1974. *Weber and Islam: A Critical Study.* London: Routledge & Kegan Paul.

Usop, Kma M. 1978. "Pasang ri Kajang; Kajian Sistem Nilai di 'Benteng Hitam' Amma Toa" (Pasang ri Kajang: A Study of The Value System in Amma Toa). Unpublished research report, Pusat Latihan Ilmu-Ilmu Sosial, Ujung Pandang.

Woodward, Mark R. 1988. "The Slametan: Textual Knowledge and Ritual Performance in Central Javanese Islam." *History of Religions* 28 (1): 54–89.

———. 1989. *Islam in Java: Normative Piety and Mysticism in the Sultanate of Yogyakarta.* Tucson: University of Arizona Press.

Afterword

Chapter 10

Islam in Contemporary Southeast Asia

HISTORY, COMMUNITY, MORALITY

Barbara D. Metcalf

The broad themes that resonate throughout this collection are ones shared by many societies in recent times. They reflect the extent to which religious symbols and issues have come to the fore in public life and provide a language for issues of citizenship, ethnicity, shared histories, and morality. Thus, even what might be thought to be intimate issues of family ceremony or dress may now be linked to corporate issues of community and political orientation. If we look for "Islam" in the late twentieth century, one arena of central importance turns out to be the institutions of the nation-state. The meaning of being "Muslim" in that sense, as the marker of a citizen or of a politicized ethnic group, is profoundly new. And just as many of the specifics of the debates described in this volume are much the same as those conducted by Muslims elsewhere, the kinds of issues engaged in these debates are ones shared by modern societies everywhere.

This argument stands in marked contrast to what is perhaps the characteristic Western interpretation of Islam in public life. That interpretation insists above all on quintessential difference and continuity, failing to recognize what is new in the meaning and deployment of Islamic symbols and failing to recognize what is shared. In that regard, Dale Eickelman's (1992) argument recognizing the modernity of the very concept of "the Islamic state" is particularly important. Europeans and Americans on the whole have a blind spot in relation to Islam and tend to posit it as a retrograde, oppressive, and anarchic threat. The essays in this volume belie that interpretation and, far from suggesting that Southeast Asia is unique ("not really Muslim"), should encourage us to rethink our approach to Islamic societies overall.

In the American case, a distorted view of Islam continues to be a serious handicap to a rational Middle Eastern policy. Nor is this interpretation only Western: there are Indians who justify the virulent anti-Muslim behavior in their country in terms of the great danger of worldwide Islamic "fundamentalism" from Israel to India itself. The essays in this volume provide lines of analysis that challenge the interpretation of a frightening, mono-lithic Islam, ones that are relevant to Muslim societies generally, not only to Southeast Asia. They encourage us to ask two sets of questions: How and in what settings is an Islamic language deployed? And is "Islam" in fact different from other historic religious traditions?

At first blush, the chapters seem to fit into the narrative of Islamic power and difference, many structured around themes of Islamic "resurgence," "reactualization," "renewal," and so forth. In each of the countries studied, the Philippines, Malaysia, and Indonesia—whether the Muslim population is 5 percent, 52 percent, or 90 percent of the whole—the story in the last two decades seems broadly the same. In each case, states or provinces have increasingly supported Islamic programs in such arenas as law and economics; individuals increasingly demonstrate public behavior marked as Islamic in behavior and dress; and Islamic organizations directed to politics, social welfare, and preaching seem to proliferate. One might well conclude that these changes demonstrate an Islamic identity and power long waiting to emerge. But by examining these changes in detail we learn, on the one hand, of the historical shallowness of politicized Islamic communities and, on the other, of the complexity and, indeed, often the familiarity of the social and ideological projects—not reducible to state terrorism or "jihad"—in which Islamic symbols find expression.

Narrating Histories

Nothing makes clearer the power of the historical myths that shape political loyalties than the fact that they are taken as natural and prima facie factual. Histories are at the core of nation-state identities and form a major strand in constructing, sustaining, and contesting those identities. Benedict Anderson has pointed to the essential irony in these stories: they are new in modern times but they must be told as if they were very old (Anderson 1983). In these stories a religion may even be equated with citizenship itself.

To cite a comparative case, India is particularly striking in the extent to which a historical myth, its fundamental lines evolved during the colonial period, has come to the fore in public life. In that story, part of virtually everyone's "common sense," "Muslims" and "Hindus" are taken as the significant markers of identity throughout the long period of the past thousand or so years. "Muslims" are "foreigners," who "penetrate" and "invade," and their monuments are deemed an extrusion symbolizing the shame of invasion. Forgotten are the pluralism and fuzziness of earlier societies, the shifting boundaries of cultural regions that render problematic notions like "foreign," the presence of Muslims in the subcontinent from roughly the same period as other migrants/invaders from what is now outside India, the shifting alliances defined not by religion but by interest, and the intermarriage and conversion that make it impossible to equate genes and culture. The British first told the story of two communities and foreign invasion as they constructed a history of "India" and justified their place in it; nationalists in turn utilized the story to explain cultural decline and to claim nationhood (Irschick 1994).

History has since become a basis for political argumentation on moral grounds by making "original" occupation (already problematic, as noted above) a justification for entitlements and rights. Against this basis, other arguments that ignore this "history"—current legal claims, the social good, justice, archeological conservation—have little play. The story ceased to be abstract on December 6, 1992, when Hindu nationalists destroyed the sixteenth-century mosque at Ayodhya and justified their action, and even the anti-Muslim violence that followed, as necessary to restore the pristine cultural shape of the nation as a whole (Gopal 1991; van der Veer 1994).

In Southeast Asia, particularly in Malaya and the Philippines, colonizers and colonized have told similar stories in which "Muslims" as a historically continuous community have played a part. The chapters on the Philippines richly illustrate the modernity, "inventedness," and utility to ethnic and national projects of this kind of linear narrative. Thomas McKenna convincingly argues that the notion of a coherent Muslim identity, forged in religious wars with Spain, contravenes substantial evidence of long periods of peace, of the lack of an *ulama* class ranged against the Spanish, and of intersultanate rivalry that meant frequent alliances on the part of the sultanates with Spain. Instead, the colonial power, in this case the United States, saw a coherent "Moro" identity—assumed on Orientalist grounds to be of necessity embryonic and only needing encouragement —as a fundamental fact of Filipino history and sought to use it as the foundation for democratic participation.

It is modern education and the opportunities of modern politics, not atavistic religious antagonism, that forge a Muslim identity, at least among certain elites, in the colonial and postcolonial state. Despite an officially secular school policy, we hear of Carpenter (governor of Mindanao/Sulu, 1914–1920) wanting to educate Muslims "in the positive aspects" of their religion and Kuder (a superintendent of schools, 1924–1941) again pushing education and links to cultural artifacts like the *Arabian Nights* so that students in colleges come to see themselves as "Mohammedan Filipinos." Boundaries are drawn to create an area with "Moro" courts and a Moro municipality. With independence, Muslim leaders focus on "rationalized emblems of a single Muslim ethnic identity," as McKenna puts it, as a way to project Muslim power; and, whether as politicians or as rebels, they deploy the heretofore pejorative Spanish label "Moro," a label Patricia Horvatich (n.d.) shows to be largely irrelevant to ordinary Muslims in everyday life.

Thus Muslim politicians and civil servants and, after 1972, rival elites give legitimacy to their claims for political clout or autonomy by reading back into history a solidarity only now, haltingly, having any meaning at all. Even today, according to Horvatich (n.d.), a Maranao, a fellow Muslim Filipino, is as foreign and frightening to a Sama as is a Christian Filipino. Sama depend on the Filipino state to protect their interests against the long-dominant Muslim Tausug. Yet Muslim politicians claim a primordial, essential Muslim nation, even as they contend with the claims of Filipino nationalists who counter with an equally primordial, pre-Christian and pre-Muslim, identity that they call on "backward" Muslims to embrace.

Although only alluded to in the essays in this volume, Malay history bears much the same burden of reified communities and the moral claims of presumed prior residence of Malays, in contrast to putative immigrants, who bear the further taint of colonial association. "Malays" are homogenized and elevated to privilege by their status as "sons of the soil." A Sumatran who arrived yesterday achieves that distinction. A Chinese whose ancestors came five hundred years back is a mere migrant.

These narratives set the framework for defining the nations in which Islamic symbols, institutions, and communities have become so significant. Even in Indonesia, whose national myths typically allowed for more pluralism, an Islamic discourse and Islamic programs have in the past two decades increasingly come to the fore.

National Politics

In each of these settings, underpinned to varying degrees by historical stories of primordial community, there has been a move from "vertical" identifications as subjects of patrons and notables to "horizontal" ethno-religious community (cf. Anderson 1983). Roy Ellen, speaking of Malaya, called precolonial Islam an "idiomatic convenience" deployed, for example, in festivals used to reaffirm loyalty to chiefs (Ellen 1983, 74). In the Indian case, the Mughal Empire, far from being an "Islamic state," operated like other early modern polities on the fundamentally secular basis of loyalty. Only if a non-Muslim went into opposition would he be signaled as a *kafir*; and Muslim as well as non-Muslim opponents in warfare would be subject to *jihad* (Eaton 1994).

The settings conducive to moving from this kind of sociopolitical organization to a pattern of religiously defined community identity are those of modernity: the colonial state, the nationalist movements, the ethnic competition characteristic of interest competition in nation-states with limited resources, and the cultural bonds forged in transnational flows of education, travel, personnel, and resources. Although some chapters in this volume treat the deeply important colonial context as laying the foundation for the new religious communities, most focus on the frameworks offered by the contemporary states that provide a context and even support for the new ethnicities.

That these Islamic movements and identities flourish in modern social contexts is suggested by the importance of educational centers, including international centers, for fostering a self-conscious Islamic religious style (Eickelman 1993). It is in colleges in the Philippines that young men come to think of themselves as Muslim Filipinos. Nur Misuari got his start through a university scholarship, and the public school supervisor, Haji Hussein, spread the teaching of the Ahmadiyya movement to receptive teachers in Tawi-Tawi. It is at al-Azhar, in the 1960s and after, that a new Filipino clerical class is forged with a vision of Islamic reform. In Malaysia, higher education not only provides the context in which modern Muslim identity is forged, but, as Shamsul A. B. shows, the academic discipline pursued actually influences individuals' response (moderate or radical) to the *dakwah* movement. The dominant figures in Islamic intellectual circles in Indonesia all seem to have U.S. advanced degrees. Beyond travel for education, we hear of travel for work to Sabah and the Middle East, and travel for pilgrimage and business. While the setting for Islamic reform and ethnicization is the nation-state, what happens in the nation-state is profoundly influenced by what happens outside its borders.

As significant as the newness of these communities is the fact that the bonds may be as much ethnic as Islamic. Here too the Philippines serves as a useful example, since the "Moro" rebellion was initially driven by a nationalist/regional program, not an Islamic program, at the elite level and by bonds of kin and community at an individual level. Outsiders may often impute a religious program—the genesis of Pakistan is a good example—when in fact goals are primarily the political interests of those who happen to be Muslim.

All three states, Malaysia, the Philippines, and Indonesia, have seen their interests bound up in patronizing and controlling expressions of Islam. Malaysia, as Clive Kessler has argued (1993), may be "secular" at the federal level, but it contains a system where provinces may well be engaged in religious activities, and, at the central level as well, there have been recent initiatives in support of an Islamic university, Islamic economics, Islamic courts, and a civil law that "implicates" *shari'ah* at the expense of a shared "life world" for all Malaysians. In the Philippines a 1976 settlement brought federal support for Muslim personal law, Islamic banking, and even a mosque built by patronage from Marcos himself. In Indonesia, after what appeared to be suppression of Islamic symbols in the first decade of the New Order, there have now been a range of initiatives supporting Islamic practices, restricting Christian missionaries, building mosques and *madrasah*s, and identifying state officials with voluntary Islamic organizations.

There has been in each state a kind of homogenizing of what is defined as Islamic, rather like what Romila Thapar has spoken of as "syndicated Hinduism" in the Indian case (Thapar 1985). In both cases, the "flattening" of local and sectarian differences is intimately linked to the project of forging a national culture. In this respect, the quotation from Wilkinson (1906) that Michael Peletz cites—"The native . . . is becoming less of a Malay and more of a Mussulman . . . his racial laws are being set aside. . . . His allegiance is being gradually transferred from national to Pan-Islamic ideals"— is, in fact, quite wrong, for the process has turned out to be the invention of the Malay "Mussulman" race as metonym precisely for the nation.

An Islamic discourse has come to dominate public space so that resistance, as Peletz argues for Malaysia, becomes the morally ambiguous resistance to Islam itself. In this Malaysia would appear to resemble Pakistan in the period inaugurated by Zia ul Haq in 1977, when all participants in public life had to embrace an Islamic vocabulary lest they be charged with opposing Islam (Metcalf 1987). In the cases described by Peletz, it would appear that people come to associate Islam with state control, tainted by U.S. government support, intruding into intimate dimensions of individual lives, including family law, surveys of economic transactions, limits on women's dress, imposition of corporal punishment, and restrictions on local customs. Martin Rössler's village-level study in Indonesia seems much the same: villagers empty the mosque when an official enjoins Ramadan attendance, and everyone resists turning over the *îd al-fitr* offerings to officials. Islamic movements, like Nahdlatul Ulama in Indonesia, that disassociate themselves from formal participation in government thus remove themselves from association with distasteful state control.

A corollary to state use and "syndication" of Islam would appear to be the traditionalizing and encapsulating of local cultural forms. *Wayang* produced in hotels and theaters, described as the embodiment of "tradition," or, in Whalley's example (1993), Minang clothes regarded as "ethnic dress" worn on special occasions, are no longer culturally central except as a necessary foil to "modernity," here in the form of "Islamic modernity."

In the case of Indonesia, it would appear that the withdrawal of organizations from active politics or the creation of new organizations with "constructive" rather than political programs has made it possible for Islamic activities and ideologies to flourish without the taint—though the tension is always there—of undue association with the state, its at least potential oppression, and its apparently inevitable corruption. Andrée Feillard argues that by this disassociation with politics since 1984, Nahdlatul Ulama has gained considerable legitimacy, proliferating organizations for women and youth, serving as a moral force to shape government policy, and stimulating Islamic change at the local level ("more mosques, fewer dogs"). Robert Hefner similarly charts the influence of ICMI, the new Association of Indonesian Muslim Intellectuals (1990), which declares itself apart from politics even while involving government figures in the quest to capture the moral imagination of the urban middle class living in a context of rapid economic change and polarization and the spread of consumer culture. It is in the context of this activity that the Indonesian state, whatever its Pancasila rhetoric, has successfully identified itself with a range of Islamic symbols and institutions.

If these Muslim communities are new, so too are the other identities, national and local, with which they interact. Patricia Horvatich has underlined how being Sama must not be understood to be the old, primal identity but is itself the result of active fostering—drawing boundaries, writing books, staging performance, creating university study programs—in the context of economic and political rivalries within the nation-state. The contested statement "I was a Malay before I was a Muslim," described by Kessler (1993), recalls another widely quoted statement by a Pakistani politician, "I am a six thousand years old Pushtoon—a thousand year old Musalman, and a twenty-seven year old Pakistani."[1] The truth is that, as markers of politicized communities, all these terms are equally new.

Moral Communities

Both the activist movements and the nation-states they operate in are engaged in defining the principles of behavior, law, and morality that guide everyday life. Overall there has been an increasing utilization of Islamic idioms within the institutional structure of the nation-states coupled with a transition within the society to more self-conscious scrutiny of what are taken to be normative Islamic practices.

In part this transition is linked to greater mobility and sociopolitical integration within a society as a whole. Put simply, there are a range of practices engaged in uncritically that serve to structure rural society: patterns of feasting and reciprocity that define social relations among the living and the dead. These practices are "Muslim" in that Muslims engage in them and may, in an unsystematic, even unself-conscious way, see them as conducive to sustaining the moral community. In contrast are a range of practices that are anything but unself-conscious: they are measured against rationalized principles of what is taken to be "Islam" properly understood. Those who identify with these "reformist" principles may often be people engaged in larger social arenas. In John Bowen's Gayo setting, those who espoused these principles as early as the 1930s typically were engaged in commerce, lived in multiethnic settings, and were fluent in the language that was coming to be called "Indonesian." Both systems can be seen as underpinned by values, even Muslim values. Both offer status and prestige in one setting but not the other.

The new values were defended, in a characteristically Islamic style but not by a defense of "Islam" as such—that comes later. Rather, arguments were conducted at a more fine-grained level. Thus, to take John Bowen's issue of *ushalli,* the objection might be that "it is against the *shari'ah* to make requisite that which is optional." The objection to feasting or *wayang* might be "it is against the *shari'ah* to waste money," "to go into debt unnecessarily," "to create a venue where men and women mix inappropriately," "to absorb people in activities that distract them from required worship," and so forth. This goal of such critical weighing, in which the issue of acting always out of good intent *(ikhlas)* and obedience, and not out of self-interest in any sense, including the pursuit of a good reputation based on following old customs, is to foster a religion of individual responsibility and "portability" delinked from local bonds of time, place, and ritual specialists. This process and the modes of argumentation are ones that cut across Muslim societies.

Muslim religious styles may seem to vary infinitely, but there are shared languages, institutions, and approaches that some members of societies may share across wide geographical boundaries at any given time. This style of *shari'ah*-based reasoning is certainly one, and may not be as specific to Gayo, for example, as it seems. Thus, the Fatiha for the dead, with accompanying food, in the Indic context is subject to much the range of interpretation as death ceremonies in Gayo. Critics will insist that it is an attempt to reach the dead, to bring them their favorite foods, or, in the case of powerful figures, an effort to win their goodwill and intervention in worldly needs, all this in ways that risk the worship owed to God alone. Those committed to the practice might insist on normatively acceptable arguments: that the Fatiha merely seeks intercession with God who is alone powerful or that it is the recitation of sacred texts whose merit accrues only to the reciter, and so forth. In the course of contention, the meaning and moral underpinnings of customary practices also change (Metcalf 1990).

The issue of the salience of social context for different religious values is nicely illustrated in Martin Rössler's vignette of the funeral of the sister of Banci, the former traditional priest who by 1991 had become involved in the "new Islam," which the local imam insisted was inappropriate in the village and belonged in the towns. Banci, it turned out, had been influenced by his own town-based brother, and, while he managed to conduct the funeral as he wished, other relatives, for whom such behavior threatened their values and networks, performed the traditional rituals secretly. Adherence to normative practices can also be a route to social mobility when those practices are associated with the pious and the well-born. Correct practice distinguishes one from peasants. We may well use Bowen's Weberian language of "elective affinity" of certain social realities for certain religious styles.

"Reformist modernism," again to use Bowen's term, may also distinguish one from the cosmopolitan, or secular, or Westernized elites, a fault line illustrated in Whalley's discussion of Minangkabau (1993). In Indonesia, as described by Hefner, a goal of the Islamically oriented has been to "convert" the secular Javanese elites. Educated professional women can distinguish themselves from such suspect values in part by their dress. This has also been true in Pakistan, where a particular target of the Islamists has been the Westernized women who are seen as a threat to all society (Metcalf 1987).

The focus of much moral argument, in both Southeast Asia and the Subcontinent, has, in fact, been issues of gender. Control of women's behavior and restrictions on women's dress have become centrally important public symbols of an Islamic society. Whalley has described the choices of dress styles available to urban, educated women, especially unmarried women, as they seek to manage a public image of themselves as both modern and moral (1993). On the whole deeply concerned with sustaining the status of their natal lineage, they now do so not in the old way of marrying appropriately, but in a new way by behaving and dressing in a morally acceptable style while earning an independent livelihood. Whalley, citing Errington, underlines that elaboration of female difference through dress is a recent development in Southeast Asia in contrast to an emphasis on distinction by class.

Bowen's study of reform in Gayo, like my own of Deoband in India, finds—surprisingly, given our stereotypes about Islam and women—that women and men are conceptualized as essentially identical, open to the same kind of teaching, responsible for the same kind of behavior. The elaboration of female difference, both bodily (undergirded with Western pseudoscience on subjects like menstruation) and moral, attributing to women the heretofore unknown quality of innate spirituality, comes with the more political movements of the twentieth century, like that in the Subcontinent led by Maududi. In Gayo, women were apparently not only invited to participate in the reformist religious style, but were themselves among the poets who spread the teachings. In Minangkabau, as early as the 1920s women were being trained to be good Muslims and civil servants and professionals: it is the Indonesian state that now wants to narrow the scope of women's activities primarily to the home. Even so, in Indonesia today women are active and well known among public preachers and preach not only to other women but to mixed audiences. The contemporary attention to distinctive women's roles is not "traditional" but embedded in the construction of national states.

What Is the Nature of Islamic Difference?

This brief review of some of the themes in this wide-ranging collection of essays may suggest some points to counter the kinds of assumptions that are so widespread in our society. First, the fact of "horizontal" Muslim solidarities, of "ethnic" or "nationalist" Islam, is as modern as the nation-states in which Muslims are embedded. Muslim communities, above all communities motivated by ideological programs, are not age-old. If many Muslims today talk of the distinctiveness of Islam as a "complete way of life," we must recognize that as one contemporary trope and then take account of the multiplicity of Islamic positions that range from those who envisage utopian communities to those who insist that to sacralize the state is *shirk*. Christianity is no more uniformly committed to a separation of religion and politics than Islam is to a single religious order. What is more totalistic than the Puritan fathers, the Spanish inquisition, or the pre-Emancipation British exclusions?

Second, the public use of Islamic symbols and the forging of Islamic solidarities are often part of profoundly modern projects shared across nations. We have seen in the Philippine case the extent to which Muslim solidarities are used as a basis for participation in the modern state, much as other ethnic solidarities are elsewhere. The Moro Islamic Liberation Front uses the language of democratic egalitarianism in opposing the *datus*: "good people with good minds have had little chance for success"—this resonates more with America as a land of opportunity than with the Qur'an. The *datu* answer similarly reflects a liberal democratic view, in this case directed to the separation of religion and politics: "if the *ulama* form the political leadership, there will be no one to preach. . . . We do not want to create ayatollahs." Islam provides a language for political participation and competition.

It also provides a language for debating values in public life and for defining the respective authority of individuals, civil society, and the state. Even without invoking Harvey Cox, the ICMI vision of individual personal ethical cultivation and the espousal of issues like "human rights" bespeak cosmopolitan moral values and would be at home with other movements challenging states and societies dominated by corruption and consumerism everywhere. An ICMI leader like Nurcholish Madjid is part of a transnational conversation, engaged in in the United States by intellectuals like Robert Bellah, who seek to foster the institutions of civil society as the locus of transcendent values and commitments that in turn influence the state. Robert Hefner suggests that Indonesia provides "an alternative ideology of what the nation should become" for those who expect secularism inevitably to triumph. But Islamic movements like this one in Indonesia are also an "alternative" to those who identify Muslim movements only with reaction and terror.

It matters that these societies are Muslim above all because of the awareness and links they have with each other. But it is, in the end, the participation in patterns common with other cultural, religious, and nationalist groups, not their specificity, that comes out most clearly in this collection. Bowen, with his interest in whether there are universal forms of the modern person; Hefner, exploring the nature of Indonesian civil society; and the authors of all these essays invite us to make the kinds of investigations of contemporary Islamic movements and styles that can profitably be compared with other, non-Muslim societies. The very process of doing that, in contrast to the stereotyping and demonizing of Islam that is so widespread, will illuminate our study of Southeast Asian societies as well as of other societies, including our own, engaged with common problems of social change and pluralism.

Note

1. The quotation is from Wali Khan in his affidavit to the supreme court in 1975, cited in Mortimer 1982, 216.

References Cited

Anderson, Benedict. 1983. *Imagined Communities: Reflections on the Origin and Spread of Nationalism*. Revised edition 1990. London: Verso.

Eaton, Richard M. 1994. *The Rise of Islam and the Bengal Frontier, 1204–1760*. Berkeley and Los Angeles: University of California Press.

Eickelman, Dale F. 1992. "Mass Higher Education and the Religious Imagination in Contemporary Arab Societies." *American Ethnologist* 19 (4): 643–655.

————. 1993. "Southeast Asian Muslims from a Middle Eastern Perspective." Paper presented at conference on "Islam and the Social Construction of Identities: Comparative Perspectives on Southeast Asian Muslims," School of Hawaiian, Asian and Pacific Studies, University of Hawai'i at Mānoa, August 4–6.

Ellen, Roy F. 1983. "Social Theory, Ethnography and the Understanding of Practical Islam in South-East Asia. In M. B. Hooker, ed., *Islam in South-East Asia*, pp. 50–91. Leiden: Brill.

Gopal, Sarvepalli, ed. 1991. *Anatomy of a Confrontation: The Babri Masjid–Ramjanmabhumi Issue*. New Delhi: Penguin Books India.

Horvatich, Patricia. n.d. "The Martyr and the Mayor: On the Politics of Identity in the Southern Philippines." Forthcoming in Renato Rosaldo, ed., *Cultural Citizenship in Southeast Asia*.

Irschick, Eugene F. 1994. *Dialogue and History: Constructing South India, 1795–1895*. Berkeley and Los Angeles: University of California Press.

Kessler, Clive S. 1993. "Reactualizing Islam in Our Times: Faith, Law, and the State in Malaysia." Paper presented at conference on "Islam and the Social Construction of Identities: Comparative Perspectives on Southeast Asian Muslims," School of Hawaiian, Asian and Pacific Studies, University of Hawai'i at Mānoa, August 4–6.

Metcalf, Barbara D. 1982. *Islamic Revival in British India: Deoband, 1860–1900*. Princeton: Princeton University Press.

————. 1987. "Islamic Arguments in Contemporary Pakistan." In William R. Roff and Dale F. Eickelman, eds., *Islam and the Political Economy of Meaning: Comparative Studies of Muslim Discourse*, pp. 132–159. London and Sydney: Croom Helm.

————, ed. and trans. 1990. *Perfecting Women: Maulana Ashraf 'Ali Thanawi's Bihishti Zewar*. Berkeley and Los Angeles: University of California Press.

Mortimer, Edward. 1982. *Faith and Power: The Politics of Islam*. New York: Vintage Books.

Thapar, Romila. 1985. "Syndicated Mokhsha." *Seminar* (New Delhi), pp. 14–22.

van der Veer, Peter. 1994. *Religious Nationalism: Hindus and Muslims in India*. Berkeley and Los Angeles: University of California Press.

Whalley, Lucy. 1993. "The Politics of Minangkabau Women's Dress." Paper presented at conference on "Islam and the Social Construction of Identities: Comparative Perspectives on Southeast Asian Muslims," School of Hawaiian, Asian and Pacific Studies, University of Hawai'i at Mānoa, August 4–6.

Wilkinson, Richard J. 1906. *Malay Beliefs*. London: Luzac.

Contributors

John R. Bowen is professor of anthropology and chair, Committee on Social Thought and Analysis, at Washington University in St. Louis. He has written on the political, cultural, and religious history of the Gayo and is currently studying legal and social change in Indonesia.

Andrée Feillard is a former Indonesia staff correspondent for Agence France Presse and Asiaweek. She now teaches Indonesian language and civilization in France and belongs to the Archipel research group at the École des Hautes Études en Sciences Sociales in Paris. She has recently published a book on the Nahdlatul Ulama.

Robert W. Hefner is professor of anthropology and associate director of the Institute for the Study of Economic Culture at Boston University. He is currently finishing a book on Islam and democratization in Southeast Asia and is directing a comparative project on democracy and civil society.

Patricia Horvatich holds a Ph.D. from Stanford University and was assistant professor of Southeast Asian studies at the University of Hawai'i at Mānoa. Her research interests and publications have addressed Sama cultural identity, religious change, and gender.

Thomas M. McKenna is assistant professor of anthropology at the University of Alabama, Birmingham. He has worked among political-economic refugees living in an urban shantytown in Cotabato. His work has focused on Muslim separatist movements as understood and experienced by the Magindanao.

Barbara D. Metcalf is professor of history at the University of California, Davis, a former president of the Association for Asian Studies, and the author of numerous works on Islam in South Asia.

Michael G. Peletz is professor of anthropology at Colgate University and the author of numerous works on the culture, history, and politics of Malaysia. His most recent book examines Malay views of gender.

Martin Rössler holds a Ph.D. from the University of Cologne and is currently a lecturer in anthropology at the University of Göttingen, Germany. He has conducted extensive field research in South Sulawesi, Indonesia, on local patterns of sociopolitical organization, religion, and cognition. Dr. Rössler is presently engaged in a project on Makassar domestic economy.

Shamsul A. B. is professor of anthropology at the National University of Malaysia and the author of numerous works on Malaysian politics, culture, and Islam. He is currently completing a book on Islam and nation building in Malaysia.

Index

Kaum Muda/Kaum Tua, 15, 159, 197, 234
Kuder, Edward, 51–53
Kuntowijoyo, 92–93

Law: *adat* and Islam, 12; colonial, 12, 150; Islamic *(shari'ah)*, 9–10, 78, 111, 236–240, 244–245; Islamic law as basis of government, 132, 137

Madjid, Nurcholish, 80, 82–85, 93–95, 110–111, 115, 116–117nn. 5–7, 268n. 20, 319
Magindanaon (Mindanao, Philippines), 58–65
Mahatir, Mohamed, 216, 220–221
Makassarese (Sulawesi, Indonesia), 276–299
Malays, 209–266
Malaysian Islamic Welfare and Missionary Association (PERKIM—*Pertubuhan Kebajikan Islam Malaysia*), 235–236
Malaysian Muslim Youth Movement (ABIM—*Angkatan Belia Islam Malaysia*), 213–215, 218, 235–236
Marriage and divorce, 79, 87, 237–238, 244. *See also* Jakarta Charter
Masykur, Kyai, 131–132
Masyumi, 78, 80–81, 129, 133
Middle class, 90–93, 234
MILF (Moro Islamic Liberation Front), 59
Minangkabau (Sumatra, Indonesia), 161, 176
Missionaries: Ahmadi, 184, 187–196; Christian, 87, 239; Muslim, 60–61, 187. See also *Dakwah*
Misuari, Nur, 56–59
MNLF (Moro National Liberation Front), 26, 56, 58–59, 203n. 3
Modernism, 15, 28
Modernization, theories of, 18–21, 27–29, 82–83, 85, 131, 157–158. *See also* Secularization
Moro identity, 43–44, 52, 56–57, 62
Moro Islamic Liberation Front (MILF), 59
Moro National Liberation Front (MNLF), 26, 56, 58–59, 203n. 3
Moro wars, 45–47
Mosques, proliferation of: in Indonesia, 88, 93, 148; in Malaysia, 236; in Philippines, 53–54
Muhammadiyah movement, 23, 150, 276–278

Murtopo, Major General Ali, 78–79
Muslimat, 138–141, 148
Mysticism: in Java, 14–17; in Malaysia, 238, 241–242, 255–259; *silat* cult groups, 212; Sufi education, 268n. 20; Sufi influences, 10–11, 17. *See also* Islam, folk/normative/traditional

Nahdatul Ulama, 23, 100–101, 129–151, 268n. 20, 314–315
Nationalism, 17, 19–26, 55–58, 90
Nation-building and Islam, 21–31; in Indonesia, 21–24; in Malaysia, 24–25; in the Philippines, 53–58
New Economic Policy (NEP), 209–210, 213–214, 234
Noer, Deliar, 100–105

Organizations, religious: ABIM (*Angkatan Belia Islam Malaysia*—Malaysian Muslim Youth Movement), 213–215, 218, 235–236; Ahmadiyya, 187–199; Ansor, 138–139, 145; Darul Arqam, 218, 221–222, 235–236, 242–243; HMI (*Himpunan Mahasiswa Islam*—Islamic Students Association), 79–82; ICMI (*Ikatan Cendekiawan Muslim Se-Indonesia*—Association of Indonesian Muslim Intellectuals), 75–77, 94–110, 130, 150–151, 315; Kaum Muda/Kaum Tua, 15, 159, 197, 234; Muhammadiyah, 23, 150, 276–278; Muslimat, 138–141, 148; Nahdatul Ulama, 23, 100–101, 129–151, 268n. 20, 314–315; Paramadina, 93, 268n. 20; PERKIM (*Pertubuhan Kebajikan Islam Malaysia*—Malaysian Islamic Welfare and Missionary Association), 235–236; PII (Indonesian Islam Students), 80; Salman, 90–91, 99. *See also* Parties and Organizations, Political

Pamungkas, Sri Bintang, 98–99, 114–115
Pancasila, 22, 88–89, 131–137, 144, 149, 275
Pan Malayan Islamic Party (PAS—*Parti Islam Se-Malaya*), 214, 217, 235–236
Paramadina, 93, 268n. 20
Parties and Organizations, Political: Generation-of-'66, 79–81, 85; Golkar,